COWARDS DON'T MAKE HISTORY

COWARDS DON'T MAKE HISTORY

Orlando Fals Borda
and the Origins of
Participatory Action
Research

Joanne Rappaport

Duke University Press
Durham and London
2020

Designed by Drew Sisk
Typeset in Portrait Text, Eurostile, and Ashley Script by
Westchester Publishing Services

Library of Congress Cataloging-in-Publication Data
Names: Rappaport, Joanne, author.
Title: Cowards don't make history : Orlando Fals Borda and the
    origins of participatory action research / Joanne Rappaport.
Other titles: Orlando Fals Borda and the origins of participatory
    action research
Description: Durham : Duke University Press, 2020. | Includes
    bibliographical references and index.
Identifiers: LCCN 2019054654 (print)
LCCN 2019054655 (ebook)
ISBN 9781478009986 (hardcover)
ISBN 9781478011019 (paperback)
ISBN 9781478012542 (ebook)
Subjects: LCSH: Fals-Borda, Orlando. | Fundación del Caribe

(Colombia) | Fundación Rosca de Investigación y Acción Social. |
Action research—Colombia. | Sociology—Research—Methodology. |
Peasants—Political activity—Colombia.
Classification: LCC HM578. C7 R37 2020 (print) |
    LCC HM578.C7 (ebook) |
DDC 301.01—dc23
LC record available at https://lccn.loc.gov/2019054654
LC ebook record available at https://lccn.loc.gov/2019054655

Cover art: Cristo Hoyos, *Cuadros Vivos*, 2011. Courtesy of the artist.

A la memoria de Ulianov Chalarka

Contents

All comics pages are reprinted with the permission of the Fundación del Sinú, the organization that replaced the Fundación del Caribe, the research collective that authored the graphic histories I analyze. Fals Borda's photographs are reprinted with the permission of the Centro de Documentación Regional "Orlando Fals Borda," Banco de la República, Montería.

The following individuals and organizations appear and reappear throughout the pages of this book. They are the protagonists of my narrative.

La Rosca de Investigación y Acción Social

La Rosca de Investigación y Acción Social [Circle of Research and Social Action] was a national network of action researchers founded in 1971 by Orlando Fals Borda and a group of co-thinkers, many of them connected to the Presbyterian Church. La Rosca's mission was to forge horizontal and participatory research relationships with popular sectors with the aim of contributing to their struggles (Bonilla et al. 1971, 1972; Rosca 1974). The network coordinated the activities of its various regional chapters, procured funding for their projects and publications, and participated on the editorial board and as columnists in the leftist weekly *Alternativa*.

Víctor Daniel Bonilla: Journalist and ethnographer based in the city of Cali, who worked with CRIC, the Consejo Regional Indígena del Cauca [Regional Indigenous Council of Cauca], the first modern Colombian indigenous organization, representing the major Native groups of the southwestern highlands in the department of Cauca. Bonilla introduced the strategy of preparing *mapas parlantes* [speaking maps] that situated major events in indigenous history in maps depicting the regional and national landscapes (Bonilla 1977, 1982).

Gonzalo Castillo Cárdenas: Sociologist originally from Barranquilla, whose activism was focused on the indigenous communities of the department of Tolima, to the west of Bogotá. Castillo edited a 1939 treatise by Manuel Quintín Lame (1971), a Nasa leader in the first half of the twentieth century, which became one of the foundational documents of the Colombian indigenous movement. At the time of the founding of La Rosca, Castillo was a Presbyterian pastor.

Orlando Fals Borda: Barranquilla-born Colombian sociologist, founder of the Sociology Faculty of the National University of Colombia. Fals conducted pathbreaking ethnographic research in the 1950s on peasant economies in the Colombian highlands (Fals Borda 1955, 1957) and participated in an advisory capacity in the Colombian agrarian reform in the 1960s. He was a supporting actor in the rise of the radical wing of ANUC, the Asociación Nacional de Usuarios Campesinos-Línea Sincelejo [National Association of Peasant Users-Sincelejo Line], developing his approach to action research at the regional level, and later at the national and international levels. Fals's personal archive is one of the major sources of evidence in this book. For a listing of his publications, see the bibliography.

Augusto Libreros: Economist and Presbyterian pastor whose friendship with Gonzalo Castillo and Orlando Fals Borda dated to their religious connections in Barranquilla. Libreros's work in La Rosca focused on Afrocolombian communities on the Pacific coast and in the Cauca Valley.

Sociologists Gilberto Aristizábal, Darío Fajardo, Alfredo Molano, William Ramírez, and Alejandro Reyes Posada, as well as economist Ernesto Parra Escobar and Swedish development scholar Anders Rudqvist, collaborated with Fals Borda by undertaking evaluations of action research on the Caribbean coast; see the bibliography for their publications.

La Fundación del Caribe

The Fundación del Caribe [Caribbean Foundation], founded in late 1972, was a chapter of the regional network established in Barranquilla, Montería, and Sincelejo by participatory action researchers working on the Caribbean coast. Its members were young aspiring researchers and activists, most of whom had grown up in coastal cities.

Ulianov Chalarka: A painter and caricaturist living in the working-class barrio of La Granja, Montería. He also went by the pseudonym Iván Tejada. Chalarka's family, originally from the highland city of Pereira, migrated to Montería when he was a teen. Chalarka drew all of the Fundación's historical comics (Chalarka 1985; Sociedad de Jóvenes Cristianos 1973).

Néstor Herrera: A development professional in Sincelejo, who in his youth in the early 1970s collaborated with ANUC's organizing efforts in the department of Sucre. Herrera was one of the key actors in the research that culminated in *Felicita Campos*, one of the Fundación's historical comics.

Víctor Negrete: Trained as a science teacher at the Universidad Libre in Bogotá, Negrete was the president of the Fundación and, along with Fals Borda, the only other researcher who worked full-time on the team from 1972 to 1974. Native to Montería, Negrete is now a professor at the Universidad del Sinú and one of the most active promoters of participatory action research on the Caribbean coast. Negrete's multiple publications are listed in the bibliography.

David Sánchez Juliao: A Lorica-born creative writer whose work in the Fundación largely centered on the production of testimonial literature recorded on cassette tapes for peasant audiences and subsequently published by the Fundación del Caribe and by national presses (1975, 1999 [1974]). In the 1980s he authored television screenplays and was ambassador to India and Egypt.

Franklin Sibaja: A Montería-based community activist, instrumental in generating rural and urban contacts for the Fundación. Sibaja discovered Ulianov Chalarka, bringing him on board as the artist of the Fundación's series of historical comics.

Other collaborators with the Fundación del Caribe who appear briefly in the coming pages include children's author Leopoldo Berdella, university student Matilde Eljach, Cereté activist José Galeano, musician Máximo Jiménez, sociologist Raúl Paniagua, folklorist Benjamín Puche, sociologist María Josefina Yance, and the regional agrarian prosecutor, Roberto Yance.

Asociación Nacional de Usuarios Campesinos (ANUC-Línea Sincelejo)

ANUC, the Asociación Nacional de Usuarios Campesinos [National Association of Peasant Users], was originally a government-sponsored peasant organization established as one of the national partners in the Colombian agrarian reform of the 1960s. In 1972, as peasants became disillusioned with official efforts at land redistribution, a substantial sector of the association took agrarian reform into their own hands by organizing land occupations; they separated from the national association, founding ANUC-Línea Sincelejo [ANUC-Sincelejo Line] at a congress held in the city of Sincelejo. ANUC-Córdoba adhered to the Sincelejo Line. Several of its leaders, especially those in the municipal chapter of Montería, participated actively in the Fundación del Caribe through a partner organization called the Centro Popular de Estudios.

Moisés Banquett: A municipal leader of ANUC in Montería, serving in various capacities on its executive committee, Banquett was a central actor in the organization of the *baluartes de autogestión campesina* [bastions of peasant self-management] in the lands occupied by ANUC in 1972, as well as being a key ally of Fals and of the Fundación. His unpublished memoir can be found in Fals Borda's personal papers in Montería (CDRBR/M, 1041–1058).

Clovis Flórez: A schoolteacher and union activist who served as president of the municipal chapter of ANUC in Montería, Flórez was an important ally of the Fundación del Caribe from 1972 to 1975. He was assassinated on 15 September 2000.

Juana Julia Guzmán: Originally from Corozal, Sucre, Guzmán was a founder of the Sociedad de Obreros y Artesanos de Montería [Society of Workers and Artisans of Montería] (1918) and the Sociedad de Obreras Redención de la Mujer [Society of Women Workers Redemption of Women] (1919), two associations of artisans, workers, and peasants that led the struggle against the *matrícula* [debt-peonage system] and a leader of the Baluarte Rojo of Lomagrande, an autonomous peasant community set up on public lands on the outskirts of Montería, ultimately serving as its administrator. Her narration of the history of socialist organizing in early twentieth-century Córdoba furnished a major source for the graphic histories produced by the Fundación del Caribe and inspired ANUC-Córdoba to found baluartes on the occupied lands of La Antioqueña in 1972. She is depicted as the narrator of *El Boche* and is a major character in *Lomagrande*, two of the Fundación's graphic histories.

Florentino Montero: Peasant leader in Sucre, and a collaborator in the research that culminated in the *Felicita Campos* graphic history.

Alfonso Salgado Martínez: Originally from Canalete, Córdoba, Salgado was one of the leaders of the municipal chapter of ANUC in Montería and an active participant in the Fundación's publication projects, authoring a primer on political economy for a peasant readership under the pseudonym Alsal Martínez (1973).

Major Figures in the Fundación del Caribe's Graphic Histories

Vicente Adamo: Italian socialist organizer, originally from Reggio Calabria, who, together with Juana Julia Guzmán, founded the Sociedad de Obreros y Artesanos de Montería and established the baluarte of Lomagrande. Along with Guzmán, Adamo was jailed for thirty months after a 1921 massacre of activists at Lomagrande and was subsequently deported.

José Santos Cabrera: Owner of the hacienda Río Ciego in San Bernardo del Viento, Córdoba, and opponent of the peasant activists of Cañogrande whose story is depicted in the graphic history, *Tinajones*.

Felicita Campos: An early twentieth-century Afrocolombian leader in San Onofre, Sucre, and the central protagonist of the Fundación's eponymous graphic history.

Juana Julia Guzmán: See above, ANUC.

Manuel Hernández, "El Boche": A peasant laborer reputed to have murdered numerous people at the hacienda Misiguay, including one of its owners, in the early twentieth century. There is scant evidence for the details of his transgressions, which have evolved into a legend that has been embellished by numerous local authors. The Fundación del Caribe produced a graphic history, *El Boche*, depicting Hernández as an early fighter against the matrícula.

Alejandro Lacharme: Scion of the Lacharme family, owners of the hacienda Misiguay and various other holdings in the Sinú Valley, assassinated by Manuel Hernández, as depicted in the graphic history, *El Boche*.

Víctor Licona: Peasant activist in San Bernardo del Viento in the 1960s and the narrator of *Tinajones*.

Bárbaro Ramírez: An elderly peasant who narrated his experience of the matrícula at workshops and in an interview with Fals Borda, Bárbaro Ramírez is cited as an oral source in *Lomagrande*.

Wilberto Rivero: ANUC leader from Martinica, Córdoba, and the narrator of *Lomagrande*.

Ignacio Silgado "El Mello": Peasant activist in San Onofre, Sucre, and the narrator of *Tinajones*.

Workshops

ACIN, Asociación de Cabildos Indígenas del Norte del Cauca Çxab Wala Kiwe [Association of Indigenous Councils of Northern Cauca Çxab Wala Kiwe], Tejido de Educación [Education Program]: Zonal indigenous organization based in Santander de Quilichao, Cauca, affiliated with CRIC, the Regional Indigenous Council of Cauca [Consejo Regional Indígena del Cauca]. The workshop was attended by indigenous educational activists and nonindigenous collaborators with ACIN.

Centro de Documentación Regional "Orlando Fals Borda," Banco de la República, Montería: Regional library and home of Orlando Fals Borda's personal papers. Participants in the workshop included surviving Fundación del Caribe activists, ANUC members, Afrocolombian educators, faculty and students from the Universidad de Córdoba (Montería) and the Universidad del Norte (Barranquilla).

CINEP, Centro de Investigación y Educación Popular [Center of Research and Popular Education]: Jesuit research institute in Bogotá. Workshop participants included CINEP researchers, members of the institute's communications team, and visiting graduate students.

Corporación Con-Vivamos: A community organization in the Comuna 1 on the hills overlooking Medellín. Barrio residents and activists were joined by members of other nongovernmental organizations and academics at this workshop.

Escuela Nacional Orlando Fals Borda: A training seminar in Bogotá attended by young activists belonging to chapters in different Colombian cities, all affiliated with the Congreso de los Pueblos, a network of leftist organizations.

IAPES, Instituto de Investigación-Acción en Procesos Educativos y Sociales "Simón Rodríguez": A chapter of the organization sponsoring the Escuela Nacional Orlando Fals Borda. The workshop was held at UAIIN, the Universidad Autónoma Indígena Intercultural [Autonomous Indigenous Intercultural University] on the outskirts of Popayán, Cauca, attracting IAPES members, UAIIN faculty, faculty from the Universidad del Cauca, and CRIC members.

Institución Educativa Técnica Agroindustrial de San Pablo: A high school in San Pablo, María la Baja (Bolívar), an Afrocolombian community. Participants were mainly students in the upper grades, as well as some indigenous Zenú activists.

RedSaludPaz: Held at the Veterinary Faculty of the Universidad Nacional de Colombia, this workshop included health professionals and educators organized into a network dedicated to building a new health system in Colombia.

Universidad Nacional de Colombia-Sede Medellín: Jointly sponsored by the Laboratorio de Fuentes Históricas [Laboratory of Historical Sources], the Corporación Cultural Estanislao Zuleta, and Con-Vivamos, this Medellín-based workshop brought together academics and members of nongovernmental organizations.

Cowards Don't Make History examines the early history of what has come to be known as participatory action research (PAR). A widely used methodology that is claimed and disputed by grassroots social movements and nongovernmental organizations, as well as corporations, bureaucracies, and international development organizations, PAR traces its origins to relationships forged between social movements and politically progressive intellectuals in the Third World and the margins of the developed world in the 1960s and 1970s. Working in numerous locations, including Brazil, Colombia, India, Tanzania, and the Appalachian region of the United States, participatory researchers constructed a methodology that would foster horizontal relationships, erasing distinctions between researchers and "the researched," encouraging a dialogue between academic and people's knowledge, and transforming research into a tool of consciousness-raising and political organizing.

As Australian participatory researcher Robin McTaggart explains, "Authentic participation in research means sharing in the way research is conceptualized, practiced, and brought to bear on the life-world. It means ownership, that is, responsible agency in the production of knowledge and improvement of practice" (1997: 28). Responsible agency is made possible by grassroots participation in setting the research agenda, collecting the data, and controlling the ways in which the information is used (McTaggart 1997: 29). It also involves alternating research with practice, so that the work of consciousness-raising feeds into the work of organizing and mobilization, which, in turn, supplies new research questions (Gaventa 1988; Vío Grossi 1981).

Paulo Freire insists in *Pedagogy of the Oppressed* that such a combination of research with activism stimulates a profound and politically effective critical awareness of reality (which he calls "praxis"):

> The insistence that the oppressed engage in reflection on their concrete situation is not a call to armchair revolution. On the contrary, reflection—true reflection—leads to action. On the other hand, when the situation calls for action, that action will constitute an authentic praxis only if its consequences become the object of critical reflection. In this sense, the

praxis is the new *raison d'être* of the oppressed; and the revolution, which inaugurates the historical moment of this *raison d'être*, is not viable apart from their concomitant conscious involvement. Otherwise, action is pure activism. (2005 [1970]: 66)

In the early years of PAR, the political action that practitioners called for was revolutionary. While it was intimately local, based in grassroots communities, the intention of participatory research was to transform the broader social system. Today, we don't use the same radical language as Freire did in the 1960s and 1970s, but PAR practitioners—at least, those involved with critical variants of PAR, those who work within popular movements and grassroots communities—continue to orient small-scale and intense research relationships toward the transformation of institutions, values, and behaviors in order to create a just society (Fine 2017). As Carlos Rodrigues Brandão puts it, the contribution made by participatory research is not so much to establish a rigorous set of research practices or analyses as it is to promote "the collective search for knowledge that will make human beings not only more educated and wise, but also more fair, free, critical, creative, participatory, coresponsible, and expressing solidarity" (2005: 45).

There is no rule book for PAR; in fact, some prefer to call it an "epistemology" (Fine 2017: 80) or "a series of commitments to observe and problematise through practice the principles for conducting social enquiry" (McTaggart 1994: 315), as opposed to a "methodology." Its lack of a concrete recipe derives from the fact that each PAR playbook evolves over time out of a dialectical relationship between the community and external researchers, as well as between theory and practice (Hall 1982, 1992). That is to say, as a participatory project unfolds, a dialogue is established between local knowledge and the knowledge that external researchers bring to the relationship, lending a specificity that is unique to the circumstances of each collaborative endeavor. In this sense, both the objectives of the investigation and the techniques researchers use grow out of the context itself, combining approaches as diverse as feminist theory (Dyrness 2008), ethnography (Fals Borda and Brandão 1986: 41–42), even quantitative methods (Fine 2017: chap. 5), with autochthonous methods of collecting information and local conceptual vehicles for making sense of reality (Archila Neira 2015; Casa de Pensamiento n.d.).

Participatory research has accumulated over time a particularly rich experience in Latin America, germinating in the social movements of the last quarter of the twentieth century among peasants, indigenous peoples and Afrodescendants, shantytown dwellers and industrial workers. Fruitful collaboration between researchers and popular movements blossomed since the 1970s, more often than not at the margins of the university or sometimes entirely outside of it in popular education collectives, grassroots organizations, barrios, and rural villages. It would be too simple, however, to state that a project is participatory merely because local people engage in some way in it, since conventional ethnographers have for decades enlisted the participation of their informants. In contrast, PAR, as it has developed in Latin America, is also participatory because the researchers themselves espouse the aspirations of the organization with which they are collaborating, both by placing people's knowledge on an equal footing with academic knowledge and by embracing the political objectives of the groups with which they are working (Brandão 2005: 56).

One of the early experimenters in participatory methodologies was the Colombian sociologist Orlando Fals Borda (1925–2008). From 1972 to 1974 he entered into a collaboration with the National Association of Peasant Users (ANUC) in the department of Córdoba on Colombia's Caribbean coast. His work involved fostering the participation of peasant cadres in conducting interviews with leaders of agrarian movements of the first part of the twentieth century. They engaged in co-analyses of their circumstances at training workshops; their stories were narrated in comics format—all with the intention that these lessons would contribute to the creation of political strategies in the present. Fals Borda called his approach "action research" (not to be confused with the action research practiced at the time in North America). Although he wrote about his experience, which was also evaluated by numerous social scientists in the decades after the project ended, there is only scant analysis of the activities in which he, his associates, and ANUC leaders engaged. Most publications highlight the theory behind this innovative attempt at redefining research and the products that emerged from it—training workshops, graphic histories, historical texts accessible to readers with minimal schooling, testimonial literature and chronicles [crónicas]—but neglect to depict the process that underlaid these achievements, despite the fact that process, and not product, was what was (and still is) at the heart of participatory action research (Reason and Bradbury 2008).

Cowards Don't Make History takes advantage of the abundant archival materials that Fals Borda left behind, reading his papers through the lens of a dialogue with many of the activists themselves, as well as with some of today's PAR practitioners. In this book, I try to make sense of what the authors of this methodology thought research was and how they organized the fusion of peasant knowledge and academic inquiry into a participatory endeavor. I probe the ways that the knowledge emanating from this extended conversation contributed to activism, particularly to ANUC's strategy of occupying large landholdings and administering them in novel ways.

When I began this project, I was not completely convinced that participatory action research held the promise that had been touted by so many. I had several decades of collaborative ethnographic research under my belt in conjunction with indigenous intellectuals from the Regional Indigenous Council of Cauca (CRIC), an indigenous organization founded in the early 1970s that was initially part of ANUC and was inspired by many of the same methodological approaches that Fals Borda employed in Córdoba. We formulated conceptual models for analyzing indigenous politics in southern Colombia at the turn of the millennium, making the results available for use by the organization's bilingual education program, some of whose activists were members of the research team. I was convinced that collaborative ethnography was superior to participatory action research, which had become a mainstay of conventional applied social science; like many academic anthropologists, I was keen to distinguish my research from that of my applied colleagues. I now know that I was blinded by the use of participatory methods by international development organizations like USAID (United States Agency for International Development) to further their own objectives, as well as by the fact that many nongovernmental organizations have appropriated techniques from PAR without paying heed to its founding principles. I neglected to recognize that many of the nonindigenous activists I met in CRIC, from whom I had imbibed collaborative research philosophies and methods, had originally begun their work inspired by Fals Borda; I worked with CRIC's educational activists without recognizing their quite obvious appropriations of his methodology. I listened to the criticisms of social scientists—that Fals Borda was paternalistic and dependent on academic models, that he never effectively reached the peasant rank and file—and lost sight of how profoundly he turned social science and activism on their heads. With the passing years, as my understanding of Fals Borda's project in Córdoba deepened through visits to the archives, conversations with his associates, and contact with PAR practitioners, I came to appreciate how unique and innovative these first attempts at participatory action research really were, even as, with hindsight, I came to identify the fissures that emerged during this early methodological experiment—frailties that I will not obscure in the following pages.

I am an ethnographer. I examine everyday practices and meanings to flesh them out in interpretations that are at once analytic and descriptive. I have conducted ethnographic research in indigenous communities where, as a participant observer, I experienced the flow of everyday life as an eyewitness, subsequently creating ethnographic scenarios in which I probed the significance of my observations. In a sense, I do the same thing in this book, only the experiences I am observing come to me secondhand from archives and interviews, information I flesh out with the help of my imagination. As I will describe in the coming pages, Fals Borda advocated an interpretive technique he called "imputation," by means of which he seized hold of historical information and gave it body through his empirically informed imagination. Imputation was not only something he availed himself of in his scholarly writings, but was for him a fundamental feature of the interstices between research and action: it was only by inhabiting the past that one could imagine the future, whether one was a sociologist or a peasant activist.

I hope that for some readers this book will expand their appreciation of how daring and transformative the social science of the global South really is. Fals Borda saw his contributions as inherently Latin American, a situated response to the social science he had learned at the University of Minnesota during his master's training and his doctoral studies at the University of Florida. The models he learned in the United States, as well as the methods he was taught to gather and analyze empirical data, did not fit the Colombian reality he lived, because these conceptual schemes were fashioned out of North American and European experience. Realizing their unsuitability, Fals Borda was forced to explore new ways of approaching the society in which he lived. *Cowards Don't Make History* documents a brief sliver of his intellectual life, when his politics blended most intimately with his identity as a Colombian and his mission as an intellectual.

The ethnographic detail I uncover comes from a process of triangulating archival materials with what I learned from interviews and my analysis of a series of graphic histories that Fals Borda and his associates produced between 1972 and 1974, drawn by a local artist, Ulianov Chalarka. I am by no means an expert at analyzing the visual language of comics. Instead, I attempt to read these graphic histories as traces of an activist research methodology. For some readers, this peek into the political use of Latin American graphic narrative may stimulate them to make deeper forays into an intellectually provocative artistic movement that is committed to social transformation and justice.

Finally, it is my hope that PAR practitioners will approach *Cowards Don't Make History* as an example of what participatory methods could and could not achieve at a particular moment in time and a specific location. That is to say, Fals Borda's experience does not afford us a model of which techniques activist researchers should adopt in the twenty-first century. Instead, it must be mined for its big ideas: What does it mean to create relationships of equality in research? What can social movements learn from history, and how can historical investigation be used to promote a more just society? How can serious research be coupled with progressive political objectives? How should social science be used to resolve violent conflict? How can the history of social science become more than an academic exercise? At the end of this book, I ask these questions of a series of teams engaged in participatory research in different parts of Colombia, bringing Fals Borda's past of the 1970s into my readers' present.

PREFACE

I have many institutions and individuals to thank for accompanying me on a journey that took more than a decade. My research was made possible by the generous support of the Graduate School of Arts and Sciences of Georgetown University, which provided me with a 2009 grant-in-aid to visit the archives in Montería and a Senior Faculty Fellowship in the fall semester of 2018; the latter allowed me to extend to three semesters my sabbatical leave, funded by a 2017–2018 fellowship from the American Council of Learned Societies. I am enormously grateful to both ACLS and Georgetown for providing me with the wherewithal to conduct research and the uninterrupted time to write this book.

The staff of the Centro de Documentación Regional "Orlando Fals Borda," of the Banco de la República in Montería, collaborated with my research in many ways. Not only did they make Fals Borda's personal papers available to me on my annual trips since 2008, but they also opened their facilities to the numerous workshops I facilitated, permitting me to discuss the significance of the archive with local activists and students; on various occasions the Banco also funded my trips to Colombia and to Montería. I am especially grateful to the Centro's staff—Diana Carmona Nobles, Ana María Espinosa Baena, María Angélica Herrera, Emerson Sierra, and Rita Díaz Sibaja—as well as to Claudia Marcela Bernal, the manager of the Banco de la República in Montería. Gabriel Escalante, the curator of Fals Borda's papers at the Archivo Central e Histórico of the Universidad Nacional de Colombia, was equally attentive to my research needs and as devoted to preserving Fals's intellectual legacy as are his colleagues in Montería. My work with the ANUC archives of the Centro de Investigación y Educación Popular (CINEP), which had been lost some years before in a flood, was first made possible when Alex Pereira gave me scanned copies of some of the documents it contained; later, Leon Zamosc sent me the entire archive in digital form. Mónica Moreno shared with me the documentation she collected at the Presbyterian Historical Society in Philadelphia. Without access to these archival holdings, this book would not have been possible.

I have been privileged to participate in a series of lively conversations taking place in a network of young scholars who are studying Fals Borda's archives: Zoraida Arcila Aristizábal, Juan Mario Díaz, Mónica Moreno, and Jafte Robles Lomeli are forging new paths in the history of social science in Latin America. Jafte, along with Nohora Arrieta, Valentina Pernett, Alfredo Poggi, and Douglas McRae, participated in a 2014 seminar I taught at Georgetown, in which we read *Historia doble de la Costa*, the Fundación del Caribe's and La Rosca's publications for peasant readerships, and worked with Fals Borda's archives, ultimately resulting in a special issue of *Tábula Rasa*, shepherded by its indefatigable editor, Leonardo Montenegro. I have been gratified to witness the recent expansion of this group with a new crop of dissertation writers, including Juanita Rodríguez and Julián Gómez Delgado. Other colleagues who have studied Fals Borda, were close to him, or have themselves engaged in politically committed research have been important sounding boards for me, including José María Rojas, Myriam Jimeno Santoyo, Elías Sevilla Casas, and Normando Suárez. My ongoing collaboration with researchers affiliated with CINEP, the Consejo Regional Indígena del Cauca, and the Asociación de Cabildos Indígenas del Norte del Cauca have kept me grounded in the real-world applications of my research; my thanks to Marcela Amador, Mauricio Archila, Graciela Bolaños, Martha Cecilia García, Diana Granados, Vicente Otero Chate, Libia Tattay, Pablo Tattay, and Rosalba Velasco.

Orlando and Utamaro Chalarca opened Ulianov Chalarka's artistic world to me. They have been gracious and compassionate guides. I dedicate this book to the memory of Ulianov, Orlando's brother and Utamaro's uncle. I never had the privilege of meeting him, but he has occupied—some would say, monopolized—my attention over the past decade.

When I first visited Montería, I was extremely fortunate to meet Víctor Negrete, one of the founders of the Fundación del Caribe and a tireless promoter of participatory research on the Caribbean coast. He has served over the past decade as my mentor. Víctor continues to remind me that the archival material I am studying was produced by activists intent on making Córdoba and Colombia a better place. Víctor and his wife, Liuber Bravo, made my visits to Montería welcoming with their hospitality, conversation, and their willingness to introduce me to other activists. Carmen Ortega Otero also opened the academic and artistic worlds of Montería, and became a close friend to me, for which I am deeply grateful.

I thank all of Fals Borda's associates, who, without exception, agreed to allow me to interview them. Their names are included in the bibliography. Orlando Fals Borda graciously invited me into his home, although he was ailing and would die a few weeks later. I met with him at the beginning of this project, when I was still unsure what to ask and in what direction my work would be going. I am thankful for his patience and *buena voluntad*. I also voice my appreciation to the following colleagues for organizing the 2018 workshops that form the basis for chapter 7 of this book: Cesar Abadía, Marcela Amador, Mauricio Archila, Eduardo Bloom, Nohora Caballero, Diana Carmona Nobles, Oscar Calvo Isaza, Martha Cecilia García, Castriela Hernández, Yamilé Nene, Laura Soto, and Libia Tattay. Pablo Guerra, Camilo Aguirre, Henry Díaz, and Diana Ojeda opened up the world of Colombian comics to me, helping me to see Ulianov Chalarka's drawings through knowledgeable eyes. Luis Pérez Rossi, the current secretary of ANUC-Córdoba, and educator María Yovadis Londoño of the *palenque* of San José de Uré in southern Córdoba, organized extremely valuable workshops with local communities in 2019, as did Víctor Negrete and Diana Carmona in Montería. The 2019 workshops were conducted with a future graphic history in mind; I am particularly grateful to Pablo Guerra for inspiring me to embark on this new project and for participating in the workshops.

My thanks to my wonderful research assistants at Georgetown University: Oscar Amaya participated in weekly sessions with Mónica Moreno and me, in which we read Fals Borda's Córdoba field notes; Verónica Zacipa went through his Saucío papers; Luis Daniel González Chavez, Diana Gumbar, Martha Lucía Jaramillo, and Edgar Ulloa transcribed many of the interviews.

It has been a great privilege to count among my friends a group of colleagues and students who have read all or parts of my manuscript. Some of them I have already mentioned, but their collaboration and my deep appreciation merit repeating. Mauricio Archila, Nohora Arrieta, Nancy van Deusen, Martha Cecilia García, Donny Meertens, and Mubbashir Rizvi read and commented on selected chapters. Mónica Moreno, who was writing her doctoral dissertation on Fals Borda's earlier research in the Colombian highlands as I traveled back and forth to the archives in Montería, was a particularly insightful interlocutor and reader. I am especially grateful to Alex Pereira, who recently returned to the academic world as a doctoral student at Georgetown, and whose perceptive readings of my manuscript caused me to deepen my analysis at many points during the writing process. My thinking was incalculably enriched by my conversations with Jafte Robles Lomeli, who just defended her magnificent doctoral dissertation on *Historia doble de la Costa*. My thanks also to the very perceptive commentaries of the two no-longer-anonymous reviewers for Duke University Press, Catherine LeGrand and Karin Rosemblatt.

Gisela Fosado of Duke University Press and Juan Felipe Córdoba of the Editorial Universidad del Rosario have collaborated with me as editors of several of my earlier books. I am indebted to them for shepherding this book to a simultaneous publication in English and in Spanish. Santiago Paredes has, once again, done an exemplary job of translating my prose into Spanish. My thanks to Bill Nelson for drawing the map and to Mark Mastromarino for preparing the index for the English edition. Cristo Hoyos granted me permission to use one of the paintings of his triptych, *Cuadros vivos*, as the cover of this book. Cristo's arresting canvas depicts coastal peasants displaced by violence over the past two decades. The fact that so many of the displaced are the children and grandchildren of the campesinos who joined ANUC in the 1970s led me to select it for the cover. I also acknowledge the permissions given me by the Fundación del Sinú to reproduce Ulianov Chalarka's comics panels and the Centro de Documentación Regional of the Banco de la República in Montería to include images from Orlando Fals Borda's photographic collection.

Portions of this book derive from, correct, and expand on earlier publications in which I made my first forays into analyzing Orlando Fals Borda's papers. They include: "'El cobarde no hace historia': Orlando Fals Borda y la doble historia de la Costa del Caribe," in Mabel Moraña and José Manuel Valenzuela, eds., *Precariedades, exclusiones, emergencias: Necropolítica y sociedad civil en América Latina*, 175-198 (México: Universidad Autónoma Metropolitana/Gedisa, 2017); "La Rosca de Investigación y Acción Social: Reimagining History as Collaborative Exchange in 1970s Colombia," in Peter Lambert and Björn Weiler, eds., *How the Past Was Used: Historical Cultures, c. 750-2000*, 231-258 (London: Proceedings of the British Academy, 2017); "Rethinking the Meaning of Research in Collaborative Relationships," *Collaborative Anthropologies* 9 (2018) 1-2: 1-31; "Visualidad y escritura como acción: La IAP en la Costa del Caribe colombiano," *Revista Colombiana de Sociología* 41 (2018) 1: 133-156; and, coauthored with Jafte Robles Lomeli, "Imagining Latin American Social Science from the Global South: Orlando Fals Borda and Participatory Research," *Latin American Research Review* 53 (2018) 3: 597-611.

For the past ten years, David Gow has put up with my obsession with Orlando Fals Borda and Ulianov Chalarka. His personal library supplied me with first editions of some of Fals Borda's reflections on action research. He has politely listened to my never-ending discourses on comics and has obliged me by reading some of my favorites. He went over my manuscript several times, offering me pointed and always relevant commentary. Afterward, he could invite me to set Fals Borda aside and enjoy a glass or two of wine and some of the exquisite cheese he hunts for on sale each week. I am a very fortunate person to be sharing my life with him.

"Cowards don't make history." So declared Juana Julia Guzmán (fig. I.1), a peasant agitator who inspired rural laborers, sharecroppers, and smallholders in the Colombian departments of Córdoba and Sucre to organize as a mass movement on the Caribbean coast during the early 1970s (*Alternativa del Pueblo* [henceforth, AP] 31: 30). In her youth in the 1920s, she led a coalition of urban artisans, workers, and peasants whose objective was to bring an end to the *matrícula*, the system of debt-peonage that bound coastal peasant sharecroppers to haciendas. At the end of Juana Julia's life, her personal reminiscences inspired ANUC, the Asociación Nacional de Usuarios Campesinos [National Association of Peasant Users], in its drive to occupy estates that were consolidated over the nineteenth and early twentieth centuries by large landowners and dedicated to cattle raising.[1] Juana Julia's story was recorded by Colombian sociologist Orlando Fals Borda and recast in comic-book form by Ulianov Chalarka, a local artist in Montería, the capital of Córdoba (figs. I.1 and I.2). Chalarka was a member of the Fundación del Caribe [the Caribbean Foundation] (henceforth, the Fundación), the activist collective that Orlando Fals Borda founded to produce research useful to ANUC's leadership.[2] The graphic adaptation of Juana Julia's autobiography was used as a pedagogical tool to instill in *campesinos*—Spanish for "peasants"—the need to organize themselves in the face of the transformation of their landscape during the second half of the twentieth century, when agrarian modernization forced them to abandon their plots to work as day laborers or move to coastal cities.

Figure I.1   Juana Julia Guzmán, in top panel, stating that "cowards don't make history" (Chalarka 1985: 22. Comic reprinted with permission of the Fundación del Sinú)

Figure I.2   Orlando Fals Borda in Córdoba, 1973 (CDRBR/M, CF, 2283. Photo reprinted with permission of the Centro de Documentación Regional "Orlando Fals Borda," Banco de la República, Montería)

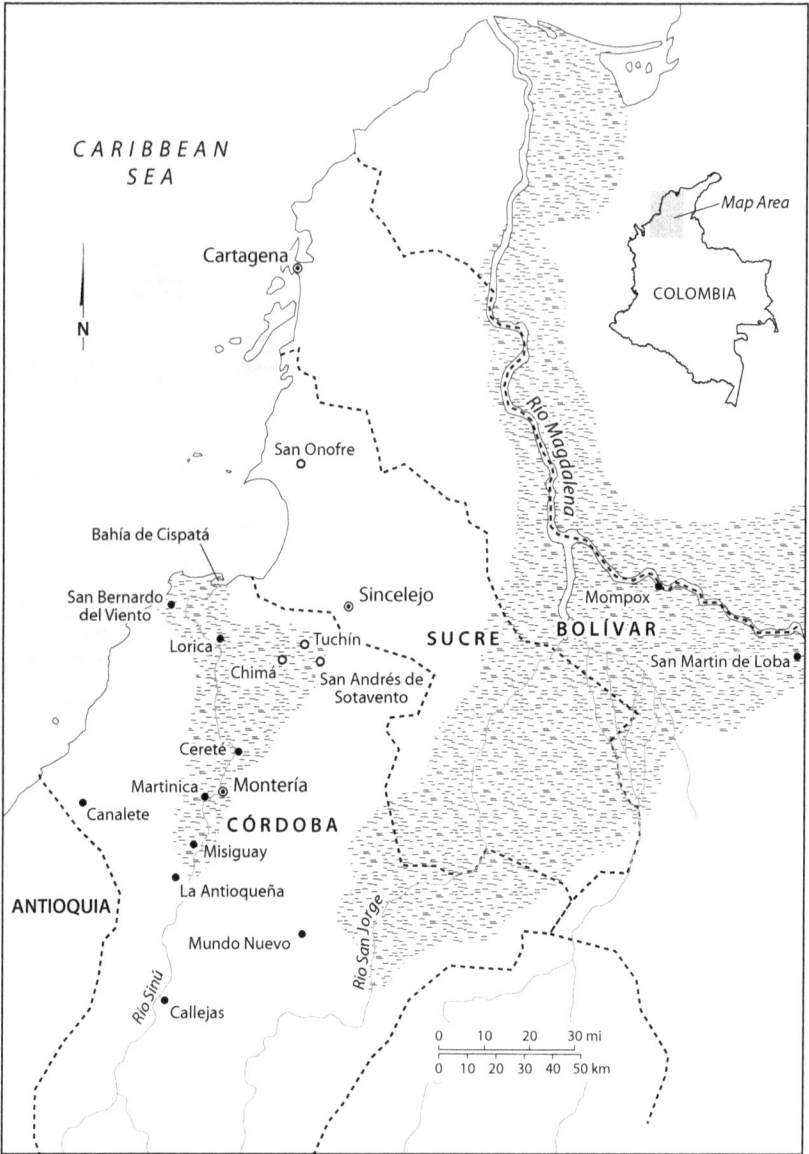

Map I.1   Córdoba and surrounding departments (map by Bill Nelson)

Figure I.3 Sinú River near Tinajones, 1972 (CDRBR/M, CF, 2151. Photo reprinted with permission of the Centro de Documentación Regional "Orlando Fals Borda," Banco de la República, Montería)

My story of the collaboration of Juana Julia Guzmán, Orlando Fals Borda, and Ulianov Chalarka unfolds in the department of Córdoba, located in the northwestern corner of the Colombian Atlantic coast, some six hours by road south of Cartagena (map I.1). Córdoba is a region rimmed by coastal mangrove swamps, a savanna leading northeast into the department of Sucre, and numerous river valleys with lush vegetation and extensive riverine wildlife (fig. I.3), the most important waterway being the Sinú River, which flows into the Caribbean. Until the mid-twentieth century the Sinú furnished the principal mode of transportation for the region (Striffler 1990? [1875]).

Fals called the peasantry of this region "amphibious" in *Historia doble de la Costa* [*Double History of the Coast*], the four-volume masterwork he published between 1979 and 1986, which narrates the agrarian history of the Colombian coastal plain and recounts in considerable detail the research methodology he used in Córdoba from 1972 to 1974 (Fals Borda 1979b: parts 1A and 1B).[3] *Amphibious* is a metaphor that conveys how the region's rural denizens live, fish, and farm on the riverbanks of the Sinú and smaller waterways. Today, many of the wetlands have been drained to make way for cattle pastures; few boats ply the waters of the Sinú, thanks to the construction of roads that link the cities and villages to one another and to Cartagena, Medellín, and beyond. Many of the children and grandchildren of Fals Borda's amphibious peasants now dwell in the working-class barrios of Montería, Sincelejo (the capital of the neighboring department of Sucre), and as far as Caracas, Venezuela, pushed out of their lands by capitalist expansion, poverty, and violence.

Córdoba in the 1970s was one of the centers of militant political action in Colombia, spearheaded by ANUC. It was also one of the places in which alternative approaches to research gestated, evolving out of a partnership forged between radical Latin American social scientists and the leaders of rural social movements. Fals Borda and ANUC formed a crucial node in a network that was emerging in the global South to transform the role of social scientists in society by incorporating popular sectors into the research process. In a sense, they all became "amphibious researchers," moving fluidly between what Fals called "people's knowledge" [*conocimiento popular*] or "people's science" [*ciencia popular*] and scholarly research, and between political action and investigative rigor.

From Reformist to Radical Scholar

It took several decades for Orlando Fals Borda to evolve into a radical scholar. His professional life began as a reformist, with a conventional functionalist research project in the highlands near Bogotá studying peasant economies (Fals Borda 1955), from whence he developed a commitment to agrarian reform following a liberal model that promoted change within the limits set by the Colombian state (Fals Borda 1959; Karl 2017: chap. 5; Moreno Moreno 2017b; Pereira Fernández 2008). He also dedicated himself to building public institutions, founding the Faculty of Sociology of the National University and attracting international funding to establish sociology as a discipline based on empirical research that followed the trends of scholarship in the global North (Arcila Aristizábal 2017; Jaramillo Jimenez 2017; Rojas Guerra 2014).

By the mid-1960s, Fals began to rethink the place of a social scientist in Colombian society. During this period, he weathered a deluge of negative public reaction to his work on La Violencia, the mid-century wave of violence that upended Colombia, taking some two hundred thousand lives from 1948 to 1958. The two-volume study, drawing on a massive archive assembled by an earlier commission made up of representatives of the Liberal and Conservative Parties, the Catholic Church, and the military, was authored by Msgr. Germán Guzmán Campos, Fals, and jurist Eduardo Umaña Luna (1980 [1962]). It flew in the face of previous literature because it offered a sociological analysis of the impunity inherent to the Colombian two-party system, investigating the social context of violence and pointing out its aftereffects. As Jefferson Jaramillo Marín notes, the book "shows the implications of reconstructing the memory and history of the war in the very midst of the war" (2012: 48). Some readers saw it as unfairly condemning the Conservative Party for the atrocities (Jaramillo Jiménez 2017: 320–331).

At the time, Fals's closest colleague at the National University, sociologist and Catholic priest Camilo Torres Restrepo, was building a popular protest movement that provoked his dismissal from his university post; he ultimately joined the guerrillas and was killed in action in 1966. As Fals mourned the loss of his friend, he also confronted a restructuring of the National University that wrested autonomy from the Sociology Faculty and weathered condemnation by a strident student movement for having obtained international funding to build sociology as an academic discipline (Jaramillo Jiménez 2017: chap. 5). He abandoned the National University in the late 1960s, taking up a temporary United Nations posting in Geneva, from whence he corresponded with other scholars in search of new forms of supporting popular movements (ACHUNC/B, caja 49, carpeta 1, fols. 3–22) and penned a theoretical meditation on Latin American social science and political commitment (Fals Borda 1987b [1970]).[4] These are the roots of Fals's radicalization.

Scholarly Research and People's Knowledge

Juana Julia Guzmán and Orlando Fals Borda are representative of the two groups that came together to engage in an unprecedented experiment in what has come to be known as participatory action research (PAR), but which in the early 1970s Fals called "action research." External researchers joined forces with social movements to harness social investigation for political ends by building an intellectual relationship between equals, what Fals termed a symbiosis between "people's knowledge" and "scientific knowledge." Juana Julia, the campesina leader, exemplifies people's knowledge, while urban intellectual Fals Borda epitomizes scientific inquiry.

Action research sought to erase the subject-object distinction that characterized the social science of the period by resignifying research as a dialogue between equals, recognizing that people's knowledge had as much to contribute analytically as did scientific inquiry. Fals argued that theory and practice exist in a dialectical relationship. On the one hand, action researchers must engage in a continuous process of reflection, thereby simultaneously occupying the roles of subject and object. On the other hand, the results of their investigations would nourish political practice while, simultaneously, activism would influence their research agendas (Fals Borda 1987b [1970]; 1978, summarized and translated into English in 1979c; 1991; 2001; 2007, translated into English in 2008a). Researcher and researched would interact as interconnected, self-conscious social agents whose political practice and analyses entered into a dialectical relationship. In the process, a dynamic synergy would evolve between the act of investigation and that of using its results to transform existing social relationships. Rigorous empirical research would contribute to the development of new political strategies, while the political agency of the coresearchers would lead them to establish novel investigative agendas.

Readers may note that I continuously appeal, not to Fals Borda as a unique figure, but to groups of researcher activists. Fals is a towering figure in Latin American social science, but the methodology he conceived could only be achieved through the work of heterogeneous research collectives in which each of the members made a particular contribution. Fals proposed a *participatory* project, not simply because campesinos had a say in the research agenda and functioned as crucial interlocutors while the inquiry unfolded, but because its objectives could not be achieved by a single researcher unconnected to a mass movement. Carlos Rodrigues Brandão, one of Fals Borda's Brazilian interlocutors, argues that participation is best understood as the simultaneous insertion of a research team into a broader social movement and the intervention of the popular organization in the research project itself (Fals Borda and Brandão 1985). In other words, participation involves more than simply inviting peasants to collect information in the service of research: it is a reciprocal process in which popular and scientific knowledge are intertwined with a political goal in mind.

Brandão's assertion brings up a further question. For several years, the Fundación del Caribe played a highly influential role in educating ANUC cadres by placing popular and scientific knowledge in a sustained conversation. How did they achieve this? The answer has a great deal to do with the heterogeneity of the Fundación's team itself, which was made up of local intellectuals, many of them of peasant or working-class origin, only a few of them with university training. This is where Ulianov Chalarka comes in as a key player. His roots were in La Granja, a barrio of Montería populated by peasants dislodged from rural estates in the 1950s and 1960s, but his political positioning was as an urban activist affiliated with the Fundación. He served as a kind of mediator between campesino knowledge and the knowledge of the urban researchers. Much of his mediation was not explicit; it emerged in his ability to capture peasant ideas in vivid visual images that could be articulated into a historical metanarrative of capitalist expansion and peasant resistance. His drawings bridged the gulf between scientific and people's knowledge.

Action Research and Historical Investigation

Action research as it was promoted by Fals and his colleagues combined political activism in support of ANUC with rigorous empirical investigation in archives and with oral narrators. Their objective was to unearth the forgotten histories of popular struggles in order to resignify them as organizing tools for social movements. Other activist intellectuals, whom I will mention in the coming pages, did not make history the center of their research: it was a particular feature of the work of Fals and his associates; it owes in part to Fals's own trajectory as a scholar, as well as the antecedents of his allies, like Víctor Daniel Bonilla (1972 [1968]), whom I will introduce in the coming pages. In his previous research among highland peasants, Fals consulted archives to lend historical depth to his analysis of rural economies (Fals Borda 1955, 1979a [1957]). Later, he consulted historical materials in his study of La Violencia (Guzmán Campos, Fals Borda, and Umaña Luna 1980 [1962]). He penned a history of subversive ideas in Colombia in the nineteenth and twentieth centuries, including the rise of the Liberal Party and of socialism, respectively (Fals Borda 1969). His writings were informed by the work of C. Wright Mills, the North American sociologist whose pathbreaking *The Sociological Imagination* (1959) fused sociological and historical analysis. By the late 1960s, like many of his Latin American colleagues, Fals had ranged far beyond his functionalist pedigree, acquired during graduate training at the University of Minnesota and the University of Florida, to engage historical materialism as one of his fundamental theoretical supports. Fals's Marxist turn further cemented his need to engage in historical research as a fount for building class consciousness, which is how the Fundación del Caribe proposed to harness history to ANUC's struggle.

Indeed, Juana Julia's statement that "cowards don't make history" lay at the heart of the Fundación's experiment. As Michel-Rolph Trouillot (1995: chap. 1) observes, history is at once a lived experience and a narrative about that process. Juana Julia made history in the first sense, by fighting the matrícula in the 1920s. In the 1970s she made history in Trouillot's second sense, when she recounted her story to a new generation of ANUC activists. Inspired by her experience, her peasant audience would make history by redrawing the agrarian landscape through the occupation of haciendas and their efforts to imagine the peasantry as a class capable of asserting its place in the Caribbean political landscape. Similarly, the story of Fals Borda's collaboration with ANUC exemplifies the double movement of history, because he and his colleagues studied the past and produced historical narratives for campesino readers in order to transform their present. History stood at the center of the Fundación del Caribe's project.

The Purpose of This Book

History also lies at the center of my interests. This book is an attempt at recovering the experiences, research process, and lessons of the Fundación del Caribe. While the research techniques and the political and intellectual consequences of the Fundación's work have been summarized and evaluated by numerous scholars, including Fals himself (Fals Borda 1985, 1978; Parra Escobar 1983; Rudqvist 1986; Zamosc 1986a), a thorough inquiry into the everyday practice and the dynamics of the Fundación as a team—how they conducted their research, how and to what purposes they disseminated it—sheds significant light on what was so innovative about their proposal and why it is still useful today as a tool to confront major social, political, and economic challenges in Latin America and beyond.

I made my first visit in 2008 to the archives of the National University in Bogotá (ACHUNC/B) where Fals donated most of his papers, which had or were being consulted by a number of graduate students (Arcila Aristizábal 2017; Díaz Arévalo 2017, 2018a; Moreno Moreno 2017b; and Pereira Fernández 2005, 2008, 2008–2009) and other scholars (Jaramillo Jiménez 2017). The following year I traveled to Montería to consult the Orlando Fals Borda Center for Regional Documentation (CDRBR/M), where he deposited his research notes from the Atlantic coast. Fals's Montería papers had only recently been catalogued and I was among the first researchers to work with them; I invited a number of my graduate students to make forays into this largely unexplored resource (Arrieta Fernández 2015; McRae 2015; Pernett 2015; Poggi 2015; Robles Lomeli 2015, 2019) and organized workshops for Montería researchers to introduce them to the archive. At the outset I thought my archival excursions would be the first step in a multi-sited ethnographic study of several collaborative research teams in Latin America through which I would analyze their dynamics, inspired by my own work with indigenous organizations in the southwestern department of Cauca (Rappaport 2005, 2008). I hoped to observe how other scholars navigated the complexities of collaborating with nonacademic researchers whose objectives and methodologies did not always mesh with those of academics.

Fals Borda is recognized as an important forebear of the recent wave of collaborative research in Latin America (Leyva Solano and Speed 2015: 453–454; Santos 2018: 255–257); for this reason, I chose to look into his activities while I continued to pursue the feasibility of conducting ethnographic research in

Argentina, Bolivia, and Mexico, where important experiments in collaboration have taken place (Briones et al. 2007; RACCACH 2010; Rivera Cusicanqui 2004). I assumed my archival visits would be perfunctory, furnishing material for an early chapter in a volume whose thrust would be ethnographic. The present book attests to my abandonment of that goal. As I perused Fals Borda's papers, I grew increasingly captivated by the novelty and insightfulness of his work on the Caribbean coast. I also began to realize that the Fundación's objectives differed from those of the more recent collaborative ethnography that had been my starting point. Although collaborative researchers also seek to establish horizontal research relationships, train local researchers, deliver crucial research materials to communities, and tackle key questions of how to interweave distinct (but not entirely incommensurate) epistemologies into a single project, much collaborative ethnography is intended, from the start, to result in academic or quasi-academic publications of one sort or another.[5] Moreover, while collaborative ethnography may support direct action, collaborative researchers are not necessarily activists. In contrast, Fals and the Fundación intimately fused research with activism. As I came to comprehend the nuances of the Fundación's work, I decided to limit my attention to this project and to abandon my ethnographic plans.

My focus on the Fundación del Caribe is particularly important today, when Colombians are navigating a peace process that the national government is intent on derailing. Participatory action research is one of the tools that grassroots, ethnic, and human rights organizations have at their disposal. Many practitioners acknowledge their genealogical relationship with Fals Borda, but much of what they recognize as his legacy are specific techniques for collecting information, not the broader objectives and the underlying philosophy of the Fundación's project. An ethnographic history of the Fundación fills in this gap. In particular, I want to probe what *participation* meant to this pioneering research team, how its members attempted to create a horizontal and politically fruitful relationship between external researchers and peasant activists, and how they implemented its guiding principles on the political stage of the Caribbean coast in the early 1970s. My purpose here is not purely academic; I hope that it will inspire participatory-action practitioners to take a second look at the contributions that Fals Borda made to their methodology.

A Critical Moment in Latin American Social Science

The story of Fals Borda on the Colombian Caribbean coast can be read as a microcosm of broader intellectual developments in Latin America in the late

1960s and 1970s. In response to a hardening of the effects of capitalist development, United States foreign policy, and the success of the Cuban Revolution, many prominent Latin American thinkers inspired by Marxism developed methodologies that fused activism with empirical research and effectively detached the locus of research from its traditional academic home. While many members of this intellectual vanguard continued to interact productively with northern academic institutions and to engage in dialogue with northern scholars, they self-consciously created innovative theoretical and methodological vehicles whose origins were in the global South (Rosemblatt 2014). Fals himself acknowledged a debt to North American varieties of action research, particularly those of Kurt Lewin and Sol Tax (Fals Borda 2001: 29), although as his interlocutor Carlos Rodrigues Brandão (2005) asserts, Latin American methodologies were different: inspired by Marxist analyses of economic inequality, they were self-consciously emancipatory, promoting radical change through political collaboration with popular movements, as opposed to Lewin's and Tax's fostering of participation by individuals in localized and more apolitical contexts (a notable exception to this distinction being the Highlander Folk School/Research and Education Center [Horton and Freire 1990]).

While a great deal of the work I draw on in this introduction originated in Latin America, it would be a mistake to focus exclusively on the intellectual geopolitics of that continent to the exclusion of the South-South and North-South dialogues that were also taking place at the time. The social scientists and activists involved in this wave of theory creation were linked into expansive networks dedicated to the propagation of alternative methodologies that extended from Chile, Colombia, and Brazil to Bangladesh, Canada, India, Tanzania, and the United States. Fals came into contact in the mid-1970s with a series of participatory researchers working on other continents as well as in neighboring countries, including Marja-Liisa Swantz and Budd Hall in Tanzania (Hall 1992; Swantz 1982), Francisco Vío Grossi in Chile and Venezuela (Vío Grossi 1981), and Rajesh Tandon in India (Tandon 1988). They and many other activist researchers came together in 1977 at an international symposium on participatory research that Fals organized in the Caribbean city of Cartagena (Simposio Mundial de Cartagena 1978). The approaches being adopted in Latin America were gestating in other parts of the Third World (McTaggart 1994), where practitioners energized by Fals's approach found that it brought together in an innovative way precisely those organizing principles they were pursuing (Rajesh Tandon, personal communication).

In the late 1960s and the 1970s, Latin American intellectuals elaborated a critique of positivist social science emanating from the global North, which, they argued, presented models that were not applicable to Latin America or other regions of the global South because they paid scant attention to the structural obstacles faced by its inhabitants. Southern social scientists had already begun to recognize that northern theories emerged out of an analysis of social realities different from their own (Cardoso and Weffort 1973). The approaches they pioneered were also different because they were not predicated on particular academic disciplines but instead incorporated anthropology, education, history, law, political science, and sociology. Social science departments were relatively new to Latin American universities (Cataño 1986), and scholars divided their attention between the academy and the public sphere (Restrepo 2002), opening the space to engage in an experiment in which academic researchers and grassroots activists operated on an equal footing, transcending the geopolitical, disciplinary, and institutional borders that were recognized by most social scientists of the period.

The materials these researchers produced went beyond scholarly writings to experiment with other modes of exposition intended for use in movements promoting radical social change. Perhaps most renowned was Brazilian educator Paulo Freire, whose methodology of *conscientização* [critical consciousness] was elucidated in *Pedagogy of the Oppressed* (Freire 2005 [1970]). Freire sought to transform the political and social consciousness of working-class people through emancipatory dialogue. In contrast to official literacy textbooks that trained adult learners through a series of generic texts organized according to the difficulty of their syllabic content, Freire advocated a program of grassroots research in which peasants and workers would collaborate to identify the relations of oppression under which they were forced to live and begin to formulate authentic, autonomous courses of action to transform the status quo, an approach in which literacy meant much more than learning to decipher print.[6] Similar initiatives at promoting horizontal relationships between researchers and the grass roots in the service of popular political action were taking place in cinema, where Andean indigenous communities collaborated in the production of films reenacting their historical struggles (Sanjinés and Grupo Ukamao 1979), and in theater, where drama workshops introduced working-class urbanites and rural villagers to socially critical theatrical methodologies for analyzing their social conditions (Boal 1985 [1974]). Participatory analysis by working-class people and peasants was undertaken in the Christian base communities that arose out of liberation theology (Gutiérrez 2012 [1971]). A new literary genre called testimonial literature created a communicative space in which a member of the oppressed class presented his or her personal story to an editor, who then shaped it for a broad readership (Achugar 1992; Barnet and Montejo 2016 [1966]; Randall 1992).

Such activist proposals resonated with Latin American academics intent on elaborating radical critiques of their disciplines. They rejected the positivist and functionalist models fashionable in North America, adopting Marxism and dependency theory as theoretical guides (González Casanova 1969), paying close attention to social class and forging relationships with organized popular sectors of society, particularly with indigenous communities and the agrarian and urban proletariat (Bartolomé et al. 1971; Stavenhagen 1971; Warman et al. 1970). The work of these academics intersected on multiple levels with figures in adult education, liberation theology, and the arts. This was a wide-ranging, pervasive body of thought in Latin America.

Fals Borda was well aware of these developments on the continental level. He was familiar with the work of the Grupo Ukamao well before embarking on his project in Córdoba (Fals Borda 1987b [1970]: 114) and, according to Víctor Negrete, had read Freire's *Pedagogy of the Oppressed* in manuscript form. He celebrated the independence of Latin American scholarship: "I believe, precisely, that what was attractive about our work was that we felt no need to appeal to any authority in the tradition called 'the Western academy' in order to achieve our approach to our own reality" (Fals Borda and Brandão 1986: 17).

Fals eventually came in contact with many of the Colombian protagonists of the democratization of research. Freire's writings had been appropriated as a guide for rethinking popular adult education in the marginal barrios of Bogotá, leading in the late 1970s to the creation of a Freirian pedagogical current spearheaded by Lola Cendales (Ortega Valencia and Torres Carrillo 2011) that explicitly engaged participatory methodologies (de Schutter 1985). CINEP, the Centro de Investigación y Educación Popular [Center of Popular Research and Education], a Jesuit research institute, sought opportunities to connect with popular classes, which they saw as a revolutionary subject with whom they could collaborate both intellectually and politically. They envisioned rigorous historical research as culminating in popular political decision-making, and their religious and lay researchers set up projects in marginal barrios in Bogotá. CINEP also worked closely with ANUC before Fals Borda arrived in Córdoba, ultimately amassing with the collaboration of sociologist Leon Zamosc an extensive archive of oral testimonies of peasant struggle (to which I will refer in the coming chapters as CINEP/B). Their researchers employed a version of action research as one of several methodologies they engaged (Archila Neira 1973, 2013, 2015).

Radical theater groups took root in Colombia's major cities, an artistic movement that a cosmopolitan intellectual like Fals could not have ignored, even if the sectarian sentiments of the time may have precluded him from developing close relationships with the most prominent of the directors

(S. García 1979; Parra Salazar 2015). Marta Rodríguez, for a brief time a student of sociology at the National University, began in the 1970s to pioneer collaborative cinema with indigenous organizations as a vehicle for recuperating their oral memory (Bedoya Ortiz 2011). Fals Borda's colleague at the National University of Colombia, the revolutionary Catholic priest Camilo Torres Restrepo, was a strong proponent of liberation theology (Torres Restrepo 1985). Fals was brought up Presbyterian and was deeply inspired by his pastor in Barranquilla, the Protestant liberation theologian Richard Shaull (1967), who was an active participant in the World Council of Churches and was familiar with Freire's writings (Díaz Arévalo 2017; Pereira Fernández 2005). Indeed, there existed a vast Latin American intellectual movement that nourished Fals Borda's aspirations.

La Rosca: Critical Recovery and Systematic Devolution

It was in this fertile terrain that Fals founded a network of Colombian activist researchers. Their umbrella organization, which also functioned as a publishing house, was called La Rosca de Investigación y Acción Social [Circle of Research and Social Action] (henceforth, La Rosca); *rosca* means "in-group" in Colombian Spanish and a kind of circle or spiral in Catalán. La Rosca came into being at a meeting in Geneva in 1970, where Fals was then working for the United Nations on a study of cooperatives and social development (Fals Borda 1971), although it was preceded by conversations with numerous colleagues and the drafting of tentative proposals (ACHUNC/B, caja 49, carpeta 1, fols. 9–11). In addition to Fals, its founding members included sociologist Gonzalo Castillo, economist Augusto Libreros, and journalist/ethnographer Víctor Daniel Bonilla (Jorge Ucrós, another founding member of La Rosca, was tragically killed in an automobile accident shortly after the collective came into existence).

La Rosca established study groups across Colombia between 1972 and 1974. Bonilla collaborated with the nascent Consejo Regional Indígena del Cauca, or CRIC [Regional Indigenous Council of Cauca], to reintroduce into the Nasa communal memory the history of eighteenth-century hereditary lords who acquired land titles for Native communities (Bonilla 1977). Castillo, working with indigenous groups in neighboring Tolima, edited and published a treatise he found in the community archives by Manuel Quintín Lame, an indigenous leader of the early twentieth century (Lame 1971 [1939]); Lame's book would become an inspirational voice in the indigenous movement. Libreros worked in the shantytowns of the Pacific Coast and the Cauca Valley. Born to a middle-class family in the coastal city of Barranquilla, Fals returned to his roots, so to speak, when he began to collaborate in early 1972 with ANUC on the Caribbean coast, accompanying peasant activists to occupations of haciendas and collecting oral and documentary histories of land struggles.

In its time, La Rosca was a somewhat unusual organization. Its members, who shared Marxism as a guiding philosophy, were never affiliated with the small leftist parties that populated the Colombian political landscape. Three of them—Castillo, Fals Borda, and Libreros—were practicing Presbyterians, an affiliation that enabled them to acquire considerable funding from the Presbyterian Church in the United States.[7] These characteristics of the research collective left its members open to biting criticism by the organized left, which was deeply mistrustful of the insertion of politically independent Protestants into the peasant and indigenous movements whose loyalties it, too, was intent on winning. It was precisely its Presbyterian funding that enabled La Rosca's projects to flourish with minimal external supervision, allowing for a full-time insertion into the social movements that the researchers had committed to supporting.

La Rosca's research philosophy guided the work of the Fundación del Caribe in Montería. Central to their approach was an objective they called *recuperación crítica* [critical recovery], which paid "special attention to those elements or institutions that have been useful in the past to confront the enemies of the exploited classes. Once those elements are determined, they are reactivated with the aim of using them in a similar manner in current class struggles" (Bonilla et al. 1972: 51–52). One of the best examples of this principle is the revival of autonomous indigenous political institutions through the reinvigoration of the councils [*cabildos*] that governed indigenous reservations [*resguardos*], an effort that was historically substantiated through archival research. As I will describe in detail in coming chapters, with the collaboration of Juana Julia Guzmán, the Fundación unearthed the story of socialist collectives in the 1920s that furnished organizing models for ANUC. Critical recovery laid the conceptual foundations for the insertion of Fundación del Caribe's historical research into ANUC's agenda, thereby transforming action research into a political process, rather than simply a research project.

The fruits of critical recovery were disseminated through what La Rosca called *devolución sistemática* [systematic devolution], whereby research results were returned to the organizational leadership and its rank and file "in an ordered fashion, adjusted to the levels of political and educational development of the grassroots groups that use the information or with whom insertion as researchers or experts has been executed, not according to the intellectual level of cadres, who are generally more advanced" (Fals Borda 1987b [1970]: 113). In the indigenous southwestern highlands, La Rosca began to investigate the possibilities of encoding the critical recovery of history in maps that would serve as props for community reflection. This ultimately culminated—several years after the demise of the La Rosca network in 1975—in a series of picture-maps called *mapas parlantes* [speaking maps] that replicate the topographical modes of remembering the indigenous past (Bonilla 1982; ACHUNC/B, caja 49, carpeta 3, fols. 61–70; see also Barragán León 2016). Since these maps were purely pictorial, they permitted viewers to discuss them collectively in their own language, to embellish on and correct what the cartographies depicted—in short, to reflect on history according to their own uses and customs. Ulianov Chalarka's historical comics fulfilled similar goals on the Caribbean coast.

Systematic devolution ensured that the products of research would have a life beyond the bookshelves, in activist practice. These materials were never meant to be final products, as occurs in academic (even much collaborative) research, as an unidentified speaker emphasized at a 1982 workshop, whose transcript I discovered in Fals's Bogotá archive:

> The mapa [parlante] is not a research result; while it is the result of a single stage of the research, the research continues afterward; when certain cases are examined, [participants] must identify other elements, and they must consider them or remember them, or stow them away, or someone told them, or that the map is a particular moment, a material basis, something they can see and touch, and they arrive at knowledge through this material basis. (ACHUNC/B, caja 49, carpeta 3, fol. 129)

La Rosca conceptualized research as a continuous activity that evolved out of the sedimentation of progressive stages of memory retrieval and interpretation, enabling grassroots information sharing and analysis. In a sense, the word *devolution* does not do justice to the scope of devolución sistemática, because it involved much more than "returning" research results to communities.

The two principles of critical recovery and systematic devolution were grounded in the conviction that external researchers were not mere observers, nor were the members of popular organizations unsophisticated informants whose words and activities would be recorded by the researchers. As Fals Borda argues, "One and the other work together, all are thinking and acting subjects in the work of investigation. One would not exploit the other as an 'object' of research, above all because the knowledge is generated and returned in circumstances controlled by the group itself" (1987b [1970]: 91). Both external and internal researchers would enjoy the same level of responsibility in a project; both would have a voice in setting the agenda and in carrying out the research. This transforms the very meaning of *objectivity* into a bi- or multidirectional process. In effect, La Rosca anticipated by decades scholars who have reconceptualized objectivity as the synthesis of multiple perspectives, as opposed to the observations of a single (white male) academic writing from the global North (Haraway 1991; Santos 2018).

Reconceptualizing Research

Augusto Libreros and Fals Borda authored a 1974 manual for would-be action researchers titled "Cuestiones de metodología aplicada a las ciencias sociales" ["Questions of Methodology Applied to the Social Sciences"], which was distributed in mimeographed form (ACHUNC/B, caja 49, carpeta 3, fols. 177–268; Fals Borda 1978: 48). In an almost messianic passage, reminiscent of their shared Protestant heritage, they lay out a dialectic in which the validity of knowledge generated by action researchers can only be proven through political activity: "Knowledge takes on a prophetic character and political praxis becomes a criterion for validating knowledge oriented toward action. Political praxis causes prophecy to become reality. For this reason, social knowledge is associated more and more with political aims" (ACHUNC/B, caja 49, carpeta 3, fol. 183). For La Rosca, knowledge would be generated and analyzed collectively in order to identify the social contradictions that propel popular struggle (ACHUNC/B, caja 49, carpeta 3, fol. 190). In the process, external researchers would articulate—but never entirely blend in—with the rank and file. Fals places participatory researchers in the Gramscian category of organic intellectuals, capable of "articulat[ing] between regional specificity and general or national theory, to produce a totalizing and integral vision of the knowledge that has been acquired" (Fals Borda 2010b: 189–190).

Consequently, if we limit our definition of research to the collection and analysis of information by trained professionals, we lose sight of the innovative character of La Rosca's project. Their experiences provide an alternative notion of what research is, one that does not negate the significance of academic rigor but, instead, places the work of experts in dialogue with other modes of inquiry. Luis Guillermo Vasco argues that the collective analysis of social reality at workshops and assemblies of the Colombian indigenous movement must be understood as a form of research (Vasco Uribe 2002: 461). He is seconded by Pilar Riaño-Alcalá (2009), who notes, in a handbook she produced for local memory workshops for victims of conflict, that although results of such encounters are ultimately summarized in published reports, the meetings themselves constitute the primary spaces in which collaborative research *among*—as opposed to *about*—victims of violence takes place. Andrea Dyrness, working with Latina mothers at a community school in California, argues that the research process provided the women with a space to share and analyze their experiences and critiques of educational reform "in light of broader patterns" (Dyrness 2008: 31). In other words, Dyrness, Riaño, and Vasco visualize collaborative forms of research as a process of thinking through ideas, not exclusively of systematically collecting data that is then subjected to analysis by the external observer to ultimately emerge as a final product.

This is a profoundly political activity that moves research away from the desk of the scholar and into the meeting venues that activists frequent, the spaces in which issues are aired and decisions are made (Hale and Stephen 2014). Of course, we academic scholars continue to collect data, because that is what we are trained to do and because we are dealing with unfamiliar social or cultural contexts that we can only come to know by studying them. Our ability to systematize new knowledge is undeniably what we have to contribute to the collaborative relationship. Insiders, in contrast, tend to engage in a more intuitive process, so that research for them is a sustained public reflection on what they and their peers carry in their personal memories and a search for where those reminiscences will lead them in the future. Consequently, collaboration between external and internal researchers evolves as a dialogue between two differently positioned participants who have distinct skill sets and conceptual frameworks.[8]

Fals Borda conceptualized research in this way in some of his reflections on his experiences in Córdoba. In 1978, with the Fundación del Caribe already in the rearview mirror, he argued that although external researchers were concerned with the collection of information, campesinos interpreted this data and inserted it into their political practice in a continuous movement between observation and theory, reflection and action (Fals Borda 1978: 34–35). In other words, he envisioned a dialogue punctuated by activism, in which participation involved using information garnered through research to make collective decisions concerning political action. In this sense, the work of the Fundación was deeply participatory in ways that are not always readily observable in retrospect.

Imputation

As I came to understand Fals Borda's particular brand of action research, I realized that what set it apart was its profound creativity. Critical recovery, systematic devolution, and the innovative techniques the Fundación del Caribe used to collect information were generated out of a deeply original impulse. Exceptional research is, of course, always creative, but it is usually produced by an individual or a small group of experts. Action research, in contrast, required not only the imaginative capacities of researchers like Fals Borda, but also the simultaneous stimulation of creative thinking among peasant participants. If ANUC was to make and rewrite history, it would take a collective effort to reimagine the past outside of the confines of conventional history and to envision how that past could be harnessed to impact the future. Action research was, in effect, a collective work of the imagination that envisaged scenarios for local history, crafted historical narratives out of stored objects and oral reminiscences, rooted peasants in the footsteps of their forebears, and constructed alternative epistemologies that could be used to build new institutions and practices. If the only creative impulses to be harnessed had been Fals Borda's, the participatory dimension of the project would have had little meaning. At all stages of the process, the peasant imagination had to be nurtured as an integral component of the methodology.

As I struggled to make sense of Fals Borda's personal archives and the reminiscences I gathered from his collaborators, I turned to *Historia doble de la Costa*, his four-volume historical narrative of the expansion of agrarian capitalism on the Atlantic coast, in which he reflects retrospectively on his methodology (Fals Borda 1979b, 1981, 1984, 1986). His text helped me to navigate the complex constellation of documents in his field notes and assisted me in generating new research questions. Each volume of *Historia doble* is framed by a semi-mythic persona originating in discussions with local narrators (CDRBR/M, 0750, fol. 4228; 0757, fol. 4246; 1108, fol. 6375).[9] For example, in the third volume, *Resistencia en el San Jorge* [Resistance in the San Jorge], Fals employs the motif of the "turtle-man" [*hombre-hicotea*], whose tremendous powers of endurance stem from his ability to bury himself below the riverbed and hibernate during the dry season, emerging with the rains to eat and reproduce; Costeño peasants exhibit similar capacities to withstand poverty, displacement, and exploitation (1984: introducción).

Fals also introduces into *Historia doble* passages in which he paints verbal portraits of the landscape and crafts imaginary dialogues attributed to his historical protagonists. He renders peasant narratives in lyric prose, sometimes combining several narrators into a single voice. For example, *El Presidente Nieto* [President Nieto], the second volume of *Historia doble*, moves between a narration of the civil wars that beset Colombia in the nineteenth century, reflected in the writings and achievements of Juan José Nieto, a mulatto from the Atlantic coast who was briefly named president of Colombia between 1865 and 1866—a presidency that was only formally recognized by the Colombian state in 2018—and the experiences of Costeño peasants during the same period (Fals Borda 1981). The peasant voice is personified by a single narrator, Adolfo Mier (also called *tatarabuelo* or great-grandfather Mier), whose long tale of suffering and displacement is recounted using peculiarly Costeño turns of phrase. But when the reader tallies the years that Fals purports Mier to have lived, the time span transcends that of a normal human being, suggesting that the tatarabuelo is a composite character (Robles Lomeli 2015, 2019).

Fals calls this strategy "imputation." At first, I assumed that his use of the techniques of literary nonfiction was solely aimed at bringing to life historical facts. Certainly, he was aware of the possibilities of the genre, given his friendship with Gabriel García Márquez, whose *Story of a Shipwrecked Sailor* [*Relato de un náufrago*] is a luminous example of Latin American journalism (García Márquez 1986 [1970]). Fals worked side by side with testimonial author David Sánchez Juliao and was close to Alfredo Molano, who began to adopt such literary techniques at the same time Fals did (Molano 1998b). All of these writers craft scenarios out of the details of the past, with the objective of drawing emotional associations between the reader and the characters, something that occurs routinely in the writing of historical novels, whose authors use the present "to create . . . emotional resonances with a theoretical past, through the reactions of . . . characters to the present," in this way fostering "a sense of the past as real and tangible" (Polack 2014: 529). In *El Presidente Nieto*, the campesino narrator recollects events from the nineteenth century as though he were an eyewitness to them, but he is portrayed in conversation with Fals, a historical impossibility.

Imputation is an accepted methodology used by quantitative social scientists to identify missing values in a data set (Rässler et al. 2003). Perhaps this was Fals's original source, although he expands upon it to such a great extent that it resembles less the work of his quantitative colleagues and more the craft of the historical novelist, where credibility trumps proof and accuracy (Polack 2014: 540).[10] Nonetheless, his appeal to experimental formats constitutes much more than a literary vehicle, because it allows "those who provided the information on the working classes to recognize it as their own" (Fals Borda 1981: 55B). That is to say, imputation is, for Fals, a politically effective strategy.

Fals writes that he employed imputation in his work with ANUC (Fals Borda 1985: 59), although he never explicitly called it that while he was in Córdoba. Some of the techniques he used to revive popular memory are good examples of how imputation became a political strategy: community meetings where elders narrated their experiences, the founding of study groups among local activists, the introduction of sociodramas through which peasants reenacted their past, and the collective perusal of objects of memory and photos stored in peasant homes. All of these techniques invoked the communal analysis of the past with an eye to immediately incorporating its lessons into the political actions of the present. In fact, if we trace an alternative genealogy of action research, not back to Lewin or Tax, but to the early twentieth-century Viennese researcher J. L. Moreno, who invented the term *sociodrama* in his work with prostitutes (Altricher and Gstettner 1997; McTaggart 1994: 316), we begin to see how peasants could become coresearchers through such exercises.

Of particular importance are Ulianov Chalarka's graphic histories, which draw on nonverbal memories and compel readers to exercise their imaginative faculties (Sousanis 2015: chap. 3). Take, for instance, Chalarka's depiction of bullfighting festivals [*corralejas*] in one of his later comics, *El Boche* (Chalarka 1985: 57). The authors of the graphic history argue that the corraleja was introduced on the Caribbean coast to placate disruptive peasants poised to confront the debt-peonage system. The comics panel is historically accurate, depicting early twentieth-century peasants in the ring confronting the bulls, while large landholders identified by their names gaze at their skirmishes from the safety of their private stalls. Two bulls wait in the pens, straining to be let loose on the crowd of campesinos. They carry names: Barraquete and Machín. Barraquete was a famously strong-willed bull from the 1950s; I learned in a 2019 workshop with University of Sinú faculty that by the 1960s, both monikers had become the titles of well-known *porros*, a musical genre typical of the plains of Córdoba and Sucre. Images from the present of Chalarka's peasant readers effectively anchor them in the past represented by the comics panels. Similarly, novelist Toni Morrison observes that her work, frequently based in the past, begins with a series of images culled from her experience of places and things, which she eventually fashions into a literary text (Morrison 1995), just as the Fundación del Caribe's vivid images of history were frequently drawn from the present. But while they depicted the past, they looked toward the future, eventually fashioned into an activist agenda.

The Organization of This Book

Cowards Don't Make History is organized according to the guiding concepts of La Rosca, which shepherded the Fundación del Caribe in its collaboration with ANUC: participation, critical recovery, and systematic devolution. I explain how to recognize them in the Fundación's practice, how Fals wrote about them, and how they are relevant to today's participatory action researchers. Numerous analysts have critiqued Orlando Fals Borda's approach to action research, pointing out his inability to discard traditional research techniques and the overwhelming attention paid by the Fundación del Caribe to schooled cadres instead of to the rank and file (Rivera Cusicanqui 2004; Vasco Uribe 2002, 2011). Notwithstanding the significance of these assessments—which I refer to in the course of my narrative—I feel compelled to underscore my conviction that it is facile to construct in hindsight a broad-brush critique, more than four decades after Fals and his associates conducted their work in Córdoba, particularly given that Fals's critics had only limited access to the details of the Fundación's activities. Certainly, Fals and the Fundación's project had obvious shortcomings of which any collaborative or participatory research must be aware. However, my fundamental objective is not to disparage, but to delve into how their methodology was conceived and executed on Caribbean soil in the early 1970s, always keeping in mind that they were pioneers who were unable to take advantage of the hindsight we enjoy today. Without a close examination of what the Fundación did on the ground—without paying attention to their process—criticisms of Fals Borda may pose significant questions but they do not provide us with answers. Fals's experience demonstrates, moreover, that alternative forms of collaborative research are "good to think," even for academics who are not activists, expanding the constellation of ideas that we have at our disposal at a time when an ever-increasing layer of those who were the traditional objects of research have become researchers in their own right (Hale 2006).

I begin this book with the historical context of the Caribbean coast in the twentieth century, detailing the various moments at which peasant organizing disrupted the spread of capitalism. Here, I return to Juana Julia Guzmán and her associates in the 1920s, tracing the linkages between her early efforts at overturning the debt-peonage system and ANUC's eruption into the political scene a half century later. Chapter 1 also introduces readers to the work of the Fundación del Caribe between 1972 and 1974, when its collaboration with ANUC ended. From there, I turn in chapter 2 to how Fals organized his personal archives, especially his field notes from the Caribbean coast between

1972 and 1974. I do not intend for this chapter to be a mere academic exercise, however. Fals classified his field notes in such a way that they enabled or supported activism, as opposed to cataloguing substantiating evidence for his academic writing. This is apparent in the categories he employed, which highlight the names of peasant leaders whose narratives were decisive in the utilization of historical information to craft ANUC strategies or underscore particular moments in the peasant struggle and the institutions that supported it. The fact that Fals's brand of action research privileged action over dispassionate research, and advocated the adoption of popular forms of narration and interpretation as opposed to hewing to standard academic formulas, is evident in how the contents of Fals's categories are assembled. Instead of proceeding from research questions to information collection and scholarly analysis, Fals's archival classification facilitated the process by which peasant forms of knowledge were brought to bear in the composition and diffusion of educational materials. This was a working archive, assembled and consulted by a group of researcher activists, with the aim of provoking political action born of historical reflection. While in subsequent chapters I draw on the archive's contents, chapter 2 explores how its form reflects the innovative methodology with which Fals and the Fundación were experimenting, providing a first look at how peasant epistemologies entered into dialogue with scientific knowledge.

Chapter 3 inquires into how the Fundación del Caribe resignified participation and research. What did Fals intend when he proposed to undertake a participatory research project in a region whose peasants were largely illiterate, living hand-to-mouth, many of them so isolated that they had never even visited nearby Montería? To what extent was the Fundación able to inspire their participation? How can we conceptualize their activities as research?

I use the process of the production of the Fundación's four graphic histories as an ethnographic scenario in which to visualize the dynamics of the Fundación's participatory methodology, examining various phases of their work: the establishment of a research agenda; the collection of eyewitness testimonies whose highlights were captured in Ulianov Chalarka's drawings; the crafting of comics panels by the Fundación collective; and the evaluation and dissemination of the educational materials. I describe how participation involved the intervention of different groups of people at various points in the process, each contributing his or her particular skill, but all collaborating in the analysis of the material. This process redefined the meanings attached to research.

The activities involved in the making of the Fundación's graphic histories were guided by the collective's goal of critically recovering the history of institutions and practices that might contribute to building a popular movement. In chapter 4, I take a second look at the Fundación's graphic histories, this time inquiring into two examples of critical recovery in Córdoba. First, the 1972 introduction of *baluartes*—communal landholdings modeled after socialist collectives of the early twentieth century—on occupied haciendas. The first of the graphic histories, *Lomagrande*, which centers on the founding of the first baluarte by Juana Julia Guzmán and her associates in the 1920s, provides an excellent platform from which to analyze the challenges and the pitfalls of critical recovery as a narrative strategy and a political tool, given that ANUC's base never entirely warmed to the concept of the baluarte, which they only imperfectly understood. Chalarka's second pamphlet, *Tinajones*, presents an alternative scenario, in which the visual dimension of the comic effectively conveys the "amphibious" nature of the river-dwelling peasant settlers, who in the 1920s constructed raised fields in the coastal mangroves to enable rice cultivation. In this instance, the Fundación effectively recuperated values from the past that continued to be central to the peasant psyche.

One of my greatest challenges has been that of visualizing a research practice whose everyday details are no longer accessible in the memory of its protagonists. My respondents remembered guiding principles, procedures, techniques, and important disputes within the Fundación, between the Fundación and ANUC, and with leftist parties. But I found it impossible to evoke more specific reminiscences, such as memories of how differences were aired as the team put together *Lomagrande*, or the constructive debates that might have preceded the creation of a workshop agenda. However, facets of the Fundación's labors can be identified using techniques other than oral testimony. Chapter 5 examines the process of systematic devolution with an eye to fleshing out the activities that accompanied the dissemination of adult education materials among the ANUC rank and file. In particular, I look at practices that might have triggered peasant participation in workshops. Following Fals's lead of using imputation as an interpretive tool, I mine Ulianov Chalarka's comics panels for clues as to how they might have influenced their readers, leading them to think along certain avenues, steering them toward specific interlocutors and particular discussion topics.

In 1975, Fals Borda began research in the neighboring department of Bolívar, which ultimately led to the publication of *Historia doble de la Costa*. That four-volume experimental history bears the imprints of action research: the forging of horizontal relationships between researchers and the researched, the search for usable historical referents, a dialogue between theory and practice, epistemological heterogeneity. The central arguments of *Historia doble* were first drafted for a leftist weekly, *Alternativa*, drawing on discussions and lectures that took place at workshops. In other words, *Historia doble* is a logical extension of the work of an activist researcher, not a purely academic contribution to the literature. In chapter 6, I look at its last volume, *Retorno a la tierra* [Return to the Land] (Fals Borda 1986), teasing out how Fals recycles the educational materials and instructional agendas of the Fundación del Caribe as intertexts in his historical narrative, showing how *Historia doble* is not only an interpretation of the contents of Fals Borda's archive, but a narrative that reenacts his activist project. Readers who are not interested in how Fals transformed his experience of action research into scholarly writing should feel free to skip this chapter.

While I hope that this book will prompt academics to pay more heed to the unique contributions to social research by Latin Americans, I am also concerned with deepening Fals Borda's legacy among PAR practitioners, only some of whom are familiar with the founding principles of La Rosca. My concluding chapter takes the results of my research to a diverse group of Colombian participatory action researchers through a series of workshops to determine what has survived of the Fundación's legacy, what is no longer applicable in the twenty-first century, and what can serve as a stimulus to further reflection at this crucial moment in Colombian history, when the signing of a peace accord with the largest guerrilla organization is threatened by renewed violence by ultrarightist factions and an intransigent national government.

I have engaged for decades in collaborative ethnography, but I do not mean for my research for this book to be taken as an example of participatory action research, since I established the research agenda on my own and did not engage in a research process in collaboration with a social movement. Nonetheless, my choice of airing my research results in conversation with Colombian activists was a political decision to engage in a process of critical recovery of the guiding principles developed by Fals and his associates in Córdoba. During the decade in which I worked in Fals's archives, I continued my collaboration with the indigenous movement in the southwestern highlands, not as a researcher but as a facilitator of research by Native activists and their allies. In the process, I became aware of the significance to indigenous researchers of Fals Borda's contribution to Colombian activism, and I began to more consciously situate my own research in this larger political framework. I made it a point to share the results of my research on Fals with indigenous organizations through presentations to groups of activists and publications in their periodicals (Rappaport 2015), which ultimately led to the workshops I later held with participatory research groups in various parts of the country. Today's participatory researchers receive sustenance from Fals Borda's work—as a teacher, writer, activist, or often, as an icon— even if they labor under political, social, economic, and ideological circumstances unlike those encountered by the Fundación del Caribe in the early 1970s. They take Fals's methodology in directions that he could not have foreseen.

1

THE FUNDACIÓN DEL CARIBE
IN CÓRDOBA

At the time of La Rosca's emergence and the founding of the Fundación del Caribe, Colombia was a country saddled with enormous inequalities in land distribution. Over the late nineteenth and early twentieth centuries, on the Caribbean coast, a region typified by large cattle ranches, peasants had been pushed to the margins of settlement and compelled to colonize forests and public lands [*baldíos*] on the agricultural frontier (which was not very distant in kilometers from cities like Cartagena). Many of these homesteaders were subsequently expelled or forced into sharecropping by the modernizing aspirations of hacendados, whose intimate connections to the local political power structure easily permitted them to grab peasant lands (Fals Borda 1986: chaps. 5A and 5B; LeGrand 1986; Ocampo 2007; Reyes Posada 1978).

Fals called this process the "law of the three steps" [*la ley de los tres pasos*]. The first step was campesino labor that transformed virgin territory into productive agricultural land; the second, the purchase of that land by more prosperous farmers; and the third, the consolidation of these farms into agrarian monopolies by wealthy regional landowners, foreign companies, and investors from neighboring Colombian provinces (Fals Borda 1975: 45–50; 1986: 113B). Ultimately, the landless were reduced to eking out a living on small plots provided by the hacendado in exchange for several days a week of labor, sealed by a contract called a *matrícula* (of course, most campesinos could not read the document, nor could they sign their names to it). The matrícula contract was time limited, but many sharecroppers immediately fell into long-term debt because they could not pay the services of the notary who validated the contract, and they ran up bills at the *tienda de raya* or company store, one of the only places they could cover basic household needs for such staples as sugar, salt, and oil to light their homes. Thus, the matrícula became a kind of bondage, made more bitter by the physical brutality of hacienda foremen and the ubiquitous use of the stocks as a form of public humiliation.

Campesino resistance to the land-grabbers who forced peasants into debt peonage comprised the central focus of the Fundación del Caribe's research strategy, which concentrated on those moments in the recent historical narrative that shed light on how campesinos organized themselves to confront the spread of agrarian capitalism. Their aim was to tell a story that would be both inspiring and relevant, a narrative that would foster the intergenerational sharing of experiences and would propel the young ANUC activists to emulate the strategies of their forebears. Correspondingly, this chapter lays out the broad contours of the moments in Costeño history that the Fundación found most compelling. In other words, I do not intend to write a narrative history of the twentieth-century Sinú region, but instead, I furnish a series of glimpses into those historical junctures that attracted the attention of these activist researchers.

The *Matrícula* and Resistance to Debt-Peonage

The Fundación del Caribe's early investigations involved the collection of eye-witness testimonies of campesino opposition to the matrícula, originating out of a series of conversations between Fals Borda and Juana Julia Guzmán. The aging activist had previously refused to permit researchers to record her story, but the sociologist's proximity to ANUC persuaded her that this particular research project would accomplish more than merely lining bookshelves. Juana Julia would become the face of historical resistance to the forced-labor regime and an emblem of the political ferment that drove peasants to collective action. The second and third decades of the twentieth century, when she became a historical protagonist, were marked by intense radical activity throughout Colombia, responding to the same forces of social change that were agitating Europe and North America. Capitalist development transformed the lives of salaried urban workers and rural laborers, the latter being the greater portion of the workforce in this era (Archila Neira 1991: chap. 2; Vega Cantor 2002). These economic transformations led to the rise of a politicized proletariat in key regions of the country, including the Caribbean coast, where workers' societies inspired by socialism and anarcho-syndicalism sprung up, culminating in the creation of socialist organizations at the national level (Fals Borda 1986: chap. 5).

Two figures are key to these developments in Córdoba, where in 1918 the founding of the Sociedad de Obreros y Artesanos de Montería [Society of Workers and Artisans of Montería] was followed the next year by the appearance of a parallel women's organization, the Sociedad de Obreras Redención de la Mujer [Society of Women Workers Redemption of Women]. It is not surprising that women were at the forefront of working-class organizing, given that in the thriving commercial center of Montería, they were active as laborers, food sellers, and servants, acting as key political players alongside male artisans (Fals Borda 1986: 143A–144A). The two workers' associations provided basic social services to their membership and organized them against the matrícula, which they helped abolish in 1921 (although sharecropping continued into the 1960s on large estates). As *Historia doble* narrates, in this period hundreds of peasant settlers who had acquired public lands in the previous decade demanded legal title to their plots in the face of encroachment by large landowners (Fals Borda 1986: chap. 5).

At the vanguard of this organizing drive were Italian anarcho-syndicalist Vicente Adamo and Costeña firebrand Juana Julia Guzmán. Adamo was originally from Reggio Calabria and passed through Mexico and Cuba, where he was employed on the railroad, in the sugar industry, and as a miner. He arrived in Colombia in 1903, working on the Panama Canal and selling coal in Cartagena before ending up in Montería, where he was in charge of sanitation at the public market and slaughterhouse. Juana Julia was a street vendor from Corozal, Sucre, born to a poor campesino family; she had worked as a servant, a barmaid, and a cleaner at the slaughterhouse before she was caught up in Adamo's socialist politics (CDRBR/M, 0866, 0929). Although he frequently identifies these activists as "socialists," Fals sometimes calls them "anarcho-syndicalists" (1999: 80).

Central to the political program of the two workers' associations was the agglutination of smallholders into *sociedades comerciales anónimas* [incorporated commercial societies], which Fals describes as cooperatives organized according to socialist principles (Fals Borda 1986: chaps. 5A and 5B; Ocampo 2014: 284–286; CDRBR/M, 0926–0928). Three of these cooperatives were founded in Callejas (renamed Tierra Libre, or "Free Land"), Canalete (Nueva Galia, or "New Galia"), and Lomagrande (Baluarte Rojo, or "Red Bastion"), all occupying and demanding title to public lands they contested with local landlords

(Fals Borda 1986: 144A–148A). The founding of these three settlements pro-voked violent reprisals, at the same time that they inspired the establishment of Peasant Leagues in other parts of the country (Uribe 1994: chap. 2).

Organized workers and peasants were continuously opposed by a Conservative government that "instead of institutionalizing civil rights . . . articulated a narrative of danger to the social and political order" by generating new definitions of delinquency and new forms of policing (LeGrand 2013: 537). The inhabitants of Lomagrande (located on the southeastern outskirts of Montería) were the object of false accusations of criminality by neighboring landlords and politicians, who provided the pretext for police incursions into the settlement. In one of the melees that ensued, some of the campesinos' supporters were assassinated and a police lieutenant was killed. Lomagrande's leadership was subsequently arrested and imprisoned for more than two years, and Vicente Adamo was banished, part of a wave of deportations of foreign-born agitators (Archila Neira 1991: chap. 3; Tejada Cano 1977: 247–248). Juana Julia returned after thirty months in a Cartagena prison to manage Lomagrande, which held on until it was attacked and finally debilitated during La Violencia in the 1950s (Machado and Meertens 2010: 210). Today, a golf course and a garbage dump stand on the site of the settlement. It is not clear to me if Lomagrande's stakeholders continued to espouse socialist philosophies during the thirty-odd years of its existence. In fact, Fals says little in *Historia doble* about how they were organized, concentrating more on their resistance to government repression and on the narratives of violent conflict Juana Julia shared with him (Fals Borda 1986: 148B).

From the 1920s to the 1960s peasant leagues, cooperatives, and other campesino organizations emerged across the coastal landscape, sometimes challenging large landholders and political strongmen [*gamonales*], at other junctures confronting foreign corporations with lumber and mining interests (Fals Borda 1986: chap. 6A). The chaos of La Violencia in the 1950s enabled land-grabbers to gobble up the plots of campesino smallholders in the upper Sinú and hired assassins [*pájaros*] destabilized life on the *baluartes* that had managed to survive for three decades (Fals Borda 1986: chap. 7).

Agrarian Reform

By the 1960s, inequities in land distribution throughout Colombia, combined with Alliance for Progress pressure to enact policies to calm the rural violence that had persisted since La Violencia, propelled President Carlos Lleras Restrepo (1966–1970) to enact an agrarian reform law and create the Colombian

Institute for Agrarian Reform (INCORA), which would implement the process of land redistribution (Zamosc 1986b: chaps. 1–2). At the time, Fals was employed as director general of the Ministry of Agriculture and helped lay the groundwork for the agrarian reform process after his recommendations, published in a preface to the first edition of *El hombre y la tierra en Boyacá* (Fals Borda 1957), caught the eye of the minister of agriculture (Pereira Fernández 2008).

The government's agrarian reform strategy included the creation in 1967 of ANUC as a semiofficial peasant association. Leon Zamosc describes ANUC as a mechanism for fostering campesino participation, something akin to an official trade union. The creation of the peasant organization allowed Lleras to harness peasant political enthusiasm while tempering the intransigence of elite agrarian sectors by deflecting reform efforts from affecting their landholdings (Zamosc 1986b: 47–54). Despite ANUC's limitations, a peasant leadership began to emerge, schooled in radical reformism by members of INCORA's staff (Zamosc 1986b: 66–67); La Rosca members Fals Borda and Víctor Daniel Bonilla were among the host of consultants who flocked to the sites of agrarian transformation during the preliminary wave of the reform (Glass and Bonilla 1967; Yie Garzón 2015).

At the same time that reformers fostered the incorporation of campesinos into new types of associations, agrarian policies impelled the massive expulsion of sharecroppers from haciendas in danger of expropriation and the cancellation of rental contracts for smallholders, thus concentrating land in ever-fewer hands (Reyes Posada 1978: chap. 2). In essence, the agrarian reform of the 1960s should be understood as a set of policies that ultimately fostered the expansion of agrarian capital, not land redistribution (Reyes Posada 1978: 141–145). Thus, it is not surprising that the smallholders of the Atlantic coast found the agrarian reform process to be wanting, given that the gears of the INCORA bureaucracy wound so sluggishly and the dispossession of campesinos was so widespread that the redistribution of lands to peasants was but a utopian dream (Zamosc 1986b: 88–89). Peasants throughout the country, but especially on the Caribbean coast and in the southwestern highlands, interpreted the creation of ANUC as an invitation to take direct action by occupying haciendas. In response to campesino initiatives, large landowners began to stage even more evictions and to press local authorities to quell agrarian unrest (Zamosc 1986b: 66–67).

In the midst of this ferment, Lleras handed the presidency over to Misael Pastrana Borrero, following the post-Violencia agreement called the National Front, under which the two major political parties, Liberal and Conservative, rotated into the national executive. Influenced by associations of large landowners, Pastrana restructured national agrarian policy by repressing hacienda occupations and generally restraining the agrarian reform process, lending his support instead to large-scale agricultural production. His presidency "approached ANUC as a Liberal clientelist stronghold whose popular ascendancy had to be strictly controlled"; he purged the staff of INCORA, hobbling its objectives through budget cuts, and replaced political appointees with his own allies (Zamosc 1986b: 69, 72–73).

As national agrarian policy shifted toward counterreform, sectors of ANUC were radicalizing. Their 1971 political platform called for land struggle and for rejecting the traditional two-party system (Zamosc 1986b: 72–73). ANUC's move to the left spurred increasing land occupations, which hit the rural landscape in several waves (Zamosc 1986b: 70–71). It also fed political divisions within the peasant movement, culminating in the 1972 split of ANUC into two lines, one more radical than the other. The Armenia Line continued to adhere to the government-sponsored policies, while the Sincelejo Line—named after the site of the ANUC congress at which it emerged—adopted a program of civic strikes, public demonstrations, peasant marches, and electoral abstention, combining their pursuit of solutions to peasant grievances with a more general strategy of overturning the social and economic system. Many of the haciendas that peasants occupied on the Atlantic coast had been carved out of campesino homesteads settled in earlier decades. ANUC activists argued that they were the prior occupants of these lands, thus providing an opening to direct action. Especially in 1971, hundreds of haciendas were occupied by peasants across the country, with a significant proportion of them on the Caribbean coast (Zamosc 1986b: 75). INCORA stepped in as an intermediary, negotiating the transfer of portions of these lands to the occupiers. In essence, the peasants were instrumental in achieving through direct action a limited program of agrarian reform (Catherine LeGrand, personal communication). These struggles legitimized a layer of radical peasant leaders.

The Sincelejo Line was shut off from the government assistance that ANUC had previously enjoyed, requiring that they seek other means of support. Progressive intellectuals like those of La Rosca were enlisted to their cause, connecting peasant organizers with a panoply of international foundations and providing crucial training to their cadres (Zamosc 1986b: 106, 113–116). With varying levels of success, a range of leftist parties developed relationships with the leadership of ANUC-Línea Sincelejo, sometimes working through organizations like the Fundación del Caribe. Participatory action research provided movements like ANUC with a less sectarian alternative, following the political objectives of the movement as opposed to promoting a party line. Cauca and Córdoba, which were hotbeds of peasant ferment in the early 1970s, constituted the laboratories in which La Rosca tested its approach to activist scholarship.

The Fundación del Caribe

Orlando Fals Borda arrived in Córdoba in March 1972, after having negotiated the terms of his presence with national leaders of ANUC-Línea Sincelejo (Fals Borda 1986: 169A; henceforth, with only a few exceptions, all further references to ANUC in this book will be to the Sincelejo Line). He immediately set to working with the peasant movement by accompanying the occupiers of La Antioqueña, one of the first large haciendas to be seized by campesinos. He also sought out local collaborators among teachers and the university community (Parra Escobar 1983: 94), leading to the founding in late November of the Fundación del Caribe (CDRBR/M, 0231; Rojas Guerra 2010).

The Fundación del Caribe was led by its president, Víctor Negrete, who was the only full-time researcher aside from Fals. Negrete studied natural sciences at the Universidad Libre in Bogotá and was trained as a schoolteacher. Another Fundación member, Franklin Sibaja, was self-employed and dedicated his life to support for civic organizations. The two were natives of Montería and grew up in families of modest means; they were shepherded into research by Fals Borda. The core group of the Fundación came to include Ulianov Chalarka, a migrant from the Andean city of Pereira, who was employed as an artist in his father's studio in a working-class barrio of Montería when he was recruited by Sibaja to participate in the drafting of the Fundación's graphic histories. David Sánchez Juliao, born in the riverine port of Lorica and perhaps the most privileged of the collective aside from Fals himself, was educated in Medellín and had recently completed an undergraduate degree in creative writing at Antioch College in Ohio; he concentrated on producing literary chronicles of the peasant struggle, which circulated both on cassette tapes and, ultimately, in published form.[1] Similar study groups were established in Barranquilla and in San Onofre, Sucre. Particularly active in Sucre were Néstor Herrera, who later went on to work as a development professional in Sincelejo, and ANUC leader Florentino Montero. Of the core Fundación group, only Víctor Negrete and Néstor Herrera are still living, although I had the opportunity to talk with Fals Borda, Sánchez Juliao, and Franklin Sibaja. The most active peasant collaborators with the Fundación were Juana Julia Guzmán, municipal ANUC leaders Clovis Flórez and Moisés Banquett (fig. 1.1), and an ANUC activist from Canalete, Alfonso Salgado Martínez, who authored a pamphlet on political economy

Figure 1.1   Moisés Banquett (center) and Clovis Flórez (on right) at an assembly, 1973 (CDRBR/M, CF, 0202. Photo reprinted with permission of the Centro de Documentación Regional "Orlando Fals Borda," Banco de la República, Montería)

(A. Martínez 1973). Of this group, Juana Julia died in the 1970s and Flórez was murdered on 15 September 2000, while Banquett disappeared several decades ago; only Salgado is still alive, although I was never able to meet him. The campesinos participated in the work of the Fundación under the aegis of an umbrella organization called the Centro Popular de Estudios, which published some of the Fundación's writings.[2]

Fundación members dedicated themselves to studying the history of land tenure and the evolution of peasant and labor union campaigns in the Caribbean region, hosting training workshops (called *cursillos*) for ANUC cadres (fig. 1.2), as well as pursuing investigations into rural health and Costeño folklore (Negrete Barrera 1981, 1983, 2008a, 2008b). Cursillos were arguably the format through which the Fundación del Caribe most profoundly touched the lives of peasant activists. Between 1972 and 1974, the Fundación authored four graphic histories for ANUC and other campesino organizations in Córdoba and Sucre (Chalarka 1985): *Lomagrande* (1972), an account of the agrarian collective founded by Juana Julia Guzmán; *Tinajones* (1973), the story of forty years of struggle between large landowners and peasant homesteaders at the mouth of the Sinú River; *El Boche* (1973), recounting an early twentieth-century massacre allegedly perpetrated by a peasant, detailing in its pages the debt-peonage regime; and *Felicita Campos* (1974), the story of an Afrodescendant leader from

Figure 1.2 Benjamín Puche (at right) facilitating a cursillo in El Vidrial, 1973 (CDRBR/M, CF, 2213. Photo reprinted with permission of the Centro de Documentación Regional "Orlando Fals Borda," Banco de la República, Montería)

the department of Sucre. A fifth graphic narrative, *¡Escucha cristiano!* (1973), was prepared for an Evangelical Protestant readership in the town of Cereté, near Montería. The Fundación's scholarly writings included a mimeographed political history of Montería authored by Víctor Negrete (CDRBR/M, 1300) and numerous reports, but they were simultaneously involved in the preparation of a variety of other materials for popular distribution, including manuals for hosting local workshops (Centro Popular de Estudios 1972), history texts accessible to peasant readers (CDRBR/M, 1918, 1923, fol. 10247; Fals Borda 1975, 1976; Negrete Barrera 1981), and testimonial literature (Sánchez Juliao 1975, 1999 [1974]). As would any research organization, Fundación members wrote numerous funding proposals (CDRBR/M, 0639, fols. 3566–3571; 0648, fols. 3588–3589; 0650, fols. 3598–3599; 0668, fols. 3629, 3633).

ANUC's Baluartes

As they expressed in a 1974 document outlining the "minimal criteria" under which their organization would operate, Fundación members envisioned themselves as activist researchers who supported popular struggles by accelerating political transformation (CDRBR/M, 0636, fols. 3559–3561). They identified and studied key moments at which social contradictions emerged to provoke popular dissent, crafting their interpretations in materials intended for peasant consumption. They sought to foster peasant class consciousness in order that campesinos did not see themselves as merely fighting for land but as engaged in a political struggle (Parra Escobar 1983: 152). La Rosca dedicated substantial funding to the Fundación in support not only of research but of local organizing activities, especially on occupied haciendas like La Antioqueña (Parra Escobar 1983: 130–134). The Fundación's commitment to combining research with activism led them to collaborate in organizing the occupiers of haciendas into autonomous self-managed communities called "bastions of peasant self-management" [*baluartes de autogestión campesina*], named after the agrarian societies founded by Juana Julia Guzmán and Vicente Adamo in the 1920s (CDRBR/M, 0639, fol. 3567). They assisted baluartes in organizing land distribution and agricultural production, as well as providing advice for the formation of a local leadership structure (Rudqvist 1986: 129–131).

The baluartes ANUC founded in the occupied lands of La Antioqueña were designed to defend the economic interests and promote the political consciousness of their inhabitants. According to Zamosc (1986b: 168–172), the resignification of the baluarte in the 1970s originated largely in Fals Borda's interpretation of agrarian history, although the particular form it took was inspired by Juana Julia Guzmán. Fals contended that capitalism developed in local enclaves on the Caribbean coast, later spreading to the broader region. He envisioned socialism as penetrating the social consciousness of Córdoba via the same path, coalescing in a small number of nuclei and then expanding throughout the countryside. Baluartes were supposed to proliferate in the same way.

Fals's Montería archive contains a proposal authored by municipal ANUC leader Moisés Banquett for a pamphlet titled *What Is a Community Enterprise or a Bastion of Peasant Self-Management* [*Qué es Una Empresa Comunitaria o Baluarte de Autogestión Campesina*]. Banquett explains baluartes primarily in the negative, by contrasting them with the *empresas comunitarias* or cooperatives promoted by INCORA, the Colombian agrarian reform agency. Unlike cooperatives, baluartes are "lands ripped from the latifundia by peasants, where we organize ourselves autonomously to work them and to continue the struggle for land and for power" (CDRBR/M, 0701, fols. 3857–3859). Baluartes, Banquett informs his campesino readers, are characterized by democracy, self-determination, free expression, personal liberty, political activism, abundant employment, socialism, and progress, among others; they function as a barrier to machine politics [*politiquería*] and unwelcome foreign influence (CDRBR/M, 0701, fols.

3858–3859). Banquett also reminds readers that the concept of the baluarte emerged in Córdoba in the 1920s and that Juana Julia Guzmán proposed it be revived by ANUC. He lays out the rules for establishing such a community, including the election of an executive council and working groups by a general assembly, determination of membership fees, distribution of subsistence plots to individuals, the identification of communal holdings, and agreement on rules and sanctions.

Notwithstanding Banquett's triumphalist tone, baluartes were not entirely successful in Córdoba, although they were fiercely defended by Fals Borda as a crucial tool for raising campesino political consciousness (*Alternativa del Pueblo* [henceforth, AP] 36: 24–25). For one, as Clovis Flórez, former president of the municipal chapter of ANUC, states in a 1980 interview with Leon Zamosc, the notion of a socialist enclave operating within a capitalist market was unrealistic and ultimately led to accusations of reformism by the Maoist left, which was also a major player in the Sinú region. There were significant local barriers to the success of the baluartes, given that the campesinos who came together to occupy La Antioqueña were a heterogeneous group, hailing from many locations, each with a different notion of how to build community (CINEP/B, doc. 14, p. 1). In fact, baluartes were never fully embraced by ANUC at the national level, although the idea was debated by the national leadership (Zamosc 1986b: 171–172). Anders Rudqvist suggests that the baluartes were also hampered by insufficient economic planning and bad handling of funds (1986: 160). Ernesto Parra Escobar states that in reality, they functioned much like INCORA cooperatives (1983: 158).

In 1980, Zamosc interviewed members of one of the baluartes in La Antioqueña, only to discover that campesinos didn't understand the concept and that it had never been fully explained to them. They observed that their former status as landless laborers (*jornaleros*) compelled them to be more concerned with acquiring land than with building socialism. They also complained that they were given the least productive lands on the hacienda and that only one of the baluartes ever acquired formal title to its lands. Some of the respondents contemplated the meaning of "baluarte" and shared with Zamosc their somewhat fuzzy impressions of its significance, which I reproduce with the original orthography: they mused that it was "synonymous with place, sector"; it meant "doing something as a community"; the idea "comes from appraising [*abaluar*] and has to do with the value [*balor*] of the soil." They told Zamosc that they had tried to look up "baluarte" in a glossary someone had found at the end of a Bible, but could not find the definition there (CINEP/B, doc. 23, p. 3).

Bridging Scientific Inquiry and Participation

At the center of this political maelstrom, the Fundación del Caribe sought to combine standard social scientific methodologies with participatory techniques, facing substantial challenges to incorporating peasants into the research process (CDRBR/M, 0637, fols. 3359-3361). They voiced their aspirations in an undated and unattributed proposal for a methodological and ideological framework, which I found among Fals's papers. The collective sought to recruit "persons suitable [*idóneas*] for working, collaborating, or assisting in portions of the research projects" (CDRBR/M, 0642, fol. 3575). Personnel would be drawn from the population of schooled local residents, who would subsequently receive methodological instruction.

Fals Borda and Augusto Libreros's 1974 "Cuestiones de metodología" crystallizes what I surmise were the methods taught these young recruits (ACHUNC/B, caja 49, carpeta 3, fols. 177-268; Fals Borda 1978: 48). The manual encourages the use of scientific techniques: "Here we apply known rules of scientific observation, such as analysis, deduction and induction, measurements, and care and equilibrium in the collection of evidence" (ACHUNC/B, caja 49, carpeta 3, fol. 214). Fals and Libreros identify historical materialism as their theoretical anchor; they advocate using scientific techniques to examine the class contradictions present in a locality. Once would-be researchers identify the social, economic, and political problems to be studied, they are encouraged by the manual's authors to conduct interviews, organize surveys, administer questionnaires, collect quantitative data, and access historical and personal archives, all of these tasks illustrated with examples (ACHUNC/B, caja 49, carpeta 3, fols. 229-244). The manual suggests further readings, ranging from Marx, Lenin, and Mao to Antonio Gramsci, Paulo Freire, Pablo González Casanova, Marta Harnecker, and Fernand Braudel. Each chapter is followed by a set of discussion questions and exercises, indicating that the text was meant to be employed in workshop settings.

What, then, of campesino participation? One of the objectives of cursillos was to bridge the distance between researchers trained by the core members of the Fundación and ANUC cadres. These educational events would introduce researchers to campesino activists "in their own words, [showing them] the location of the zone, its population, the large haciendas that stifle it, and from there the masses will discover the origins of their poverty and exploitation." In the process "a knowledgeable cadre would be created, with a new understanding, the process of knowing generated through their direct contribution to the research endeavor" (CDRBR/M, 0642, fol. 3575).

The fact that the Fundación del Caribe advocated the training of a small number of ANUC cadres does not, however, imply that a significant number of peasants participated as researchers on projects dedicated to the recovery of historical, political, or economic knowledge. Rather, the author of the Fundación memo recommends that campesinos serve as *facilitators* of research, which would be conducted largely by the academic cadres. Witness, for example, the following definition of who can be a researcher. It tends to privilege university- or, at least, high school–educated candidates:

> In my opinion these persons should have some prior knowledge of some research methodology. At this moment there are many young people who have completed their coursework at various universities, who could join the Fundación. There are also students, workers, and peasants. Once the personnel are chosen their names will be presented to the assembly or executive council, those who we think can serve will be summoned, and once he or they have accepted, will be assigned tasks. They will be observed over a period of one or two months, and those who truly demonstrate the ability and desire to work will be accepted as members of the Fundación. (CDRBR/M, 0642, fol. 3376)[3]

While the document does raise the possibility of peasants assuming researchers' tasks, its author questions whether rural farmers are truly capable of blending their agricultural pursuits with research activities: "Can a researcher combine the very labor of research with the work of the countryside, such as: planting manioc, rice, etc.? Personally, I think not, given that each of us is involved in what he is involved in; he who is meant to grow rice will grow rice; he who is meant to conduct research will conduct research" (CDRBR/M, 0642, fol. 3376). Fals was asked to recommend instructors who could teach campesino researchers how to keep records of surveys on land use, but there is no indication in the archival holdings that this was a habitual practice (CDRBR/M, 0643, fol. 3581).

A small number of campesino researchers sent Fals reports from the field (CDRBR/M, 0211, fols. 774–775) after having been trained in "simple techniques for social and economic research, placed within their reach, to allow them to conduct and indefinitely continue their own studies with minimal processing and analysis, without the need to consult advisors or seek external assistance" (Fals Borda 1978: 47). A similar goal, now expanded to the grass roots, is expressed in an undated note from a meeting of the various La Rosca study groups on the Caribbean coast:

Create researcher-cadres: giving concrete tasks to the rank and file so they can do the work, will give them more self-confidence, that the campesino is valued and is capable. They can collect data, make recordings, take counts, reports.

Other things: surveys, statistics, photographs (Instamatic 350), read maps, type, make biographies (case studies). (CDRBR/M, 2199, fol. 12516)[4]

Fals called this process *autoinvestigación* (1978: 47), which I would translate as *autoethnography*, for lack of a better term. He proposed that cameras and tape recorders could be used to record information in the event that autoethnographers did not possess sufficient literacy skills (ACHUNC/B, caja 49, carpeta 3, fols. 240–243). He anticipated that in the long run, campesinos would achieve a proficiency permitting them to conduct research without the intervention of external collaborators (ACHUNC/B, caja 49, fol. 243).

Notwithstanding such long-term goals, the purpose of autoethnographic exercises was, primarily, to raise campesino consciousness:

Autoethnography, taken as an experience in collective education, has the virtue of revealing the myths created by the oppressor's ideology, opening the eyes of communities, not only to their objective situation, but to their critical capacities and techniques for understanding reality and taking action to transform it. As such, it constitutes a revolutionary educational experience. (ACHUNC/B, caja 49, carpeta 3, fol. 242v)

Research was, therefore, essentially considered to be a political act, a process of training peasants to analyze their surroundings in order to take action to transform them. No matter how proficient campesinos actually were in replicating the techniques taught to them, and no matter how fully they participated in the research project, the fundamental objective was to foster political decision-making.

In many ways, the Fundación's research appears to have been a one-way conversation with local people or, better stated, a dialogue controlled by only one of its participants. This contradiction is noted by researchers close to Fals, who were practicing action research in other parts of Colombia. For example, Leon Zamosc observes that the exigencies of the political context in which Fals and his associates were operating—the occupation of haciendas and other forms of civil disobedience met by intense repression—forced the research group to pay more heed to political action than to research. The hoped-for synergy between research and action was frequently inhibited by the political needs of the moment. As a result, Zamosc argues that "it was the researchers who ended up defining the research objectives" (1986a: 29).

While I find the work of Fals Borda and the Fundación del Caribe to be pathbreaking and profoundly innovative, I do not intend for this book to be celebratory; instead, I must signal their failures and the gaps in their work alongside their accomplishments. The Fundación was only partly successful in balancing its scientific approach with the establishment of a horizontal research relationship with campesinos and a real recognition of the power of people's knowledge, a weakness that is still to some degree an ongoing issue for participatory and collaborative researchers, as I will elaborate further in chapter 7. The research process continues to replicate the hierarchical relationships present in the broader society, despite the best intentions of its practitioners. By pinpointing some of the mistakes that Fals and his collaborators made, I hope that today's politically and socially committed researchers can begin to identify their own lapses.

On the other hand, the moments of success of the Fundación's melding of academic methodologies with popular participation are most apparent in the four graphic histories of Costeño peasant struggles published during the three years of the Fundación's existence. These comics lie at the center of my analysis in subsequent chapters, where I examine the procedures they used to conduct research in a participatory manner, how they struggled with the implementation of their goal of critical recovery in both the visual space of the comics page and the political space of land occupations, and the role of graphic narrative as a tool for consciousness-raising. I could not see this when I first read the comics; I needed to juxtapose them to the archival record and to the memories of the Fundación team in order to read them as methodological tools.

The End of the Experiment

Fals's long-term objectives were never achieved on the Caribbean coast, not only because the Fundación struggled with reconciling its reliance on professional expertise with the political needs of campesinos, but because, in the end, political factionalism shattered their relationship with ANUC. These middle-class urban intellectuals saw themselves as presenting an independent alternative to leftist political parties and to state agencies like INCORA. However, some Fundación members were also sympathetic to the PCML (Marxist-Leninist Communist Party), a Maoist (pro-China) political current that advocated armed struggle, harbored a profound distrust of intellectuals, and deployed a radical discourse that was in large measure incomprehensible to the peasants of Córdoba; these militants saw the land struggle as an opportunity to provoke a revolution. Maoism was, in spite of its idiosyncrasies, a major force in the countryside on the Atlantic coast as land occupations surged in 1972 and 1973, although by 1974 its radicalism had alienated ANUC's regional leadership; Maoists never penetrated the peasant movement at the national level (Archila Neira 2008; Zamosc 1986b: 114–117).

In the early years of the Fundación, PCML sympathizers were active in coordinating its training workshops, but later, cracks began to appear in the relationship. By 1974, some Fundación members had moved from being PCML sympathizers to party members who bitterly confronted Fals and his colleagues. Alberto Gómez, a University of Córdoba faculty member and former Fundación supporter, openly attacked Fals Borda in a vituperative critique of his use of Marxist theory that so offended Fals that he consulted with his Fundación colleagues and with ANUC leaders before drafting an open letter in response (CDRBR/M, 0632–0634). Although perhaps the most public voice on the left, Gómez was joined in his attacks by a host of other Marxist-Leninist critics who denounced Fals and the Fundación for being insufficiently revolutionary, lambasting them in particular for their role in establishing the baluartes (Parra Escobar 1983: 179–184; Rudqvist 1983: 18–21). The Fundación was branded as an imperialist institution with foreign funding, led by an outsider whom they accused of being a CIA plant (Rudqvist 1986: 165–167).

Simultaneously, deep divisions had emerged in ANUC's national executive committee over whether the peasant movement should support the creation of an agrarian political party—a move that was opposed by Fals Borda (Rudqvist 1986: 165)—as well as the extent to which the organization should be receptive to the left. The national organization, following the decision of its Second Congress (ANUC's policy-making body), issued recommendations in favor of adopting a political line independent of both traditional and leftist political parties, the latter in an effort to placate those sectors of the peasantry who had been alienated by the Maoists' radical strategy of orienting the struggle only to the landless (Zamosc 1986b: 116–117). The national executive committee subsequently purged independent leftists and PCML members from the organization, although the Maoist left never directly attempted to influence ANUC at the national level (Zamosc 1986b: 116).

While factional struggles over party politics brewed at the national level (Zamosc 1986b: 174–177), ANUC replaced its departmental leadership in Córdoba, removing most of those cadres who had been mentored in the cursillos sponsored by the Fundación del Caribe. This move alienated at least half of the organized peasants of Córdoba, particularly those in the municipality of Montería, who had allied themselves with Fals, leaving him without a base in the national or regional organization (CDRBR/M, 1058, fols. 6273–6275; Negrete Barrera 2008a: 88; Parra Escobar 1983: 193–194; Rudqvist 1986: 168). ANUC-Córdoba subsequently fragmented into pro- and counter-Fals Borda factions, the former called *falsistas* (CINEP/B, doc. 14; Parra Escobar 1983: chap. II; Rudqvist 1986: chap. 6). Condemnations of La Rosca's work in Córdoba were aired in the national leftist press, most prominently in *Alternativa*, the magazine that Fals had founded in early 1974 in collaboration with novelist Gabriel García Márquez (Agudelo 2007; *Alternativa* [henceforth, Alt] 20: 5; Alt 20: 20–21; Alt 21: 22). La Rosca vociferously defended itself in a manifesto (Rosca 1974) and in *Alternativa del Pueblo*, the magazine they founded to take the place of *Alternativa* for their readership (although *Alternativa* continued to appear on newsstands).

Anders Rudqvist, one of Fals's allies invited to evaluate the strengths and weaknesses of La Rosca in Córdoba, observes that the three contending political forces—ANUC-Córdoba, the Fundación, and the PCML—differed in their goals, organizational structures, political styles, and relationships with the peasant rank and file: ANUC was an organization whose leadership represented its rank and file, with decisions made at periodic congresses; the Fundación was a small collective that functioned democratically; the PCML saw itself as a vanguard of agrarian revolution, paying little attention to the needs and aspirations of the peasantry. This was a struggle over control of progressive politics in the region, one that the Fundación ultimately lost because it could not foresee that it would come at loggerheads with the left; they had only gauged the dangers presented by their enemies on their right flank. Consequently, Fals and the Fundación could not successfully navigate the factional skirmishes taking place both around them and in their midst (1986: 171–173).[5] By mid-1974, the Fundación del Caribe closed its doors and Fals Borda left Córdoba in December. The following year, La Rosca, itself beset by internal differences and the desertion of some of its members, ceased to exist as an organization (ACHUNC/B, caja 49, carpeta 1, fols. 193–196, 207). This ended a brief but seminal era that had only lasted three years, during which participatory action research was conceived and took root in Córdoba.[6]

2

ARCHIVES AND REPERTOIRES

Orlando Fals Borda's personal archives can be read as a map of his activism. In fact, this is probably the best way to approach his papers. I didn't recognize this the first time I visited the Centro de Documentación Regional in Montería. The archive had been described to me as containing the historical evidence that Fals used to write *Historia doble de la Costa*, source material for his scholarly writing. Upon arrival, I encountered a fragmentary and episodic collection of papers that reflected his activism more than his scholarly objectives. I dutifully worked through the subfonds that were relevant to the work of the Fundación del Caribe from 1972 to 1974, but I gained little sense of how I would ultimately use them.[1]

The logic of Fals's papers was thus not initially transparent to me. Sometimes, he scribbled his notes on the backs of flyers or paper bags, occasionally in partially filled notebooks of the sort used by schoolchildren in Colombia, always in the small, tight, neat handwriting I associate with penmanship classes from my primary school days in the 1960s (while Fals's hand was a schooled one, it was not always legible). His notes were usually classified by subject or place and were sometimes identified by date, but the categories he used sometimes hewed so closely to the contents—"Tuchín de Aguasvivas April/73"—or were so expansive—"Beliefs and Customs" or "Mompox"—that they did not help me to make sense of how the vignettes fit into the overall scheme of things. Typed transcriptions of the numerous interviews Fals conducted with local knowledge bearers and former activists demonstrated to me his abilities as an interviewer, but the transcripts were infuriating, since they almost never indicated who was speaking with whom and the written versions did not always replicate the utterances I suspected were recorded on the reel-to-reel tapes that, in their great majority, are no longer part of the archive (most of the extant recordings are from Fals's later research in Bolívar). I gazed, curious but unsatisfied, at agendas for meetings of the Fundación del Caribe: they were never accompanied by minutes of the discussions that transpired, informing the reader which topics were considered but not what was said about them. How would I weave a narrative from the disconnected skeins of Fals's field notes?

I encountered many of the same difficulties that scholars confess to having experienced when they confront the ethnographic field notes of other researchers (Larcom 1983; Lutkehaus 1990). Fals's papers are not polished documents but instead provisional texts recorded at the instant he came to know something, or in a moment of inspiration. You are reading over his shoulder, so to speak, as his indefatigable gaze captures the most minuscule details of the weave of a fishing net or the history of ownership of a plot of land, but you don't have an inkling as to why this information is significant. Then, pages (or boxes) later, you observe Fals thinking through what he noted down earlier: now that he is stepping back to abstract from experience (Barz 1996: 49; Heinrich 2011: 38–39, 44–45), he is recasting his observations as quasi-literary works. The result is what James Clifford called in his study of French anthropologist Marcel Griaule's field notes a tangle of "various levels of textualization" whose origins are not always transparent (Clifford 1983: 125). The penetrating portraits of individuals and the expansive portrayal of a vibrant but conflict-ridden region, full of pain and of dreams, is eloquently depicted in *Historia doble*, but remains fragmented into disconnected miniatures in his archive.

The fact that second users have no access to Fals's memory—where the notes were originally embedded, lending them more coherence—colludes in rendering his papers opaque. Some scholars distinguish the written record as *field notes* and the remembered but unwritten context as *head notes*, the latter inaccessible to future readers. Head notes are always in flux. The ideas we keep in our heads are not static—they change over time—while what is on paper is fixed (Ottenberg 1990: 144–146; see also Behrensmeyer 2011: 90; Sanjek 1990a, 1990b). We must take account of this when we approach Fals Borda's notes. His jottings took on new dimensions as he came to understand ANUC more deeply and as he entered into conflict with a segment of its leadership. Even more to the point, his archive needs to be understood as a period piece. It is imperative to keep in mind that he recorded his notes over forty years ago. We must be ever vigilant to not allow *our* head notes, dating from the third decade of the third millennium, to guide our reading of his late twentieth-century archive (Smith 1990: 362). Instead, we must acclimate to the head notes of a man who recorded them in an era before computers and cellular phones, when the USSR still existed and a significant layer of activists in Latin America still believed it was possible in their lifetimes to overturn the capitalist system. Moreover, in the 1970s peasants were determined by mainstream researchers to be relics of an abandoned stage of historical development, as opposed to social actors coeval with scholars. Of course, Fals was prescient in his objective of redirecting historical narratives so that they would be guided by peasant values and aspirations.

But it is not only Fals Borda's personal field and head notes that are at stake in this documentary collection, because this was not the archive of a lone researcher. Its contents were produced by multiple hands, including other members of the Fundación del Caribe, peasant leaders, and local intellectuals with whom Fals and his associates maintained communication. The notes—at least, those collected between 1972 and 1974—were intended to be accessed by the research team. In *Historia doble* Fals identifies this collection as the archives of the Fundación del Caribe (Fals Borda 1986: 183B). Presumably, he inherited them in 1975, when the Fundación closed its doors. At some point, he added to the Fundación files his personal field notebooks and the documentation that he and his wife, María Cristina Salazar, had collected in notarial and historical archives in Córdoba, Cartagena, Bogotá, and Seville, much of which was consulted in preparation for writing *Historia doble*. As a result of this process of sedimentation, parts of the archive appear to be pieces of historical evidence gathered by Fals or his personal reflections on the research process, while other sections, particularly Fundación del Caribe and ANUC documents, transcriptions of interviews, and workshop agendas, were produced by or for the Fundación or were collected by them in the course of their work. Certainly, this corpus was intended to be much more than the notes of a scholar preparatory to writing a book.

Archive and Repertoire

It took me eight years of rooting through Fals Borda's papers before I realized that they constitute more than an archive. They contain the traces left behind of a practical repertoire, a series of activist performances that are only imperfectly captured on paper. I borrow the distinction between the archive and the repertoire from performance scholar Diana Taylor, who draws a comparison between what she calls "the archive of supposedly enduring materials (i.e., texts, documents, buildings, bones) and the so-called ephemeral repertoire of embodied practice/knowledge (i.e., spoken language, dance, sports, ritual)" (2003: 19). Taylor understands the repertoire to be a series of "meaning-making paradigms that structure social environments, behaviors, and potential outcomes" (2003: 28). Her main concern is with artistically oriented political performance of the sort one might see in public demonstrations or in street theater. I have appropriated her notion of the repertoire with the aim of reading the archival entries through the lens of the Fundación's collaboration with the peasant movement, including land occupations, the sharing of knowledge at public assemblies or in workshops, Fundación meetings: all that "ephemera" that is only partially recorded in Fals's papers. The archived documentation served as a guide to and as source material for the myriad political activities in which the Fundación participated. It is my contention that this is the best way to read Fals's papers: as a gateway to activism. The archive is a space in which we catch glimpses of what was in the Fundación's repertoire. It is really the repertoire that I am after, because this is where La Rosca's objectives of participation, critical recovery, and systematic devolution became political tools, spaces in which I can reconstruct the process of action research.

The intentionality—the performativity—of Fals's archive is unmistakable when we examine how its contents are arranged. Its classificatory scheme tells us a great deal about what he and his colleagues thought they were doing and how they proposed to accomplish their objectives. I will examine this classification in more detail below, but, for the moment, it suffices to say that many of the subfonds are identified by the names of major campesino protagonists, sites and types of ANUC activities, and the organizations that entered into collaboration in the project. The Centro de Documentación adapted Fals's categories from the typed or handwritten labels he affixed to the manila envelopes in which his papers were transferred to the library in 1986. The classifications on the envelopes constitute what archivists call the "original order," the organization of an archive at the time of its donation (Douglas 2013; Douglas and MacNeil 2009; MacNeil 2008; Meehan 2010). In Fals Borda's case, the original order was probably assembled with the help of a personal assistant in the period before he made the donation (Douglas 2015).[2] Nonetheless, I suspect that the scheme began to take shape at some point between 1972 and 1974, insofar as it reflects many of the concrete activities that the Fundación was involved in. Fals probably adjusted the classification when he took possession of the archive in 1975 and added his own papers to it. I tend toward this conclusion on the basis of an entry in Fals and Libreros's mimeographed methodological handbook, which instructs would-be investigators to organize their personal archives by theme, in alphabetical order (ACHUNC/B, caja 49, carpeta 3, fols. 230–230v). This is precisely how Fals's papers were organized when he delivered them to the Montería repository.

Not only the contours, but also the contents, of Fals Borda's archive betray the activist repertoire that underlies it. The entries were not intended as a simple register of the activities of an organization, nor can they be presumed to have served strictly as evidence substantiating the researchers' historical interpretations. Instead, Fals's categories and the documentation contained in them are organized into a series of steps for taking action. This explains why most of the ethnographic and historical materials Fals collected during his first three years on the coast concerned land tenure and labor arrangements. The coastal hacienda economy was in flux at the time, its cattle ranches undergoing a process of restructuring to accommodate the expansion of agrarian capitalism, leaving in its wake a large and mobile landless population (Ocampo 2007; Reyes Posada 1978). This is in part what made Córdoba and Sucre ground zero for the radical current of ANUC, the Línea Sincelejo. Fals's archives contain lengthy transcripts of interviews with campesinos who had experienced the matrícula and a plethora of handwritten notes on the various other voluntary and involuntary labor arrangements that characterized the hacienda system—advances on wages [*avance*], contracts for household workers [*concertaje*], day laborers [*jornaleros*]. The archive documents the day-to-day work of hacienda peons. There are maps of large landholdings and notes on how land was consolidated in the hands of the few, copies of legal papers documenting the expansion of latifundia, and interviews with activists who through direct action contested the hacienda system at various junctures over the twentieth century. Even Fals's photographic collection gives emphasis to the peasant movement and to agrarian labor, featuring images of land occupations, ANUC training courses, and peasant livelihoods. Countless ANUC documents are compiled in the archive, including memoranda, proposals, pamphlets, correspondence, legal papers, and notes from meetings, traces of the repertoire of practical action that emerged in response to the conditions the researchers and their peasant allies uncovered in the course of their historical research and activism.

Fals conceived of ANUC as a laboratory, a space in which he hoped to test his newly honed methodology. His archive constitutes a sort of "epistemological experiment" more than strictly a source of evidence (Stoler 2002: 87). There is an intentionality about his corpus, a purposefulness, an attempt to break new ground both inside and beyond the academic world. This chapter looks at the form of the archive, reading it "along the archival grain" (Stoler 2002), as a means of accessing the repertoire that governed it. I begin with a brief historical detour into how Fals Borda organized his field notes in the 1950s, when he engaged in functionalist sociological research in the highland peasant community of Saucío, Cundinamarca (ACHUNC/B, cajas 1–14). My aim is to juxtapose the mental map of the Costeño corpus to his earlier conceptualizations of research, thereby revealing how closely related his organizational model was to his methodological innovations.[3] From there, I examine how Fals's papers from 1972–1974 can be read as evidence of a repertoire. I end with a look at one of the archival categories—a small compendium of research on strategies for recruiting Evangelical Protestants to the peasant movement—which furnishes further evidence of the unusual ways his empirical research fostered activism. In other words, I "counter-engineer" Fals's personal papers, not only to reveal a research project, as other studies of scholarly field notes have done (Guber 2013), but to uncover an activist process.

How Fals Borda Organized His Archives: Saucío in the 1950s

Fals's research in the Andean highlands was published as *Peasant Society in the Colombian Andes* (Fals Borda 1955), a pioneering work in Colombian sociology and one of the first studies by a Colombian researcher to draw on the functionalist methodology of U.S. rural sociology to construct a holistic and rigorously empirical portrait of a highland agrarian community. His research plan was unusual for the 1950s, when Colombian sociology was characterized by an impressionistic essay tradition that largely ignored empirical study (Jaramillo Jiménez 1996). Fals began working in Saucío, some 70 kms north of Bogotá, in the late 1940s, when he was employed by the Winston Brothers Company, which was constructing the nearby Sisga dam. He had read T. Lynn Smith's work on the organization of agricultural labor in nearby Tabio (Smith, Díaz Rodríguez, and García 1944) and was anxious to apply similar survey methods in Saucío, whose inhabitants he met when they were hired as construction workers. Fals used Smith's survey schedules to collect information on family and household structure, schooling, land tenure, and the nature of agricultural work and crop yields in Saucío, arguing that the cultural similarities between the Saucitas and Smith's respondents permitted him to ask them the same questions (Fals Borda 1955: 249–251). (Smith would later direct Fals's doctoral dissertation at the University of Florida.) He balanced his survey data with fine-grained ethnography based on observation and interviews conducted during a long-term residence in a Saucita peasant household.

In his methodological appendix to *Peasant Society*, a monograph based on his 1951 master's thesis at the University of Minnesota, Fals noted:

> Field notes were classified under the following headings: Climate, Transportation, Ecology, Flora and Fauna, The House, Furniture and Household Items, Domestic Economy, Property, Household Occupations, Industry, Agriculture, Tools, Animal Husbandry, Weight and Distance Measurements, Somatic Characteristics, Costume, Health and Diseases, Food, Education, Religion and Folk Beliefs, Music and Dance, Sports and Recreation, and Social Psychology and Customs. (Fals Borda 1955: 251)

The subfonds of Fals's archive at the National University in Bogotá that are dedicated to his research in Saucío maintain this classification. The chapters of *Peasant Society* loosely conform to groupings of these categories, combining a sociological emphasis on social stratification, institutions, and organizational forms with a keen ethnographic eye that captures the everyday lives of these mestizo peasants (Jaramillo Jiménez 1996: 70–71). The organization of the Saucío archive resembles the recommendations of Bronislaw Malinowski, one of the fathers of functionalist ethnography, who proposed that field notes be used as a space in which to map out social structure and to draft the basic contours of social institutions (Malinowski 1965 [1935]: 317; 1984 [1922]: introduction).

Fals continued to collect information in Saucío after completing his master's thesis, during the course of his subsequent doctoral dissertation research, and as part of an ongoing collaboration in the 1960s with Colombian and international institutions dedicated to the dissemination of modern agricultural technologies. In particular, he engaged peasants in a series of experiments involving the introduction of modern agricultural implements, new planting techniques, and chemical inputs, which, as Mónica Moreno infers, placed Fals's peasant interlocutors in the position of coinvestigators rather than passive recipients of new technologies (Moreno Moreno 2017a). Moreno points out, on the basis of a textual analysis of the Saucío archive, that his notes flag the themes of each entry with terms in brackets, such as "diffusion," "innovation," "cultural contact," "demonstration," "mechanization," "resistance," "acceptance," and "introduction," thus permitting his experimental model to frame his observations (2017a: 3–4). One might say that with these labels, Fals converted the stable categories (the nouns) by which he classified his notes into types of action (verbs). His agricultural experiments drew on a methodology called "participant experimentation," originally developed by Nelson Foote and Leonard Courell (1955: chap. 6), which he translated into Spanish as *experimentación por participación* (Fals Borda 2010c [1959]: 67). The experiments Fals promoted in Saucío were never intended to incite the peasants to call for radical structural change. To the contrary, they were geared to promoting reform within existing social structures. This would change radically in Córdoba.

How Fals Borda Organized His Archives: The Caribbean Coast, 1972–1974

The founding of La Rosca the year before Fals's move to Montería in 1972 led him along more politically and intellectually radical paths. No longer would he advocate insertion into communities for the purpose of observation and fostering induced change. Now, inspired by Marxism, he promoted activism as an integral feature of his research plan: the study of the ideological and cultural components of the class struggle in a specific region with the objective of motivating political action geared at systemic change, guided by the concepts of "critical recovery" and "systematic devolution," to be determined by ANUC's political priorities, just as would the mechanisms for its diffusion (Parra Escobar 1983: 19; Bonilla et al. 1972). His insertion as an activist researcher into the peasant movement was meant "to increase the velocity of transformation, or to raise the level of class confrontation, thanks to the greater effectiveness that organized groups obtain through such ends, which can lead them in practice to articulate or reinforce a vanguard movement and political organization" (Fals Borda 1987b [1970]: 91–92). His language may appear doctrinaire to today's readers, but it speaks to the intimate intertwining of social science and leftist politics in the Latin American intellectual landscape of the 1970s, and for this reason it is worth quoting.

In effect, Fals considered his project to be "subversive" (Fals Borda 2001) because it was organized to support a utopian movement for structural transformation that drew on a long historical tradition in Colombia (Fals Borda and Rahman 1991: vii) and because it turned positivist social science on its head. The Caribbean coast was, to his mind, an excellent fit for a subversive intellectual experiment: a site of revolutionary turmoil, replete with peasant land occupations, guerrilla groups, trade union activism, and student movements, precisely the sort of context in which subversive thought could gestate (Bringel and Maldonado 2016: 408–410).

We can recognize the subversive nature of Fals's Caribbean project in the categories into which he classified his field notes. They reveal a major shift in how he came to conceptualize research since the 1950s. No longer was he concerned with compiling a holistic panoramic portrait of a bounded campesino community, as he had in Saucío, where the organization of his notes had laid bare his intentions to document the wide range of interrelated economic, political, and cultural activities of highland peasants. Instead, he embraced the broad sweep of history of the Caribbean coast, with a primary focus on its southwestern portion, including Córdoba, Sucre, and, after 1975, southern Bolívar. As soon as he arrived in Córdoba, Fals was invited by ANUC to participate in the occupation of La Antioqueña (Parra Escobar 1983: 111-131). His initial field notebooks (CDRBR/M, 0392-0396) contain general information on land occupations, songs of struggle recorded in peasant hands, descriptions of local characters exemplifying the various social groups of the region, interview notes, studies of material culture, and ANUC communiqués. But very quickly, he made sense of the vast and complex panorama that lay before him and began directing his attention to particular actors and specific historical moments at which peasants and workers organized to impede the spread of agrarian capitalism. These became the principal categories organizing his field notes. In a word, peasant activism was a major determinant of his classificatory scheme. As occurs in many activist archives (Meehan 2010: 38; Pell 2015: 48-49, 51-56), his intellectual categories reflect the political activities in which he and his Fundación associates were involved over time.

Some of these historical markers are identified by the names of their peasant protagonists, including key actors in ANUC's struggle. The dossier titled "Juana Julia Guzmán" (CDRBR/M, 0852-0866) contains documentation relating to the political trajectory of the founder of the Sociedad de Obreros y Artesanos de Montería and the agrarian collective of Lomagrande that provided a model for the organization of ANUC-occupied lands. Juana Julia's story anchors the graphic history *Lomagrande*. In addition to a taped interview with her (one of the few that survives from the period), Fals filed away transcriptions of the ANUC training courses at which she spoke; mimeographed biographies that circulated in political circles, authored by peasant and student activists; poems; and some of what he called her *archivo de baúl*, her personal papers, consisting of letters, fading photographs, armbands, medical identification cards, contracts, and receipts, which became tools for eliciting reminiscences at public assemblies (Fals Borda 1985: 58, 60-61). Another important dossier is "Moisés Banquett" (CDRBR/M, 1041-1058), named for a leader of the municipal chapter of ANUC in Montería; it contains his handwritten memoirs, which Fals cites in *Historia doble* (Fals Borda 1986: 183B) but never published, perhaps because Banquett dropped out of sight in the 1980s and could not therefore give his permission for the publication. A third important archival category is "Bárbaro Ramírez"

(CDRBR/M, 0246–0247), which collects the experiences of the matrícula of an 85-year-old campesino, recorded in 1972. These were all individuals that the Fundación worked with: not so much "informants," they were allies or participants in workshops, so that the contents of their dossiers are not simply archival sources but tools for engaging the Fundación's political repertoire.

Similarly, place was an essential vehicle for conceptualizing the scope of the Fundación's activism: not mere geographical location, but rather the sites of significant peasant mobilizations. For example, "Tinajones" (CDRBR/M, 1912–1925) comprises several hundred pages of documentation relating to the struggle of landless homesteaders at the mouth of the Sinú River to retain public lands they had carved out of the mangroves in the first half of the twentieth century. Documents that fall under this category range from transcribed interviews to official government reports and legal documents, field notebooks, and a series of time lines of events, all ultimately culminating in the graphic history *Tinajones*. "San Onofre-Chichimán-Rincón" (CDRBR/M, 1768–1787) records summaries of the story of Afrocolombian leader Felicita Campos as told by activists from San Onofre, Sucre, material that ultimately was condensed into the graphic history *Felicita Campos*.

The most urgent historical milestones were the land occupations led by ANUC, in which Fals and the Fundación participated. Documentation of some of the first occupations in 1972 are classified by titles like "Hacienda La Antioqueña (Baluarte Adamo)" (CDRBR/M, 0678–0708, 0719), "Hacienda La Floresta" (CDRBR/M, 0710–0715), and "Hacienda Mundo Nuevo" (CDRBR/M, 0271–0272). La Antioqueña and Mundo Nuevo were occupied in early March, just at the point Fals arrived in Córdoba, and he agreed to provide financial, legal, and educational assistance to ANUC in support of direct action (Parra Escobar 1983: 111–131). These dossiers mark the evolution of Fals Borda's relationship to the ANUC leadership. They contain handwritten reports of visits by municipal leaders of the organization to the newly constituted baluartes, as well as baluarte statutes and regulations. The land occupations spawned other related dossiers. La Antioqueña was protected for a period by a legal document called an *agencia oficiosa*, a juridical formula through which individuals could assert control over, but not ownership of, an uncultivated property. Fals encouraged the occupiers of La Antioqueña to draw up such a writ, which helped them to stave off eviction and force the landowner to ultimately cede a large piece of property to them (Rudqvist 1986: 133–134). One of the dossiers in the Fals papers is called "Agencia Oficiosa" (CDRBR/M, 0196–0209) and includes correspondence, denunciations, press clippings, ANUC acts, and the agencia oficiosa document itself.

The two organizations with which Fals Borda worked, the Fundación del Caribe (CDRBR/M, 0678–0708, 0719) and ANUC (CDRBR/M, 1996–2185)—the latter classified as "Users" ["Usuarios"], after the organization's name, the National Association of Peasant Users—round out the categories, containing meeting notes and agendas, proposals, outlines of training seminars, newspapers, and printed booklets, numbering in the hundreds of pages. These classifications are not ethnographic or historical per se, but pertain to spaces of ongoing political collaborations.

This is, then, an activist archive. It simultaneously serves as a record of peasant efforts at direct action and a source of evidence for the adult education materials on the history of the peasant struggle that the Fundación produced. It constitutes an itinerary of the Fundación's interventions in ANUC. Although it does contain field notes and interview transcripts, the archive does not resemble Fals's Saucío collection. While the latter maps the social institutions of a peasant community, the Caribbean archive is anchored in a series of activist projects that were identified according to sites and nodes of political struggle, producing materials, legal documents, and events destined for a nonacademic public.

La Rosca disbanded in 1975 and Fals Borda retooled himself as an action researcher disengaged from the ANUC-Córdoba leadership. He developed a less intense relationship with civic activists in Bolívar, where he organized a study group intent on reconstructing local history to promote the creation of a new administrative department on the Caribbean coast, the Departamento del Río, encompassing the inland water lands of the Magdalena and San Jorge basins (Fals Borda 1979b: chap. 1A). His attention moved east to the vicinity of Mompox and back in time to the colonial period, when the hacienda system was just beginning to take root in the region. He reenvisioned the purpose of his research, now oriented to writing a book, *Historia doble de la Costa*, which would come out in four volumes from 1979 to 1986. His archive continued to be centered on individuals and places, following the scheme established in 1972–1974, but now the individuals were historical figures—such as the nineteenth-century mulatto politician Juan José Nieto, about whom he would write in the second volume of *Historia doble* (CDRBR/M, 0797–0836; Fals Borda 1981)—not the ANUC activists with whom he had collaborated. The places were the locations of historical events—like Mompox (CDRBR/M, 1074–1249)—unconnected to struggles in which he had participated.

As Fals moved into the Mompox Depression and the San Jorge River basin after 1975, he became consumed with myriad facets of Costeño rural life and thought. This is especially apparent in his notes archived under the rubric of

the place-name "Jegua" (CDRBR/M, 0749–1796), where we find a plethora of detail on the periodic flooding of the wetlands, the flora and fauna of the region,
and peasant strategies for turtle fishing [galapagueo], as well as accounts of early
twentieth-century murders, descriptions of witchcraft, copies of poems, forms
of popular religiosity, and archival documentation of nineteenth-century indigenous rebellions. The contents of these categories more closely resemble
the field notes of an ethnographer or oral historian, insofar as they are exhaus-
tive, vivid, and far ranging, furnishing abundant evidence for an argument
or anecdotes for a book. Nonetheless, they are catalogued according to the
activist scheme that governed the organization of Fals's papers during his collaboration with ANUC from 1972 to 1974.

Inside an Archival Category

Fals Borda's archival classification was organized around peasant protagonists
on the Caribbean political stage and the spaces in which the social transformations they wrought unfolded. We might say, then, that the classificatory
scheme of the archive both reflects and enabled the Fundación's activist repertoire. Nonetheless, it is not sufficient to examine the broad contours of the
archive. If we are to understand how Fals and his associates used these papers
in practice, it is also necessary to inquire into how each of these categories
functioned as an engine for steering research toward activism. Just as the
organization of the archival categories evinces a radical reconceptualization
of the Fundación's research process, the contents of the files mark a profound
change in Fals's research practice: what kinds of documents are included, how
they were compiled, who produced them, and who enjoyed access to them—in
other words, what Steve Wright (2012), who worked with the archive of an Italian student organization from the 1960s, calls a "genre repertoire."

Many of the dossiers in Fals's corpus contain too many items for me to describe and analyze briefly, so I have chosen to look at one of the less-populated
categories, "Evangelical Church" ["Iglesia Evangélica"]. This is a small collection containing an ethnographic report, correspondence, religious publications, and proposals for work with a Protestant youth group in the town of
Cereté, just outside of Montería. Cereté not only boasted a large Protestant
population but was home to important ANUC leaders and the headquarters of
the Marxist-Leninist Communist Party (PCML), the Maoist organization that
exerted great influence in Córdoba.[4] Cereté's Protestant youth were eager to
recruit Evangelicals to ANUC's cause (CDRBR/M, 0731–0743). Their project ultimately culminated in a pamphlet composed in comics format, titled ¡Escucha

cristiano! [Listen Up, Christian!], which juxtaposes biblical quotations to images of Costeño peasants (Sociedad de Jóvenes Cristianos 1973).[5]

The dossier is particularly interesting for several reasons. First, Evangelical and Pentecostal congregations placed uncompromising barriers in the way of leftist organizing throughout Colombia and across Latin America. The faithful depended on the Bible for inspiration in their daily lives and exercised their religious doctrine as a means of deflecting the organizing efforts of politicized peasants, whom they deemed to be Godless. The task of convincing a group of hard-core opponents of ANUC to support the peasant movement was certainly of political utility, but it also afforded what would be a valuable experiment in gauging the usefulness of action research, which it appears is what led the Fundación to Cereté.

Second, as I mentioned in the introduction, Fals Borda, as well as La Rosca members Gonzalo Castillo and Augusto Libreros, were all practicing Presbyterians. They and their donors espoused strong ecumenical sentiments and were sympathetic to liberation theology, lending a moral tone to their activism but also spurring the conservative Colombian synod to condemn them as leftist extremists (CDRBR/M, 0733) who should never have been funded by the U.S. Presbyterian Church. Arguably, this group of Protestant researchers was among the very few who could successfully insert themselves into an Evangelical context (Poggi 2015), also making them uniquely qualified to denounce the various foreign missionary organizations operating in the countryside (AP 26: 12–13; AP 34: 18–19; CDRBR/M, 1416).

Finally, the documents in the dossier constitute clear evidence of how authority over research results was effectively ceded to the community by action researchers. The grassroots organization took the lead in determining the contents of the materials that were produced and their subsequent distribution and use. Furthermore, the dossier is noteworthy insofar as there is little of Fals Borda himself in it: none of his handwritten notes or commentaries on the progress of the project, even though similar sorts of documentation abound in other folders. Fundación members other than Fals appear to have been the major players in this instance. This indicates how the new methodology was a team product and not the result of the efforts of a single individual.

While the Fundación's collaboration with Evangelicals was in many ways a sideshow to their participation as activist researchers in ANUC, it embodied many of their core values and presents a good introduction to how they were put into practice. A perusal of the contents of "Evangelical Church" supplies evidence of how Fals's papers were compiled and used in furthering the Fundación's core mission. The documents in this dossier demonstrate a radically different progression from what can be found in most scholarly field notes, which generally proceed from a hypothesis or a research question to a period of gathering material, accompanied sometimes by preliminary reflections, and, finally, to a descriptive or analytical publication. There are fourteen documents in the "Evangelical Church" category, which begins with a 1973 ethnographic study of a Pentecostal community in El Retiro de los Indios, near Cereté, by Fals's wife, María Cristina Salazar (CDRBR/M, 0731); her paper is complemented by Fundación del Caribe commentaries on her research (CDRBR/M, 0738). Supplementing the research report is a series of news articles and records of the activities of Evangelical missions and youth organizations (CDRBR/M, 0732, 0733–0735, 0740–0741, 0744) and documentation of the 1972 dispute between the Presbyterian Synod of Colombia and La Rosca de Investigación y Acción Social over funding of the latter by the U.S. Presbyterian Church (CDRBR/M, 0733). Fals also inserted into the folder various articles and proposals concerning ecumenical integration in the Caribbean region (CDRBR/M, 0736–0737). Central to the dossier is a 7 June 1973 memorandum concerning the contents and use of the comics pamphlet ¡Escucha cristiano! (CDRBR/M, 0739) and a draft of its verbal contents (CDRBR/M, 0743). The file is clearly oriented toward the task of consciousness-raising among Protestants in Cereté, with the goal of working with them in spite of their recalcitrance and of recruiting them to ANUC's cause.

Experiments in Research

The project's origins lie in María Cristina Salazar's research into Protestantism on the Caribbean coast. A trained sociologist (and a practicing Catholic) with a doctorate from the Catholic University of America who occasionally collaborated with her husband, Salazar began to inquire into Pentacostalism in 1956 in El Retiro de los Indios, but she did not undertake comprehensive field research until 1972, when she spent three months there at the request of ANUC. The dossier includes Salazar's 1973 report (CDRBR/M, 0731) but no field notes, suggesting that her research project was not conceived as being the central objective of the Fundación's intervention but, instead, as one of several supporting documents (similar to the articles about Evangelical missions and Caribbean ecumenism). Composed in a conventional academic format in language accessible to nonacademic readers, Salazar describes a small congregation of Pentecostals affiliated with the Presbyterian Church, made up of landless laborers inhabiting a locality surrounded by latifundia dedicated to cotton cultivation that supplied only temporary employment. The lives of

congregation members, especially those of the women, were profoundly influenced by their religious practice. They frequently cited biblical verses to
influence the personal behavior of family members and looked to Pentecostal-
ism to liberate them from vices like alcohol, which disrupted family life. These
women viewed ANUC's land occupations as disobedience in the eyes of God.

Notwithstanding the seemingly finished quality of Salazar's report, it was
but a prelude to the Fundación's participatory project, which was conceived as
a kind of a revolutionary experiment, as were all of the Fundación's activities.
Fals wrote in retrospect that Fundación projects "involved conducting very
preliminary experiments, or soundings, about how to connect historical-social
understanding and its resulting studies to the practice of self-conscious (labor
and/or political) local and national organizations within the context of the
class struggle in the country" (Fals Borda 1978: 13). In their manual, Fals and Libreros more explicitly characterize the Fundación's research agenda, including
the phase of returning accessible materials to the community, as a "scientific
experience" (ACHUNC/B, caja 49, carpeta 3, fol. 257v). It is in this sense that I
want to interpret the Evangelical dossier: as an experiment whose every phase
constitutes a political activity, moving toward a finale in which the efforts of
the various actors coalesce into a result intended to inspire political action. In
other words, the way the dossier was compiled reveals the repertoire it enabled.

Fals and his associates were deeply aware of the fact that Evangelicals vis-
cerally feared Marxism, "so that it is necessary to communicate with them
in the manner in which they are familiar, *to begin with*, and from there steer
them toward new ideological concepts and action" (CDRBR/M, 0739: fol. 4162;
underlining in original). The first step in consciousness-raising was to be accomplished through the illustrated pamphlet *¡Escucha cristiano!* (Sociedad de
Jóvenes Cristianos 1973), whose text was authored by the Evangelical youth
and subsequently illustrated by Ulianov Chalarka, the artist who drew the
Fundación del Caribe's four other graphic narratives. *¡Escucha cristiano!* combines biblical quotations with panels depicting the exploitation of the peasantry. The activists involved in the project envisioned "the pamphlet as a first
experiment. . . . Other pamphlets should keep in mind the results, in order to
modify the presentation and contents. Although it is not a Marxist pamphlet,
it should be conceived as coming out of dialectical Marxism, as it points out
and utilizes biblical contradictions between ideology and religious practice
that demonstrate or lead to the class struggle" (CDRBR/M, 0739: fol. 4162).
This was a controlled exercise, its reference group carefully delimited. A joint
agreement stipulated that the resulting publication would not be sponsored by
ANUC but by the Evangelical youth group and that it would be produced under

their supervision for their internal use (CDRBR/M, 0739: fol. 4163), although the dossier contains nothing concerning the publication's use or afterlife.

The dossier contains a verbal script—a draft of the written contents of what would become the graphic narrative—prepared by the Sociedad de Jóvenes Cristianos and dated 14 May 1973 (CDRBR/M, 0743). A comparison of the script with the comic (Sociedad de Jóvenes Cristianos 1973) that came out several weeks later reveals that the verbal channel of the comic and the script are identical. This suggests to me that the youth group chose the biblical quotations and began analyzing them before Chalarka made the drawings. Exegetic exercises continued as the artist worked with the youth group to prepare the images that accompanied the biblical quotations. Each page of ¡Escucha cristiano! features biblical quotations and their interpretation, the latter grounded in the needs and rights of an impoverished Caribbean peasantry. The verbal text is juxtaposed to Ulianov Chalarka's illustrations depicting the exploitation of peasants by the elite and Costeño workers and peasants in direct union with Christ, God, and other celestial beings (figs. 2.1 and 2.2), indeed, a sort of an illustrated sermon (which is how the Centro de Documentación inaccurately catalogued it).

"Evangelical Church" documents the research process that gave rise to ¡Escucha cristiano!—or the experiment, as the Fundación called it—illustrating how it unfolded across a range of media, featuring a distinct set of participants at each step of the process: first ANUC and Salazar, then the Cereté youth group, and finally, Ulianov Chalarka. It presents an excellent example of how the external researchers ceded their authority to local knowledge bearers, erasing the distinction between observer and observed in significant ways. Notably, the campesinos who participated in the project did not assume the role of the "observed" at any point during the process; they were never the object of study, given that Salazar's research was conducted in a different church community that presumably exhibited many of the same values as did the families of the young people who wrote the script of ¡Escucha cristiano! In short, the documents contained in the dossier were generated by an array of social actors who were all fully integrated as researchers into the investigation. There is no single agent controlling the process, although the final word is left to the Evangelical youth.

If this were a set of field notes kept by a conventional ethnographer, the empirical evidence would have predated the drafting of a research report, with the latter as the culmination of the project (or, at the least, as advance notice of a more polished article). In contrast, "Evangelical Church" works in what at first glance appears to be the reverse order. It begins with a research report

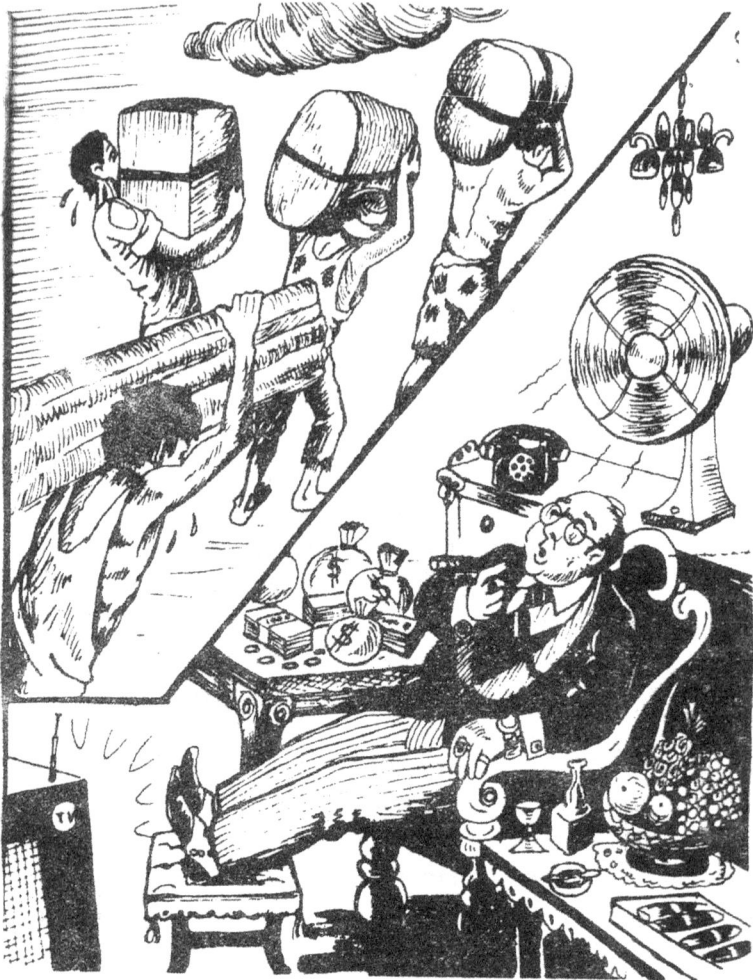

Por fortuna, DIOS ESTA JUZGANDO A ESTOS OPRE—
SORES, A LOS RICOS Y A LOS PODEROSOS. El ha
dicho:

"Con el sudor de tu frente comerás el pan". Y esto
no lo hacen los ricos. Por eso Dios los ha condenado
así:

"Veamos ahora, ricos ! Llorad y aullad por las mi-
serias que os vendrán. Vuestras riquezas están po-
dridas y vuestras ropas están comidas de polilla.
Vuestro oro y plata están enmohecidos ; y su moho
testificará contra vosotros y devorará del todo vuestras carnes como fuego".

(Santiago 5:1-3).

5

Figure 2.1 Greedy rich men and miserable workers (*¡Escucha cristiano!* p. 5. Comic reprinted with permission of the Fundación del Sinú)

Por eso es necesario que la gente humilde y trabajadora, de dentro y fuera de la Iglesia, se una entre sí —los obreros, los campesinos, los menesterosos, los perseguidos, los lu-' chadores por la justicia— para que ganen la libertad y la verdadera libertad en la nueva Jerusalén. El Señor lo ha ordenado :

"Porque vosotros, hermanos, a libertad fuisteis llama - dos... Si os mordéis y os coméis unos a otros, mirad que también no os consumáis unos a otros".

(Gálatas 5:13-15).

Por eso han aparecido organizaciones de los humildes y explotados, que los defienden en sus derechos y que van en busca de la justicia, que es amor.

Son los
SINDICATOS DE OBREROS,

los USUARIOS CAMPESINOS,

y otras organizaciones del pueblo trabajador.

Figure 2.2 God and the angels gaze down on peasant and worker protest (¡*Escucha cristiano!* p. 11. Comic reprinted with permission of the Fundación del Sinú)

that furnishes the empirical context of the project and subsequently lays the ground rules of a participatory endeavor in the form of a written agreement. It uses a research methodology that departs radically from established academic forms of analysis, namely, by employing biblical exegesis instead of sociological, historical, or economic methods of inquiry; this is a method that was commonly used by Christian base communities inspired by liberation theology and by Marxism, but it clearly has more ancient origins. The extent to which the local community exerted epistemological control over the project was, perhaps, unusual, even for the Fundación del Caribe, whose other pamphlets did not diverge as radically from the conceptual models that characterized Marxist-inspired agrarian histories of the period. *¡Escucha cristiano!* provides a useful introduction to the experimental nature of early action research and the multiple possibilities it opened. This is not research in any standard sense of the word, although it constituted research in the Fundación del Caribe's new understanding of the investigative process.

The Archive and the Repertoire

A reading of Orlando Fals Borda's archives "along the archival grain" reveals traces of the epistemological and political experiments to which the Fundación del Caribe was committed. They opened new vistas for researchers around the world, but Fals never supplied a recipe for replicating his methodology. This is evident in the organization of Fals's papers. His classifications are local and historically specific. They furnish a road map for tracing the Fundación's activities but cannot serve as a guide for those who aspire to apply the same methodology in other venues. The localized and personalized nature of Fals's classification reveals one of the central principles around which action research was conceived. Its starting point was located in the concrete reality in which researchers found themselves, not in a preordained set of questions and approaches. What Fals and his associates saw as transferable were their basic premises: research that privileged the knowledge and political needs of popular sectors, horizontal relationships between researcher and community, a ceding of intellectual authority to the popular organization, and the collective production of widely accessible materials. The archive embodies a repertoire that was inspirational but was never intended to be replicated verbatim.

Because activism is the motor behind Fals's archive, leading him to organize his papers so that they reproduce the trail of the Fundación's activities, the archive only took me so far, requiring that I move beyond its holdings to think through the dynamics of peasant participation in the research process and how the Fundación implemented its project of critical recovery. Likewise, the archive contains only brief mentions of how educational materials were disseminated in campesino communities. Participation must be inferred from Fals's papers; it is not unmistakably evident in its pages: the repertoire must be imputed to the archive. I begin to pose this challenge in the next chapter, which meditates on how Fals and the Fundación fostered participation, through an examination of the making of Ulianov Chalarka's graphic histories.

3

PARTICIPATION

In volume 4 of *Historia doble* Orlando Fals Borda underscores the Fundación del Caribe's four graphic histories as one of the collective's major accomplishments (Fals Borda 1986), as do Fals's collaborators (Negrete Barrera 1983, 2008a; Parra Escobar 1983). *Lomagrande, Tinajones, Felicita Campos,* and *El Boche* are identified in these texts by their titles and the dates they were published, but virtually nothing is said about how they were composed; they are described as research products, as part of the archive. Nonetheless, the four graphic narratives were critical spaces in which participation and horizontality were achieved, making them also part of the Fundación's repertoire. If we read between the lines (or the comics panels) of the four graphic histories, confronting their texts with the traces of action recovered from Fals Borda's archive and the reminiscences of activists, they become fertile ground for comprehending what research might have meant to campesino narrators and their audiences, insofar as they demonstrate how the Fundación team engaged peasants as much more than informants.

This chapter examines the division of labor among campesinos and external researchers at various stages of the production of the graphic histories, examining in particular the initial encounters of narrators, ANUC leaders, researchers, and artists, which resulted in a collection of written and graphic notes that would be organized by the Montería research team. From there, I look at how these materials were fashioned into comics panels and put together into a grid. My intention is to use the graphic histories as a point of entry to gain a deeper understanding of what participation meant in practice. I am aware that the Fundación del Caribe produced materials in a wide array of media for use by ANUC, including history texts (Fals Borda 1975, 1976) and semi-fictionalized chronicles (Sánchez Juliao 1975, 1999 [1974]), and that they organized and facilitated workshops in rural and urban settings (Centro Popular de Estudios 1972); I will examine these other venues in later chapters. Notwithstanding, the graphic histories open a singular window into participation, one that is worth exploring in depth. Fals's archives contain source materials that help us to trace how research was channeled into user-friendly publications. Furthermore, since the graphic histories were created by groups of people, the nature of their production process clarifies the roles played by the rank and file, ANUC cadres, Fals Borda, and the other members of the Fundación. But before I do that, I want to introduce readers to Ulianov Chalarka, the artist who harnessed the language of comics to the Fundación's activist research agenda.

Looking over Ulianov Chalarka's Shoulder

I begin by meditating on a series of photographs taken by Fals Borda in the early 1970s in Montería and San Onofre, Sucre, during the preparation by members of the Fundación of one of their historical comic books. The first photo (fig. 3.1) is of a mustachioed man wearing a beret—somewhat of a Che Guevara look-alike—cigar in his mouth, seated at a table with a map of Colombia in the background. He is beginning to apply ink to a drawing; onionskin sheets filled with sketches are strewn before him on the table. He is Ulianov Chalarka. That is his birth name, but he also went by the pseudonym "Iván Tejada" to protect him from the government repression that bit at the heels of ANUC during the escalation of land conflicts in this period.[1] Chalarka was born in Pereira, some 600 kms south of Montería, in the coffee-growing area of the central highlands, which Costeños call the "interior." Chalarka migrated in his youth to the Caribbean city of Montería, where his family of itinerant artists settled and opened a studio in the working-class barrio of La Granja. La Granja was a planned neighborhood, founded in the 1960s by one of Montería's mayors in response to the pressure of community leaders to erect their dwellings on the grounds of a by-then-abandoned experimental farm (a *granja experimental*), hence its name (Durango Padilla 2012: 79, 84; Puche Puche 1998: 159–161). Many of the inhabitants of La Granja were campesinos uprooted by agrarian conflict, former sharecroppers and other rural workers expelled from

Figure 3.1 Ulianov Chalarka at work (CDRBR/M, CF, 1405. Photo reprinted with permission of the Centro de Documentación Regional "Orlando Fals Borda," Banco de la República, Montería)

the countryside during the transition to cattle raising, which required less labor input than the previous agricultural economy (Ocampo 2003, 2014).

Chalarka earned his living reproducing images of Christ, the saints, and historical figures. He learned his craft at home after being plucked out of high school to help support the growing household. As Orlando Chalarca, Ulianov's brother, showed me on one of my visits to his studio, Ulianov's commercial canvases were mass-produced through the use of stencils. The paintings were widely available in Montería. One of the most popular was of Galileo, but the Chalarca family studio also reproduced paintings of Christian figures, such as an image of Saint Jude I saw in the modest household of a Montería journalist. Numerous families hang these paintings in their living rooms, unaware of Chalarka's collaboration with ANUC; to wit, the Catholic Church commissioned from him portraits of their local hierarchy. Chalarka's talent transcended the limited repertoire of the family business, however. I have located portraits of family members and neighbors, copies of classical paintings, and Montería landscapes gracing the walls of both elite and working-class households. There is a striking image of Christ on the cross, comforting a Colombian guerrilla. Probably the most well-known canvas Chalarka painted is of folk saint Domingo Vidal Villadiego, a mid-nineteenth-century teacher from Chimá, Córdoba, who advised smallholders victimized by land-grabs (Durango Espitia n.d.: 22; Fals Borda 1986: 89–93) and who is the subject of a novel by Fals's interlocutor Manuel Zapata Olivella (1974 [1964]); notwithstanding, it is one of Chalarka's least remarkable canvases. I listened to countless recollections of Chalarka murals that have vanished over the years, painted on the walls of various public and private buildings; most remembered is a be-feathered indigenous *cacique* [hereditary lord] cradling a naked white woman hostage, his shield resting on the ground to his right, a dead dove spread-winged at his feet.

Chalarka enjoyed passing a few evening hours at a Montería bar called El Percal that was a hangout for poets and writers (Garcés González n.d.), where he made portraits of local characters (respondents always call them *personajes*), images that he either gifted or sold to the owner of his favorite watering hole (I have not been able to gain access to this collection). A deteriorating copy of one of his caricatures, titled *Chicharrón con Pelos*, is kept by Orlando Chalarca. Drawn in 1962, it depicts a large-headed, unshaven, barefoot man carrying a bottle of holy water and a sack, with a massive crucifix hanging from his neck. The Chicharrón's given name was Benigno, and he was a mainstay at Montería wakes, a *rezandero* adept at reciting prayers for the dead, who had the habit of hurling religiously tinged insults at adolescent passersby (Díaz Arrieta 2010; Garcés González 1992). Chalarka was a talented caricaturist.[2]

According to his brother, Ulianov was an autodidact who was very well read, notwithstanding the limitations that geography and class placed on his access to books and reproductions. Despite never finishing high school, he was well informed about classical art. In Orlando's studio, located in the back of what was once the family home, hangs a self-portrait in early modern costume in which Ulianov imagines himself in the clothing of Rembrandt. The lintels of his house and some of the walls feature reproductions by Ulianov of Aztec, Maya, and Muisca motifs (fig. 3.2), which are obscured by the fronts of a grocery store and a restaurant currently renting the premises. There used to be an angel on the front roof, while on the corner of the gutters there was a gargoyle, which is why the house is still known by many as the "Esquina del Diablo," the "Devil's Corner." Orlando showed me a news clipping with a photo of the house in its better years, featuring a hedge that hid its adornments from public view: a taxi driver whom I asked about the family confessed that when he was a child he had been caught peering between the bushes.

Ulianov Chalarka caught the eye of Orlando Fals Borda and his associates at the Fundación del Caribe in the early seventies. More precisely, he was discovered by Franklin Sibaja, the Fundación member who enjoyed a broad range of contacts, both rural and urban, and who was skilled at locating interview subjects and collaborators. The team had been on the lookout for an artist who could assist in producing illustrated pamphlets, which they hoped would

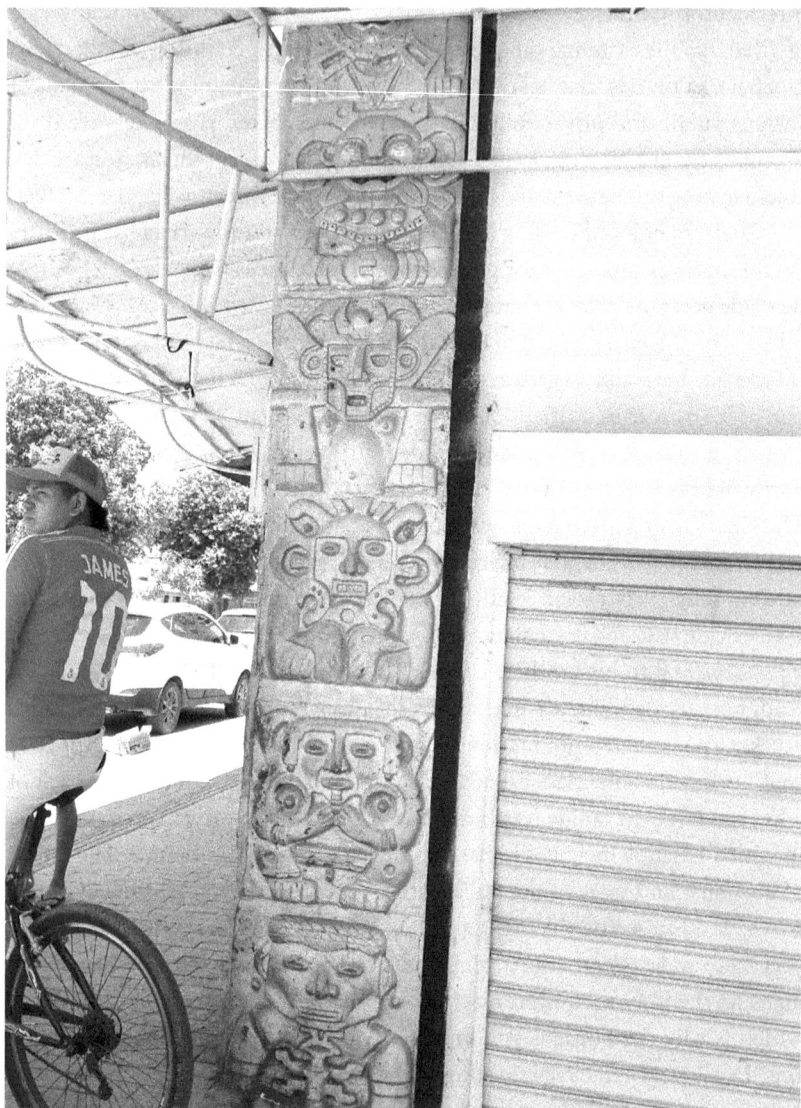

Figure 3.2 La Esquina del Diablo, Barrio La Granja, Montería (photo by author)

be accessible to a largely illiterate readership. At first, a Montería art professor named Álvaro Mendoza was tapped. He provided a script—a mock-up of the illustrations and texts of the panels of a comic—depicting the occupation of the Baluarte Rojo of Lomagrande (CDRBR/M, 0680, 0681). The script is rather flat, to my mind, and presumably to Fals's and his associates' as well, because, ultimately, they recruited Chalarka to their team instead of Mendoza. Chalarka produced four graphic histories between 1972 and 1974, each ranging from fourteen to eighteen pages in length. They were published in collaboration with various agrarian organizations, some of them affiliated with ANUC. Printed on low-grade paper, with pages measuring approximately 20 by 25 cms, each of the pamphlets took approximately six months to prepare from the preliminary research to its publication.[3]

When I initially looked at Chalarka's comics, they seemed to be a fait accompli, a polished work that at first glance resisted my analysis of its conditions of production. There was only minimal documentation among Fals's papers on how the Fundación put the graphic histories together: some time lines summarizing the contents of interviews and archival sources, Mendoza's failed script, and a mock-up of the last few pages of *Felicita Campos*. It was only when I began to ask Víctor Negrete and others for details on the process (using my growing review of the literature on comics as a basis for asking specific questions), when I learned to look at Fals's photos for the evidence they contained instead of as illustrations, and when I engaged comics artists who could help me to analyze the images that I discovered I could make good use of a combination of my visual and verbal sources. In this chapter, I begin this process, framing the graphic histories as an ethnographic scenario through which I decipher the participatory conditions of their production. I read my evidence as an ethnographic observer, constructing a thick description of the setting, the people who populated it, and the procedures they used to prepare the text.

The Making of *Felicita Campos*

The initial photograph of Ulianov Chalarka at work (fig. 3.1) depicts the artist plying his craft in solitude. In fact, in this photo he is putting the finishing touches on materials whose process of authorship was profoundly participatory. His historical comic books originated in a series of collaborations by a range of activists with dissimilar talents and life experiences, who engaged one another in a chain of conversations. ANUC activists set the research agenda, sending Fundación researchers and Fals Borda to comb local archives and to participate in community meetings at which they interviewed elderly campesinos who had been active in the 1920s to 1960s. Chalarka took visual notes at these events and shared his sketches with his rural audience, receiving constructive criticisms from them, as well as new information to supplement the drawings. A Fundación del Caribe/ANUC committee laid out the graphic history, using Chalarka's illustrations as a starting point and adding speech balloons and captions.[4] After ANUC approved the final version it was taken to assemblies and workshops, where it was read and discussed by campesino audiences, sometimes with the participation of the narrators depicted in its pages. The work of dissemination expanded the knowledge base of the graphic histories by incorporating the personal experiences of the readers, in addition to informing peasants about their forebears.

How this process functioned on the ground is depicted in another series of photographs. Ulianov Chalarka, with his characteristic beret, is seated in front of a thatched hut, a group of children peering over his shoulder as he sketches a portrait of an elderly Afrocolombian man dressed in a striped shirt, clutching a machete. The man sits wearily on a chair placed in front of a white Toyota jeep (fig. 3.3); the jeep belonged to Fals Borda, who, I surmise, was the photographer. The sitter is identified on the back of the photograph as "El Mello" ["The Twin"], a nickname for Ignacio Silgado, a community activist from Aguas Negras, a hamlet in the municipality of San Onofre, Sucre, which in the colonial period was a *palenque*, a community of refuge for escaped slaves. Silgado shared his personal reminiscences with the Fundación researchers (CDRBR/M, 1770) and would eventually be given a prominent role in the history project as the narrator of *Felicita Campos* (fig. 3.4). Each of the graphic histories features a semi-fictional narrator, a persona based on a leader who was well-known in the locality. I identify the narrators as "semi-fictional" because they combine the testimonies of multiple storytellers interviewed by researchers from the Fundación del Caribe. In this case, the interview with Silgado was augmented by a series of other conversations with narrators from neighboring hamlets (CDRBR/M, 1784, 1785, 1786). Néstor Herrera, a young urban activist affiliated with the Fundación, led the research team that collected information for the comic among the peasants of San Onofre. He fondly remembers Silgado as enormously hospitable and an inspiring community organizer.[5]

El Mello's reputation as a local leader made him an excellent spokesperson to share the story of early twentieth-century community organizer Felicita Campos, a woman who braved assaults by armed authorities and took her case in defense of community lands all the way to Bogotá (Chalarka 1985: 65–78). Herrera did not tape his testimony; he summarized it in five typescript pages. As in so many other parts of the coast, the campesinos had settled the

Figure 3.3   Ulianov Chalarka sketching a portrait of "El Mello," Aguas Negras, San Onofre, 1973 (CDRBR/M, CF, 1945. Photo reprinted with permission of the Centro de Documentación Regional "Orlando Fals Borda," Banco de la República, Montería)

public lands of Aguas Negras in the late nineteenth century, cultivating rice, manioc, and plantains; colonization was described by Herrera as a process of "civilizing" the land. Although Silgado was very young during the years when Campos mobilized the community, he remembered myriad details about the families that settled there, the fights that erupted among them, skirmishes with the police, the price of plantains, and how some homesteaders lost their plots during the War of the Thousand Days, the last of the civil wars that beleaguered postindependence Colombia (CDRBR/M, 1770, fol. 9701). In 1928, Rafael Enrique Prieto arrived from Cartagena, at the time the provincial capital, some 73 kms to the north, claiming that the lands had been assigned to him. One of his acts was to require widow Felicita Campos to mark her cattle with his brand, provoking a conflict that unfolded over the early 1930s, bringing police into Aguas Negras and neighboring hamlets, where they demolished and set fire to campesino huts.

These acts propelled Campos to travel by foot the more than 500 kms to the national capital of Bogotá, from whence she returned three months later, only to discover that the police had burned down the hamlet. Ten times she traveled to Cartagena in defense of her lands, while neighboring landlords

Figure 3.4 "El Mello" as narrator of *Felicita Campos* (Chalarka 1985: 67. Photo reprinted with permission of the Centro de Documentación Regional "Orlando Fals Borda," Banco de la República, Montería)

brought in indigenous scab labor from San Andrés de Sotavento and seized peasant lands and cattle; eventually, the Zenúes from San Andrés refused to collaborate further with Prieto, who in the end, mysteriously contracted a ghastly illness that culminated in dementia and death. Felicita Campos was never to obtain title, Aguas Negras lands remaining in the public domain. (CDRBR/M, 1770, fols. 9702-9704). ANUC arrived in Aguas Negras in 1970, in the person of Florentino Montero, commencing a year of hacienda occupations that ended when the agrarian reform agency bought the lands for the peasants (CDRBR/M, 1770, fol. 9705). Ulianov Chalarka condensed El Mello's narrative into fourteen pages of comics panels. This was his last graphic history, and its illustrations are more complex and detail laden than his earlier attempts at graphic narrative, which I will describe in coming chapters.

The presence of El Mello, a respected knowledge bearer, in the pages of *Felicita Campos* reminded campesino readers that the protagonists of earlier struggles still resided in their midst. A comparison of figures 3.3 and 3.4 underscores Ulianov Chalarka's ability to capture Ignacio Silgado's personality. As they experienced the immediacy of these images, populated by the identifiable visages of their neighbors, campesinos began to see themselves as historical protagonists, "project[ing] themselves *into* the [experience of the] people about whom they're reading," in the words of comics artist Nate Powell, coauthor of *March*, an award-winning graphic history of the civil rights struggle in the United States (Eil 2016; cf. Lewis, Aydin, and Powell 2013-2016). Matilde Eljach, a university student who accompanied Fals for a time in Córdoba, told me that the campesinos "were moved when they saw their portraits of history in the pictures."[6]

In another photo in Fals's archive, we are ushered into a working meeting of the collective that produced *Felicita Campos* (fig. 3.5). Chalarka—seated at a table and dressed in a soccer jersey, with his ubiquitous beret perched on his head—takes visual notes while at his right a local activist, the grandson of Felicita Campos, raises his hand to accentuate a point. The two men who frame the composition listen passively, while two others at the center rear, both wearing the characteristic woven hats [*sombreros vueltiaos*] of the Caribbean coast, are engaged in a private conversation. These two are ANUC leader Florentino Montero (in the button-down shirt), the activist who set in motion the land occupations in San Onofre in 1970, and Fundación del Caribe member Néstor Herrera (in the pullover). Montero was a campesino activist, one of the peasants, like Juana Julia Guzmán and Alfonso Salgado, whom my interlocutors identified as a close Fundación collaborator. In this photo, we observe firsthand what constituted research for this team: a group of agrarian leaders

Figure 3.5   Study group for *Felicita Campos*, 1973 (CDRBR/M, CF, 1946. Photo reprinted with permission of the Centro de Documentación Regional "Orlando Fals Borda," Banco de la República, Montería)

and schooled collaborators directing a conversation with knowledge bearers, their aim to transmit to potential community activists the inspiring history of struggle of their forebears, conveyed in a visual language that they could comprehend and that would become food for thought. There is no single authoritative voice in this dialogue, but instead, we see a merging of academic and people's knowledge, with the objective of crystallizing campesino points of view in the framework of a user-friendly vehicle for stimulating further political action.

The Language of Chalarka's Comics

Latin American graphic narratives have always been connected to the North American comics industry that historically supplied magazines and comic strips to Spanish-speaking readerships (Campbell 2009; Guerra 2010; Merino 2003; Vázquez 2010). Notwithstanding the flowering across the continent by the end of the 1960s of alternative comics generated by community organizations (Acevedo 1981), educational graphic narratives by state agencies and development organizations (Flora 1984; Parlato et al. 1980), and independent Latin American graphic narratives like *El Eternauta* in Argentina (Oesterheld and Solano López 2013 [1957–1959]), noncommercial comics rarely reached the Colombian provinces. Ulianov Chalarka was more familiar with translations of the North American comic strips *Woody Woodpecker* [*El Pájaro Loco*], *Little Lulu* [*La Pequeña Lulú*], *Donald Duck* [*El Pato Donald*], *Tarzan*, *The Lone Ranger* [*El Llanero Solitario*], and *Batman*, as well as the Mexican superhero Kalimán (Hinds 1977), which were easily accessible in Spanish at newsstands in Montería or in businesses that rented out comic books (colloquially known as *paquitos*) by the hour.[7]

Chalarka's comics follow the typical conventions of the genre (Acevedo 1981; McCloud 1993): a story organized in panels laid out on a page organized in a grid, each panel separated from the others by a gutter, the empty space or line between panels. Panels are frequently captioned by an external narrative that is visually distinguished from the contents of the panels by its positioning along the frame, sometimes encased in a box. They also feature speech balloons containing the words or thoughts of the characters. Comics as a genre requires a sequential reading of the panels, compelling readers to follow a series of images through which the action develops.

Unlike many of the comics with which readers may be familiar, which are sequential in the sense that single episodes are chronicled over a series of panels, the Fundación del Caribe graphic histories are only sequential insofar as their panels march from year to year, with explanatory captions marked by date. In other words, Chalarka's rendering of each panel represents an event, inserted into a chronological series. There are hints at more complex sequentiality in the last two of the four comics, something I will come back to in chapter 5 with reference to *El Boche*. The late introduction of a fine-grained sequentiality suggests that the two years of comics production constituted a learning process for Chalarka. The strategy of confining historical events to single panels probably coincided with campesinos' lack of experience with the medium. I would guess that their reading consisted of digesting a single panel at a time, instead of their eyes moving over a sequence, something Mauricio Archila told me occurred when peasants near Bogotá perused comics created by CINEP (COPRORCO n.d.), which were inspired by the Fundación's graphic histories.

Chalarka's four graphic histories contain two or three panels on each page, identified by dated captions. Their stories generally begin in the pre-Columbian period depicting a primordial aboriginal autonomy that was subsequently violated by the Spanish invasion. Images of the nineteenth-century voyages of discovery by foreign investors in search of raw materials and the rise of cattle raising comprise the next chapter of these booklets. Panels illustrate the introduction of the matrícula in the early twentieth century and socialist organizing against debt-peonage. They lend a visual embodiment to campesino experiences of La Violencia, the mid-twentieth-century interparty conflict that unleashed an assault by the elites on the peasantry and, on the Caribbean coast, contributed to the dissolution of the agrarian collectives that had sprung up in previous decades. They always end with depictions of ANUC's demands and its victories, showing activists in peasant garb shouting slogans and carrying protest signs. That is to say, they conclude in the present of their readership, who would carry history into the future, in a utopian trajectory culminating in ANUC.

Chalarka's panels contain a wealth of sub-narratives (Spiegelman 2011: 168). His unpretentious drawings produce an ethnographic "sense of time and place through 'incidentals'" (Brown 1988: 99): the crops that typified rural existence—plantains and rice, for instance—the barbed-wire fences hacienda owners erected to demarcate the lands they had usurped from smallholders, the humiliating punishment of the stocks, everyday tasks of fishing or lumbering, mobilizations bristling with protest signs. Their details are repetitive, intended to bring to mind how monotonous and wretched were the living conditions of the mid-twentieth-century peasantry (Sacco 2002: 13). Haciendas are always clearly identified by their names on signs hung from trees or on walls.

The reader of any comics text is an active participant in the task of making sense of the narrative. She must reconstruct in her imagination a world represented in the panels by a small constellation of icons and phrases. Deciphering this world involves not only the careful processing of each panel but also an appreciation of the comics grid that orders each page (Groensteen 2007: chap. 1). This is true for any comics reader, although only to some degree for campesinos, many of whom depended on others to convey the verbal content to them. I want to go beyond this commonplace, however, to examine in depth how these texts were created and how they functioned as a vehicle for participation, with the objective of discovering how Fals Borda's notion of imputation—the harnessing of the imagination to the analysis of historical referents—functioned as a political strategy.

Taking Graphic Notes

Generally, the author of a comic is the person who writes the script—the visual and verbal plotting of the organization of panels on the page (Bredehoft 2011: 98; Pekar and Crumb 1996; Sacco 2002: 36; Sacco and Chute 2011). The script, which may be very abstract, usually precedes the drawings. This is explained by Art Spiegelman, author of one of the most influential English-language graphic novels, *Maus* (Spiegelman 1973, 1986). *Maus* narrates in comics form the (bio)graphical story of Spiegelman's father during the Holocaust. His father's narrative is framed by drawings depicting the interview sessions in which Spiegelman collected his father's testimony decades later. Spiegelman recalls that he transcribed the taped interviews into a notebook and then looked "for a logical narrative unit of information to form a drawn page out of key scenes." He composed and rewrote the text on a transparent grid to test out various page schemes. Finally, he drew a series of studies for each panel, outlining the final draft set on a light table and applying ink to the image (Spiegelman 2011: 172–174).

At first, I assumed that the Fundación del Caribe followed a similar model. I found time lines in the archive that roughly reproduce the scenes narrated in some of the graphic histories (CDRBR/M, 1916, 1917); Víctor Negrete told me these documents, culled from research materials, guided the crafting of the comics panels.[8] Matilde Eljach recalls how Juana Julia Guzmán's memories were collected:

> We programmed two or three meetings with the peasants, depending on the immediate conditions, because at times security concerns impeded our meetings, or it was raining heavily. And the meetings were in groups with the people. We sat in circles. They gave us their stories, we all carefully took notes, and at the end of the afternoon the working group met to confront the notes and try to make a first draft of the narrative. . . . Then we compared what one person wrote, and what another wrote. And then, Orlando decided on the final version.[9]

I infer that the drafts to which Eljach refers are not scripts for the graphic histories but time lines synthesizing events based on information gathered through interviews and archival research. Eljach calls this work an exercise in translation:

> The people spoke and we copied, reread, put together the narrative. So the narratives were voluminous, extremely long. And to put together this story, to synthesize it in graphic form, took a tremendous effort, because it could extend for pages and pages, and we had to make the pamphlets like a film-script. That's what we had to do: we had to help in the task of synthesizing it all into a sentence, in simple language, without distorting it, without mutilating the idea.[10]

As Negrete revealed to me, the Fundación's production process was distinct from that of other comics, because there were no scripts prepared ahead of the drawings.[11] His reminiscences helped me to visualize in what follows how Chalarka's act of imputation and that of the campesinos were combined in practice.

The first step was to determine which events and historical processes would be incorporated into the graphic histories. This took place in discussions between ANUC leaders and the Fundación del Caribe. The research group then collected documentary and bibliographic materials from archives, libraries, and personal collections, accompanied by the taping and transcription of eyewitness testimony in selected communities. It is worth citing Negrete's recollection of how Chalarka accompanied the researchers to assemblies and meetings, where he took visual notes as he listened to the protagonists:

> The artist accompanied us to the villages and to the meetings we held with organizations and communities. He generally took notes by making drawings and written reminders. He paid a great deal attention to peoples' physiognomy, the expressions they used, the details of the surroundings, that is, houses with visible objects, construction materials, animals, plants, that is to say, soil, rivers, everything that would give him a complete picture of the moment in which he found himself. (Rappaport and Negrete 2015: 37)[12]

Then, Chalarka would meet with members of the community to prepare a first draft of his drawings, which may be what we see in the photo of the *Felicita Campos* working group. As Negrete recounts: "At the end of the meeting he would get out the onionskin paper and begin to draw in the presence of the participants. The people would draw near him and he would show them what he had done. He would ask them for their evaluations and suggestions. The people would ask, correct, augment, reduce, laugh, clarify, argue" (Rappaport and Negrete 2015: 37). Chalarka took advantage of the surroundings in which he found himself and his campesino interlocutors to construct an image of a Cordobés past-in-the-present: "When Ulianov went to places, he would begin to draw and he was surrounded by peasants, and he had some models— faces, physiognomy, clothing. And then the jokes would begin: 'Look, paint this man's nose like this, his mouth like this.' And they'd say, 'Why don't you put in that parakeet that's there, that thing that's there?' They helped flesh these things out."[13] Needless to say, Chalarka also enjoyed access to historical materials collected by the Fundación del Caribe researchers—photos, maps, and other items—permitting him to produce historically plausible drawings.

Chalarka took the lead in determining the visual contents of the comics based on his preliminary sketches, but they emerged in dialogue with the peasants. His visual notes were subsequently transformed as they were laid on the table for evaluation by the Fundación team, which ultimately decided what would go into the panels. After the collective had transformed the sketches into finished panels, they added captions and speech balloons. The contents of the panels were debated, as Negrete remembers, "word by word, gesture by gesture, drawing by drawing"; unfortunately, I could not get Negrete to dredge up the details from his memory.[14] Negotiation of the visual components of the panels and the addition of the verbal channel was a painstaking enterprise:

> On the basis of this draft made by [Chalarka] and by those who partici-
> pated in the meeting, there were more meetings with those responsible for
> research. One by one, we would review the initial drawings or illustrations,
> seeking maximal expression and representativity, we would eliminate,
> change, and add new ones. We began to write the texts, short sentences
> really, easy to understand, precise, which could explain the messages with
> clarity. So, at meetings with us [Chalarka] went on elaborating the text,
> the drawing, a little more, and we began to add short sentences. In ad-
> dition to the participation of the artist and the people, this other draft
> included our participation, through which we partially modified the draw-
> ings and added the context and the texts. (Rappaport and Negrete 2015: 37)

While Negrete does not remember the particular issues that provoked discussion among the team that laid out the graphic histories, Fals's archive provides a clue to at least one of the points at which negotiations over the comics' contents took place. I found a partial script of *Felicita Campos* that appears to have been reviewed, or perhaps written, by the Fundación (CDRBR/M, 1787, fols. 9710-9711), detailing action taking place in 1970. Ignacio, Felicita's son, is pictured in a land occupation that eventually led to the founding of a local chapter of ANUC in San Onofre. An organizing meeting is depicted in both the script and the final version of the comic, with a man pictured leading the discussion; he is not identified in the published booklet (Chalarka 1985: 77). The script—which contains no drawings, only notes about where images are to be inserted—reads, "Florentino presiding over the meeting—his face, but don't put his name" (CDRBR/M, 1787, fol. 9710, underlining in original). The scriptwriter is referring to Florentino Montero, who would lead the research team at Aguas Negras and who instigated the introduction of ANUC in the locality. The fact that the script underscores the need to hide Montero's name suggests to me that this was one of the points of discussion, perhaps even of disagreement, among the group that mapped out the graphic narrative. Note that the decision to obscure his identity was a political one, as many of the issues discussed at these meetings undoubtedly were. I would assume that the process of compiling was uneven and involved some degree of disagreement.[15]

Negrete speaks of the act of composing the verbal text of the graphic narratives "as though he were writing with" the campesinos. Peasant narrators inspired the writing process, which took place after the oral narratives were collected, but incorporated direct quotations from campesino stories in speech balloons. As he explains in a 1980 pamphlet coauthored with José Galeano for the community of El Cerrito, they strove to capture the style of peasant narration, replicating the tone of the conversations they had with narrators: "the work . . . is written to be read aloud; its writing style is similar to that of the peasants who were interviewed; its language is simple, characteristic [of the region], and a bit literary; the chapters are brief and with sufficient illustrations" (CDRBR/M, 0576, fol. 2764). This local history employs photographs instead of comics panels, since it was produced after Ulianov Chalarka's death.

The working group for *Lomagrande, Tinajones,* and *El Boche* was led by Ulianov Chalarka, Víctor Negrete, Orlando Fals Borda, and Franklin Sibaja (as mentioned in note 10, *Felicita Campos* may have been outsourced). Drafts of the final texts were subsequently vetted by ANUC: "We once again took this second draft to meetings with activists, the leadership, and the rank and file. Here, together with them, we made the necessary changes after receiving clarifications and analysis. Once we were in agreement, the artist would give it his final touch and it would go to print" (Rappaport and Negrete 2015: 37).

Background research was essential inasmuch as it supplied documentary evidence backing up the oral narratives, indispensable given the unstable political moment and the probability that the veracity of the graphic histories would be contested by the local elite. Notwithstanding the centrality of narratives of twentieth-century campesino experience to these comics, they also depicted events from earlier historical periods with which the storytellers were unfamiliar and thus had to be collected from other source material. Even more important than substantiating oral testimony, the collection of historical sources placed the Fundación researchers on a horizontal plane with campesinos. Both they and ANUC members had information to share with one another. The Fundación's bibliographic research entered into a reciprocal relationship with peasant testimonials, complementing peasant knowledge. The comics were, consequently, the result of a dialogue, not the traditional research methodologies that privilege the academic voice, but instead an interpenetration of numerous voices, something like the testimonial literature that was beginning to be produced at the time across Latin America (although, like in testimonial literature, this dialogue is erased from the final product).

It is difficult, nonetheless, to reconstruct the dynamics of the meetings at which eyewitnesses narrated their experiences, which were taped by Fals Borda or recorded in notebooks by Fundación researchers and captured as sketches by Chalarka. While participants recollect these meetings as having been horizontal dialogues, there is only limited historical evidence to demonstrate the interpenetration of numerous voices. Transcripts of the interviews used in *Lomagrande, El Boche,* and *Tinajones* do not appear to deviate from standard interview procedure: they record questions and answers, as though a single interviewer and a single narrator engaged in a formal conversation. In fact, when I read the transcript of Fals Borda's 17–18 April 1972 interview with Juana Julia Guzmán, I concluded that it was a particularly stilted encounter, since Juana Julia appears to provide only cursory responses to Fals's questions (CDRBR/M, 0864). At first glance, a subsequent 23 May 1972 interview (CDRBR/M, 0866) was a more successful attempt at eliciting her life history, with the narrator responding to the interviewer with more detailed stories. I would later discover that I had misconstrued entirely the context of the first interview.

Few of Fals's reel-to-reel tapes dating from the early 1970s survive, but fortunately, I had access to his 18 April conversation with Juana Julia (CDRBR/M, CG, C/OFB/GM II). I learned from listening to the recording that this was not a standard interview. Numerous men and women interceded in the discussion, in a conversation that took place over the space of a day, moving from the hamlet of San Isidro to Lomagrande itself, adding interlocutors at various locations. As Fals recounted to Ernesto Parra, "I remember at least some ten elderly men and women who had belonged to the era of Vicente Adamo. Of course, they were there waiting their turn for the recording, so things had gotten more interesting" (Parra Escobar 1983: 139).

Admittedly, some of the speech in these recordings is very difficult to comprehend, given the heavy regional accents of the respondents—even for a Costeño transcriber familiar with the staccato intonation, the dropping of *s*'s, and the local idioms of campesinos—so that entire exchanges are left out of the transcript. More important, the diverse participants in the conversation are not identified by the transcriber, who lays out the interview as though Fals Borda were speaking only to Juana Julia. When I listened to the tape I was startled to discover that the brief sentences were not all uttered by Juana Julia. Other voices constantly broke in to add details, correct some of her errors, or answer questions when her memory failed her. In other words, this was a lively conversation *among* Costeño peasants, not an interview directed *at* them, a dialogue in which Fals only intervened occasionally. The tape gave me a deeper appreciation of how eyewitnesses and Fundación researchers interacted:

in a spirited dialogue among equals, a process of campesinos collectively making sense of their own history. I returned to other transcripts, such as an exchange between Víctor Negrete and Bárbaro Ramírez that furnishes key historical detail for *Lomagrande* and *El Boche* (CDRBR/M, 0247), where I also came to recognize the participatory character of what I had thought was a standard interview. I could now see why Negrete calls them "conversations" (Negrete Barrera 1983: 14).

These encounters constituted privileged moments at which campesinos engaged in communal reflection. This part of the process of "systematic devolution" occurred at many moments during the research process, not only at the moment of delivering a final product. It

> consisted of an effort to refresh the memory and remembrances of the people, principally the most elderly. For them, the devolution of a reconstructed past allowed for reminiscences and for bringing up to date what they partially or completely knew and/or what they themselves lived and did in the days of their youth, or what they were able to hear from their parents and grandparents. For the youngest, this information would allow them to learn something new, about which they had no idea or had only vaguely heard their elders comment. This procedure permits a reencounter of the most recent generations of the exploited classes with their own history. (ACHUNC/B, caja 49, carpeta 3, fol. 248v)

These were occasions for a critical analysis from below and for intergenerational dialogue. The collective nature of this process is obscured in Fals's field notes and, notably, in the comics format. Discovering it requires excavation.

Designing Comics Panels

My conversations with Víctor Negrete gave me an idea of how the narratives inspired the artist to make his initial sketches, but I still needed to learn more about how the sketches were transformed into panels. I decided to seek out new interlocutors in hopes that they would see in the panels all of the things I hadn't noticed. In early July 2016, I convoked a meeting with comics scriptwriter Pablo Guerra and artists Camilo Aguirre and Henry Díaz, coauthors along with geographer Diana Ojeda, of *Caminos condenados* [Dead Ends] (Ojeda et al. 2016), a graphic novel based on scholarly research by a team of geographers (Ojeda et al. 2015) evaluating the consequences of the complicity of paramilitary agents and agribusiness in Montes de María, a vast region located on the northeastern coastal plain of Colombia. (San Onofre, the setting of *Felicita Campos*, is one of the many municipalities comprising Montes de María.) Many of its inhabitants—people who might have listened in as children at the meetings that gave rise to the 1974 graphic history—were driven from their homes by armed agents or deprived of access to land and water by palm oil plantations and have since dispersed to Sincelejo and as far afield as Venezuela.[16] Allied with the paramilitary, narco-traffickers gave the finishing touches to the decomposition of the region's social fabric (Becerra Becerra and Rincón García 2017b: 31–38). *Caminos condenados* captures the essence of Ojeda's scholarly research without repeating its contents verbatim. I hoped that its authors could bring to a reading of the Fundación's graphic histories that same sense of how history can be narrated in a unique way through comics.

Over four hours we slowly contemplated the panels of *El Boche*, *Felicita Campos*, and *Tinajones*, which we projected onto the wall of a conference room at the Universidad Javeriana. Pablo, Camilo, and Henry clarified some of the artistic influences governing Chalarka's depictions: they repeatedly noted where Chalarka was inspired by *The Lone Ranger*, *Tarzan*, and *The Phantom*, as well as pointing out those panels inspired by popular caricatures, such as the ubiquitous image of a heavyset and prosperous shop owner who declaims, "Yo no fío" ["I don't sell on credit"], a print one encounters occasionally in neighborhood bodegas. They commented on Chalarka's attention to the vagaries of costume: how he carefully rendered images of policemen and soldiers from different moments in history in appropriate period uniforms. They also helped me to analyze how Chalarka grew as a comics artist over the two years he worked on the graphic histories by walking me through his incremental appropriation of comics language—sequentiality, split panels, English-language onomatopoetic inserts (like *bang*), and other techniques. They pointed out his increasing ability to draw complex and coherent compositions that became progressively less panoramic and more convincingly displayed characters interacting with one another.

I am especially interested in their close readings of how the graphic histories were put together. They were able to identify which parts of Chalarka's images were drawn first and which were added later, thereby revealing how his preliminary sketches were combined into panels. They concentrated on a series of pages from *Tinajones*, depicting hacienda owner José Santos Cabrera's early encounters with the homesteaders of the littoral marshes and the repressive actions he took against them. When I juxtaposed my interlocutors' analyses to source materials from Fals's archive, I discovered I could identify the particular scenarios that provoked Chalarka to put pen to paper. Then, with my interlocutors' help, I uncovered the rationale behind combining these sketches into panels. I could only accomplish this through imputation, because Chalarka's visual notes no longer exist.

Tinajones tells the story of the 1961 confrontation of the campesinos of San Bernardo del Viento with José Santos Cabrera, a mulatto politician and owner of the hacienda of Río Ciego, located near the mouth of the Sinú River (Chalarka 1985: 40). The peasant smallholdings described in the comic were public lands, mostly mangrove swamps that landless settlers began to transform in the 1920s, constructing a human-made waterscape of canals feeding strips of arable land on which they cultivated rice, much like the pre-Columbian raised fields of the nearby San Jorge basin (Plazas and Falchetti 1981) or the *chinampas* of central Mexico. Beginning in the late 1920s, Cabrera initiated a legal crusade to usurp lands from the smallholders, enabled by his political ties in what was then the regional capital of Cartagena and in the courthouse of nearby Lorica. When homesteaders did not heed his warnings he turned to violence.

This is a story that would be repeated throughout the coastal plain: landless peasants transform public lands into usable property, only to be cheated out of their homesteads by well-connected large landowners (Fals Borda 1986; LeGrand 1986; Ocampo 2007) either by legal theft or by very cheap purchase (Leal and Van Ausdal 2013; Van Ausdal 2008, 2009). According to ANUC-Línea Armenia leader Juana de León, who presided over the San Bernardo del Viento chapter in the late 1970s, peasant settlers were required to cut down the mangroves and sow pasture, which would then be expropriated by the large landowners. In turn, they ejected the smallholders from their land. This was called "making farms for the terratenientes" [*haciendo finca al terrateniente*] (CINEP/B, doc. 7).[17]

In Chalarka's rendition of the 1961 meeting of Cabrera and the smallholders of San Bernardo del Viento, the landlord is dressed in city garb as befits a successful politician (a guayabera and slacks) and is buttressed by two battle-ready officers armed with machine guns (fig. 3.6). He angrily gesticulates in an effort to legitimize the questionable tactics he has employed to divest a group of homesteaders of their lands. A semi-naked child trapped between the soldiers and Cabrera cries, "Mami ay!" and calls for his mother to rescue him from the towering interlopers, one of whom threatens to kick him. The peasants—men and women in worn and patched clothing, sombreros vueltiaos on their heads, in iconic contrast to Cabrera's apparel—are poised at the ready, their children clinging in terror to their legs, mirroring the young boy behind Cabrera. Their fists and machetes are held high in a revolutionary posture ubiquitous to 1970s political art and spectacle. Campesino power salutes deflect Cabrera's pointing finger, defiantly conveying their refusal to abandon the homesteads they built four decades earlier.

Figure 3.6   José Santos Cabrera meets the peasants of Tinajones, top panel (Chalarka 1985: 40. Comic reprinted with permission of the Fundación del Sinú)

Landlord and peasants are separated by a mediator, Padre Ignacio Arroyabe. Grasping his Bible, the local parish priest threatens to abandon the priesthood (*dejar la sotana* or, literally, "take off his cassock") if Cabrera wins his legal case. This is a visual reference to one of the oral histories collected by Fals in 1972, in which Federico Fiordanengo recollected that "the Father had some words with Dr. Cabrera, Dr. Cabrera telling him that he preferred to remain poor and not lose those lands, while the Father said to him that if he won back the lands, he would abandon the cassock. Those were the words of offence they shared there" (CDRBR/M, 1913, fol. 10177). Chalarka crystallized the event into a confrontation between two towering iconic figures. The faces and attire of the peasants and the soldiers betray no signs of their unique personalities. While Father Arroyabe's priestly identity is represented by his cassock, only Cabrera is clearly identifiable as an individual: a well-fed and domineering man whose face bears some resemblance to a youthful portrait I found in Orlando Fals Borda's personal archive (CDRBR/M, CF, 1352) and who is depicted using stereotypical black facial features.[18]

As Chalarka listened to narrator Fiordanengo's reminiscences, he sketched an imaginary rendition of the words shared by the two central figures. I have no direct evidence of why he chose this sentence from Fiordanengo's lengthy exposition, but I surmise that its iconicity was attractive to an illustrator charged with rendering the complexities of political alliances in simple but striking images. Cabrera is backed up by the army, while Arroyabe stands in defense of the campesinos, his very identity as a priest at stake in the encounter. A dichotomy is drawn between good/priest and evil/ hacendado, one that is common to both the graphic histories and to *Historia doble* (Archila 1986). The other inhabitants of the *Tinajones* panel—the soldiers and the peasants—were probably added afterward, based on Chalarka's personal knowledge of how the military and small farmers dressed in the period. The poses grow out of the artist's careful observation of the people surrounding him during his visit to the coastal wetlands, his experiential knowledge of how soldiers comport themselves at public disturbances (which he observed at land occupations), his familiarity with priests, and his understanding of the subtleties of social interaction among members of the Montería elite who commissioned his reproductions of saints' images for their living rooms.

Chalarka had a hand in assembling the panel out of his preliminary sketches. This is evident in the care he took to balance the figures surrounding the hacendado and the priest, with small children appearing as mirror images on either side of the pair and the composition brought into a dynamic equilibrium by the intersecting diagonals of Cabrera's pointing finger and peasants' raised fists and machetes. I doubt that the other Fundación members would have been as aware of this essential aspect of the pictorial composition. But a close look at the panel suggests that he was not working alone. Pablo, Camilo, and Henry brought to my attention the fact that the soldiers in the foreground are rather incongruous. One of them looks like he is kicking the child, but his posture is somewhat wooden. He was probably added into a composition that had already been constructed; perhaps his image was lifted from another panel (the graphic histories contain several repetitions of this sort). This is not the only scene in which soldiers occupy planes disconnected from the rest of the composition. In several of the panels of *Tinajones*, soldiers are added without situating them firmly in the space occupied by other actors; instead, they appear to be floating in other planes.

Small errors crop up in other panels, again clueing us to the production process. Cabrera's newfound political powers allowed him to unleash a wave of repression to dislodge the homesteaders from Río Ciego. In figure 3.7, the middle panel of the right-hand page vividly captures this moment in the hamlet of Sicará. We see a series of small vignettes, not exactly a sequence: more like a juxtaposition of simultaneous moments, a swirl of events, which is something that the comics medium is good at (Sacco 2002: 28). A thatched hut on the left is engulfed in flames, with a pregnant woman, identified by an arrow and labeled as "Sergia," emerging from the conflagration, pursued by a soldier. At the center of the frame, a man named Juan Blanco pleads for his life as a man armed with a

Figure 3.7   José Santos Cabrera in Tinajones (Chalarka 1985: 34–35. Comic reprinted with permission of the Fundación del Sinú)

club reproaches him with the words, "This is for messing with the doctors!" On the right-hand side of the panel, another figure is beaten by two soldiers, with a second hut consumed by fire in the background. In the left foreground, a hatless man is held in a stranglehold, and to the right, we see a dead pig (animals frequently serve in these comics as a Greek chorus of suffering). Pablo, Henry, and Camilo concluded that this panel is a montage of various scenes from Chalarka's visual notes, which I can substantiate with archival references.

Ignacio de la Rosa, an activist from the hamlet of Cañogrande, described these incidents to the visiting researchers:

> Down there was an inlet they call El Soldado, where he sent an employee of his, Espitia, and took a woman out of the cabin where she lived, having just given birth, and they took her outside and they burned her house. The woman was named Señora Sergia and the husband was called Juan Blanco. They left her without a house, they burned her house: that was Felipe Espitia, who [Cabrera] had as a peon. And from there they continued committing atrocities all over the place. (CDRBR/M, 1913, fol. 10186)

These scenes were probably assembled into a single panel by the project team in Montería, but only imperfectly. The size of the groups depicted gives the reader little sense of their relative positions in the landscape. The central figures appear to stand on the same plane as those on the right, but the latter are smaller than the former, suggesting that they should be farther in the distance. Sergia, who is an important character in the narrative, is depicted as half the size of the other actors, implying that she is a distant figure somewhere in the background, although this is belied by the inclusion of the arrow pointing to her, just as she is emphasized in de la Rosa's narrative. Chalarka knew to depict objects and people proximate to the viewer in a larger scale than those who were more distant. That doesn't happen in this panel, which fuses a series of visual notes, leaving the sutures readily apparent, which suggests to me that other members of the Fundación collaborated in mounting this panel.

Participation

Once the layout of *Tinajones* was complete and ANUC had approved its publication, it was sent to the printer. This was not, however, the end of the participatory process. Crucial to the methodology of action research was the post-publication stage, which was also considered to be research and was also participatory in nature. As the graphic histories circulated at workshops, their contents projected on screens as filmstrips or recounted in puppet shows for those who could not read (fig. 3.8), the participatory dialogues that went into making the illustrated pamphlets were expanded to include discussions with readers. At these events, campesinos shared their personal experiences and analyzed the implications of the histories they had studied. The narrators depicted in the pages of the comics, particularly Juana Julia Guzmán, participated in their diffusion, delivering speeches and interacting with workshop participants; Juana Julia's mere presence elicited applause and even tears, Víctor Negrete told me. If some of her speeches I found in Fals Borda's archive are any indication, Juana Julia's interventions at these events transcended the contents of the graphic histories. For example, in a 1972 speech to the municipal leadership of ANUC in Montería, she built on her experience at Lomagrande to admonish her listeners to learn from the experience of the Sociedad de Obreros y Artesanos (CDRBR/M, 0865, fol. 5178) by rejecting alliances with traditional machine politicians [*politiqueros*]. Thus, it was not only her visage in the graphic histories but her subsequent analysis of her experience and its significance for peasants in the 1970s that summoned readers to appreciate Juana Julia as a bridge between the past and the present. As Matilde Eljach

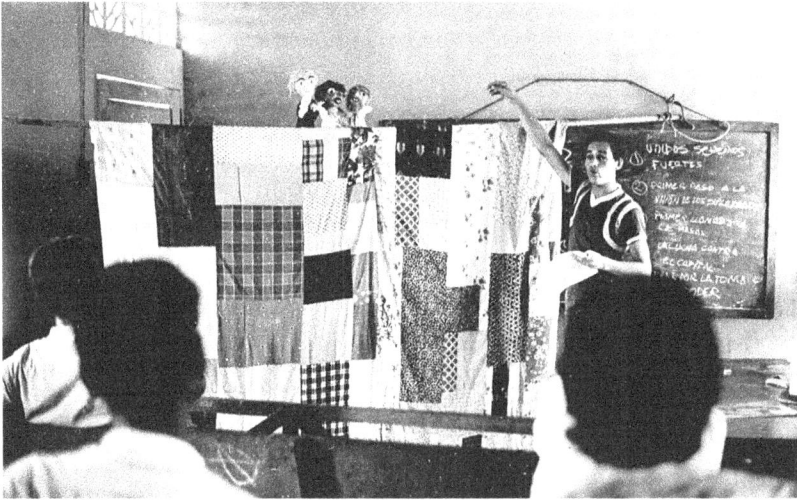

Figure 3.8 Puppets at a school for cadres in Montería, facilitated by Raúl Paniagua, 1973 (CDRBR/M, CF, 1392. Photo reprinted with permission of the Centro de Documentación Regional "Orlando Fals Borda," Banco de la República, Montería)

recounts: "People felt they were the protagonists of the history of Juana Julia. And that has political value."[19]

Action research inspired a text with no clear authorship but, instead, a chain of authors that extended well beyond the completion of the publication. The ANUC leadership chose the topic and Fundación researchers conducted background research. Elderly campesino narrators were invited to tell their stories in front of a multigenerational audience while Ulianov Chalarka listened and made preliminary sketches; he submitted his drawings to the public for commentary and criticism and then perfected them at his Montería studio. His drawings were combined into panels, and speech balloons and captions were inserted at meetings held at the Fundación headquarters in Montería. The drafts of the pamphlet were critiqued by campesino leaders before being given the ANUC imprimatur that permitted it to be published. The final link in the chain was forged at workshops, where the graphic history was read, summarized, and embellished by the reminiscences of participants, who were as immersed in the research as were the makers of the pamphlet.[20]

This chapter fleshes out, at least speculatively, how the Fundación del Caribe "transform[ed] the interview into a participatory experience" (Fals Borda 1978: 23). Fals describes this as a process of "reflective action" [*reflexión-acción*], in which researchers and community activists came together to share information, then withdrew to their own spaces to process it in light of their political activities: "The idea was to promote an exchange between concepts and acts, adapting observations, concrete action, or relevant practice in order to determine the validity of what was observed, then returning to a reflection based on the results of practice" (Fals Borda 1978: 35). Given Fals's conceptualization of his methodology, the movement of the team's activities from a circle of peasant narrators in a village to the Fundación offices in Montería and then back again was precisely what he had envisioned. Moreover, given the penury in which the peasantry lived and the constant threat of police incursions that frequently broke up workshops and meetings, it would be unrealistic to imagine that the research team could put together an entire pamphlet in a rural setting.[21]

Notwithstanding Fals Borda's aspirations, reflective action was not as successful as he had hoped it would be when he first proposed it. Leon Zamosc suggests that while the Fundación achieved a close working relationship with certain members of the ANUC leadership, it was not as successful with the campesino base (Zamosc 1986a: 29), who to some extent filled the traditional role of informant or, alternately, consumer of materials researched and written by others. This opens a crucial question regarding whose voice is privileged in the Fundación's graphic histories: external researchers, the organizational leadership, or the rank and file? Schooled researchers, whether external to ANUC's organizational space or campesinos, were all, to some degree, distanced from the base. My collaborative work with intellectuals from the Consejo Regional Indígena del Cauca was accompanied by an ongoing and lively debate as to whether trained indigenous researchers were positioned "inside" or "outside" the community, whether they were an elite that spoke for indigenous communities or an internal intelligentsia (Rappaport 2005: chap. 1). My colleagues were reticent to call themselves "intellectuals," for fear that the label would distance them from their communities of origin. Forty years earlier, the Fundación might have given equally ambiguous answers to the same question.

Fals sidesteps this dilemma by arguing that action researchers did not intend to "speak for" the peasants but to "speak as" organic intellectuals enmeshed in the everyday struggles of ANUC (Fals Borda 1985: 26). "What justifies the presence and the work of a researcher among the people? Or stated in another way: on the basis of what foundations does a researcher achieve the acceptance and collaboration of the researched?" asks Leon Zamosc at a 1985 seminar, and he responds that acceptance is an outgrowth of political collaboration, itself only possible when the researcher adjusts to people's own perception of their situation, when he or she adapts to their ideology and uses scientific knowledge to modify these representations (1986a: 33–34). In other words, the external researchers' willingness to engage in activism enabled the (admittedly only partially successful) multi-sited, multivoiced chain of conversations I identify as key to the process of composing the graphic histories. This should not be equated with the buzzword *rapport*, as it is used nowadays by anthropologists, because action research of the 1970s was more instrumental, more intent on producing an impact in the political sphere than on the research itself. The chain of research encounters was punctuated by links in which researchers and community cooperated in land occupations and set up baluartes. Ostensibly, this would involve interaction not only with the leadership but with the rank and file—although the nature and quality of dialogue with the campesino base appears to have been rather piecemeal and mediated by those ANUC leaders who were in closest communication with the Fundación. Notwithstanding this quandary, participation was a multifaceted process: a vital component of the task of collecting information, a building block in the construction of knowledge, key to the thoughtful and purposeful dissemination of this knowledge, and central to the political project that was the foundation upon which research took place. The next chapter examines how the graphic histories communicated the political project to their peasant readers, taking a closer look at critical recovery.

4

CRITICAL RECOVERY

At the center of La Rosca's conceptualization of action research was critical recovery [*recuperación crítica*], a mechanism for harnessing historical interpretation to the formulation of organizing strategies. The reintroduction of baluartes—the communal agrarian societies established on public lands during the socialist struggles of the 1920s—is the clearest example of how the Fundación used critical recovery as a guide to arriving at its research priorities, although as I argued in chapter 1, social, political, and economic conditions ultimately prevented the agrarian collectives from effectively taking root in the coastal landscape of the 1970s. Other values that Orlando Fals Borda saw as fundamental to the Costeño peasantry, such as their relationship to the waterways and the wetlands that defined their environment, were also susceptible to critical recovery. We can follow the evolution of the notion of critical recovery through Ulianov Chalarka's graphic histories, which provide fertile ground for exploring how the researchers made legible to the rank and file those narratives that were most strategically significant to the movement. This chapter will explore this process through a series of close readings of *Lomagrande* and *Tinajones*.

Pablo Guerra, the comics scriptwriter who helped me to interpret Ulianov Chalarka's graphic histories, told my Georgetown comics seminar that in order to produce a graphic narrative based on scholarly research it is necessary to "reverse engineer" [*contraingeniar*] it. I asked him to elaborate and he sent me the following explanation in a 10 March 2017 email message: "I speak of reverse engineering because I understand it as a process of discovering the functioning of something that is already completed in order to be able to replicate it." Guerra's goal as a comics author is, then, not the verbatim reproduction of an academic narrative but, instead, its reorganization in order to get at how it was put together. *Caminos condenados*, the graphic novel for which Guerra was the scriptwriter, condenses the research experience of a group of geographers studying the introduction of commercial palm oil plantations in Montes de María (Ojeda et al. 2015). In the space of the comics page they depict the everyday experiences of campesinos, whose sphere of movement was restricted by encroaching palm fields and whose sense of hearing was disrupted by the continuous barrage of the sound of palm fronds hitting their tin roofs. In contrast, researchers sought in their scholarly writing analytical avenues to examine the social and economic impact of agribusiness on peasants. The comics version of the research highlights experiences of sound and feeling.

Most pieces of academic writing generally avoid engaging feelings, but comics as a medium depends on them. Juan Acevedo, a Peruvian cartoonist, told me that his fundamental goal is to use the spare but convincing details of his comics panels to evoke emotions in his readers. Even when his imaginary characters travel to distant places and time periods, readers are enjoined to access sentiments from their own lives in order to connect with the strip's protagonists. The comics medium bridges the lives of narrators and readers in immediate and moving ways. The same occurs in testimonial literature. Alfredo Molano, a former student of Fals Borda, explains that his own personal history is interwoven with that of his peasant interlocutors in his chronicles of the victims of violence in the Colombian countryside. Life history, for Molano, "represents the growing self-awareness of the people themselves, and also on the part of the researcher" (Molano 1998b: 105). There is a moral or ethical project at stake here (Chute 2017), one that is at the root of the Fundación's graphic histories, just as it is central to action research as a whole. The harnessing of sentiment is key to this process, as is the streamlining of history so that it points to the political tasks of the future.

We need to pay close attention to Ulianov Chalarka's drawings to comprehend how this was achieved. How did Chalarka craft his sketches into iconic representations of a history narrated by campesinos? How did they reflect a Costeño ethos, combining a rural worldview with that of the urban researchers of the Fundación del Caribe, thereby merging people's knowledge and scientific inquiry? How did they function as scenarios in which peasant narrators, listeners, and readers could recognize the connections between that history and political action? What did comics contribute to arousing emotions and convictions among campesinos in a way that other media could not? In short, how did they exemplify the process of critical recovery?

Graphic Narratives as a Form of Looking

In the last chapter, I worked through several panels from *Tinajones*, analyzing depictions of the first encounter between landowner José Santos Cabrera and Father Ignacio Arroyabe and the repression that the hacendado unleashed against the homesteaders of Sicará. I pointed out that while the panels were partially based on oral and archival evidence, they also drew on Ulianov Chalarka's personal experience: the landscapes he traveled through, the postures and features of the peasant narrators, the threatening stance of police at a land occupation. Images like Chalarka's are thus not depictions of actual happenings but carefully constructed renderings of a combination of memories and observations.

A drawing is not a snapshot, observes artist and critic John Berger. The artist's pencil doesn't reproduce a fleeting moment like a camera does. Instead, Berger insists that "to draw is to look, to examine the spectrum of appearance. A drawing of a tree shows, not a tree, but a tree being-looked-at. Whereas the sight of a tree is registered almost instantaneously, the examination of the sight of a tree (a tree being-looked-at) not only takes minutes or hours instead of a fraction of a second, it also involves, derives from, and refers back to, much previous experience of looking." A picture is something crafted, meditated on, a kind of a fiction that "has a plenitude of actuality that we experience only rarely in life" (Berger 2001: 43–44).

What was that "plenitude of actuality" that Ulianov Chalarka crafted into his comics panels? Matilde Eljach, the university student who worked as Fals Borda's assistant, recalled that "the stories about what happened in the past were sort of flavored, qualified, by the narrative of the present."[1] The challenges that campesino readers faced in their everyday lives were not all that different from those of the 1920s, the 1940s, or the 1950s as depicted in the graphic histories: they were still impoverished, malnourished, and landless, prey to large landowners, police, and moneylenders. The presence of the past in Chalarka's graphic histories can be best understood, then, as a present in the past, a past that was still being lived by its narrators. The lived past is embodied in the visages of narrators, like "El Mello" Silgado in *Felicita Campos*, in the characteristic lacustrine landscape, and in the hardscrabble lives of the campesinos.

Ulianov Chalarka created first-person narratives of experiences that he heard secondhand. Nonetheless, when we look at his panels, it is as though he were an eyewitness to everything he drew. He was, in fact, an eyewitness to the conditions of the present. He took hold of what he observed and merged it with what he was told, what he recognized in historical photos, what he read in the voluminous archive collected by Fundación researchers. Out of this blend of observations he crafted what appears to the reader as a first-hand account, a visual narrative that makes us feel as though we are walking to Bogotá with Felicita Campos or standing side by side with Juana Julia Guzmán as the police attack Lomagrande. Only, we're not sure who, exactly, the eyewitness is. Is it the storytellers whose words were captured on tape and whose names are cited in a list at the beginning of the booklet? Is it the narrator whose face is depicted every few pages? Is it Ulianov Chalarka? Or is it us, the readers?

At a public talk shortly before I interviewed him, *cronista* Alfredo Molano asserted that the eyewitness testimony that Fals Borda inserts into his books is written in the third person, in the sense that it is framed as the reported speech of one of his interlocutors (much like how ethnographers and oral historians generally quote their respondents). I didn't entirely understand Molano's argument and asked him to explain it further. He began by telling me that he, in contrast to Fals, writes in the first person, and that testimonial literature's emotional impact owes to its insistence on narrating in the first person. Molano's first-person narrative is not presented in his books as the reported speech of the storytellers whose words he taped. Instead, the cronista crafts a fictional narrator who speaks in the first person, an individual with whom readers can empathize:

> My argument is very simple. The third person impedes you, it impedes you from entering the most subjective, the most emotional part, that which is closest to sentiment. From the outside, you can say that someone is sad, but you cannot speak of the sadness I feel, for example. The first person permits you to enter this world, let's just say a subjective one. But I think that it's—better put—emotional, sentimental, in a good sense, with everything that has to do with the spiritual life, if you wish, of a person. You can't enter there from outside: you must be inside, you must place yourself inside. How can I put it? You cannot enter if you speak in the third person. You have to enter in the first person. So that lets people feel that the person you are interviewing can feel, can express his sentiments, his emotions. It's not the same thing to say that a person felt an aversion to blood,

as it is to describe this from the inside. That is my argument. In the first person I can enter and in the second person I am stuck in the doorway.[2]

Molano also recalled an interview with a man called "El Tuerto Gallardo" ["One-Eyed Gallardo"], who lost his hands in an explosion, and whom he discovered, blind and maimed, waiting on a street corner to confront his enemies as they passed by. Molano had to craft El Tuerto's story to make it convincing, and he could only do this, he told me, if he rendered it in the first person: "All of what happened to him, what he told me very superficially, is material that I had to seize upon and amplify, deepen it. With what? With what I feel, with what I feel in a situation like that." The first-person narrative merges narrator El Tuerto Gallardo with Molano, the author. It involves much more than simply using the first-person singular: it involves *inhabiting* the person whose voice is being projected.[3]

How does a comics artist like Ulianov Chalarka construct a first-person narrative of the sort advocated by Molano? In part, by melding past and present in the very bodies of his fellow researchers. Víctor Negrete remembers how he posed as an artist's model whenever Chalarka needed to achieve a natural pose in his depictions of people. One might say that members of the research team had to *inhabit* the bodies of the characters in order to make them believable. Julia Watson (2008: 38) describes this practice as a form of empathetic imagining; it is a common procedure among comics authors (Bechdel 2006; Spiegelman 2011: 35; cf. Chute 2006). In the interest of achieving verisimilitude in the comics panels, Fundación researchers relived historical moments, assuming the postures of angry campesinos with raised fists, terrified children, stalking policemen, the self-important landlord, and the dignified padre. Of course, this was a much more literal form of mimesis than that advocated by ethnographers (Stoller 1994), or even the imaginings of comics artists, because the Fundación researchers were also simultaneously living the ANUC occupations: they were exposed to similar emotions and circumstances as were pictured in the graphic histories.

Chalarka used his own body to guide his pen, another approach common among cartoonists (Trudeau 2017: 20). Juan Acevedo observes that comics are often self-portraits: "I wanted to make the comic based on photos but it didn't work out. One thing is a photograph, reality, and another is the character you construct. The one you construct almost always has to do with you; in one way or another you are making your own self-portrait" (2015: 32). Chalarka painted several self-portraits, depicting himself as an early modern painter, in a muscular half-body pose wearing his beret, and in a close-up of his face that looks almost like a death mask. Indisputably, his own body was an object of medita-tion, as his brother, Orlando, told me, motioning with his hand in front of his face, as though he were looking at it while drawing a comics panel.[4] Nonethe-less, I suspect that the artist found it easier to inhabit the bodies of some actors as opposed to others. His representations of peasants are more fluid than his drawings of the elite or of armed agents, the latter frequently standing in awk-ward poses. Campesinos appear more comfortable in their bodies, as though Chalarka were imagining his own physique as he drew them. I will return to the source of such resemblances at the end of this chapter. For the moment, let us imagine Chalarka fleeing the police as agents descend on the huts hastily raised by ANUC at La Antioqueña, only to incorporate his experience into one of the panels of his comics as he sits at his drawing table in La Granja.

Critical Recovery of the Baluarte

The process of researching, writing, and disseminating the graphic histories made critical recovery comprehensible to peasants. The dialogue between campesinos and researchers produced concepts—abstractions—that both crystallized the major tropes in the narratives of peasant eyewitnesses and pro-vided avenues for making their stories relevant to the present. I take this to be an adaptation of Paulo Freire's pedagogy, which defines praxis "as an act of knowing" that moves from concrete reality to abstraction, to action, and back again (Freire 1970: 213). An example of how this movement was subsumed in the process of critical recovery is the reinvention of the institution of the balu-arte, the socialist landholding collective established by Costeño working-class and peasant activists in the 1920s (which I recount very briefly in chapter 1). At Juana Julia Guzmán's urging, Fals determined that baluartes could serve as an organizing tool for ANUC-Córdoba. The adoption of baluartes was only arrived at over countless meetings at both the national and the regional levels, where arguments for and against the strategy were generated and compromises were made. The crafting of *Lomagrande*, prepared during the occupation of La An-tioqueña, furnished one of several scenarios in which the Fundación and local ANUC leaders found a space to think through what a baluarte had been in the 1920s and what it could potentially become in the 1970s.

As the conflict over La Antioqueña heated up, Fals made overtures to Juana Julia Guzmán, who had in the past refused to share her testimony with external researchers. Her reminiscences formed the centerpiece of *Lo-magrande*, published in September 1972. The history of the Baluarte Rojo had already been told in varying degrees of sensational detail by two conservative writers, Montería educator Jaime Exbrayat Boncompain (1994 [1971]: 197–199) and journalist Carlos Velasco Puche (1963: 61–73), who, needless to say, bitterly condemned the organized peasants as violence-prone revolutionaries wracked by internal dissent. In contrast to the local elite, the Fundación version recounts in visual format a revisionist history of socialist organizing and the confrontation over Lomagrande, capturing numerous sentences from Juana Julia's testimony as comics panels and setting the tone for all subsequent retellings (Valencia Salgado 1980). A young ANUC leader from Martinica, Wilberto Rivero, was depicted as the narrator, with Juana Julia as a protagonist.

We could say that the story of Lomagrande was written on the bodies of activists: campesino organizers and their supporters who were imprisoned or killed by the police in 1921 and whose names were appropriated in 1972 for the baluartes of La Antioqueña (Vicente Adamo, Urbano de Castro, Juana Julia Guzmán) and ANUC members who put their bodies on the line as they illegally cultivated plots and built houses in La Antioqueña.[5] Their bodies are depicted in the pages of Chalarka's graphic history, based on Chalarka's manipulation of the postures of his Fundación models, his observations of campesinos at work, and his witnessing of land occupations. The act of looking at campesino bodies instantiated an intensely political and historiographically revisionist process that redefined what research could be under a participatory rubric.

As I noted in the previous chapter, multiple interlocutors participated at various moments in the research process, which unfolded in a series of phases that linked Fundación and campesino activists into a chain of collaborations. In the first phase, Chalarka took visual notes at rural assemblies, quietly inhabiting the sidelines of these gatherings, a thoughtful but silent observer and an astute analyst. Néstor Herrera recalls that Fals Borda took a more public role, initiating conversations by putting the campesinos in dialogue with the artist, only to disappear into the background as the exchange unfolded: "Fals placed the people in conversation. So that the people would tell Chalarka how things had been, the details, anecdotes. Their memories: maybe a photo, some document or other. Then, the people would start bringing him [these] things. What we did was something like idealizing things, in order to make them a reality."[6]

Here is Juana Julia's recounting of the beginnings of Lomagrande, which Chalarka would commit to paper as he listened to her recordings. We can picture her telling her story with Pacha Feria, her comrade from the Sociedad de Obreras, by her side (fig. 4.1):

Figure 4.1 Juana Julia Guzmán (standing) and Pacha Feria, 1972 (CDRBR/M, CF, 0833. Photo reprinted with permission of the Centro de Documentación Regional "Orlando Fals Borda," Banco de la República, Montería)

What [Vicente Adamo] said was that "workerism [*obrerismo*] has to organize to defend wages, because you don't earn anything around here, or we don't earn anything, because I also earned nothing where I was a washerwoman in the market, in the slaughterhouse, and we must unite to demand a wage-raise." And when the peasants came to make demands for the uncultivated land, then we began the struggle to defend it. . . . So, you see, [Adamo] got those people together and he organized them, he organized them and there they'd been working those lands in Loma Grande, and then [hacendado] Turko [*sic*] Malluk [claimed] that they belonged to him, they belonged to him, and that he was going to turn the police on the people, to throw them out, because the people were in the way, you see? The peasants worked over here, that's how it was, this was scrubland, it was uncultivated, all of it without owners, and they thought they had title. (CDRBR/M, 0866, fol. 5185)[7]

Note that Juana Julia says nothing about the baluarte and how it functioned. The soft-spoken Ulianov Chalarka listened thoughtfully to her recorded testimony and rendered in pen and ink visages well-known to him, hardened by years of labor in the brutal sun of the Caribbean coast; he imputed to the rural narrators his own visual reconstruction of the past. At the same time he analyzed their historical experience and abstracted it into iconic images, based on their testimony and on the articles of incorporation of the Baluarte Rojo that the Fundación unearthed in notarial archives (CDRBR/M, 0926–0928).

Depicting the Baluarte Rojo

It is worth meditating on how Chalarka captured the historical moment of the founding of the Baluarte Rojo, since the Fundación's "idealizing" of this event would become an organizing tool for ANUC's land occupations. Juana Julia herself does not describe the functioning of the agrarian community in detail in the tapes Fals made with her, so Chalarka had to imagine the story from the vantage point of the present. It is depicted on a single page of *Lomagrande* (Chalarka 1985: 15; CDRBR/M, 0683, fol. 3838), extending across three panels (fig. 4.2). The uppermost panel juxtaposes four vignettes announcing the demands of the Sociedad de Obreros y Artesanos de Montería. "Tierra! Trabajo!" ["Land! Work!"] is depicted as a seated man wiping sweat from his face, a shovel in his left hand. "Salud!" ["Health!"] is represented by a couple, the man clutching a sheet of paper, listening to another who gestures with outstretched arms. In "Guerra a la matrícula (esclavitud)" ["War on the matrícula (slavery)"], a man shows a document to a woman who is carrying a saucepan; I assume that it is a matrícula document, since bondage was initiated by drawing up a legally binding contract (Dávila Flórez 1912: 95). "Unión! Educación!" ["Unity! Education!"] has three men in a huddle. Chalarka obviously struggled to depict some of these ideals. He was most successful at the first demand, on the left-hand side, since it is relatively easy to depict land and work through an iconic representation of agricultural labor. The drawing showing the signing of a matrícula contract was probably also convincing, since rural readers knew from their parents that the establishment of relations of debt-peonage involved signing a document. But

EL PROGRAMA:

TIERRA! TRABAJO!   SALUD!   GUERRA A LA MATRÍCULA (ESCLAVITUD)   UNIÓN! EDUCACIÓN!

LA MUJER TAMBIEN PARTICIPÓ.

7 DE AGOSTO 1919

PACHA-FERIA (FISCAL)

SOCIEDAD DE OBRERAS "REDENCIÓN DE LA MUJER"

JUANA JULIA GUZMÁN (PRESIDENTA)

AGUSTINA MEDRANO (SECRETARIA)

OCUPARON LOS TERRENOS DE LOMA GRANDE QUE BAUTIZARON **BALUARTE ROJO** TAMBIEN OCUPARON TERRENOS EN CANALETE Y CALLEJAS.

EL TURCO MALLUK SE CREE DUEÑO DE ESTAS TIERRAS. LOS ÚNICOS DUEÑOS SOMOS NOSOTROS!

BALUARTE ES UNA POSICIÓN QUE SE CONQUISTA EN UNA LUCHA Y QUE HAY QUE DEFENDER.

Figure 4.2   The Baluarte Rojo of Lomagrande (Chalarka 1985: 15. Comic reprinted with permission of the Fundación del Sinú)

health, unity, and education are demands that could only be depicted obliquely, by ambiguous drawings of campesinos meeting with agitators—people like Vicente Adamo, whom Juana Julia recalls in the quotation above.

The middle panel informs readers that a year after the founding of the Sociedad de Obreros y Artesanos, a sister organization was established, the Sociedad de Obreras Redención de la Mujer. A photograph of an elderly Juana Julia Guzmán, the president of the Sociedad de Obreras, is juxtaposed to a drawing of a group of young women in early twentieth-century period dress; some of the participants, including treasurer [*fiscal*] Pacha Feria and secretary Agustina Medrano are identified by name. I will come back to this panel in the following chapter, when I look at the incorporation of photos into the graphic histories. For now, let it suffice to say that the two upper panels provide historical background for the bottom illustration, which is the panel I want to concentrate on here.

Chalarka's depiction of the Baluarte Rojo opens with a caption that synthesizes the essential facts of the historical moment. "They occupied the lands of Lomagrande, which was baptized BALUARTE ROJO, they also occupied lands in Canalete and Callejas," as Juana Julia told Fals in the interview. The three drawings that comprise this bottom panel crystallize the creation of the Baluarte Rojo at three simultaneous moments, all of which depict agricultural labor, which was, after all, the defining feature of the community. At the left, three men with their backs turned retreat from the viewer, one carrying a machete and another a stick. We know they are peasants, because they are wearing patched clothing and carrying *mochilas*, woven bags, and we can guess that they are on their way home from their labors. This vignette replicates a drawing from the previous page (Chalarka 1985: 14), where a panoramic panel depicting the early organizing drives of the Sociedad de Obreros includes two of the same men walking toward a recruiter, presumably Vicente Adamo (see fig. 5.10). The vignette on the right draws on Juana Julia's testimony, when she observed that "they'd been working those lands in Loma Grande, and then [hacendado] Turko [*sic*] Malluk [claimed] that they belonged to him." In the comics image, two shirtless men, shod in the thong sandals that are still worn by rural people on the coast, are at work in the fields, one wielding a shovel and the other carrying a spade; the worker with the shovel declares, "Malluk the Turk thinks he's the owner of these lands. The only owners are us!"

The center image shows two men carrying large branches—perhaps they have cleared a field, or maybe they will use the lumber to build houses—while a third one chops wood. It does not appear to have been prompted by sentences in Juana Julia's taped interviews. The men cutting wood and hauling branches are more like a present-in-the-past, an example of Ulianov Chalarka's effort to render visually an idea he has conceptualized on the basis of the narrators' recollections of their personal experience, but for which he has no concrete historical referent or coherent visual icon to serve as a basis for his depiction. Where does the image come from? After studying Fals's photos, I infer that the agricultural laborers occupying La Antioqueña in 1972 may have furnished the models for Chalarka's depiction of the Baluarte Rojo (fig. 4.3). La Antioqueña was where the artist could observe the peasants at work, fusing the image of Baluarte Vicente Adamo of the 1970s with the early twentieth-century icon of the Baluarte Rojo. I don't think this was out of mere convenience. Surely, it was a conscious effort to capture visually what peasant readers knew from personal experience. The panel entreats readers to comprehend what happened in Lomagrande in the 1920s by comparing that event to their own occupations of haciendas. The images invite them to apply this knowledge to the present by building a functioning baluarte in a somewhat elliptical caption at the bottom: "Baluarte is a position won in a struggle and it must be defended."

The caption would have posed significant problems for campesino readers. It inspires action in the present, but it never adequately explains what a baluarte was in the 1920s, nor what it should become in the 1970s. As I indicated in chapter 1, Leon Zamosc discovered in his 1980 conversations with baluarte members that insufficient effort was made to clarify the concept to the rank and file, whose understanding of the institution ranged from a simple topographic marker to a measure of monetary value. The members of the former baluarte named after Juana Julia told Zamosc that "Fals came and told us to make a baluarte, but he explained it to the educational cadres and not to us, not directly. The cadres explained it to us but we didn't understand. Then, they left. Fals took photos and talked about other things and not directly about the baluarte" (CINEP/B, doc. 16, p. 2). The members of the former baluarte Vicente Adamo affirmed that they never really functioned as a collectivity because the land wasn't suitable for growing food, so they rented out the pasture and worked as day laborers on other farms, and their children migrated to other regions of the coast (CINEP/B, doc. 19). That is to say, there was no concrete practice associated with the baluartes that might permit campesinos to comprehend its significance as an organizing concept.

In retrospect, then, critical recovery of the baluarte and the graphic history that rendered the research process visible to peasant readers were by no means entirely effective as political tools. The text sometimes struggles with difficult abstractions and does not always succeed in explaining them sufficiently. It may be that these discrepancies were resolved at the workshops at which the comics were read and discussed, but Zamosc's interviews intimate that the

Figure 4.3   Occupation of La Antioqueña, 1972 (CDRBR/M, CF, 0089. Photo reprinted with permission of the Centro de Documentación Regional "Orlando Fals Borda," Banco de la República, Montería)

shareholders in the baluartes rarely consulted the publications (CINEP/B, doc. 23, p. 3), their misinterpretations never rectified. Nonetheless, in these scenarios we can grasp most clearly how politics and research were supposed to function in an open-ended dialogue, even if the Fundación's methodological objectives didn't always mesh with their political aspirations.

Tinajones: Unvoiced Master Narratives

Tinajones is an especially pliable text, thanks to the extensive body of evidence that Fals and his colleagues amassed: several hundred pages of interviews with the peasants of San Bernardo del Viento, land titles and sales contracts, press clippings, mimeographed compendia of information collected by local politicians, and INCORA reports. Fals also took numerous photos during his brief visit, especially of the process of rice cultivation, which undoubtedly provided evidence for Chalarka of the daily activities of the protagonists, particularly the bodily poses of people harvesting rice and preparing bundles of rice stalks, the act of husking rice with mortars and pestles, the process of winnowing the grains (CDRBR/M, CF, 2163–2178). These extensive resources facilitate the identification of the choices made by the Fundación del Caribe team as they composed the panels of *Tinajones*. We can distinguish the information they selected for depiction in interview transcripts and we can gauge how much they drew on other sorts of materials, such as archival documents and novels. We can also identify those themes that were so deeply embedded in the campesino psyche that they did not have to be articulated verbally by campesino narrators but could be eloquently translated into the visual channel.

It is this last point that I want to explore in the remainder of this chapter. Ulianov Chalarka's depiction of the Baluarte Rojo supplies me with a scenario for analyzing how Juana Julia Guzmán's narrative was translated into abstract—and therefore, portable—concepts. By quarrying Chalarka's drawings in *Tinajones*, I want to scrutinize the artist's rendering of values that were so central to the worldview of the peasant narrators that they did not voice them in their oral testimony. This *cosmovisión*, in which the Sinú River was central to campesino lives and livelihoods, bound them ineffably to the aquatic landscape they were fighting over—Fals calls it "amphibious culture" in *Historia doble* (Fals Borda 1979b: part 1). The primacy of the river undergirds how San Bernardo activists narrated their experiences and what they thought was significant about their struggle. It tells us a great deal about what the peasants of Tinajones may have visualized in their imaginations as they told their stories. Ultimately, amphibious culture determined how Ulianov Chalarka would depict the story of Tinajones, transcending the reminiscences of campesino resistance to corrupt landowners and politicians, to arrive at the very epistemological foundations of the peasants' political project.

The two narratives, environmental and political, are closely related. Jesús Pérez, one of the leaders of ANUC in Sucre in the 1970s and the author of a recently published memoir (Pérez 2010), recounted to me how campesinos first settled on small floodplains [*playones*] whose fertility was ensured by the annual overflowing of the river, which deposited rich silt on its banks. The playones were later fenced in by the landlords' barbed wire, isolating villagers from the hacienda and resulting in narrow hamlets with a single, long street.[8] The peasants' riverine lifestyle determined which lands the agrarian movement would defend and how they could explain the process of land loss to a broader public. These two tropes, amphibious culture and militant struggle, did not always fit into a single narrative; it was necessary to emphasize one over the other, depending on the audience. We can observe this trade-off in the making of *Tinajones*.

At the same time that the graphic history was in production, another booklet was written by Orlando Fals Borda, Víctor Negrete, and María Cristina Salazar, recounting the political history of the peasants of San Bernardo in an extended prose narrative. Both pamphlets were published in 1973, sponsored by the Sindicato de Agricultores de Palermo, the grassroots rural syndicate with which the Fundación was collaborating.[9] Negrete recollected in a 14 December 2016 email that activists distinguished the graphic narrative from the prose version bearing the same title by calling the latter the "Tinajones booklet." The prose narrative was meant for use in cursillos for advanced ANUC cadres, and it circulated among local allies, including teachers, unionists, and university professors. We can glimpse one of its several intended audiences in Fals Borda's photo of two campesinos in a classroom, their work-hardened hands grasping the prose booklet (fig. 4.4), whose cover depicts a canoe named "El Caimán," the vessel in which hacendado José Santos Cabrera's agents traveled around the region collecting payment in kind in return for sharecroppers' rights to work their plots. The comic's cover is different, showing campesinos engaged in agricultural labor, machetes in hand.

The two publications document the same story, highlighting many of the same episodes, roughly in the same chronological order. They differ, however, in their framing of the major protagonists in the conflict. While the central agents of history in the prose narrative are all human beings—peasant activists, José Santos Cabrera, other politicians, INCORA functionaries, and bureaucrats—Ulianov Chalarka's comic inserts the Sinú River into the story as a major protagonist, an enemy who is as—or more—dangerous than the landlord. This divergence between the two publications, associated as they were with a single production team and a unified political struggle, exemplifies two modes of looking, two complementary and situated worldviews, which were different but also in constant dialogue with each another. A comparison of the two gives eloquent testimony to the power of the comics medium, which, with its series of static images arrayed in space and its emphasis on portraying action embedded in social and geographical contexts, encourages unique processes of reading and of making sense of the world. In this particular case it gave voice to a campesino epistemology that is invisible in the prose account.

Both versions of *Tinajones* were valuable political tools for ANUC, but only one—the comic—provides us with a window into the power of participatory

Figure 4.4   Peasants at a cursillo in Montería, 1973 (CDRBR/M, CF, 2276. Photo reprinted with permission of the Centro de Documentación Regional "Orlando Fals Borda," Banco de la República, Montería)

methodologies, despite the fact that similar techniques and values guided the two publications. Unlike the prose narrative, the graphic history conveys a Costeño ethos that situates the human beings who inhabit the Sinú region in a distinctive riverine environment. Fals Borda only appears to have conceptualized this ecological connection in writing when he published his monumental *Historia doble de la Costa*, christening the culture of the Sinú watershed as "amphibious." Certainly, he was aware of the nature of their riverine existence during the preceding decade, since it is vividly described in his field notes (McRae 2015). Nonetheless, when I asked Víctor Negrete about how the Fundación used the concept of an "amphibious culture" in practice, he told me that it was not an idea they engaged in their work with ANUC, nor was it voiced by the campesino leadership. But it was something that was indubitably felt (in Fals's parlance, *vivenciado*, or experienced in the course of everyday life).

While not voiced in the interviews, the ecological dimension is explicitly incorporated into Chalarka's graphic history. This is highly significant because it resituates the agrarian struggle, not as a fight for land but as "the reclaiming of a productive agricultural space embedded in a regional environment, an ecology with deep (historical) roots" (McRae 2015: 83). I see this as a further example of how the research process converted a narrative of personal experience into a cogent abstraction, grounding ANUC's ideology in the relationship of the peasants of the Caribbean coast to a particular territory. In Córdoba, the Sinú River and its tributaries were a central fact of their existence, determining the itinerary of their land struggle. Their appeal to the cultural underpinnings of rural activism was as much a part of the process of critical recovery as was the narrative of the Baluarte Rojo.

Life on the River

In *Mompox y Loba*, the first of the four volumes of *Historia doble*, Fals introduces the concept of the amphibious culture of the inhabitants of the marshlands of the Atlantic coast. This cultural complex "combines the efficient exploitation of resources from land and water, of agriculture, animal husbandry, hunting, and fishing" (Fals Borda 1979b: 19A; see also 21B). Peasant adaptations to the lacustrine environment are exemplified by a very particular characteristic of the waterscape: the presence of raised fields. The Sinú delta floods annually, forming new landmasses as rich alluvial soil is deposited by the retreating waters. Lorica-born Manuel Zapata Olivella captures this in a series of vibrant metaphors in *Tierra mojada* [Sodden Land]. The words of the novelist are well worth reproducing here, since he is cited as a source on the opening page of *Tinajones*:

> The river, like a water-snake, tries to muscle its way into the bay, pushing back the sea, which poisons its waters with saltpeter. That channel [which the narrator points to] . . . was another outlet, which [the river] was searching for, in desperation. Then it opened a path on the other side, at a place called Leave If You Can [Sal Si Puedes]; in short, almost every year it looks for a new exit, out of pure spite. You'll see it yourself in the summer, when the sea overcomes the weak current—and he continued—but in winter, as you saw the other night, the river takes its vengeance and beats the sea all the way to the bay. It's as though it were saying: "If my love doesn't move you and it surprises you, take this, darn it, go back to your pool, alligator," and the sea does just that. The river isn't happy just throwing it out, but pushes silt, and more silt, wherever it is able to open a path and it channels, it channels. That's how it seizes control of the bay, which, as you see, is now just a little bit of nothing. (Zapata Olivella 1964 [1947]: 63)

The human inhabitants of the Atlantic coast learned early to mimic the natural process of the river, constructing raised fields fed by canals that expanded human access to cultivable land. Along the San Jorge River to the east, the Zenú and their ancestors constructed a complex system of channels and raised fields [*camellones*] over a vast area of fifty thousand hectares, a monumental set of public works that lasted for some two thousand years and supported a considerably higher population density than would have been possible without them (Parsons 1970; Plazas and Falchetti 1981; Plazas et al. 1988). These pre-Columbian canals and camellones can still be observed in aerial photographs. The peasants who colonized the public lands near Tinajones in the 1920s transformed their landscape in a similar fashion, although on a much smaller scale.

Zapata Olivella paints a verbal portrait of the process of transforming into cultivable land the mangrove swamps that hug the coast. The campesino homesteaders who are the protagonists of his novel built their homes atop the mangrove roots, along the network of small channels leading off the river. Some lived off the sale of mangrove bark, but others used the mangroves as a platform on top of which to construct their raised fields:

> Once more they split the mangroves, but this time the roots and stocks were not for sale, but used to fence off the surface of the two dry planting beds. They hammered stakes into the sides, where the current crashed with greater force and they marked a small path with earth for a seed-bed.
>
> . . . .
>
> As the rains became more intense, the dry beds were submerged by the current, and the fences, reinforced with new poles and plants, protected the lands. They transplanted rice seedlings and with joy watched them peek over the surface of the water. Women, children, and men all adjusted the stakes and lost sleep with the worry that they would be toppled. There were times when they stayed up all night watching for rainstorms and the violence of the river. (Zapata Olivella 1964 [1947]: 97–98, 102–103)

Fals Borda registers this process less poetically in his field notebook, identifying it by the term used by the peasants of Tinajones, *calce* (for which I cannot find an adequate English translation): "*Technique of calce*, very well practiced with 'little channels' [*cañitos*] that, by gently carrying the river-water, allow the mud to be deposited, slowly filling the beds with this mud" (CDRBR/M, 1921, fol. 10247, p. 8r). We might say, then, that the peasant homesteaders built their environment canal by canal. Their channels can still be glimpsed on Google Earth and are still farmed by their descendants.

As the two versions of *Tinajones* document, hacendados like José Santos Cabrera coveted this constructed landscape, since all the work to convert it from mangrove swamp into arable land had already been completed by the campesinos. Mid-nineteenth-century elites had somehow obtained title to the lands adjacent to the mangroves decades before (or, at least, they used their political connections to fabricate legal titles), but these territories required too much labor for them to be immediately exploited by absentee landlords residing in the nearby port city of Lorica or in the more distant city of Cartagena. Once the mangroves were tamed by campesinos, however, the hacendados swooped in, using both legal legerdemain and brute force to introduce the matrícula, confining the peasants to tiny plots of less than a hectare and leaving ample territory for cattle grazing (Leal and Van Ausdal 2013; Van Ausdal 2008, 2009). But they never legally established the boundaries of their pastures. The smallholders, who argued that the territory they had colonized was publicly owned land, countered by stubbornly refusing to abandon their rice plantings, even when hacendados forced them to turn over their teenage daughters for sexual favors in exchange for the right to eke out an existence on their minuscule plots (CDRBR/M, 1912, fols. 10170–10171).[10] When INCORA representatives Carlos Duica and Camilo Torres—the same Camilo Torres who was Fals's colleague at the National University—visited the region in 1961 to investigate the need for agrarian reform, one of their peasant interlocutors underscored his personal justification of his rights to the land: "Showing his hardened hands crisscrossed with scars, one of the peasants said 'our titles are our hands'" (CDRBR/M, 1914, fol. 10203).

The natural process of annual flooding in the Sinú delta, to which campesinos accommodated as a fact of life, was occasionally interrupted by more catastrophic events. In 1942 a new mouth of the Sinú opened in Tinajones. Aerial photos from 1938 to 1989 graphically illustrate how a bend in the river located immediately to the south of the coast broke open and deposited enough silt to form a new delta that protruded into the Caribbean (Serrano Suárez 2004: 629). The emergence of this new mouth of the Sinú triggered massive flooding at the end of the 1940s, bathing the colonized mangroves in salt water and frustrating the labors of the rice farmers. As Fundación del Caribe member David Sánchez Juliao writes in the 9 December 1973 Sunday magazine of the Bogotá daily El Tiempo, channeling the voice of his campesino guide: "That was twenty-thousand hectares, as I'm saying. All rice. After so much struggle for these lands, a long struggle, which lasted years, which seem like centuries, to have the sea ruin it all. And, tell me: who can defeat the sea?" (CDRBR/M, 1920, fol. 10246). Many of the carefully tended camellones reverted seasonally to marsh: "Don't fool yourselves. All of what looks like scrub, dry land, is water covered with vegetation concealing the silt, with stubborn plants that tiptoe across the wetland, the salt water."

From that moment onward, the battle between peasants and landlords centered on the possibilities of reining in the Sinú. The smallholders called for dredging, which at one point they attempted by hand to close the new river mouth, although the national government also half-heartedly sent in a dredger that never completed its assigned task. The hacendados were content to let the river remain as it was, since their cattle pastures, which were not on the riverbanks themselves, were not affected by salinization and the flooding freed up peasant labor to tend their herds. This spurred a nascent agrarian organization in the 1940s, led by Alberto Licona and the formation in the 1960s of the Sindicato de Agricultores de Palermo [Syndicate of Palermo Farmers], which coordinated a series of land occupations that were greeted with repression by the landlords. Víctor Ávila recalls in an interview by Fals Borda how in 1961 the recalcitrant occupiers were shut for days in a corral without food or shelter. It was only thanks to the heroism of their wives, who slipped into the enclosure under cover of darkness bearing food, that the men didn't starve to death:

> The first to arrive at the corral was Manuela, Francisquito's wife . . . Manuela Blanquiset. (How did the police treat her?). Well, they didn't mess with her because she followed the riverbank and when they asked her where she was going she said to [San Bernardo del] Viento, to Viento, and when we saw her she'd arrived at the same riverbank where we were imprisoned and then the other women began to arrive, because there were many of them who were distant relatives. There was Cristina de la Rosa, my first cousin, and others from El Balsal who arrived later. So there were some 30 women by the end of the night, when it was 1 in the morning almost all the peasants had eaten what the women brought. (CDRBR/M, 1913, fol. 10185)

Surprisingly, this dramatic scenario did not make it into the graphic history (nor does it appear in the prose narrative), although it was the first reminiscence that the children and grandchildren of the Fundación's narrators shared with me during a 2019 visit. This is the moment at which Padre Arroyabe interceded as a mediator between the peasants and Cabrera, a scene depicted in one of the panels analyzed in the previous chapter.

The intervention of INCORA resulted in a windfall for Cabrera, who managed to extract several million pesos from the government in recompense for turning over his hacienda of Río Ciego despite his lack of substantiated title or evidence of legally established boundaries (CDRBR/M, 1915). The campesinos who formed a cooperative under the supervision of INCORA were obligated to pay for the lands they had been awarded. As David Sánchez Juliao reports: "So now look at the double-edged sword that is cutting at us—the canoe pilot tells us—INCORA wants to charge us for land we built with our own hands and

CRITICAL RECOVERY

the salt that kills it, which we cannot pay because the land isn't productive" (CDRBR/M, 1920).

Two Looks at Tinajones

Marshlands are ubiquitous to the Caribbean coast. Alsatian mining entrepreneur Luis Striffler was overwhelmed by the vegetation he encountered on his voyage along the Sinú River in search of gold mines:

> The picture presented by the riverbanks of the Sinú on its uninhabited stretches gives lively and brilliant testimony to the fertility of the valley that is irrigated by its waters. The tropical vegetation has collaborated in reproducing fantasies such that art will never achieve. The leafy trees bent over the waters and, attached only by a few roots to soil that is undercut by the current, let hang from their branches draperies and garlands of dark-green vines glazed with brightly colored flowers.
>
> On the banks, the slightest breeze stirs the immense leaves of those aquatic plants that grow with such vigor and acquire such giant proportions, even in such a watery base. All around, you find the land blanketed by an accumulation of vegetation that competes for space, each plant stifling the other. (Striffler 1990? [1875]: 30–31)

These were, for Striffler, untamed territories, full of insects and snakes. Their mutability—the annual cycle of flooding, the profusion of tiny canals interlacing the landscape—made them treacherous to traverse (Striffler 1920 [1880]: 6).

Striffler's descriptions of the coastal marshes leave little room for their human inhabitants. For him, this was a natural landscape, not a human one. In fact, he saw those who peopled it as "barbaric," "dirty," and "savage." As Nohora Arrieta interprets the ethnographic depictions by the French entrepreneur, the Costeño peasant was "a lethargic man, dead, incapable of modifying his surroundings or of producing something from them," his savagery justifying foreign exploitation of the territory. When Arrieta turns to Fals Borda's field notes, a different picture emerges. Here, topographic space is not a protagonist, but it is depicted as intimately linked to human activities like fishing or turtle hunting (Arrieta Fernández 2015: 118–119). His field notebooks from Tinajones pay close attention to the waterscape and how its campesino inhabitants made use of it, particularly in his notations concerning the building of raised fields and the harvesting of mangrove bark for dyes, as well as in his descriptions of the varieties of rice the peasants cultivated (CDRBR/M, 1921, fol. 10247, pp. 8r, 9v, 11r, 12r). This was a natural environment shaped by and shaping human activity.

But the human aspect of the landscape—how homesteaders harnessed its mutability to survive in what for both Striffler and Fals Borda was a hostile environment—is not as evident in the prose version of *Tinajones*, which depicts a fertile wilderness that was "at once magnificent and terrifying" (CDRBR/M, 1921, fol. 10249, p. 9). The reader hardly recognizes the peasant face of the Sinú delta in the opening pages of the prose narrative, only its wild visage. Humanity only peeks out occasionally from behind the dense green curtain:

> The dangers were many, because almost the entire region was virgin jungle. The river itself played tricks, changing course or carrying submerged tree-trunks that filled up its strands and [created] islands where they had not existed before. . . . The jungle was dense and wild. There were great stands of ceiba and oak that, together with camajon trees, campanos, fig-trees and tagua palms, invited workers to produce wealth and cultivate foodstuffs. Toward the sea, there were immense mangroves. A few clearings along the river, full of small-scale plantings of maize, manioc, rice, and fruit trees, gave new evidence of the fertility of the region. (CDRBR/M, 1921, fol. 10249, p. 8)

In this telling, the peasant settlers suffered from fevers and fought dangerous animals. They found only limited space on the riverbanks where they could eke out their precarious existence, their labors ultimately thwarted by catastrophic flooding that left the rice fields bathed in salt water (CDRBR/M, 1921, fol. 10249, pp. 12–14, 30). After the opening pages the authors pay only fleeting attention to the environment, moving on to the real purpose of the booklet: the history of peasant resistance.

The prose version of *Tinajones* provides rich historical evidence of Cabrera's legal maneuverings over time, the stirrings of agrarian opposition, the saga of the battle over the dredger in the Boca de Tinajones, the recommendations for new land tenure arrangements made by INCORA representatives Duica and Torres, and how INCORA ultimately took over the role of hacendado, exercising a similar level of control over the peasant economy. The pamphlet's fluid prose is journalistic, but it was not an easy read for a campesino who had barely completed primary school, if that. Indeed, it was meant to be read and discussed in groups, providing advanced cadres at cursillos with a comprehensive introduction to the major political actors in the conflict. The facts narrated in the pamphlet, particularly the legal details, would be potentially useful for the ANUC leadership as it navigated the court system and public opinion. For this reason, the Sinú River and the mangrove swamps are only bit players, a barely cited landscape to ground the human protagonists: this is a *political story* (McRae 2015: 83).

Ulianov Chalarka's graphic history takes a different tack. Almost half of its panels incorporate the Sinú River, either as background or as a central protagonist, so that we are constantly reminded of its riverine setting. This is something that the comics medium is expert at accomplishing: repeated imagery conveys ideas to readers without having to voice them verbally (Sacco and Mitchell 2014: 60). But I think we can go further than championing one of the generic characteristics of comics. Chalarka's fascination with the Sinú, his repeated portrayal of the river, seems to be an example of his ability to empathize with campesinos, to hear what was behind their words. Would he have been any better at this than university-trained ethnographer Fals Borda? As I perused the interviews that Fals conducted in Tinajones it became evident to me that his interlocutors only occasionally mentioned the river, which was more an enduring fact of life than an object of conversation (Arrieta Fernández 2015: 125–126)—except when they referred to the catastrophic flooding that resulted in the loss of their lands. Of course, Fals was aware of the peasants' amphibious culture, even if he didn't call it that in 1973, but his priority in framing the prose narrative was political.

Chalarka didn't make the same choices as Fals. I would guess that his constant sighting on the Sinú in his drawings was likely the result of a connection he already had with the peasant ethos, even though he wasn't a campesino himself and wasn't even Costeño (remember, he was from Pereira, the coffee-growing belt of the Colombian interior, although he lived in Montería). When I commented at a 2016 archival workshop in Montería about how ubiquitous the river was in the drawings, my interlocutors immediately responded that the Sinú was as central to the lives of Monterianos as it was to the peasants in Tinajones. Montería was built along the Sinú. Until the construction of roads in the mid-twentieth century, the river connected the city to smaller but wealthy urban populations like Lorica and the vast expanse of rural cattle ranches, as well as to the oceanic route to Cartagena (Durango Padilla 2012). Montería is thus similar in its layout to the small riverine ports like San Bernardo, whose urban plan follows the river. Its inhabitants eat fish on the banks of the Sinú and are ferried back and forth across its waters on rafts [*planchones*] that glide from one side to the other via a system of cables and pulleys. The river traverses the entire city, its major landmarks no more than a block or two from its banks. Only the more recent working-class barrios—like Ulianov Chalarka's La Granja—are deprived of a river view. The primacy of the Sinú is evident in the graphic history, expressed in a range of ways. Leaving aside the panels in which the river is simply a waterway on whose banks critical scenarios unfold, there are several visual formats in which the Sinú becomes a major protagonist in this very human story, sometimes depicted via the usual comics icons, while in other cases appearing in panels that look like illustrations or maps.

Visualizing Amphibious Culture

Tinajones opens with two panoramic scenes of fluvial traffic on the Sinú (Chalarka 1985: 31). It is narrated by the aging agrarian leader, Víctor Licona, whose interview transcript is in Fals Borda's archive (CDRBR/M, 1912), although his story incorporates the voices of other storytellers, as well. The graphic history of peasant settlement at the mouth of the Sinú begins with the depiction of two vessels, one traveling along the Sinú and the other approaching the riverfront at San Bernardo del Viento (fig. 4.5). The sailboat in the top panel— named *Dios Me Salve* [*God Save Me*], evoking the dangers of the Sinú—glides along an uninhabited stretch of the river; its sails have not been unfurled, and one of the deckhands pushes it along with a long pole in what may be the shallows. The *Dios Me Salve*'s path is framed by egrets in flight and feeding in the water. A pair of parrots nuzzles on a tree branch while a snake slithers up its trunk, almost indistinguishable from two vines that entwine the tree. A monkey clings to a bough, and a rodent—perhaps a *guatinaja* (*Agouti paca*)—sits expectantly at its foot. There is a *caimán*, a variety of alligator, whose head has surfaced in front of the craft's stern.

The natural world is portrayed with considerable care in this panel, even while the crew aboard the *Dios Me Salve* is sketched as stick figures. The egrets, in particular, are depicted in a variety of poses that betray Chalarka's familiarity with the flora and fauna of the Sinú. Comics authors Pablo Guerra, Henry Díaz, and Camilo Aguirre commented on how this image is more like a book illustration than a comics panel, like the frontispieces that you see nowadays in some graphic novels. More laden with detail than most of the other panels of *Tinajones*, the drawing sets a scene in which the natural world is meant to be experienced directly by the reader. This is an environment in which humans are only protected by God, as the name of the sailboat so cogently declares.

A later panel reveals how dangerous this water world could be (Chalarka 1985: 38), again, more of an illustration than a comics panel (fig. 4.6). In white-on-black, rendered as though it were a woodcut, the bottom panel depicts the flood that broke open the mouth of the Sinú at Tinajones, propelling seawater

Figure 4.5 Opening pages of *Tinajones* (Chalarka 1985: 31. Comic reprinted with permission of the Fundación del Sinú)

Figure 4.6 "Y se vino la creciente!" ["And the deluge came!"] (Chalarka 1985: 38. Comic reprinted with permission of the Fundación del Sinú)

into what had been a tranquil riverscape. We see a canoe, its five passengers clinging to one another—one of them, a small child—navigating floodwaters bursting with debris. Wild waves crash in on the port side and buffet the canoe's starboard, while the headwinds pommel a palm tree in the opposite direction, an ill-fated man clinging to its trunk. Chalarka clearly preferred illustrations to comics when it came to portraying nature in its most raw form, revealing his origins as a painter. (Note, however, how the committee that laid out the graphic history raised the right-hand side of the gutter between this panel and the one above it in order to make room for a redundant caption.)

In contrast to these two illustrations, the bottom panel on the opening page, a panoramic view of the San Bernardo riverfront, is considerably more iconic, more comics-like (fig. 4.5).[11] The campesino homesteaders embarked from here on their journey to colonize the wild marshlands. The natural world has been conquered in San Bernardo del Viento, exemplified in the name of the boat: *Vencedora* [*Victor*]. I would argue that this bottom panel supplies background information, while the top panel is the space in which the narrative takes place; it is also where Chalarka inserts a portrait of the narrator, Víctor Licona.

Thierry Groensteen reminds us in *The System of Comics* that not only individual panels but the architecture of the grid organizing the comics page is intended to be deciphered by the reader. Our eyes move from one panel to another. We notice how facing pages mirror each other and we follow the last panel on the left-hand page to the top of the page on the right (Groensteen 2007: chap. 1). In Ulianov Chalarka's rendition, we exit the port of San Bernardo and abandon the *Vencedora*. We turn the page to embark on a humble canoe (Chalarka 1985: 32) and enter the world built by the campesino homesteaders (fig. 4.7). The page contains three panels, all in comics style. The illustrations progress from an intimate view at the top of the page to a panoramic image at the bottom, so that the sequence retrocedes, like a film or video, to display an ever-widening waterscape. The sequence displays how the peasants transformed their environment over time, in what Scott McCloud would call a "scene-to-scene" transition that "transport[s] us across significant distances of time" within a single space (McCloud 1993: 71).

The page begins with a canoe drifting on the Sinú, probably in the shallows, because directly behind the canoe is a figure up to his ankles in water, hacking away at the mangrove with his machete. The three men in the canoe are just arriving, as the caption tells us: "1924 We arrived from San Bernardo and San Antero to work these public lands." The speech balloons let us know why these men have made such a perilous journey: one man insults the large

Figure 4.7 The world the peasants built in Tinajones (Chalarka 1985: 32. Comic reprinted with permission of the Fundación del Sinú)

landlords they are escaping when he declares, "The large landowners should eat shit!," while the other endorses their newfound autonomy, "Here no one gives us orders!" A third man safeguards their agricultural implements, a water lily at his left peeking out of the water. Behind him in the distance, two others—stick figures whose paddles emerge as slivers on the top side of a thin oval that stands in for their canoe—propel their craft to an unknown destination. The panel embodies the possibilities the comics medium affords to say a great deal with a tremendous economy of expression. It would not have been as easy for prose to focus in and out of the details of this scene; it could never say so much using so little. The panel is intimate, homing in on a small group of men whose names we never learn; however, their story is not told in the third person (as it would be in prose): they are first-person flesh and blood, voicing strong opinions. The panel affords readers hints at why these men undertook their journey (to escape the tyranny of the matrícula), the world they encountered (wild and uninhabited), and how they began to transform it (with their muscles and machetes), all in a single iconic image. At the same time, it conveys a big story about the colonization of the coastal frontier: the first phase of the "law of the three steps," as Fals Borda puts it.

A great deal of work went into building the campesinos' environment. Their labors fill pages of Zapata Olivella's 1947 novel, *Tierra mojada*. His protagonist learns by trial and error how to tame the river and manipulate it to achieve his own goals. In the graphic history, that labor is left to the imagination of the readers, embedded in the gutter—the black line separating the panels—which conveys the reader from the scene of arrival to the next panel, depicting a finished homestead that we imagine was built by the very men we met in the canoe. A thatched hut on stilts planted above a rice paddy drawn in as bunches of blades, shaded by palms and plantains, a canoe moored nearby—perhaps the same canoe on which the homesteaders arrived—laden with burlap bags and coconuts. A photograph taken in the San Jorge Basin three years after the comic was published (fig. 4.8) underscores the iconicity of Chalarka's image. In Fals Borda's photo we see the river, the moored canoe (a more recent model with an outboard motor), and a thatched hut bordered by plantains. Both the panel and the photo display a productive environment forged by human hands, as Chalarka's caption declares: "Despite great difficulties we made the land produce." This middle panel is a pullback shot, which moves the reader from the intimate to the merely local. It also transports us from the past to the present, although the present of the image was already being eroded in the 1970s by the transformation of many of the coastal wetlands, drained in the late 1960s and early 1970s in many parts of Córdoba by the Agrarian Reform

Figure 4.8 Río San Jorge, 1977 (CDRBR/M, CF, 1664. Photo reprinted with permission of the Centro de Documentación Regional "Orlando Fals Borda," Banco de la República, Montería)

agency (Negrete Barrera 2007: 36; 2018: chap. 1). But since we can repeatedly shift our gaze from one panel to another and back, the scene persists, always in the present.

Crossing another gutter, our eyes move to a panoramic view, where three thatched huts sit atop bands of cultivated land dotted with plantains. Bundles of rice hang suspended on a pole next to the hut at the center. The homesteads are separated by small man-made canals (cañitos) connected to the river, along which a produce-laden canoe sails, piloted by two stick figures. We know these raised fields were constructed atop the mangroves by the campesinos, because one of the canoeists says, "This year I have a half a hectare more to work," alluding to the ever-expanding agricultural landscape he and his companions are forging. When Víctor Negrete and I examined this panel, he told me, "This is what it really looked like." Víctor remembers it that way, but it is difficult to discern the cañitos in Fals Borda's photos because they are obscured by vegetation, as they were when I visited Cañogrande.[12] They are rendered visible in the comics panel: this is not what Chalarka saw with his eyes, but what he saw in his imagination after repeated observations. The comics panel enhances the reader's appreciation of the landscape in the same way that eighteenth- and nineteenth-century botanical drawings focus attention on particular features of plants that are generally obscured but in the watercolors are larger-than-life and constructed out of composite viewings (Bleichmar 2012).

Mapping Tinajones

Most stunning, to my mind, is an aerial map depicting the zone of settlement affected by the flooding of the Sinú (fig. 4.9). The riverine village of San Bernardo appears at the bottom of the page, complete with houses, church, and nearby farmsteads. The viewer follows the curves of the Sinú as it flows up the page, toward the Caribbean. At the top left, there is an oxbow lake, the encircled land on the brink of becoming an island, where the meandering river has deposited silt. Just a bit further in the background, we see the course of the Sinú flowing past Cañogrande, whose raised fields are lightly crosshatched along the river that moves on toward the Bay of Cispatá. Precisely at this last curve before the river enters the bay, a new mouth emerges at Tinajones. This panoramic view could only come from the artist's imagination, as there would be no high ground from which to observe it on the flat coastal plain (and there is no indication in Fals's archives that the team had obtained aerial photos). But in the comic, there is someone looking at the scene from above. Víctor Licona, the narrator, explains the image to us, emphasizing that the new mouth of the river will expose the cultivated lands of Cañogrande to the salt water that is making its way toward Cispatá.

Many comics incorporate cartography into their pages. The Fundación del Caribe routinely inserted maps into their graphic histories, as did ANUC comics produced at the national level (ANUC n.d.). With the exception of *Lomagrande*, the first of the Fundación's pamphlets, published in 1972, all of the other three graphic histories include maps that identify local agrarian struggles within broader regional or national contexts. While the vast majority of ANUC activists at the time were illiterate, maps had become important props in the movement, especially for determining the boundaries of baluartes and reclaimed lands, as is attested by photos in Fals Borda's collection (CDRBR/M, CF, 0179). So at least some of the graphic histories' readership knew how to read the cartographic documents inserted into their pages, which were included to provide peasants with a sense of the broader regional and national scope of their efforts.

Nonetheless, this bird's-eye view of the Sinú delta is different from the other maps inserted into Chalarka's comics. Víctor Negrete told me in a 29 December 2016 email that the aerial map was Ulianov Chalarka's initiative. It is similar to the picture-maps of pre-Columbian and colonial-era Nasa and Misak chiefdoms that the La Rosca affiliate in the department of Cauca incorporated into its history of indigenous organizing to depict the various towns founded by the Spaniards, marked by images of churches connected by footpaths, with in-

1.942

MIENTRAS TANTO
UN NUEVO PROBLEMA
SE NOS VENÍA ENCIMA:
UNA NUEVA BOCA DEL RÍO
SE ESTABA ABRIENDO
EN TINAJONES.
AL SUCEDER ESTO LAS TIERRAS
DE CAÑOGRANDE SE SALARÍAN
AL ENTRAR EL MAR POR LAS BOCAS DE CISPATÁ.

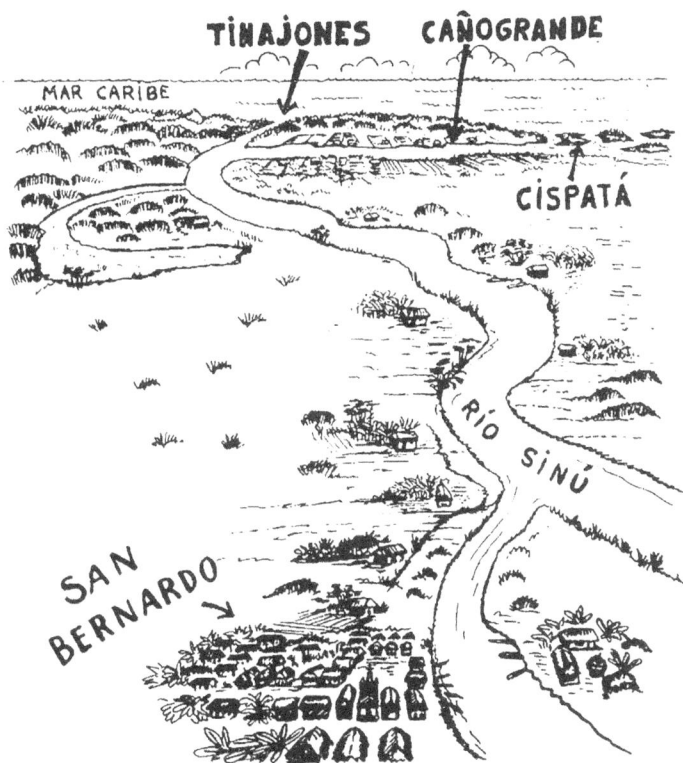

Figure 4.9   Aerial map of Tinajones (Chalarka 1985: 37. Comic reprinted with permission of the Fundación del Sinú)

digenous migrations and military movements drawn as arrows across the land-scape (Bonilla 1977); these picture-maps were precursors to the mapas parlan-tes developed by former Rosca member Víctor Daniel Bonilla, which stimulated the oral retrieval of communal memories among the Nasa of Jambaló, Cauca (Barragán León 2016; Bonilla 1982). Chalarka's aerial rendering was completed before the Rosca affiliate in Cauca published its first pamphlet. His picture-map of the Sinú delta was not meant to stand on its own. It was a prop intended to stimulate rank-and-file dialogue and to guide campesino imaginings of the topographic space they were struggling to control, which the amphibious activists would necessarily envision as anchored by the river.

Chalarka's aerial view of the Sinú delta also functions as the fulcrum of *Tinajones*. It lies at the center of the booklet, separating in comics space two envi-ronments that, in real life, were arranged in a temporal progression. First comes a landscape built and defended by the peasant settlers. After the map follows a territory soaked by salt water, stolen by latifundistas, and defended by organized peasants. In this sense, the map organizes time into before the flood and after the inundation, what comics author Dylan Horrocks (2010: 86) calls a "geography of time" that superimposes the location of things in space onto their positioning in time. The time-space of *Tinajones* revolves around an imagined bird's-eye view of a landscape at the moment before it was irrevocably altered.

To understand this better, we need to examine the pages immediately after the map. The work of graphic journalist Joe Sacco is particularly helpful in comprehending the progression of the panels (Sacco 2000). Sacco is well-known for juxtaposing Cartesian images of the topography of war to human experiences drawn from "a grounded perspective that inserts the reader into the action and attempts to replicate the experience of war through the visual negotiation of the conflict landscape" (Holland 2015: 85; Sacco 2000: 148). Likewise, Ulianov Chalarka's aerial view of the Sinú delta opens a path to sub-sequent panels that track an itinerary of events. On the page following the map (fig. 4.6), the doomed peasants attempt to stave off the flood by passing sandbags from hand to hand, while a dredger (the *Chichau*) carries on its deck a stick figure who revels in his power to destroy the precarious man-made bar-rier: "Stupid peasants, now we're going to destroy the levee with a jet of water." His companion responds with a telling statement: "Yes, Capitan, now we have the money that the landlords gave us" (Chalarka 1985: 38). The ensuing tor-rent hurls a canoe to certain disaster in the bottom panel, which I already noted is more like a woodcut than a comics image. Geographers call this sort of itinerary a "mapping," as opposed to a "map," because it privileges practice over gaze, a grounded perspective over an abstract panorama (Crampton 2009;

Holland 2015: 88–89), something like Michel de Certeau's distinction between "itinerary" and "map" (de Certeau 1984 [1980]: 117–122). Chalarka effectively fashions his readers' imaginations around a nostalgic waterscape and precipitously drops them into the reality that both peasants and readers had recently experienced during the campesino struggle to hold back the waters of the Caribbean from inundating the delta and their laboriously constructed parcels rescued decades before from the mangroves. They are ultimately foiled by a conspiracy led not only by the landlords but by the river itself.

Conclusion

John Berger contrasts three different types of drawings: "There are those that study and question the visible; those that record and communicate ideas; and those done from memory. Even in front of drawings by the old masters, the distinction between the three is important, for each type survives in a different way. Each speaks in a different tense. To each we respond with a different capacity of imagination" (Berger 1987: 58). His first category contains drawings that were produced in the past to represent what was visible, which he calls "the indicative tense." The second grouping communicates ideas by setting scenes: "Such drawings are visions of *what would be if*. . . . Most record visions of the past which are now closed to us, like private gardens. When there is enough space, the vision remains open and we enter. Tense: Conditional." Third come drawings from memory, which are declarative: "I saw this. Historic Past Tense" (Berger 1987: 59–60).

Ulianov Chalarka's sketches communicated what he heard at assemblies and meetings, producing emblematic visual representations that would be immediately comprehensible to his peasant readers. They are Chalarka's reaction to eyewitness narratives—by someone who did not see the action but has created scenes that evoke an eyewitness account and that turn readers into eyewitnesses. Thus, by combining narrators' recollections, other evidence (such as Zapata Olivella's novel), and his own imagination, Chalarka's drawings fall into Berger's second category, conveying speculative ideas in scenarios in order to craft an alternative future made possible by activism: what we don't entirely know, but what should have, or could have, happened. Chalarka leads viewers to imagine "what would happen if . . . ?" What if campesinos could correct history? He forges a "sense of belonging to what-has-been and to the yet-to-come" (Berger 2015: 44). The question of how to redirect the consequences of past actions would ultimately be answered by the collective agency of the ANUC rank and file.

The comics version of *Tinajones* is a redemptive narrative. Its simple, archetypal images lay bare the ongoing confrontation between campesinos and landlords, opening room for local narrators and activists to fill in the gaps at public assemblies. The graphic history links the activist present to the narrated past through the persona of Víctor Licona, the narrator, who appears at critical moments of the story, inviting further recollections and discussion. But the graphic history does something else. It cogently captures the ethos of the peasants of the Sinú delta by elevating the river to the role of protagonist. It reveals, in its depiction of the labor of erecting the raised fields and its portrayal of campesino efforts to close the new mouth of the river, the crucial fact that this was a dual struggle, not only against the landlords but against the environment itself, a perilous and fragile landscape to which the landless and land-poor had been displaced in the early twentieth century. If these were "amphibious men," it was not entirely by choice. The waterscape so prominent in *Tinajones* did not function as a political demand, as did the baluarte depicted in *Lomagrande*, but it buttressed an ethos that grounded the political action of the campesinos of San Bernardo. This is also a kind of critical recovery, perhaps ultimately more successful than the baluartes, because it fostered a sense of commonality and belonging.

As I already mentioned, Chalarka was a working-class migrant with only an informal education. He came of age in a barrio created through land invasions by displaced smallholders and the landless who had been forced to adapt to an urban environment (Mora Vélez 2010; Ocampo 2003: 246). La Granja was thus at once rural and urban, peopled by peasants camped out on terrain that had once been an experimental farm. In Chalarka's lifetime La Granja was greener and less developed than Montería's urban grid skirting the Sinú (today, there is parkland along the river, while La Granja is largely a sea of cement). The artist was someone who was betwixt and between, someone who didn't quite fit within any category. Matilde Eljach told me that he was somewhat of a hippie, but then again, he wasn't: "I remember Chalarka. Many funny things happened to Chalarka because he was a stocky man. . . . He wore necklaces. . . . He said . . . [that] he was a hippie. And the people said that a hippie doesn't have that physique. So, once someone told him: 'You keep saying you're a hippie; hippies are thin.'"[13] Chalarka looked to the campesinos like one of them, not like a hippie, occupying the ambiguous space between the urban peasants of La Granja and the intellectuals of the Fundación del Caribe. In addition, he was a liminal figure in La Granja: not a Costeño but a *Paisa*, a migrant from the interior, yet very much a part of the fabric of Montería, well-known across the city's barrios.

Ulianov Chalarka thus occupied a crucial position. He bridged peasants and researchers, country and city, coast and interior, oral and written means of expression, and verbal and visual narratives. All of the collaborators in the research project—ANUC activists and Fundación researchers—had a particular role to fulfill, and all of them, Fals included, were obliged to cede their individual authority to the collective. This was particularly imperative in the production of a graphic history, since comics is frequently a collaborative medium. But aside from his role as an artist, Chalarka's positioning in the collective filled a deeper need. If Fals preferred to think of the campesinos of Córdoba as "amphibious men," Chalarka was undoubtedly an "amphibious researcher," a quality that was key to his ability to grasp concrete ideas conveyed by the narrators and transform them into abstractions. He was not entirely successful in depicting the Baluarte Rojo, but his visualizations of the primordial status of the Sinú River were highly effective. We know this from Zamosc's notes from La Antioqueña, where baluarte members from the former agrarian collective Urbano de Castro told him they especially liked *Tinajones* but weren't as excited by the other comics (CINEP/B, doc. 23, p. 3). Thanks to his talent and his intermediate position between campesino and researcher, Chalarka was adept at capturing "people's knowledge"—campesino epistemology—that undergirded the struggle of ANUC. This is why he could reveal so eloquently how the people of Tinajones fought for their marshes. He could see that profound connection with a landscape that was, after all, much deeper than politics and was what ultimately drove Costeño peasants to action.

5

SYSTEMATIC DEVOLUTION

Víctor Negrete recently reminded me that the graphic histories, slideshows, videos, history texts, and cursillos sponsored by the Fundación del Caribe were intended not merely to enlighten people but to spur them to action: "Young people need to do more than read, they need to act. That's what we're interested in: the changes being promoted. They shouldn't only read. That's only part of it. What we want is for people to have these ideas, to develop them, and to get involved in them. That is the objective of participatory action research."[1] In keeping with Víctor's assertion, this chapter inquires into how the Fundación engaged campesinos in understanding the relevance of history to their struggle, fostering ideological maturity, and spurring activism. Regrettably, it is almost impossible to gauge in hindsight the direct impact of the Fundación's adult education program because we no longer have access to the peasants who participated in the activities they sponsored. Many of them were killed, died of old age, disappeared for one reason or another, or were displaced by the ongoing conflict.

Montería, where the Fundación was most active, was without dispute the municipality that most broadly and enthusiastically embraced ANUC's cause (Rudqvist 1986: 105). Rudqvist's interviews with peasant leaders indicate that cursillos played a significant role in the ideological formation of the municipal leadership (1986: 124–126). However, the few rank-and-file commentaries gleaned by Leon Zamosc indicate a certain degree of ambivalence, hinting at a lack of sufficient emphasis on the dissemination and analysis of educational materials, a task that was left to overburdened ANUC leaders. Zamosc concludes that the distance between external researchers and the grass roots was never entirely bridged, even as close relationships were established with the leadership of the peasant movement (1986a: 28–29).

I don't want to lay all the blame on Orlando Fals Borda and the Fundación, however. Quite simply, three years was not sufficient lead time for the Fundación's research to be assimilated by the ANUC membership before the Rosca/Fundación del Caribe/ANUC experiment came to an end. This point was driven home to me by my experience in Cauca, where the work of La Rosca took at least a decade to reach into the indigenous villages that dot the mountainous landscape, propelled by an expanding and increasingly influential indigenous movement. In Córdoba and Sucre, in contrast, ANUC was progressively weakened by government repression and internal factionalism, so that the movement that could have sustained the dissemination of the Fundación's materials was no longer capable of doing so.

Absent any means to evaluate the immediate, or even the midrange, success of the Fundación's educational strategy, I have opted to inquire into the mechanisms the group used to disseminate its message. Close attention to the elements of reception that were built into educational materials provide a glimpse, at the least, of how the Fundación expected to impact the Costeño peasantry. In this chapter, I explore some of the tools they used to guide campesino assimilation of historical research, focusing on the cursillos facilitated by external researchers and the tools embedded in the graphic histories. My exploration requires that, once again, I submit Ulianov Chalarka's comics to a close textual analysis, but my objective, as in previous chapters, is to go beyond the texts in and of themselves to impute to the comics those practices they may have inspired: I examine the archive to speculate what the repertoire could have contained.

In this chapter, I inquire into the pedagogical guidelines that were harnessed to train a politically conscious base, understanding them as part of the Fundación del Caribe's broader activist repertoire. To this end, I meditate on the intentionality of the Fundación's educational program, in particular, how it functioned as a bridge between knowledge and action. How was participation in cursillos arranged and to what extent did these training seminars foster a kind of intellectual democracy? How did cursillos contribute to the process of instilling a brand of radical literacy among an illiterate peasantry? What did it mean for illiterate campesinos to "read" graphic narratives? How did the Fundación organize the layout of the pages with the aim of leading readers' attention away from the past and into the present? In short, what sorts of interventions were necessary to transform the Fundación's contributions from mere entertainment to pedagogical and political tools?

I will take a four-pronged approach to answering these questions. First, using Fals's archive, I will assume a bird's-eye view of the training workshops sponsored and facilitated by the Fundación. Cursillos were the space in which the Fundación's educational materials were studied and discussed, where campesino cadres received a basic ideological grounding to undergird their assimilation of history and guide their political activities. Then, I will turn to the graphic histories as a scenario in which I can impute the pedagogical tools that were brought to bear at the workshops. I interpret selected comics panels in order to comprehend how real-life narrators were used to connect peasant readers to the past as it was presented in Chalarka's drawings: Who were these narrators? What was their role in preparing and disseminating the comics? What did the Fundación hope to achieve by fictionalizing their personas in the comics panels? I already hinted at my interest in how campesinos with minimal exposure to the comics medium may have deciphered the graphic histories. I suspect that they did not move from panel to panel, filling in the gaps in the comics sequence—commonly called "gutters," both in English and in Latin American Spanish—because they had never learned to do this, having limited access to reading matter in their communities. How, then, did they process the fracturing of time and space that occurs in a series of comics panels? What did they fill the gutters with? One of the later comics, *El Boche*, helps me to answer these questions.

Finally, I look at archivos de baúl, which I will sometimes translate as "kitchen archives" (Behar 1986). They are the documentary traces and mementos that peasants stored in their homes, which the Fundación used as *aides-mémoires* to stimulate oral narrative. The contents of these personal treasure troves motivated researchers to compose written materials in a language that not only was accessible to peasants but also embodied a local historicity, one with its own distinct narrative arc and landmarks of memory. *Lomagrande* contains panels that I infer functioned as portable archivos de baúl, reproducing some of the objects that are mentioned in my archival sources and in published accounts. How were they used in cursillos and study groups to encourage campesino audiences to relive the research process? In particular, I want to examine the role played by photographs in stimulating and guiding peasant memory, focusing on how they not only constituted evidence of the past but gave impetus for campesinos to analyze their position in the present, thus extending the work of research into a post-publication phase.

This is what La Rosca called the process of "systematic devolution," the creation of educational vehicles geared to their audience's capabilities and needs. Fals Borda describes systematic devolution as a participatory strategy for stimulating grassroots analysis:

> There is an obligation to return this knowledge systematically to the communities and workers' organizations because they continue to be its owners. They may determine the priorities concerning its use and authorize and establish the conditions for its publication, dissemination or use. This systematic devolution of knowledge complies with the objective set by Italian socialist Antonio Gramsci of transforming "common" sense into "good" sense or critical knowledge that would be the sum of experiential and theoretical knowledge. (Fals Borda 1991: 9)

Systematic devolution aims at taking what people know and showing them why it is important. It is "systematic" because its materials and pedagogical approaches are geared to particular audiences. "Devolution," on the other hand, is a somewhat misleading term, because it implies that the researchers are "returning" finished products to a passive popular audience that has not participated in the process of its compilation. Víctor Negrete once remarked to me that if a research process is truly participatory, "it isn't being 'returned,' but is disseminating work produced by the people."[2] Keeping in mind his corrective, but also remembering that the Fundación exercised substantial intellectual, if not political, control over the research process, I will inquire into how the researchers took hold of common sense and transformed it into critical knowledge.

The Social Landscape of Córdoba and Sucre

I have encountered a series of challenges to analyzing the reception of the Fundación's educational program, most significant among them being the identification of their audience. The peasantry of Córdoba and Sucre was not a homogeneous mass of landless campesinos, even if this is the picture given in the graphic histories. Its population was diverse; different sectors enjoyed varied types of access to land and differing articulations with government institutions, and their historical experiences were, correspondingly, distinct. In addition to the hacienda peons and landless day laborers who are depicted in the graphic histories, there were small property owners, some of them affiliated with INCORA cooperatives. Some of these people had participated in the budding socialist movement of the 1920s, although their political sensibilities fifty years later cannot be determined by the activism of their youth. There were also residents of the small towns that dotted the landscape, people who may or may not have supported ANUC, depending on their politics and their social networks. Some were evangelical Protestants or Pentecostals, who by doctrine opposed the peasant movement and whose history in the region went back to proselytizing by agents associated with nineteenth-century foreign investors (Fals Borda 1986: chap. 5A). Even these Protestant communities, however, were heterogeneous in their political aspirations and inhabited towns and villages where many neighbors and family members were ANUC supporters. Other campesinos were fierce adherents of the mainstream Liberal or Conservative Party in a period when Colombian politics was still controlled by a two-party system. ANUC itself was a heterogeneous organization. As I have suggested already, there was sometimes a great distance between the political aims and knowledge base of its leadership and that of the rank and file. As former ANUC activists impressed on me, the Fundación was closer to some of its leaders than others.[3] To complicate the situation even further, the Maoist PCML was active in the region, as were the EPL guerrillas [Popular Liberation Army], each with its own peasant following.

The complexities of rural Costeño society confound a naive analysis of how the Fundación del Caribe approached its audience. We cannot paint a one-dimensional portrait of a united and homogeneous multitude of campesinos confronting a government oppressor. Yet, there is scant information available on how the Fundación navigated the heterogeneity of the Costeño landscape in the preparation and dissemination of its educational materials. Silvia Rivera Cusicanqui—a Bolivian scholar activist who spent a period in exile at CINEP studying the history of ANUC—argues that the Fundación's embrace of Marxist theory led its members to espouse a homogeneous image of the peasantry and to believe that the organizational objectives of ANUC were indistinguishable from those of the peasant base (Rivera Cusicanqui 2004: 21–22).

These caveats hold significant implications for how to interpret the Fundación's educational activities. To some extent, embedded in its materials is an artificial and romantic notion of who were peasants, what they aspired to, and what motivated them. These preconceptions determined to a degree how the Fundación expected to engage its audience, including the types of activities it employed to ensure their participation in the collective interpretation of history. However, for lack of information, I can only gauge campesino reception to a limited extent and am forced to concentrate on what the Fundación expected from its audience, as opposed to what it actually experienced.

Cursillos

In 1972, the Centro Popular de Estudios, one of the partner organizations of the Fundación del Caribe, published a manual to guide the coordination of cursillos at the local level. Fals Borda's archives contain the preliminary notes for this publication in the form of a list of subject headings (CDRBR/M, 1922), as well as a typescript draft to be sent for critical commentary to the municipal chapter of ANUC in Montería (CDRBR/M, 2177); the published manual is available in the archives of the Fundación del Sinú (AFS/M) and is cited in the bibliography. The manual's preface, authored by the departmental leadership of ANUC in Córdoba, describes the cursillo as a vehicle for "fulfilling the purpose of liberating the peasant according to the dispositions in the Mandato Campesino, the Plataforma Ideológica, and the second National Peasant Congress of Sincelejo" (Centro Popular de Estudios 1972: 7), the three keystone documents of the Sincelejo Line of ANUC. The "Plataforma Ideológica" ["Ideological Platform"], adopted at a national junta meeting in 1971, demarcated ANUC as an organization dedicated to transforming unequal relations of land ownership through redistribution, expropriation of large landholdings without indemnification, and support of land seizures by peasants. The 1971 "Mandato Campesino" ["Peasant Mandate"] laid out a concrete program for achieving these goals under the slogan "land without masters" ["*tierra sin patronos*"] (Zamosc 1986b: 72–73). The second National Congress, which took place in 1972 in Sincelejo, marked the formal split of ANUC into two lines, the government loyalists of the Armenia Line and the radical Sincelejo Line; the latter, which was the majority of the Association, was the line to which ANUC-Córdoba adhered (Zamosc 1986b: 101). Cursillos thus fulfilled a distinctly ideological function, inculcating in ANUC activists the basic precepts of the organization.

The cursillo manual was designed to assist local cadres in organizing their own training events, without the need for external facilitators. It includes instructions for even the most minimal of logistical details, assuming no prior experience on the part of local activists: the type of paper to use as a visual aid, where to place the Colombian flag in the classroom, how to organize a procession at the end of the seminar. It also lays out a model cursillo agenda, commencing with a diagnosis of local problems, touching on land tenure, health, education, and the state of the peasant movement (Centro Popular de Estudios 1972: 20–21). The agenda encourages the study of ANUC's central documents followed by a summary of recent news of peasant organizing and governmental repression (1972: 21–22). Each cursillo should include a critical analysis of the history of the peasant struggle using Fundación del Caribe pamphlets as supports. The final agenda item is a summary account of agrarian legislation (1972: 22–23). Sessions are to be structured by plenary sessions, punctuated by small-group meetings in which the main points of the plenary are explained and debated (1972: 26). As the manual recommends, the final session of the cursillo ends with a summary of the proceedings and an evaluation of how its conclusions contribute to an awareness of the class struggle, followed by a procession and a closing ceremony (1972: 30–33).

These rank-and-file training workshops functioned parallel to other events organized for the ANUC leadership, which were called the Escuela de Cuadros [Cadre School] (CDRBR/M, 0639, fol. 3568). There is substantially more evidence in the archive for the Escuela de Cuadros, since the Fundación was intimately involved in its planning. The Escuela was organized to deepen leaders' knowledge base: "We see a cadre enriched by knowledge, enlightened anew, leading to knowledge mediated by research conducted with their direct support" (CDRBR/M, 0642, fol. 3375). The personnel organizing these events was recruited by the Fundación del Caribe from the Costeño intelligentsia, including folklorists, sociologists, and lawyers (CDRBR/M, 0643; see fig. 1.2). Some cursillos were dedicated to teaching specific techniques and procedures, such as production of legal documents to legitimize land occupations, organization of collective labor in occupied lands, or puppetry (CDRBR/M, 0687; see fig. 3.8). The Fundación's 1973 work plan called for monthly cursillos in addition to their other activities, which included research, writing, and the production of educational materials (CDRBR/M, 0648). The significance of this training program cannot be overstated: the municipal leadership of ANUC-Montería emerged out of the Fundación's cursillos (Rudqvist 1986: 105).

Moisés Banquett, one of ANUC-Montería's municipal leaders, reminisces in his memoirs about various cursillos he attended. He remembers that they varied in size, ranging between five and fifty participants (CDRBR/M, 1058, fols. 6244–6246), following similar agendas to the model cursillo offered by the Fundación's manual (CDRBR/M, 1058, fols. 6243–6244). He argues that cursillos produced political results: they expanded ANUC's membership and provided basic knowledge necessary for planning land occupations (CDRBR/M, fol. 6244). Cursillos were already being held before the appearance on the scene of Orlando Fals Borda, but as the Fundación del Caribe/ANUC partnership took root, these events became more frequent, taking place in more locations. Banquett writes that not only campesinos but also teachers and students attended cursillos. In 1973, he was invited to a regional cursillo in Cartagena. His memories of this experience underscore the rigorous ideological training that he received there:

> It was here that I began to learn that Colombia was facing a class struggle between the exploited and the exploiters, but that there were two types of politics, which were bourgeois and proletarian, that there were two ideologies, bourgeois and proletarian. That in Colombia there were two leftist groups that for many years have striven to promote socialism in Colombia, but that they all had flawed methods of promoting the revolution. . . . Each one of them proposed to promote the revolution in its own way and for that reason these groups were wasting their time, while the enemy took advantage of all of the critical moments [*coyunturas*] created by these groups to destroy them. (CDRBR/M, 1958, fol. 6364)

Fals's notes for cursillo presentations look like lecture notes by any educator (CDRBR/M, 2186, 2190, 2197). Víctor Negrete remembers them as following a traditional lecture format, something that, in hindsight, he confesses inhibited the active and creative participation of campesinos (2008a: 87–88). Nonetheless, if my experience with CRIC workshops is at all relevant to 1970s Córdoba, rural audiences demonstrate a tremendous capacity for withstanding long, drawn-out lectures, certainly more than my own students would tolerate. When I have spied the notes they take as they listen to invited speakers, they record only scant details from the lectures. I suspect that many of the peasant listeners only partially understood what the Fundación facilitators were telling them, requiring repetition of the same materials on various occasions. A 1974 set of Fundación minutes records Juana Julia Guzmán's complaint that she could not understand the explanation given of the concept of "mode of production," suggesting that the lectures were not always immediately comprehensible to their heterogeneous audience.[4] Despite the fact that many cursillos were closely orchestrated by the Fundación, they were always subject to critique by the collective. At a March 1973 meeting in Cañoviejo, for example, the facilitators were requested to use clearer and simpler language, and it was suggested that since the students were campesinos, their instructors should hail from the "exploited classes"; the attendees also urged that more women be encouraged to attend (CDRBR/M, 2183).[5] Notwithstanding their shortcomings, the effectiveness of cursillos as tools for consciousness-raising is evident in Banquett's memoirs, particularly notable being the extent to which they contributed to his awareness of the class struggle gleaned from the writings of Marx, Lenin, and other authors whose work was explained at these events (CDRBR/M, 1058, fols. 6243–6244, 6263–6265).

Fals Borda's photographic collection affords a closer look at what transpired at cursillos. Figure 5.1 was taken at a 1973 event held in Montería (CDRBR/M, CF, 1391). It depicts a man making an oral presentation: he is Aniceto Pereira, a campesino leader from the outskirts of Montería. At his side, another man consults a notebook. Papers are strewn over the desktop, indicating that cursillos demanded a modicum of reading, at least on the part of its campesino facilitators. A third participant takes notes on a blackboard, where we spy a combination of verbal and visual elements, awkwardly mirroring Ulianov Chalarka's comics. In the drawing, a face in profile points to a discussion topic titled "Critique and self-critique of the peasant movement," presumably part of the evaluation of the event. Below appears a slogan, parts of which are obscured by the presenter: "Workers-peasants-students, united we will defeat . . . the enemies of. . . ." Pereira may have been summarizing plenary conclusions while simultaneously raising audience fervor. Other photos indicate that participants were guided in their readings of movement publications. Figure 4.4 captures a communal reading in 1973 of the prose version of *Tinajones* (CDRBR/M, CF, 1399). One of Fals's photos of a 1972 cursillo in Cañoviejo shows campesinos reading an early pamphlet prepared by the municipal chapter of ANUC, *Así luchamos por recuperar la tierra!* [*How We Struggle to Recuperate the Land!*] (AMUCM 1972; CDRBR/M, CF, 0402), which employed photographs instead of drawings.[6]

Making sense of the written word posed challenges, even for the most politically committed cadres, as Moisés Banquett's autobiography reveals. He reminisces about the difficulty of the texts he was introduced to at the 1973 workshop he attended in Cartagena, although despite his limited schooling, he devoured Marxist writings and developed his own conclusions regarding how they would guide his politics:

> At that meeting in Cartagena some compañeros cited Marxism-Leninism, all those great teachers who have left us their revolutionary theses in writing. At that meeting I got a copy of the Communist Manifesto and other books that we each purchased. Since then I began to put things in their places and to analyze all of the arguments of groups on the left. I began to study the manifesto. That was how I oriented myself, because I was a dissenter [*inconforme*]. I saw that compañero Marx's thesis was being developed in practice. . . . That was when I began to study politics and prepare myself in political ideology and locate all of the political groups on the left, and what the great teachers proposed. I could not find any group that promoted things as they should have, according to the great teachers. For

Figure 5.1   Cursillo in Montería, 1973 (CDRBR/M, CF, 1391. Photo reprinted with permission of the Centro de Documentación Regional "Orlando Fals Borda," Banco de la República, Montería)

that reason, up to 1978 I declare myself independent within revolutionary ideologies. I could not affiliate myself with any of the leftist political groups because there never appeared a true, unified socialist party that would be the one that would break all of the chains that have humiliated us nowadays. (CDRBR/M, 1058, fols. 6255–6256)

Like his Fundación colleagues, Banquett advocated an approach to politics that was independent of the major leftist political parties. But while he struggled with ideas, other campesinos were challenged by the written medium they were asked to confront. The Fundación's response was to seek out alternative modes of exposition for unschooled attendees of their workshops. Two of Fals's photographs illustrate how cursillos were friendly to nonreaders: a puppet show in a 1973 Escuela de Cuadros in Montería (fig. 3.8), which appears to be narrated by the facilitator, Cartagena sociologist Raúl Paniagua, and a group of participants at the same event engaged in what looks like a sociodrama, a dramatization exercise used as a vehicle for social analysis (fig. 5.2). The photos convey how campesinos were motivated to engage in analysis by means of performative vehicles in which they embodied the scenarios conjured from the memories of elderly narrators and fashioned into comics panels by Ulianov Chalarka.

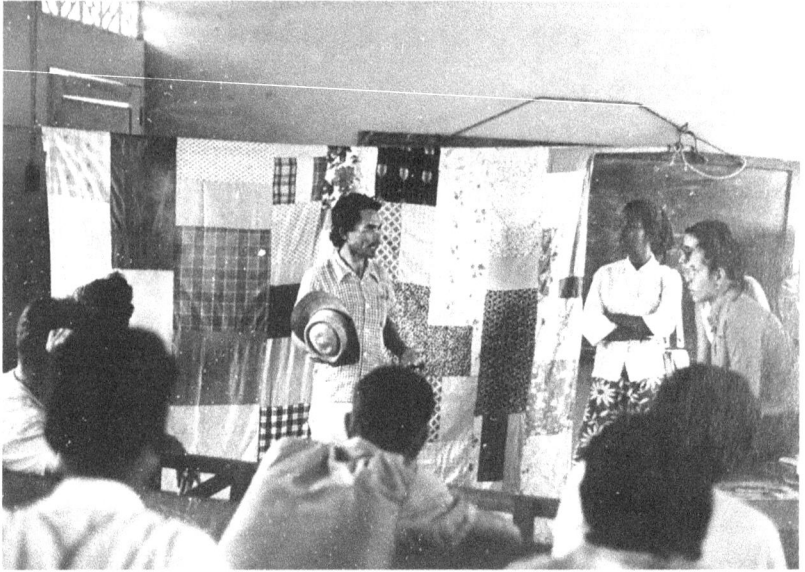

Figure 5.2   Sociodrama at a cursillo in Montería, 1973 (CDRBR/M, CF, 1395. Photo reprinted with permission of the Centro de Documentación Regional "Orlando Fals Borda," Banco de la República, Montería)

The Narrators

The stories of *Lomagrande*, *Tinajones*, *El Boche*, and *Felicita Campos* are anchored by narrators who accompanied ANUC and whose headshots appear at crucial moments in the graphic narratives as a reminder that these stories of the past are very much relevant to the present (fig. 5.3). *Lomagrande*'s story is told by Wilberto Rivero, a young ANUC leader from Martinica (fig. 5.4), who was active in the occupation of various haciendas in the early 1970s. The narrator of *Tinajones*, Víctor Licona, was one of the 1960s activists interviewed by Fals and his associates on their visit to San Bernardo del Viento (CDRBR/M, 1912); he was a member of the Licona clan that led many of the early peasant struggles in the region (CDRBR/M, CG, C/OFB/GM 33). Juana Julia Guzmán (fig. 4.1), whose name has come up repeatedly in this book, narrates *El Boche*. The story of Afrocolombian activism in Sucre, *Felicita Campos*, is told by Ignacio ("El Mello") Silgado (fig. 3.3), the esteemed elder from the municipality of San Onofre who was interviewed by Sincelejo-based Fundación researcher Néstor Herrera and local ANUC leader Florentino Montero (CDRBR/M, 1770).

These four individuals were chosen to embody the vital connection between the struggles of the past and those of the present, to imbue history with familiar faces. Only three of them—Guzmán, Licona, and Silgado—were

Wilberto Rivero, *Lomagrande*   Víctor Licona, *Tinajones*

Juana Julia Guzmán, *El Boche*   Ignacio Silgado, *Felicita Campos*

Figure 5.3   The narrators of the graphic histories (comic reprinted with permission of the Fundación del Sinú)

eyewitnesses to the historical events they narrate; Rivero was chosen because of his reputation as a young leader of ANUC. All are real people, but the stories told by their comics personas combine information culled from interviews with numerous storytellers who are listed at the beginning of each of the graphic histories. In other words, the narrators are composite characters crafted out of the voices of many storytellers, the fictional doubles of people who were well-known to the campesino readership.

Composite characters are a central feature of testimonial literature, generalizing personal experience so that it seems to arise from the collectivity as

Figure 5.4   Wilberto Rivero and Orlando Fals Borda at a 1973 cursillo in Montería (CDRBR/M, CF, 2275. Photo reprinted with permission of the Centro de Documentación Regional "Orlando Fals Borda," Banco de la República, Montería)

opposed to any single individual (Gómez Buendía 2007: chap. 3; Randall 1992). Alfredo Molano explains the purpose of this literary (and political) move as "placing in brackets the singularity of the accounts in order to capture the generalities of the story they were telling . . . , while maintaining an absolute respect for the people's language" (Molano 1998b: 104). He concedes that he is in the business of producing fictions—*inventos* is the word he uses in Spanish— but he also argues that his imaginings have an objective basis: "not the mere subjective whim or egotism, but a re-elaboration of people's stories with analytical elements" (1998b: 105).

Many graphic novels feature fictional narrators, who generally perform the same role as do narrators in literary fiction. They inhabit the boundaries of the simulated world of the comic and, as such, are understood by readers to be as fictional as the other characters (Thon 2013). Some recent graphic memoirs feature their authors as narrators (Bechdel 2006; Spiegelman 1973, 1986). The narrators of the Fundación's comics also evoke real people who appear to be in control of the story they are narrating, just as they would be when recounting their experiences orally to a peasant assembly. The difference between Guzmán, Licona, Rivero, and Silgado and the narrators of today's graphic memoirs is that the campesino narrators enjoyed close relationships with their readers and participated in events at which the comics circulated.

These fictional-real narrators function as vehicles for the process of abstraction through critical recovery, which I analyzed in the previous chapter. They implicate the events of the graphic histories in the readers' present. They stand in for the process of critical analysis that is directed more at present concerns than at the past, as Fals and Libreros explain in their unpublished research manual: "The uses of history should be accommodated to the needs and the urgencies of the present, without limiting it to a simple and curious anecdote about the past. The 'narrator' can thus take on the role of critic of society or share appropriate political demands during the narrative or at the end of the pamphlet" (ACHUNC/B, caja 49, carpeta 3, fols. 259–259v). Figures like Juana Julia Guzmán thus bridge past and present; they are represented as active participants in ANUC who have something to say, not only about their experiences but about the politics of the peasant movement in the 1970s.

The intentionality of the Fundación's narrators differs, therefore, from that of other graphic memoirs, or even *testimonios*, which are intended for general distribution, not as organizing tools in the communities of origin of the narrators (Robles Lomeli 2019; Yúdice 1992). This was a conscious choice, one the Fundación shared with other affiliates of La Rosca. Carlos Duplat, a filmmaker and theater director who collaborated with La Rosca on the Pacific Coast, made the following argument in a series of talks organized by the research collective for educators in Barranquilla in 1971, the year before Fals Borda began his work in Córdoba:

> A performance by an actor who lives entirely in its context is thus more effective. At this moment, theatrical performance integrally and truly fulfills its function: ". . . The son of Mr. So-and-So is not really the exploitative rich man nor the big-bellied bishop, he is playing that character." After the performance he will continue to be the son of Mr. So-and-So who gave them a critical picture of reality. And if this reality is their own reality, the result will be doubly positive and dynamic. If the paintings shown to them or the songs sung to them speak to them of their concrete reality, that is to say, of their neighborhood, of their houses, of their streets, of their factory, they will see reality there, but presented in another form. Behind this performance the public will begin to critically perceive its position within the relations of production. Subsequent work, in more depth, will permit them to become interested in understanding the mechanisms that govern our society, mechanisms that they can show and begin to transform. (Bonilla et al. 1971: 95–96)[7]

The superimposition of the real world with a fictional world made the narrators of Chalarka's comics more convincing, while persuading readers to rethink the relationships governing the world they inhabited and to imagine their own agency in transforming it. The narrators' role in the graphic histories—and in the activities surrounding them—was to guide peasant readers through the various steps of consciousness-raising, which I will explore in the following pages through an examination of some of the tools used to elicit reflection and further testimony from campesino readers.

Reading *El Boche*

My first task is to think through how peasant audiences were expected to read and process Chalarka's comics. I will use *El Boche*, one of the later graphic narratives, as the ground on which to base my speculations. Published in 1973, it depicts the beginnings of the peasant struggle against debt-peonage at the dawn of the twentieth century. Unlike *Lomagrande* (1972) and *Tinajones* (1973), the panels of *El Boche* are carefully crafted and visually complex, containing fewer errors than Chalarka's earlier work. This is not surprising. Prior experience led the Fundación team to refine and deepen its appropriation of the language of comics. For example, unlike the earlier publications, whose panels present cameos of historical events identified by dated captions that move in chronological order, *El Boche* experiments with sequentiality. Its readers piece together a narrative by navigating panels separated by spaces or lines commonly called "gutters" (as I already mentioned, the same word is used in English and in Latin American Spanish). We are meant to fill the gutters with action conjured in our imagination linking one panel to the next, in an act that comics writers call "closure," the creation in the mind of the reader of a whole from a discontinuous series of images (McCloud 1993: 63, 67). The discontinuity of comics panels requires the reader to become an active participant in making sense of the text (Groensteen 2013: 36). While the gutters of Chalarka's comics did serve as spaces in which campesinos' imaginations were given play, I think they fulfilled a different role than do the gutters in conventional comics. They not only connected the actions of one panel to another but opened new narrative spaces into which the personal reminiscences of their campesino readers were given voice.

I have consistently referred to Ulianov Chalarka's comics as "graphic histories" in an effort to underscore the fact that they are not fictional accounts but historical interpretations based on empirical evidence, narrated in a comics format. Of course, they are fictional in the sense that they are crafted in an iconic visual language and their stories are mediated by semi-fictional narrators who stand in for multiple eyewitnesses and documentary sources. Nonetheless, the contents of their narratives are verifiable: the events of *Loma-grande*, *Tinajones*, and *Felicita Campos* really happened and Fals Borda's archive contains documentation of the veracity of these narratives. They are similar in this sense to today's graphic journalism, which condenses complex news stories into evocative, empirically based images (Sacco 2002, 2012) or historical analyses condensed into comics formats (D'Salete 2019 [2017]; Getz and Clarke 2016; Laurent, Egea, and Vega 2013; Schecter and Clarke 2014).

El Boche differs, however, from other Fundación comics. It reimagines and reconfigures a legend that had been circulating in Córdoba since the early twentieth century and transforms it into a vehicle for conveying information about the abuses of the matrícula, the debt-peonage system. Given that the story line of *El Boche* is the stuff of myth and not of history, we might think of it as a kind of graphic novel.[8] Its story functions as a literary vehicle for transmitting a historical lesson about the matrícula, and the documentary and oral research conducted by the Fundación was meant to substantiate this historical detail, not the plot itself.

"El Boche" is the nickname of the comic's campesino protagonist, Manuel Hernández, a *negro sabanero*, a term used to refer to certain rural populations of the savannas of Sucre. Fals describes this segment of the population as "not of African features but mixed-race people [*quinterones*] with olive skin, straight noses and wavy hair, the result of the mixture of Indians and mestizos" (Fals Borda 1986: 74). Hernández reputedly emigrated to Córdoba to work as a peon on the hacienda Misiguay, some 18 kms south of Montería along the Sinú River. Misiguay and several of the surrounding farms belonged to the Lacharmes, a family of French origin that settled the Sinú in the nineteenth century (Polo Acuña 2018). Hernández is by legend said to have become jealous of his wife's trysts with other men, especially with Alejandro Lacharme and his overseers, and to have gone on a frenzied and bloody rampage at Misiguay, slaughtering numerous bystanders and finally murdering Lacharme, before being killed himself.

The original account of the event, which reputedly took place on 5 October 1908, came out a week later in an extravagantly narrated article published in a Cereté newspaper (Berrocal Mendoza 2017). Over the years, several members of Montería's lettered elite, some of them relatives by marriage of the Lacharmes, embellished the original story. Their texts enumerate a series of lurid details about the rampage and make a series of wild allegations. They recount, for instance, that the bullet that ultimately killed Hernández had been bitten into the form of a cross. They report that he was buried with his arm raised, as if he were still wielding his lethal machete (Díaz 1935: 62–66; Exbrayat Boncompain 1939: 109–126; 1994 [1971]: 194–196; Velasco Puche 1963: 74–98). In short, they conjure a legendary demon, whom they call a *boche*, seizing on a French slur against Germans, which came to be used in Córdoba to identify a violent person (not a surprising appropriation, given that the Lacharmes were of French extraction). It is not by accident that El Boche was also identified as a *negro sabanero*. While the appellation does not exactly signify an African descendant—the racial typologies on the Atlantic coast are complex, taking note of multiple degrees of mixing—elite authors used El Boche's race to "other" him, effectively equating black masculinity and campesino poverty with savagery and danger. Velasco Puche's rendition of the story is the most racially charged of the lot, featuring a woodcut of a heavily muscular, shirtless, and very black man brandishing a machete (74).

In 1962 the Barranquilla-based journalist and Montería native Jorge Valencia produced a sixty-episode radio-play [a *radionovela*], *La pesadilla del Boche* [*The Nightmare of El Boche*], which was immensely popular; some of the peasants who later joined ANUC might have tuned in to it. Valencia calls his script a "work of protest" (Valencia Molina 1987: 16) and in his conversation with me expressed his sympathies for Hernández as a "good man," a hard worker driven by jealousy who did not deserve to die as he did.[9] Notwithstanding Valencia's protestations, the Fundación del Caribe excoriated him, along with Jaime Exbrayat and Carlos Velasco Puche, on the first page of *El Boche*, asserting that they "made it their aim to deform the character of EL BOCHE and his struggle, broadcasting all the old-wives' tales invented by the large landholders to discredit his memory and block anyone from following his example" (Chalarka 1985: 47).

The Fundación del Caribe turns the story of El Boche upside down, recasting Hernández as an early hero of peasant resistance to the matrícula, a campesino bursting with revolutionary fervor who killed his hacendado only after being provoked by him. *Lomagrande* was also a retelling of a time-worn legend forged by the Montería elite (Exbrayat Boncompain 1939: 137–146; 1994 [1971]: 197–199; Velasco Puche 1963: 63–73), but the Fundación's revisionist history of the Baluarte Rojo was based on the oral testimonies of Juana Julia Guzmán and other campesinos, as well as on documentary evidence. In contrast, I found nothing about the legend of El Boche in Fals Borda's archives, and there is no evidence that its story line was the subject of his interviews with peasants. That the Fundación had been toying with the prospect of tackling the story of Manuel Hernández for at least a year before the comic's publication is evident from the naming of one of the baluartes created after the 1972 occupation of La Antioqueña for El Boche. A panel of *Lomagrande* that depicts Vicente Adamo delivering a public address includes the following remark by a member of his campesino audience: "I've been a matriculado [bound to a matrícula] of the Lacharmes for 15 years. With an organization, they won't fuck us over like they did to El Boche" (Chalarka 1985: 13).

In *El Boche*, Ulianov Chalarka experiments with sequential narratives to a greater degree than he did in his previous comics. A two-page sequence in *El Boche* depicts Manuel Hernández as he kills the hacendado (Chalarka 1985: 59–60). In the top two panels of the first page (fig. 5.5), Lacharme hurriedly grabs his rifle, which is propped up against the wall of his office; he then moves onto the porch, where he aims the rifle at a distant figure. We discover who this figure is in the bottom panel, when Manuel Hernández arrives at the house, just as Lacharme's gun blocks and the hacendado tries to unload the bullets. On the following page, the two men wrestle in the first panel and the hacendado is felled by Hernández's machete in the second, provoking anger and mayhem among Lacharme's men, depicted at the bottom of the page (fig. 5.6).

This two-page sequence may appear obvious to us, but I'm uncertain whether Costeño peasants in the 1970s read it as we would. Because many campesinos were illiterate, someone else would have had to read the verbal text to them, creating a collective reading event quite distinct from what we generally experience as solitary consumers of comics. What probably transpired was a communal analysis of single panels, transforming the reading of the comic into a conversation between readers. If this was the case, then the sequential progression of panels establishing a plotline would not have been the primary vehicle lending meaning to the comic. Meaning derived, more likely, from readers' personal experiences elicited during the act of reading. Navigating the gutters of the comic would thereby take on a different purpose than it does for most comics readers. It would lead peasants to look for historical facts in their own lives, supported by factual details in the comics panels—not factual details concerning the life of Manuel Hernández, but those surrounding the institution of the matrícula.

The Fundación recast Hernández as a hero capable of identifying the exploitative nature of debt-peonage and enlisting his fellow peons in a campaign to end it. Its comic refocused the story of El Boche, transforming the villain into a hero. A caption depicting the dead Lacharme reads, "And in the name of the matriculados justice was done" (Chalarka 1985: 60). Manuel Hernández is reimagined here as a savior. Juana Julia Guzmán, in her guise as the comic's narrator, explains why ANUC appropriated a popular villain, transforming him

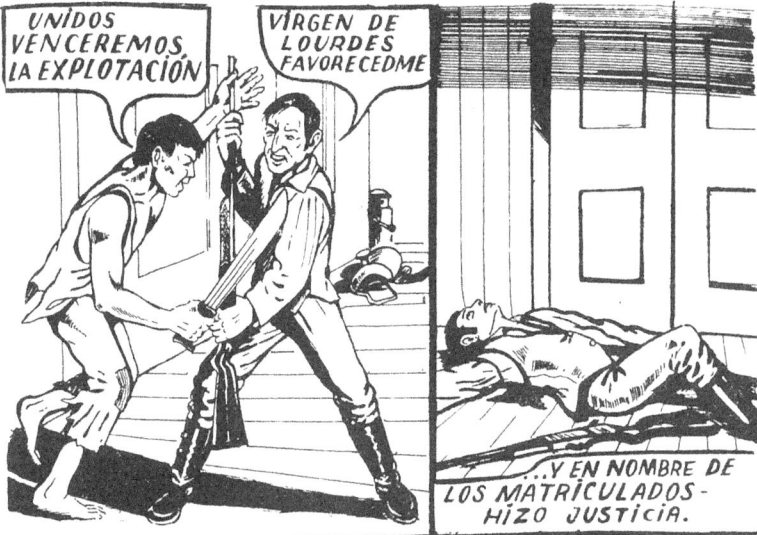

Figures 5.5 and 5.6   The death of El Boche (Chalarka 1985: 59, 60. Comics reprinted with permission of the Fundación del Sinú)

Figure 5.7 Correcting the myth of El Boche (Chalarka 1985: 61. Comic reprinted with permission of the Fundación del Sinú)

into a hero: "You must have understood, compañero, that we have our own heroes. Compañero Hernández showed in practice that the large landowners can be defeated" (1985: 64). The comic gives the lie to the exaggerated sensationalism of previous accounts in one of its final panels (fig. 5.7). As Hernández's cadaver is dragged through the streets of Montería, all of the falsehoods uttered by previous authors are depicted as a swirl of rumors: "They say he made the musiu into chopped meat" [*monsieur*, used to refer to foreign hacendados, like the Lacharmes]. "They say he killed out of jealousy." "They say he burned down the hacienda." "They say he killed 10!" "We'll bury him outside of the cemetery!" "They say they killed him with a bullet in the form of a cross." "They say he drank rum with gunpowder." These falsities are juxtaposed to the truth broadcast by the comic: "I knew him: he fought for the exploited!" (1985: 60).

The Fundación's rendering of *El Boche* was a call to arms against the Montería elite, but instead of being based on historical narrative it confronts head-on the stories that hacienda owners used to justify their superior position in society. As Joe Sacco argues, "the cartoonist draws with the essential truth in mind, not the literal truth" (2012: xii). The depiction of Manuel Hernández as a hero of an incipient agrarian struggle is more of an essential truth than a literal one, given that El Boche was always a fictional character. The factual dimension of the graphic novel is, rather, woven into the supporting details of the panels, which recount what it meant to live under the matrícula; this information is documented in Fals's archive and drawn from oral and published sources. In other words, the core lesson of *El Boche* is all about the matrícula, which is the principal antagonist of this story, not Lacharme. The fictionalized story of Manuel Hernández touched a nerve, both among campesinos and in urban areas, in a region in which everyone was familiar with earlier versions of the story, but not everyone was cognizant of the institution underlying it. The story of El Boche was the hook; the facts about the matrícula provided the lesson. Manuel Hernández's story still provokes strong emotions. When I sponsored a public reading of *El Boche* at the Banco de la República in 2019, I discovered that the Fundación version was still under vigorous debate by local historians, over four decades after its publication, although no one disputed the realities of debt-peonage. One might even venture to say that the Fundación's objective of critical recovery met its greatest success in *El Boche*.

Navigating the Gutters of *El Boche* with Peasants

How were peasant readers to assimilate *El Boche*? Did they focus on the story line or did they concentrate on their experiences of the matrícula? The answer to that question hinges on the methodology the Fundación used to study the graphic novel with peasants. Víctor Negrete told me that the Fundación frequently projected panels onto a screen, one by one, and discussed them with workshop participants.[10] In effect, those campesinos who read the graphic novel at public events did not always have the opportunity to follow it panel by panel, filling in the gaps in the narrative with their imaginations to flesh out the story of El Boche. In this case, the gutters had a different purpose. They were not so much vehicles for developing a story line as they were moments at which an oral reading of the verbal text was paused, so that rural audiences could own the story by sharing their own reminiscences of the matrícula and reflect on their actual experiences as landless sharecroppers or day workers. In other words, it was not only Juana Julia's visage—the face of a living woman who embodied agrarian struggle against debt-peonage—that connected readers of *El Boche* in the 1970s to Manuel Hernández; it was also how they related his experiences to their own sufferings. I wonder, therefore, whether the discussions following readings of *El Boche* concentrated on the comic's protagonist or if, instead, they steered peasants into an extended series of reminiscences about the role of activists like Juana Julia in ending debt-peonage and the campesinos' own responsibility to confront the modern system of land tenure that sustained their extreme poverty and marginalization. It is revealing that the Fundación distributed copies of *El Boche* on the occasion of the founding of a baluarte in Martinica, which is located near Misiguay, suggesting that they intended to reinforce support for the occupation by introducing a familiar story (Fals Borda 1986: 183A).

El Boche certainly provided peasant readers with such an opportunity. An early page of the text (Chalarka 1985: 53) explains the matrícula, introduced by a dated caption: "1898 Manuel Hernández arrived in Montería" (fig. 5.8). His belongings slung in a sack over his shoulder, Hernández chats with the administrator of Misiguay, who remarks, "You look strong. Talk to the white 'Musiu' Lacharme. We're needing matriculados," to which Hernández responds by thinking: "Matriculados? And what might that be?" (Elite hacienda owners were often called "whites," even if they were mulattos like José Santos Cabrera or Syrio-Lebanese like Malluk, the owner of Lomagrande.) In the background, men are caring for livestock and in a caption at the bottom, readers are informed that the matrícula was a continuation of slavery, codified in law in the department of Bolívar in 1892—one of the authors' citations of their historical sources.[11] Below, we become bystanders to Hernández's meeting at the notarial office with the hacendado, Alejandro Lacharme, just after his matrícula contract was issued. In this encounter, Hernández demonstrates subservience to his social superior, his sombrero vueltiao clutched to his chest out of respect. Lacharme informs him that a contract has been signed for him, implying that Hernández does not know how to affix his name to the document. The hacendado also lets him know that he owes ten days of work for the fifty-centavo cost of the notarization. A police officer stands at attention behind Lacharme, reinforcing his authority.

The bottom panel describes the matrícula in a language that is both accessible and tinged by condemnation:

With the matrícula the rich and large landowners could:
- Hold us as slaves for our whole lives.
- Lend us [to others], sell us, or rent us out as though we were just a thing.
- Use [our women] and our daughters freely.
- Punish us, torture us, even kill us, on the slightest pretext.
- Enslave our children or relatives if you escaped, died, or didn't pay back the debt. (Chalarka 1985: 53)

I translate "matrícula" as "debt-peonage" because although matrícula contracts were signed for a determined period of time, their completion was delayed, sometimes interminably, by the debts that matriculados accrued at the

Figure 5.8   Explanation of the matrícula in *El Boche*, bottom panel (Chalarka 1985: 53. Comic reprinted with permission of the Fundación del Sinú)

company store and for multiple other reasons cited by the hacienda management, such as the cost of the notarization of the contract, as the panel narrates. "Matrícula" is used in the graphic histories as an umbrella term that also covered other labor arrangements through which funds were advanced to peons in exchange for labor (Fals Borda 1986: 119B–127B; Ocampo 2007: 232–247). Gloria Isabel Ocampo argues that such contracts exemplified a hybrid system in which large landholdings coexisted alongside smallholders' plots (2007: 248).

The Fundación conducted a series of interviews to gather facts about the matrícula (virtually none of the eyewitness conversations cited on the first page of *El Boche* are recorded in Fals's field notes). They also consulted a 1912 police code that lays out the procedures for contracting rural laborers (Dávila Flórez 1912: 95–100), which is, presumably, the legal code cited in Chalarka's panel (fig. 5.8). *El Boche* brims with information about the matrícula: the use of stocks to punish laborers, the forced recruitment of peons during the Guerra de los Mil Días (the War of the Thousand Days, the civil war that devastated Colombia at the turn of the twentieth century), the cooperation of religious authorities in maintaining the debt-peonage system. Lacharme's tryst with Manuel Hernández's wife is undoubtedly a reference to the derecho de pernada that I mention in chapter 4, whereby hacendados forced peasant women under their control to grant them sexual favors. The Sociedad de Obreras Redención de la Mujer, led by Juana Julia Guzmán, was at the vanguard of the fight to end the matrícula, so it is no surprise that she is *El Boche*'s narrator.

Ernesto Parra and a group of sociologists (including Darío Fajardo, Gilberto Aristizábal, Anders Rudqvist, Alfredo Molano, William Ramírez, and Alejandro Reyes) were enlisted in 1976 to evaluate the work of La Rosca in Córdoba and Sucre (Parra Escobar 1983: 9–10). The evaluation committee convoked informal meetings in rural communities to collect histories of land ownership, to comprehend the nature of the relationships latifundistas established with peons, to reinforce campesino knowledge of the struggles of the past, including how they were steadily impoverished over the decades, and to evaluate whether ANUC was succeeding in reversing historical trends. They read the Fundación comics with people in the localities, provoking intense political discussion and remembrances of how movement leaders facilitated local training sessions. According to Parra, the comics were not so much a focus of discussion in these events as a point of departure for recollecting campesinos' own experiences.[12]

Similar oral exchanges probably transpired at the ANUC workshops at which *El Boche* was read or viewed. No transcripts of these encounters survive in Fals's archive. The only documentation I have discovered is a 14 May 1972 cursillo in Buenos Aires, Córdoba. The event was organized for various local ANUC chapters and took place before *Lomagrande* came out in print, so the transcript is not so much a confirmation as it is a hint of what might have occurred as campesinos gazed at panels from *El Boche*. The four points to be covered in the seminar were peasant history, rules of conduct and responsibilities of ANUC members, finances, and cooperativism (CDRBR/M, 0246, fol. 1079). Discussion of the first two items was facilitated by Víctor Negrete. He delivered a summary of the history of capitalist expansion in Córdoba, emphasizing many of the points that would later be taken up in the graphic histories, including the nineteenth-century entrance of French and North American companies into the Sinú Valley to exploit wood, mine for gold, and grow tobacco and cacao on large landholdings; the introduction of the matrícula as a form of institutionalized slavery; the history of the elite landholding families of Córdoba and how they acquired their wealth; and the story of Vicente Adamo and the Sociedad de Obreros y Artesanos de Montería (CDRBR/M, 0246, fols. 1081–1090).

Bárbaro Ramírez, an elderly campesino from Buenos Aires, Córdoba, interceded repeatedly to share his memories of the matrícula, which other participants embellished. He recounted how peasants were charged money for breaking tools and what transpired when matriculados tried to escape their bondage. Of special interest to the assembly was the series of punishments meted out to the matriculados, including the stocks. While we cannot see the unnamed narrator of the following quotation, we can sense his movements as he speaks: "It was an apparatus made of wood with holes in the center, the two flaps opened more or less in this way, with a hinge here, and so, they put the workers in by their feet and closed it up with a lock here" (CDRBR/M, 0246, fol. 1083). Another speaker offered further corroboration, observing that women were put in the pillory (CDRBR/M, 0246, 1084). The stocks and pillories would later be captured by Ulianov Chalarka in a panel of *El Boche* (Chalarka 1985: 55), undoubtedly a talking point for group discussion.

Bárbaro Ramírez also recalled how the matriculados fell further and further into debt. They carried around sticks into which notches were carved to keep a record of what they owed the company store, which Ramírez equates with account books: "They would go adjust their accounts any day they wanted to pay their accounts, and they would say, 'Ok,' they would say, 'Let's do the accounts. You owe me in sugar: so much, in refined sugar: so much.' They would note it down 3 times in that folder, understood? . . . And in that system they were never owed anything, but instead they were always in debt, and that's how things were done" (CDRBR/M, 0246, fol. 1084). Ramírez remembered how one day, two bounty hunters arrived at his hut with a pair of matriculados they had taken prisoner and demanded that his mother feed them. Ramírez was astounded: Why were they prisoners when they were just like us? He delivered meals to them for two or three weeks. He concluded his story by stating that that was the moment at which he joined the Liberal Party in order to give purpose to the intense emotions that the experience provoked in him (CDRBR/M, 0246, fol. 1085).

Víctor Negrete interceded in the discussion with what he called the "true story of Lomagrande," a history he said would supersede those written from the perspective of the victors (Exbrayat Boncompain 1939: 137–146; 1994 [1971]: 197; Velasco Puche 1963: 61–73). Negrete's argument hinges on the assertion that history has to be rewritten because "the people who don't know their true history . . . won't organize as they organized, nor would they struggle as they had, nor would they understand who their true enemies were. So this is one of the objectives of the people: to write their own history, because history is made by the people" (CDRBR/M, 0246, 1093). This is how ANUC members filled the gutters of the graphic histories: by taking the first steps toward writing that history. Although the comics vividly retold inspiring stories, their function was undoubtedly more of a stimulus for peasants' introspection, reminiscence, and, ultimately, organizing than for their making sense of the story line. The graphic histories served as exemplary vehicles for moving from archive to repertoire, from collecting historical evidence and fashioning it into a narrative to creating contexts in which peasants could begin to analyze their circumstances as a prelude to action. The resignification of the gutters of the graphic histories afforded one of the necessary tools for motivating such a process.

Archivos de Baúl

In their unpublished research manual, Orlando Fals Borda and Augusto Libreros encourage public acts of witnessing by elderly narrators in order to prompt young people to "re-encounter" their history (ACHUNC/B, caja 49, carpeta 3). While oral narrative was certainly a crucial facet of popular consciousness-raising, the Fundación employed various innovative techniques to generate such reminiscences. Perhaps the most ingenious example is its use of what they called "archivos de baúl" [kitchen archives]. Fals describes archivos de baúl as "the documentary treasure that, by chance, can be found in the hands of families in towns, whose members had the foresight to save historical mementos, deeds, letters, pamphlets, broadsides, old books, artistic and mechanical objects, drawings, and old photographs that can illustrate a historical era through its concrete regional expression" (Fals Borda 1979b: 42B). He termed these keepsakes "indispensable elements" for seizing hold of the past. Kitchen archives furnish crucial evidence that can be transformed subsequently through a process of "inference" [*ilación*] into tangible, emotionally laden, and inspiring stories (Fals Borda 1981: 57B; 1984: 45B, 47B; 1986: 69B). I take "inference" to be a cognate of "imputation" in Fals's writing; both "inference" and "imputation" require the use of the creative faculties of a group to produce new narratives that are based not only on empirical information but also on popular common sense. The objects contained in an archivo de baúl helped to ground such narratives in lived experience.

The Fundación del Caribe's insistence on archivos de baúl represents an effort to resignify existing research methods as a means of achieving novel objectives. Objects that elicit narrated memories have always been part of oral historians' tool kit. This is especially true for photographs, whose condition (faded, torn, annotated) and style (rigid figures and unsmiling faces) are as significant as tangible links to the past as is the historical information they contain. Marianne Hirsch and Leo Spitzer (2006) call them "testimonial objects." In an effort to distinguish their innate power, they engage Roland Barthes's notion of the "punctum," which the French semiotician defined as the details, frequently unintended, that captivate the imagination of the viewer of a photograph (Barthes 1981 [1980]). Hirsch and Spitzer appropriate the concept to draw attention to the point in space and time that "puncture[s] through layers of oblivion, interpellating those who seek to know about the past" (2006: 358). They continue on the same page:

> A point is also small, a detail, and thus it can convey the fragmentariness of the vestiges of the past that come down to us in the present—partial recipes on scraps of paper. In addition, such remnants are useful for *purposes of remembrance*—in order to help generate remembrance—another meaning of the term "point." And points of memory are also *arguments* about memory—objects or images that have remained from the past, containing "points" about the work of memory and transmission.

Archivos de baúl effectively "punctured through layers of oblivion." Juana Julia's medical records, an insignificant receipt somehow stored with more important papers, and, above all, the photos she and her associates saved over the decades still have the power to evoke powerful emotions in viewers, as I observed when I introduced participants in a Montería workshop to parts of her archivo de baúl. Kitchen archives and the objects associated with them also have the ability to reconfigure historical narrative so that it conforms more closely to the shape of local memory: this is why objects like the stocks are so prominent in Bárbaro Ramírez's recollections of the matrícula.

Archivos de baúl not only guided the creation of historical accounts following campesino narrative conventions but also generated sentiments of belonging to a group. La Rosca saw appeals to sentiment as fundamental to their task of coalescing grassroots political sensibilities, as was asserted by its founders at a workshop in the early 1980s:

> In a strict sense, there are no disarticulated objects of knowledge, as academic thought recommends, but, instead, multilateral reflection in the service of action. Multilateral, because it is active thought; it is active thought because its points of departure are a people's most vital expressions. It takes in BEING but also FEELING, their DESIRES, the depth of their sentiments. For this reason, this type of thought is not cold. When it is expounded, it bursts out from the actions themselves, gathering up, as in a cry, all of the repressed rebelliousness and because of this it is invested with history and the symbols of the masses. (ACHUNC/B, caja 49, carpeta 3, fol. 109)

Framed in the militant language of the times, the author of this passage recognizes that politics, research, and sentiment go hand in hand. Fals Borda would later articulate the centrality of sentiment to radical politics in his notion of the *sentipensante*, the "thinking-feeling" actor who was a protagonist of history (Fals Borda 2009).

It took some navigation through Fals Borda's archive for me to discover the location of some of the archivos de baúl he had accessed, because it wasn't always clear where he had saved them—or even if he archived them, given many of them were undoubtedly returned to the wooden trunks [*baúles*] tucked under villagers' beds, from which they had emerged in the first place. If they were photographs, the Fundación sometimes made copies. However, many of the photos were reclassified at some point before the archive was bequeathed to the Banco de la República and are now stored in the photographic collection instead of in the archival categories—which were also action items—in which they initially appeared. Since so many of the photos are identified by only minimalist captions (written by an employee of the Centro de Documentación), it is not always possible to ascertain their origins.

For example, the collection contains a photo of Vicente Adamo, a sepia print of a young, bearded man saluting the photographer (CDRBR/M, CF, 1421). Its edges are torn, Adamo's visage is blurred and stained, as though the original had been touched by many hands. It is a remnant encoding a tactile memory as much as a visual one, a reminder not only of Adamo himself but also of the individual who repeatedly looked at the portrait. It was presumably copied from a kitchen archive, perhaps Juana Julia Guzmán's. But Fals seems to have left only bits and pieces of documentation collected from Juana Julia's archivo de baúl in the dossier titled "Juana Julia Guzmán" (CDRBR/M, 0854-0856), mainly receipts and identification cards dating to her later years, documents not directly germane to the story of peasant resistance in the 1920s. He mentions other more relevant items in *Historia doble*, such as an armband (Fals Borda 1985: 60-61), but I never found it. Víctor Negrete told me that Juana Julia showed them a letter from Vicente Adamo that was written after he went into exile—Negrete remembers it had been posted from Jamaica—asking her to sell his rights to his plot in Lomagrande, but I never uncovered it. Many of the most significant objects in Juana Julia's archivo de baúl were, undoubtedly, photos, but how many of the historical photographs of the Sociedad de Obreros y Artesanos de Montería and of the Sociedad de Obreras Redención de la Mujer that are stored in Fals's photographic collection come from Juana Julia's kitchen archive, and not from other archivos de baúl, is not clear to me. For example, the family of Agustina Medrano, another leader of the Sociedad de Obreras, also supplied the Fundación with some photos of these organizations.[13]

What interests me most about the Fundación's kitchen archives is how they were employed as components of a participatory methodology, fostering the collective interpretation of history, engaging popular sentiment and historical knowledge, and mobilizing bodies to occupy haciendas and to march in the streets. If the contents of archivos de baúl functioned as a kind of a punctum through which campesinos could access and control the past, it is useful to examine how these exercises in collective memory were organized. Unfortunately, Fals saved very little evidence among his personal papers of the Fundación's uses of the technique, undoubtedly because work with archivos de baúl was more an activist performance than a collection of things. In and of themselves, these objects were inconsequential; their significance was in how they were deployed in the work of memory. Consequently, Costeño kitchen archives are most appropriately situated in the repertoire and not in the archive. A letter, a photo, or an armband was converted into a punctum through its display at a communal setting. Ulianov Chalarka's comics supply a venue for extrapolating the process by which kitchen archives might have been read. The contents of various archivos de baúl were purposely inserted into the graphic narrative, transforming the pamphlets into portable kitchen archives. This is most obvious in Chalarka's collages, where photos are juxtaposed to texts and drawings.

Portable Archivos de Baúl

In the years since the publication of the Fundación comics, authors of graphic novels have increasingly incorporated photographs into the comics medium, particularly in works of nonfiction (e.g., memoirs). In some instances, such as Alison Bechdel's *Fun Home* (Bechdel 2006) or Art Spiegelman's *Maus* (Spiegelman 1973, 1986), the actual photo is not placed in the panel, but instead, readers confront an image of the photo drawn into the comic, its heightened realism frequently contrasting with the iconicity of the rest of the panel (Watson 2008). Occasionally, cartoonists insert photos directly into their panels, so that they can function as evidentiary fragments (El Refaie 2012: chap. 4; Ernst 2015; Hirsch 1992–1993; cf. Sontag 1973). The presence of actual photos or drawings of them in a comics panel draws readers' attention because they usually contrast visually with the rest of the panel. They are a kind of an archive inside a comic. Indeed, as Hilary Chute has observed, the comics form itself is a kind of an archive insofar as it "literalizes the work of archiving: selecting, sorting, and containing in boxes" (2012). However, there are also examples of quite the opposite: when the drawn comics illustration is needed to explain an ambiguous photo. This occurs in *The Photographer* (Guilbert, Lefèvre, and Lemercier 2009), which narrates the experience of Didier Lefèvre, a photographer who accompanied a Doctors Without Borders expedition to Afghanistan. Drawn after his death, the graphic novel incorporates Lefèvre's photographs into a pictorial narrative by Emmanuel Guilbert. Here, the comics panels clarify and complement the photos (Pedri 2011).

Latin American authors were already incorporating photos into comics in the 1970s, building on a long tradition of *fotonovelas*, sequential narratives illustrated by photos instead of iconic drawings, which were frequently used in popular education programs (Flora 1984). *La increíble y triste historia de la reforma agraria y su INCORA desalmado* [*The Incredible and Sad History of the Agrarian Reform and Its Heartless INCORA*] (ANUC n.d.), a sophisticated graphic pamphlet produced for ANUC, narrates a revisionist agrarian history and accuses INCORA, the agrarian reform agency, of complicity in the continuing unequal distribution of land. It includes a number of inserted photos of heroes of the Colombian left.[14] The merging of comics and photographs was not thus entirely new to the Fundación del Caribe. In fact, before Chalarka embarked on his project, ANUC-Córdoba produced materials whose visual components were largely photos. The municipal chapter of ANUC in Montería published an informational pamphlet, *Así luchamos por recuperar la tierra!* [*This Is How We Fight to Reclaim Our Land!*], using photographs instead of drawings (AMUCM

1972). Two years later, an ANUC-sponsored primer, *Nuestra cartilla* [*Our Primer*], featured photos of a young boy as its narrator (Centro Popular de Estudios 1974); the only drawn illustrations are the cover—a group of ragged, barefoot children playing music, shouting in a megaphone, and carrying signs bearing ANUC slogans and the Colombian tricolor flag—and two portraits of the narrator wearing a sombrero vueltiao (1974: 8, 28), all by Ulianov Chalarka, who is identified in the introduction to the primer by his pseudonym, Iván Tejada.[15]

The incorporation of photos and objects into historical comics, a graphic technique with which external researchers and ANUC leaders were already familiar, created a portable archivo de baúl. Collective readings of kitchen archives required not only the saved objects themselves but also the presence of their owners, Fundación researchers, and a listening public. Given the advanced age and infirmity of many of the narrators, the perusal of their personal archives could only be indulged in occasionally, perhaps even only once. The incorporation of archivos de baúl into the Fundación's graphic histories, in which the narrators are pictorially present, permitted the technique to be more widely disseminated. Fragments of kitchen archives are scattered throughout the four comics: a profile portrait of Tinajones leader Alberto Licona that appears to be a newspaper caricature (Chalarka 1985: 36), the retouched photo of Felicita Campos (1985: 71). However, the most interesting examples come from *Lomagrande*, which is not surprising given that Juana Julia's kitchen archive was most frequently mentioned by my interlocutors and in Fals's writings.

First, an anecdotal example: a lovely story about one of Chalarka's insertions of an imaginary archivo de baúl into *Lomagrande*. When the Lomagrande leadership was imprisoned in Cartagena, a flurry of protest letters from all over Colombia, as well as from Latin America and Europe, was sent to the Colombian government. Matilde Eljach told me in our 15 July 2009 conversation in Popayán that in one baúl they discovered a copy of a letter about Lenin by Juana Julia Guzmán. Eljach didn't specify that it was a protest letter written by Lenin, but it appears in this form in a *Lomagrande* panel depicting the imprisoned socialists, who are conversing behind a large barred portal, with an armed guard standing outside the heavily fortified prison. The image is framed on the left by a cascade of envelopes representing protest letters, with the names or locations of their senders (the "R/" is an abbreviation of *remitente*, or "sender," including R/Santo Domingo—from Santo Domingo—R/Mexico, R/Argentina), and one of them reads "Lenin R/Russia" (Chalarka 1985: 20).

Most illustrative, however, are the photos associated with Juana Julia's kitchen archive, which interact in particularly interesting ways with the surrounding comics panels, furnishing clues as to how they might have been used as props in an oral narrative. I will focus here on two sets of photographs. First, a photo of the headquarters of the Sociedad de Obreros y Artesanos de Montería (fig. 5.9), inset at the top right into a panel containing a drawing of the same building (Chalarka 1985: 16). The photo is very small, blurred, and difficult to decipher. It depicts a side of the building and the street corner; the front of the building is marked by a series of large doors and two windows, all of them closed. A woman stands at the corner, barely visible because her white dress merges with the white background. There are similar photos in Fals Borda's collection showing Juana Julia Guzmán at this very location, dressed in similar clothing (CDRBR/M, CF, 1428). In sensu stricto, the photo was probably not extracted from an archivo de baúl but was taken by Fals or one of his associates. But I would argue that the photo is turned into an archivo on the comics page. This tiny image acts as a punctum, a link to the past, a kind of a talisman connecting readers to a fuzzy memory that can only be fully retrieved by looking at Chalarka's drawing, located directly below it.

The iconic depiction of the Sociedad headquarters is three times larger than the photographic image, considerably more detailed, and full of human activity. Above the doors of the building, Chalarka identifies two of the functions of the organization, which housed a Worker's School [*Escuela Obrera*] and a Socialist Hospital [*Hospital Socialista*]. Two horses stand near the door of the hospital; even in the 1970s, there were many horses on the streets of Montería. Directly below the photograph, Chalarka identifies the building's location—Calle 28 and Carrera 7, Montería—so that any reader could visit the edifice, which had different tenants by the 1970s but has since been demolished. As in *The Photographer*, Chalarka's comics panel renders the photograph legible. Cursillo facilitators probably drew readers' attention to the two images. What would they have talked about? Perhaps they would be reminded of the functions of the Sociedad de Obreros and how they could be replicated by the peasant organization in the 1970s. Some of the older participants might have shared stories about visiting the building in its heyday. They would have noticed Juana Julia, leading them back into the narrative of the Baluarte Rojo and the baluartes established in La Antioqueña.

Two facing pages immediately before the page bearing the snapshot of the Sociedad headquarters (Chalarka 1985: 14–15) display a more complex scenario (fig. 5.10). In chapter 4 I worked through the right-hand page to illustrate the difficulties of representing the institution of the baluarte as an abstraction. Now, I want to contemplate how the two facing pages prompt readers to follow a particular itinerary to construct a narrative out of the juxtaposition of archivos de baúl and drawings. First, note that there is a kind of a "solidarity"

Figure 5.9   Headquarters of the Sociedad de Obreros as depicted in *Lomagrande* (Chalarka 1985: 10. Comic reprinted with permission of the Fundación del Sinú)

Figure 5.10 How Ulianov Chalarka guided the memory of his readers in *Lomagrande* (Chalarka 1985: 8–9. Comic reprinted with permission of the Fundación del Sinú)

between these two pages (Groensteen 2007: 34–37), which mirror each other. The top-left and bottom-right panels depict almost identical groups of men walking away from the reader, thereby forcing the viewer to take in the two pages as a single composition. The two-page spread is both chronological and simultaneous. It moves us through a series of events associated with the workers' organizations of the early twentieth century at the same time that it juxtaposes the past with the present through the use of photographic images from far-flung time periods, namely, the group photo from 1918 and the portrait of Juana Julia in the 1970s. It holds time and space in a kind of "electric tension" (Sousanis 2015: 63).

My intention here is to use the organization of the comic's pictorial space to uncover hints of how peasants might have read *Lomagrande* and talked about it. It is important to remember that many of them could not read its verbal contents. Readers of graphic novels sometimes assume that comics are easier to decipher than verbal narrative texts, but the pages of *Lomagrande* were probably not consumed as hurriedly by campesinos. It would have taken more time to read them aloud than silently, and in those minutes nonreaders had the opportunity to examine the illustrations more closely. Their gaze would have been guided by the rhythm that the artist established for the two facing pages, their eyes directed back and forth between pairs of images. For example, they might have fixed their gaze on the two photos, or perhaps on the juxtaposition of the photo of Juana Julia placed next to her younger self, or they might have noticed the almost identical depictions of the departing workers positioned on a diagonal over the two pages. They might have slowed down to dwell on a single panoramic image; one is located in the top panel of the left-hand page, and two are on the facing page.

I don't think the pages were arranged this way by accident. Ulianov Chalarka ensured there was a certain directed cadence to their reading (Groensteen 2013: 134–154). I am not aware of whether the entire Fundación team was conscious of how the layout controlled the readers' eyes, or if Chalarka alone was responsible for establishing the visual tension between photos and drawings. I assume the latter; the team probably selected the historical referents and the photos and suggested what should appear in the panels, but I suspect that only Chalarka knew how to arrange them so that they interacted successfully on the page. Once he got it right, it would have clicked unconsciously with the rest of the team.

The reader's eye tacks back and forth between the 1918 photo of the Sociedad de Obreros y Artesanos on the first page and the photo of Juana Julia in her senior years. The two photographs catch the reader's attention because they are darker than the surrounding drawings. Then, look at the drawn image next to Juana Julia's portrait, of the women activists in 1919, with Juana Julia at its center, gesticulating to her comrades. Tangible evidence of the past is reimagined in the present: the photo of the Sociedad de Obreras is blurry, its characters indecipherable, but Juana Julia's portrait is easier to make out. In the drawing that accompanies her photo, the officers of the Sociedad de Obreras are identified by name; they become individuals. Moreover, two of these historical agents—Pacha Feria and Juana Julia Guzmán—erupted into the temporal context in which the readers were located: they were historical actors whom the readers of the 1970s knew and trusted.

But the punctum here is neither the historical photo nor the drawing. The lead actor is Juana Julia and it is the photographic image of ANUC's elderly mentor whose presence powerfully unites past with present. Her portrait pulls the eye away from the portrait on the facing page of narrator Wilberto Rivero, the young leader from Martinica; the reduced size of his visage does not capture the eye quite as effectively as does Juana Julia's photo. She is positioned near the center of the two pages, her face is the largest, and the darkness of its background attracts readers' attention. The aged Juana Julia steers the 1918 photo and Chalarka's iconic sketch of the Sociedad de Obreras into a constellation of images of which she is the center. Her significance carries readers into the bottom-right panel, where we see members of the Baluarte Rojo, which she founded. As I observed in the previous chapter, the verbal and visual texts of this panel conceptually superimpose the Baluarte Rojo of the 1920s with the baluartes established in occupied lands in the 1970s, a political decision that she inspired. The organization of the pages transports readers from the past into the present.

The spread lends significant hints to how archivos de baúl might have been read. Their purpose was not so much to reveal the past as it was to engage the past in generating a new future, with narrators like Juana Julia forming the axis that connected past and present with what lay ahead. Her portrait stands in for the well-known person. Potawatomi philosopher Kyle Whyte conjectures that Native Americans think through strategies for surviving climate change by reflecting on how their ancestors might have analyzed their current predicament, since, as he argues, climate change is not a new phenomenon for colonized people but a cyclical occurrence. Just as planning for future generations involves "going back to the future," so does learning from the elders (Whyte 2017). One might say that this is, precisely, what the workshops featuring archivos de baúl achieved, with the distinction being that the elders of the past who were being consulted by the peasants of Córdoba and Sucre were present at the meetings or stood in as pictured narrators, supplying direct conduits to the past.

Systematic Devolution

Were these tools for fostering campesino participation as successful as they appear in retrospect? More precisely, did they effectively promote a deeper knowledge of local history and a critical framework for analyzing the present? Did they inspire peasants to become more active in ANUC? It is difficult to respond to these questions with certainty, as neither the archives nor my interlocutors provided me with sufficient evidence. Instead of dwelling on what I can never find out, over the past three chapters I have accessed the Fundación del Caribe's graphic histories as a space in which I can give flesh to the narrative of their methodology, which is only skeletal in what has been written about them. Chapter 3 reconstructs the process of writing the comics to reveal the social dynamics of participation between the Fundación, ANUC, and its rank and file. I compare the research process to a chain of conversations between differently positioned actors whose participation takes place at different moments. In chapter 4, I turn to the comics panels themselves to tease out the meaning of "critical recovery," through which political concepts were abstracted out of the vast array of available narratives and cast in a pictorial language that would be politically meaningful to its campesino audience. In this chapter, I have fleshed out what La Rosca called "systematic devolution," examining in particular how campesinos who participated in cursillos were led by the Fundación's materials to assume in their own right the role of social analysts.

The unpublished research manual written by Fals Borda and Libreros argues that the devolution of research results occurs throughout the research process, beginning with the audiences at community assemblies who listen to the narrators who walk among them. Nonetheless, this freewheeling notion of devolution becomes more pointed when the research results are subject to what the authors call a process of "systematizing" or "logical ordering" (ACHUNC/B, caja 49, carpeta 3, fol. 257v). La Rosca and the Fundación del Caribe identified four distinct levels of systematic devolution: simple pictorial materials for the illiterate grass roots; comics combining easy-to-read verbal contents with images, meant for local activists; more complex and abstract written materials—still accessible to peasant leaders—like the *Tinajones* pamphlet in narrative prose I described in chapter 4; and theoretically sophisticated writings like the synthetic agrarian history texts presented at the Escuela de Cadres (Fals Borda 1975, 1976), which I will introduce in the following chapter, or like *Historia doble de la Costa*, meant for consumption by intellectuals (ACHUNC/B, caja 49, carpeta 3, fols. 259–260; Low and Herrera 1988: 46). In other words, they conceived devolution as a systematic process that combined scientific rigor with political purpose and was directed at particular audiences, always keeping in mind the public's level of ideological sophistication and command of the written word. In addition, they believed that the very process of systematic devolution would ultimately leave them with scientific results on the basis of which they could further develop their methodology; this was another facet of the method's "systematicity."

Fals and his associates never imagined that the products of systematic devolution, such as Chalarka's graphic histories, would be entirely transparent to their audiences. They were meant to be studied at communal gatherings in which their arguments could be questioned, analyzed, and evaluated in light of the needs of the present and the personal experiences of the participants. The use of living narrators to connect past with present; the transformation of the gutters into spaces for recounting personal experiences; and the archivos de baúl that guided the audience to draw specific conclusions about the history they had seen, read, or heard were tools that ensured that materials like the graphic histories would be transformed into *vivencias*—lived experiences. Ultimately, as campesinos occupied haciendas, they would embody what they had read or heard. Whether, in actuality, they achieved that goal is something I don't think we will ever know entirely. I will return to this quandary in the final chapter of this book.

6

ENGAGEMENT AND REFLECTION

Orlando Fals Borda's conceptualization of action research combined investigation and activism with moments of reflection, when the researchers would step
back to evaluate their research, their insertion in political activities, and their future goals (Fals Borda 1978:
35). Ultimately, his experience with ANUC and the Fundación del Caribe stimulated him to write more complex pieces aimed at broader audiences. Based on his
notes from cursillo presentations and the discussions
that ensued at them, Fals penned a series of histories
of the expansion of the hacienda system, aimed at a national readership—including not only leftists but also a
campesino and proletarian audience who could digest
relatively uncomplicated prose texts. He first tried them
out as biweekly columns in 1974 in *Alternativa* and from
late 1974 through 1975 in *Alternativa del Pueblo*, the two
leftist magazines he edited (the columns are listed in the
bibliography). After the Fundación closed its doors, La
Rosca—which, itself, was soon to fold—published Fals's
magazine columns in book form as *Historia de la cuestión
agraria en Colombia* [*History of the Agrarian Question in Colombia*] (Fals Borda 1975). A year later, Fals adapted the
topics of his national history to the regional setting of
the Atlantic coast in *Capitalismo, hacienda y poblamiento*
[*Capitalism, Hacienda, and Settlement*] (Fals Borda 1976).
As I will show in this chapter, *Historia doble de la Costa*,
Fals Borda's four-volume history of the Atlantic coast,
marks the final step in this process of activism punctuated by reflection.

Fals retreated in 1975 to the department of Bolívar, where he continued to conduct research with campesinos but was not as closely associated with the peasant movement as he had been from 1972 to 1974. Over the next decade, he wrote the four volumes of *Historia doble*. Fals considered this lengthy period of reflection to be an integral component of his methodology. Action research didn't require continuous commitment to an organization but could, instead, "contribute to the global process of social change, seeking out convergences" with social movements (ACHUNC/B, caja 49, carpeta 3, fol. 194). On the one hand, he anticipated that *Historia doble* would have an impact on processes of social change, insofar as it elucidated what was still a new activist research methodology. On the other hand, Fals found in Bolívar a space in which he could begin to think about his next project, which proposed an administrative restructuring of the Colombian state (something I'll return to presently). *Historia doble* thus represents more than the written culmination of his work on the Caribbean coast or the end of an academic research project. Instead, he conceived of the book as a step in a continuing progression of action research.

For this reason, I have dedicated a chapter to exploring how Fals's masterwork reproduces his research process. *Historia doble* is a historical narrative that channels peasant voices through an exposition—or perhaps better stated, a reenactment—of his innovative methodology. As such, its writing cannot be entirely separated from Fals's activist period in Córdoba between 1972 and 1974, because it is during this period of reflection that he evaluated what he and his colleagues in Montería had accomplished. Consequently, this chapter is not so much an addendum to as it is a continuation of my examination of the emergence of action research in the first half of the 1970s.

I approach *Historia doble* as a process of "sedimentation," the progressive consolidation of the Fundación del Caribe's activities into written materials that were subsequently recycled into action. In turn, political activity led to the production of further writings that quote from, paraphrase, and build upon earlier works and are aimed at ever-wider audiences. To clarify this point, I draw on the work of Italian archivists, who explain archival sedimentation as a conscious process of layering, ordering, and sometimes even disposal of documents in an archive over time (Bologna, Foscarini, and Sonnewald 2017; Mata Caravaca 2017). In this chapter, however, I am less concerned with how Fals's archive was readied for its permanent home in the Banco de la República in Montería and more with how it was sedimented into educational, political, and scholarly materials in a continuous process of systematic devolution. In essence, the writing of *Historia doble* is part of the same dialectical process that I examine in previous chapters. The sediments that Fals continuously recycled in later writings are not always obvious; they have undergone radical textual transformations that to some degree occlude their collective authorship—just as occurs in the Fundación's graphic histories. But if we read *Historia doble* as the successive depositing of a series of activist research products, their collective nature is revealed and Fals's magnum opus is comprehensible as a participatory-action field narrative embedded in a history text.

It is useful to consult Michel-Rolph Trouillot's four moments in the production of history (Trouillot 1995: 26) as a framework for thinking about the process of sedimentation that characterizes Fals Borda's work. The Fundación del Caribe created what Trouillot calls "facts" when they identified and recorded historical sources, like Juana Julia Guzmán's life narrative or the written documentation they collected for the history of the Baluarte Rojo. Subsequently, they assembled these sources into an "archive": written and photographic evidence was classified according to the needs of the organization and stored in filing cabinets; archivos de baúl were used as props at interviews and were sometimes archived, either as originals or copies. The Fundación's repository furnished source material for cursillo presentations and for crafting written and visual narratives, the third of Trouillot's moments. Both peasants and external researchers analyzed these stories at workshops, in the proposals they wrote for pamphlets promoting the baluartes, and in all sorts of political activities, in the process lending the narratives retrospective significance that transformed them into what Trouillot calls "history." Unlike conventional historical writing, which bestows retrospective significance through the production of scholarly narratives, the Fundación and its allies in the ANUC leadership accomplished this goal by embedding their historical interpretations in ANUC's political repertoire.

Trouillot asserts that all four moments—fact production, creation of archives, making of narratives, attribution of retrospective significance—unfold simultaneously, not always in succession. We see this occurring, once and again, in the relationship between the Fundación's archive (a set of tangible and permanent records) and their political repertoire (embodied in their activism). Their goals of critical recovery and systematic devolution stimulated a cross-fertilization between the archive and the repertoire that yielded an ever-expanding constellation of historical texts. The process culminates with *Historia doble*, where Fals combines the contents of his archive with the Fundación's repertoire of actions in ever-wider geographic spheres that range across the entire Caribbean coastal plain and move from the pre-Columbian period to the 1970s, resuscitating the voices of not only peasants and proletarians but also urban and rural elites from various historical periods. Both archive and repetoire were visited and revisited over the fifteen-odd years of Fals's experience on the Atlantic coast. Each time the activists read or reread a document, or when they created a new one that drew on the existing corpus, they left "fingerprints" that altered the meanings of the existing documents (Ketelaar 2001: 137–138) so that we can trace the life cycles of these archival traces. Thus, the process of sedimentation exhibited in *Historia doble* in some ways replicates the model of his working archive.

An Introduction to *Historia doble de la Costa*

The four volumes of *Historia doble* proceed in a loose chronological order: *Mompox y Loba* (henceforth, *Mompox* or, in parenthetical references, HDC I), published in 1979 and based on extensive archival investigation, is concerned with the creation of a colonial agrarian order on the Caribbean coast from the sixteenth to the eighteenth century; Mompox and Loba are two localities, the former the epicenter of the regional elite and the latter the rural village whose storytellers are positioned in Fals's text as a narrative counterpoint to the hacienda founders. *El Presidente Nieto*, which appeared in 1981, recounts the civil wars by means of which the nineteenth-century Colombian elite struggled to consolidate its rule in the postindependence period and the impact of these wars on the peasantry; the volume juxtaposes campesino oral narrative to the writings of President Juan José Nieto, the eponymous protagonist of the volume. *Resistencia en el San Jorge* [*Resistance in the San Jorge*], published in 1984, examines the introduction of agrarian capitalism and extractive industries to the Atlantic coast, highlighting the beginnings of resistance to hacienda expansion; at the same time, it paints a vivid ethnographic portrait of riverine life. *Retorno a la tierra* [*Return to the Land*] (henceforth, *Retorno* or, in parenthetical references, HDC IV), the 1986 volume that most closely hews to Fals's experiences with ANUC in Córdoba, narrates the peasant struggles of the twentieth century and evaluates the contributions made by action research to the peasant movement. Notwithstanding Fals's nod to historical chronology, even those chapters dedicated to the colonial period and the nineteenth century are permeated by the voices of twentieth-century Costeño storytellers, who, like the narrators in Ulianov Chalarka's comics, revitalize the lessons of the past in the present.

Historia doble is the culmination of a unique research project that was neither individual nor strictly scholarly. Correspondingly, Fals's history of the coast is profoundly shaped by his collaboration with ANUC in the early 1970s; the four volumes are explicitly framed by action research. He opens *Mompox* with the story of how he established a study group in Loba, near Mompox. He closes *Retorno* with an evaluation of his methodology and brief allusions to its continuing use in Córdoba and Sucre. *Historia doble* reenacts Fals's research strategy by staging conversations between researchers and peasants and by highlighting the critical recovery of key moments in Costeño peasant history. Fals consciously draws on many of the documents he and his Fundación associates generated during their collaboration with ANUC as source material, sedimenting the historical interpretations of multiple social actors. He registers eyewitness narratives and layers on top of them the Fundación del Caribe's graphic histories. The serialized history Fals penned for *Alternativa* (henceforth in citations, Alt) and *Alternativa del Pueblo* (henceforth in citations, AP) in the second half of 1974 and in 1975, *Historia de la cuestión agraria* (Fals Borda 1975), and *Capitalismo, hacienda y poblamiento* (Fals Borda 1976) are all reutilized in *Historia doble*, where images, motifs, historical accounts, and peasant voices are recycled and refashioned so that they interact in synergy with his narrative.

The four volumes of *Historia doble* carry little resemblance to conventional histories of the time or even to today's historical monographs. Channel A, on the left-hand pages, narrates the process by which the evolution of the Costeño landholding system divested small cultivators of their lands to establish large landholdings and the ways in which campesinos resisted this encroachment. Channel B, on the right-hand pages, provides a historiographic, methodological, and theoretical context for Channel A, but its thematic content is dependent on the plotting of events and historical voices in the left-hand channel (Robles Lomeli 2019). Channel A appears to be directed at a broad audience, while Channel B might be read as a text destined for an intellectual readership (Bergquist 1990: 160). Although the contents of Channel B do not stand on their own, Channel A can be read in isolation as a continuous narrative. This is but a handy gloss of the book's format; it would be a gross simplification to distinguish the two channels by their readerships, given how they interpenetrate, reflect, and comment on each other.

The language of the two channels differs noticeably. Channel A is colloquial in tone. It juxtaposes Fals's rendering of history from below, an often graceful narrative based on bibliographic, oral, and documentary sources, to oral accounts that he rewrote to be more appealing to readers, as is common in literary nonfiction. It contains vivid descriptions of places and reconstructs imaginary dialogues between protagonists, employing the technique that Fals calls "imputation," through which he fleshes out the bare bones of the historical record by exercising his empirically anchored imagination. There are indented paragraphs on many of the pages of Channel A, signposting alternative story lines and protagonists who are not always identified by name. The indentations usually evince orality, although if we compare them to the interviews collected in Fals's archive we discover that his rewrites are sometimes composites of the testimonies of multiple storytellers (Robles Lomeli 2015), just as occurs in the graphic histories. At times, Fals situates his narrators in historical periods that are entirely different from the temporal locus of the main narrative. For example, *El Presidente Nieto* takes place in the nineteenth century, but twentieth-century narrators appear in the indented paragraphs of Channel A in an attempt to contrast the experience of political-military leaders [*caudillos*] in the civil wars with the challenges faced by peasants. There are no footnotes in Channel A, no sense of the sources on which the narrative is based. The reader is faced with unattributed conversations that sometimes coincide with and at other times contradict each other, covering vast expanses of space and time. Of course, this polyphony is deliberately fashioned; it is not haphazard. Notwithstanding, it is sometimes difficult to decipher.

In contrast, Channel B is written in a more recognizable academic format. It contains bibliographic and archival references, as well as sections dedicated to historiography, theoretical discussion, and methodological observations. Occasionally, Channel B seems to repeat Channel A in academic prose, but in reality it expands on Channel A by intellectually or historically contextualizing its narrative. Channel B contains fewer words than Channel A; it is where Fals placed the numerous photos that grace the four volumes. Sometimes, the photographs mirror the text with portraits of the narrators or photos of the landscapes from which the narrators are speaking; the right-hand pages also contain charts and maps that clarify the arguments of Channel B.

The reader is asked to alternate between channels, reading a chapter of Channel A and then moving to its counterpart, Channel B. The epilogue of *El Presidente Nieto* and various chapters of *Retorno* break with this convention by presenting the argument in a single channel that reads like a conventional book (I will identify my citations of these chapters with asterisks). The two channels are meant to interact in a dynamic exchange of theory (Channel B) and practice (Channel A), evoking the process of critical recovery, inasmuch as the narratives of the left-hand channel contain ideas embedded in stories that are subsequently conceptualized and historicized in the right-hand channel, thereby forcing theory to take note of—or even defer to—local epistemologies (Robles Lomeli 2019). Just as Fals's archive is an intentionally organized repository of traces of activism that culminate in educational materials, his book narrates, reenacts, and expands on the activities compiled in the archive, although in chronological instead of alphabetical order.

The two channels are connected by a series of "personifications," metaphors that condense features that Fals identifies as central to Costeño culture and that serve as conceptual tools organizing the historical narrative. I will concentrate here on only one of them. *Mompox* revolves around the concept of "amphibious culture," which Fals argues embodies peasants' relationship to a landscape punctuated by wetlands and savanna. At the time of the writing of the first volume of *Historia doble*, local Montería intellectuals had just founded a literary collective, El Túnel, to support folkloric research into what they called "sinuanology" [*sinuanología*] (Valencia Hernández and Márquez Meza 2012: 23; cf. Grupo El Túnel n.d.). I infer that Fals's use of metaphors like "amphibious culture" probably did not occur in a vacuum but originated in conversation with Montería's poets and essayists; in fact he quotes the most well-known of them, "Compae Goyo" (Guillermo Valencia Salgado), various times in *Retorno*.

Personifications bridge past and present, grounding the historical narrative in the daily lives of peasants and connecting the two channels. Channel A of *Mompox* contains a lyrical description of the "alligator-man" [*hombre-caimán*], recalling a moment at which Fals spied an alligator on his first river trip to Loba. He asks: "Or is it the wandering alligator-man, who would prefer the shade of the *uvero* vines and ceibas [*cantagallos*] of the tranquil swamps behind the town, to the wild currents of the great river that is crisscrossed today by boats and canoes?" (HDC I: 16A). In this quotation, the hombre-caimán is situated in the distant past, like the colonial haciendas described in association with the legend, but Fals also uses the motif to characterize the present in which he is writing, even though the Sinú River had by then become an artery for industrial transportation. Fals first heard the story in Mompox, when he was told of a man transformed by a witch into an alligator so that he could surreptitiously gaze at his lover while she bathed in the river. The woman eventually left for Barranquilla, as did the alligator (CDRBR/M, 1108), as is recorded in "Se va el caimán," a famous *porro* (a Costeño musical genre similar to *cumbia*) known by most Colombians. Channel B analyzes the metaphor through an exploration of the concept of region, which in the case of the Caribbean coast, Fals argues, embodies a culture specifically suited to a wetland environment.

Historia doble's personifications are thus not isolated from their political context. Undeniably, they constitute an exercise in critical recovery of the key tropes of Costeño culture. In his movement from Channel A to Channel B,

Fals grasps hold of a story and transforms it into a politically useful concept. Indeed, one of the purposes of the study group he established in Loba was to lay the historical basis for proposing the creation of a department comprising the riverine territory at the intersection of Bolívar, Córdoba, and Sucre, which he hoped would replace the existing administrative structure of the current departments of the southern portion of the Caribbean coast (HDC I: part 1). Fals contends that it is well worth looking at the coast as a coherent regional formation, because "it holds important implications for political practice, ideological alliances, and economic and social planning" (HDC I: 16B), a set of concepts he would eventually promote as a delegate to the Constituent Assembly that rewrote Colombia's constitution, which includes important articles on territorial restructuring (Fals Borda 2010a [1993]).

Historia doble and Action Research

Fals explains in a 1988 interview that the two channels of *Historia doble* correspond to four levels of action research: the first two levels, comprised of those who are illiterate and those able to read simple texts that mix verbal and visual elements, which stand in contrast to the second two levels made up of activists, who can read texts composed in a language accessible to nonspecialists, and intellectuals, who are equipped to read theory (Low and Herrera 1988: 46). There were campesinos in all four readerships, although only a small number at the fourth level. Charles Bergquist interprets the organization of the volumes literally, as materials directed at distinct groups of readers, and criticizes Fals's tendency to "dichotomiz[e] abstract and concrete modes of thought and discourse," which, in the end, he argues, are equally abstract because they are both crafted products of interpretation (1990: 172). I wonder, however, whether Fals really aimed at two distinct readerships for the channels of *Historia doble*, and I infer that his reference to the two more demanding levels of participatory action research are better understood as metaphors he employs to illustrate how his book evokes his research methodology by placing people's knowledge in dialogue with academic science. Indeed, the two channels are not meant to be read separately. In fact, Channel B is incomprehensible without Channel A, and for those of us not from the Atlantic Coast, Channel B places Channel A in more familiar contexts. Rather than viewing them as discrete communicative channels, I prefer Jafte Robles's interpretation of the parallel narratives as operating in a counterpoint, variations on a common theme (Robles Lomeli 2019). Together, they fuse theory and practice into a single composition. Moreover, both of the channels contain paraphrases of the Fundación's graphic texts produced for campesino audiences, so that in the end, there is no single channel that embodies theory and another that represents practice, just as action research only functions when theory and practice are engaged in chorus.

Thus, *Historia doble* is a reenactment of a deep, wide-ranging, and intensely political conversation between equals. In framing his historical narrative within the precepts of action research, Fals strains the limits of historiography, which traditionally channels the voice of a single author according to an agreed-upon metanarrative (Chakrabarty 2000); it was greeted by intense criticisms of its structure, its lack of footnotes, its neglect of the historiographic literature, and its resort to imputation (Bergquist 1990; Martínez Garnica 2008–2009). But it would be a mistake to concentrate solely on the ways Fals defied historiographic conventions, because he also turns ethnography on its head. Anthropologists generally insert native voices into a hierarchical conceptual structure in which local knowledge is framed by ethnographic interpretation, thereby making it legible to its readers (Dilley 2002: 452). Collaborative researchers, in contrast, are forced to seek out alternative frameworks if they expect the groups they collaborate with to make sense of their writing. The divergences between our frameworks and those of our respondents are eloquent examples of why our work is not uniformly celebrated by the very communities with whom we purport to be collaborating. If we are to make collaboration possible, we must recognize these differences and work with them, not against them (Briones 2013).

Fals Borda attempts to reframe local knowledge but does not entirely succeed, perhaps because of the fragmentary nature of his text and the difficulties it presents to readers. The intellectual framework he uses as a general scaffolding for the four volumes has much in common with the Latin American historiography of the period, but it also corresponds to the ways in which Latin American activists conceptualized history. Fals embeds the knowledge he acquired over his three years of collaboration with ANUC in a Marxist interpretation of history that employs a discourse of peasant resistance. However, he teases his narrative out of the voices of his narrators and the educational materials with which campesinos were familiar, so that the historiography of Channel B is to some degree determined by the narrative of Channel A. His framework also determines who is permitted to speak in Channel A, privileging those individuals who have been promoted as local heroes, thereby replicating the language and contents of the Fundación's graphic histories. This is why, in an effort to reflect the preoccupations of political allies and recognize the intellectual contexts in which collaboration took place, *Historia doble* sediments writings originally destined for nonliterates. Thus, although the two channels of *Historia doble* are written in different registers, they originate from a common source that determines how the various voices they contain are to be represented. But they are not, in a strict sense, distinct voices, since both registers were crafted by the author and do not reproduce verbatim a "pure" campesino voice free of intervention. The narrators of Channel A sound like they are Fals's peasant interlocutors, but there has already been a political intervention that converts their voices at once into politically usable utterances and into intellectually malleable propositions, as well as a literary intervention making them more readable, just as occurs in the Fundación's graphic histories. This is particularly evident in *Retorno a la tierra*, which is my primary focus in this chapter. It narrates the twentieth-century history of peasant movements on the coast with Juana Julia Guzmán as its central character.

Fals Borda's Muse

Without Juana Julia Guzmán as its guide, *Retorno a la tierra* would have been a different book. Unlike most Colombian historical monographs published in the 1980s, the last volume of *Historia doble* includes an index of persons and places. Juana Julia is the individual with the largest number of entries, although her role as a protagonist in the history of peasant resistance is limited to a few years in the early 1920s. In order to comprehend the ubiquitous presence of Juana Julia Guzmán in *Retorno*, we need to return to *El Boche* (Chalarka 1985: 46–64), the graphic history for which she serves as the narrator, in which her visage appears four times. After the obligatory list of oral and written sources that opens all of the Fundación's graphic histories, Chalarka inserts a map of Colombia bearing the names of indigenous, Afrocolombian, peasant, and proletarian heroes from various historical periods. The map is accompanied by a slogan: "The people also have their own heroes!" (1985: 48). Before the reader is immersed in the graphic rendition of the story of El Boche, we meet Juana Julia (fig. 6.1), who introduces the volume by cautioning that although the popular classes have their own heroes, they don't know them because the ruling classes have concealed their stories (1985: 49). History has been censored, denying the masses the examples set by Benkos Bioho, founder of the maroon community of San Basilio; José A. Galán, the leader of the late eighteenth-century insurrectionist movement of the Comuneros that was a prelude to the independence wars; twentieth-century indigenous leader Manuel Quintín Lame (whose writings were published by La Rosca); and socialist María Cano, whose ideas inspired Juana Julia and Vicente Adamo. Juana Julia narrates what

ESO ES VERDAD COMPAÑEROS!
PERO NO LOS CONOCEMOS BIEN.
POR QUÉ? PORQUE LOS RICOS
Y TERRATENIENTES
DE COLOMBIA Y EL EXTRANJERO
HAN PROCURADO OCULTARLOS.
DE ELLOS NOS HAN DICHO MUCHAS MENTIRAS
PARA QUE NO SIGAMOS SU EJEMPLO DE LUCHA.
PERO NOSOTROS LOS EXPLOTADOS SÍ NECESITAMOS
CONOCER LA HISTORIA DE ESTOS COMPAÑEROS
PARA APRENDER DE ELLOS
Y LUCHAR MEJOR POR LA TIERRA Y EL PODER.
POR ESO TE CONTAREMOS
LA VERDADERA HISTORIA
DE MANUEL HERNÁNDEZ, EL BOCHE.

Figure 6.1   Opening speech of *El Boche* (Chalarka 1985: 49. Comic reprinted with permission of the Fundación del Sinú)

she calls the "true story" of Manuel Hernández, "El Boche," revealing him to be an unrecognized champion of the peasants of Córdoba and Sucre.

Readers of *El Boche* are reminded that Juana Julia will be accompanying them on this historical journey, because her portrait is inserted again on the following page (the same portrait is repeated throughout the pamphlet, as is Chalarka's practice in all his comics). Here, Juana Julia narrates the history of the migration of landless campesinos to the Sinú Valley in the mid-nineteenth century (1985: 50). She doesn't crop up again for some six pages, in the course of which the text depicts how peasants tamed the jungles only to lose their lands to latifundistas, the same landlords who later imposed the matrícula. Manuel Hernández, the protagonist of the graphic history, is featured in these intervening pages. Juana Julia briefly interrupts his story at the bottom of a page that depicts how peasants were forced by landowners to serve as cannon fodder in the War of the Thousand Days at the turn of the twentieth century (1985: 56). After the campesino conscripts limp back from the battlefields, they are subjected once again to the debt-peonage system. Juana Julia firmly warns her readers to take note of the terratenientes' subterfuges. She recounts how the landowners evaded burgeoning peasant protest by distracting them with *corralejas*, or bullfighting festivals (cf. AP 26: 30). It was at one of the first corralejas held in Córdoba that Hernández reputedly learned of his wife's infidelities, leading ultimately to his skirmish with hacendado Lacharme. The graphic history ends with a panel depicting a 1921 demonstration of the Sociedad de Obreros and the Sociedad de Obreras celebrating the abolition of the matrícula, followed by a list of the places where peasants successfully organized over the mid-twentieth century. Juana Julia bids her readers farewell on the last page of the comic with another page-long discourse cautioning them not to give up hope in the face of the death of El Boche. She warns that the struggle will take decades and that some heroes, like Manuel Hernández, will fall, but the organized peasantry must persist, united against its oppressors (1985: 64).

Juana Julia's role in *El Boche* is twofold. Unmistakably, she binds a hidden history to the present of ANUC in her opening and closing discourses, but she also functions as a vehicle for moving between the plot and a broader interpretation of historical process. This is most clear when she intervenes in the panels themselves as someone who can insert Manuel Hernández's experience into the history of peasant migration, the dispossession of their lands at the hands of the hacendados, and their subjugation under the matrícula. This is an example of critical recovery, whereby peasants are ushered into an abstract and wide-ranging analysis of their circumstances to contextualize their political participation in the present. (It is also what Fals does in Channel B of *Historia doble*.)

Juana Julia's positioning in *Retorno* is very similar to her role in *El Boche*. Fals dedicates an early chapter to discerning the ability of a late seventeenth-century Spanish noblewoman, doña Francisca Baptista de Bohórquez, to amass extensive landholdings and harness Native labor to work them (HDC IV: chap. 4A). It is not by accident that Fals backtracks to the colonial period in the last volume of his history, which ostensibly focuses on the twentieth century. Doña Francisca presents a point of departure for a diverse series of vignettes depicting women as major protagonists of Costeño popular history over the centuries. The Spanish noblewoman is juxtaposed to Gilma Gómez, a twentieth-century campesina leader from Chuchurubí, near Cereté (HDC IV: 31A–32A), and to Bernabela Reondo, the *cacica* (female leader) of the Zenú community of San Andrés de Sotavento (HDC IV: 25A–26A), whose photo appears in Channel B (HDC IV: 25B). The three female protagonists come together in Juana Julia's first monologue in *Retorno*, where she reacts to a question regarding the prominence of women in the history of Córdoba and Sucre:

> "It had to be a woman," explained another champion of the people, the half-mulatta from Corozal Juana Julia Guzmán. . . . "In this machista paradise that is the Coast, we women are stronger than you might think. Look at Gilma and the other compañeras who fight for the land, shoulder-to-shoulder with their husbands. Although the so-called men won't admit it, without us they'll never make the revolution!" (HDC IV: 32A)

In later pages, Fals brings to life socialist firebrand María Cano (HDC IV: 144A, 147A) and reminds readers of Felicita Campos, the protagonist of Chalarka's comic about San Onofre (HDC IV: 158A–161A). He reminisces about María Barilla (HDC IV: 131A–139A), a dancer whose likeness graces the cover of the first edition of *Retorno*, reproducing a portrait originally commissioned by Fals from the Sincelejo painter Wilfredo Ortega (CDRBR/M, CF, 2237); the portrait was later rendered as a statue that stands on the Montería waterfront. Fals identifies Barilla as a socialist activist, although others have repeatedly told me that she wasn't; this was a case in which Fals took imputation a step too far, mistakenly interpreting popular culture as inherently antiestablishment (Archila 1986: 109). He then proceeds to supplement the story of Tinajones with a female protagonist, Petrona Barroso, whom he met in Lorica in the late 1970s, well after the Fundación published the two versions of *Tinajones*. Barroso's voice is incorporated into Fals's narrative, where he lauds her not only as a Catholic mystic but also as a political leader (HDC IV: 152A–154A).

The juxtaposition of all these female actors underscores a trope that runs through the pages of *Retorno*, in which women are among the book's major protagonists and some of Fals's most often quoted interlocutors. He asserts that women display particular forms of independence throughout Costeño history and that it is the *female* ethos that has historically fostered resistance, from the pre-Columbian period to the present. One could say that Fals takes Juana Julia's "It had to be a woman" and, following her lead, transforms it into a conceptualization of the historical process, with Juana Julia at its center. After Fals introduces her in his chapter on the colonial conquistadora, she crops up again and again, punctuating his narrative and directing him toward his narrative goals. When he describes how displaced indigenous and mestizo peasants colonized the Sinú Valley in the nineteenth century, she is held up as representative of this emerging rural class (HDC IV: 108*), filling the same function as she does in her role as narrator in *El Boche* by taking a local experience and reconceptualizing it as part of a regional historical process. A lengthy description of the establishment of socialist organizations in early twentieth-century Montería revolves around Juana Julia and her partner-in-struggle Vicente Adamo (HDC IV: 140A–153A).

Juana Julia's voice is an essential facet of *Retorno*'s rendition of the mid-twentieth-century experience of La Violencia in Córdoba. Fals highlights the violent attacks on Lomagrande as emblematic of this horrific period in Colombian history, when large landowners took advantage of interparty strife to divest peasants of their lands (HDC IV: 164–165*). The concluding chapter of *Retorno*, "Rebuilding the Ant-Hills," appropriates Juana Julia's metaphor of ANUC as an army of ants that surges, relentlessly, across the countryside (HDC IV: chap. 9*). Readers are reminded of her contributions to the peasant struggle in the conclusion to the volume (HDC IV: 205*), emphasizing yet again the central role of women in the history of the coast (HDC IV: 207*). Ultimately, Fals confesses that he only comprehended how to frame campesino history as a political tool with the help of Juana Julia (HDC IV: 180A).

It is almost as though Juana Julia Guzmán were the driving force behind *Retorno a la tierra*, she is so key to the unfolding of its narrative. She is Fals's muse, a living memory whose voice guides the narrative in the same way that her visage permeates *El Boche*. Ernesto Parra concludes that the ANUC–Fundación del Caribe agrarian history project only became a reality once Juana Julia agreed to be interviewed and introduced Fals to multiple storytellers, who took turns sharing their reminiscences with him (Parra Escobar 1983: 138–139). Fals reflects with hindsight on her significance in an article published in the late 1980s:

Juana Julia held the key to the critical, untapped historical knowledge of those years. She had not wanted to share it with local conservative or liberal politicians who constantly urged her to tell her story. She only relented when she saw that her own class had re-emerged in the peasant movement which had inspired her in her youth and took part herself in the new struggle, attending meetings and assemblies along with the others. Juana Julia's presence in the peasant meetings was like seeing history in the flesh. In these special circumstances her word carried the additional magic of real experience and the weight of the exciting experiment which had defeated the land-owners of the coast for the first time. In the same way, it can be said that the rediscovery of Juana Julia (and other contemporary figures) was one of the ideological factors which most stimulated the struggle for land between 1970 and 1976 in Córdoba. (Fals Borda 1987a: 340–341)

It is not only Juana Julia's narrative voice that drives *Retorno a la tierra*. She fiercely spurred her fellow campesinos to action. She was an active member of the Centro Popular de Estudios, the ANUC-sponsored organization that collaborated with the Fundación del Caribe to produce the graphic histories (AP 30: 31). She was not Fals's "principal informant" in the standard anthropological sense of a key community member who mentors the researcher and shares crucial information with him, oftentimes playing a prominent role in the ethnographic monograph (Casagrande 1960). Juana Julia's memories were certainly decisive in the Fundación's research, but even more significant was her political impact: how she incarnated the past in the present by virtue of her mere presence at meetings and her political and intellectual interventions, which influenced ANUC's political choices, particularly in La Antioqueña.

There is a sedimentation going on here of the political discussions in which Juana Julia participated and the process of critical recovery whereby her narrative was fashioned into a political argument. She shared important lessons with her comrades through her public speeches, culminating in the creation of the baluartes she championed on the occupied lands of La Antioqueña. Her ideas would be condensed into *Alternativa* columns and history texts intended for peasant leaders. Subsequently, these writings made their way into *Historia doble*. This is not so much an example of an individual scholar, Fals Borda, paying heed to the words of his main informant as it is an example of a process of co-analysis whose conclusions are recorded and encoded in various media in tandem with their implementation as political tools, a merging of theory and practice.

Comics Panels and Historical Vignettes

Bergquist surmises that the Fundación's graphic histories should be considered a missing third channel of *Historia doble* (1990: 160), but the comics are very much present in *Retorno a la tierra*, their visual contents sometimes reproduced verbatim and sometimes recast in literary form. Chalarka's panels provide a space in which the process of critical recovery is transformed into a pedagogical tool. It is no surprise, then, that his portraits of some of the main protagonists of the graphic histories—Manuel Hernández, "El Boche" (HDC IV: 120B), Alberto Licona of Tinajones (HDC IV: 154B), and Felicita Campos (HDC IV: 159B)—are reproduced in Channel B. They are not mere illustrations occupying unused space but represent carefully thought-out abstractions of campesino history in a text whose narrative channel is crafted out of a series of vignettes, akin to the panels of the graphic histories. So much for the criticism that Fals filled Channel B with images for lack of enough to write!

All four of the graphic histories appear in Channel A as verbal sketches, some more lengthy than others. Fals's literary rendition of their story lines follows the comics panels so closely that these segments of Channel A might be interpreted as ekphrastic versions of Ulianov Chalarka's drawings, verbal narrative descriptions of visual images. For example, Manuel Hernández's arrival at Misiguay (HDC IV: 120A) is described just as the comic portrays him meeting with the overseer (Chalarka 1985: 53). Fals visualizes the work of Hernández cutting lumber and his wife's labor as a washerwoman (HDC IV: 120A) much like Chalarka renders his two panels depicting the toils of hacienda peons (Chalarka 1985: 54). Both Fals and Chalarka insert images of the stocks into their narratives (HDC IV: 120A; Chalarka 1985: 55) and depict the corraleja at which Hernández discovers that one of the obligations of a matriculado is to allow his social superiors access to his wife's sexual favors (HDC IV: 120A; Chalarka 1985: 57). Likewise, both narrate how Hernández organized the Misiguay workers against debt-peonage (HDC IV: 120A; Chalarka 1985: 58) and the moment at which El Boche flees into the nearby wetlands, to be felled by a bullet whose tip is bitten into the shape of a cross (HDC IV: 121A; Chalarka 1985: 61). Fals cites the comic as one of his historical sources in Channel B (HDC IV: 123B), but *El Boche* is much more than mere source material: it furnishes a frame-by-frame template for his literary rendition of early peasant resistance to the matrícula. The same occurs in *Historia doble*'s recounting of the founding of Lomagrande, which, like the comic, homes in on the 1921 storming of the Baluarte Rojo by the police, the imprisonment of the peasant activists, and the deportation of Vicente Adamo (HDC IV: 147A; Chalarka 1985: 17–21). Likewise, *Retorno* reproduces *Tinajones* in prose (HDC IV: 152A–154A; Chalarka 1985: 33–36). Felicita Campos as a historical actor occupies only a sound bite (HDC IV: 159A), a sentence or two of Fals's text, but the three narrative moments recounting her imprisonment, her voyages to Bogotá, and the death of the evil terrateniente from a strange and disfiguring illness faithfully reproduce Chalarka's comics panels (1985: 72, 74). It is as though Fals were consciously rewriting Chalarka's graphic histories in prose.

But we can go deeper than that. The comics function as more than sources, or even outlines, for *Retorno*. They also drive the narrative of several chapters of Channel A that touch on historical events Fals learned about after he left Córdoba. The stories he collected during his subsequent research in Bolívar fall into patterns determined by the comics. This is most evident in Fals's use of *Lomagrande* and *Tinajones* to frame his description of activism in Loba. Much of the material of the first three volumes was researched in Bolívar after 1974, and a great deal of the action of *Historia doble* takes place in, or is narrated by storytellers from, the Mompox Depression. But when Fals arrives at the last volume of *Historia doble*, whose central theme is peasant activism in the twentieth century, the materials and interviews he collected in Loba no longer occupy a prime position. Instead, they are rearranged so that they accommodate to what he already knew about Córdoba and Sucre, information that had already been encoded into the graphic histories.

For instance, Fals's description of the founding of socialist agrarian societies in Callejas and Canalete and the Baluarte Rojo of Lomagrande all use *Lomagrande* as their major source. His chronicle of their appearance on the political stage opens the door to a recounting of the organization of peasant leagues, defense groups, and other local organizations in the Mompox Depression, highlighting the contributions of campesino leader Francisco J. Serpa, a prominent activist into the 1960s (HDC IV: 149A–152A). Fals collected a series of penetrating interviews about Serpa (CDRBR/M, 0873, 0874, 0875); he had enough material so that his narrative of campesino resistance in Bolívar could have stood on its own. Nonetheless, *Lomagrande* stands as the entry point to Serpa's story, the latter conforming to the plotting established by the events that took place at the Baluarte Rojo. Serpa's organizing efforts are presented as yet another example of the tenacity of Costeño peasants, their strong communitarian and antiestablishment leanings, first expressed in the 1920s at Lomagrande.

Cursillos and Cartillas

Even before he began to write *Historia doble*, Fals recognized the fruitfulness of his strategy of sedimenting activist documents and accomplishments in a rewritten format. He began layering his writings in the mid-1970s as he meditated on where he would take activist research after leaving ANUC. In the prologue to his 1975 *Historia de la cuestión agraria en Colombia* (henceforth, *Cuestión agraria*) he informs readers that his synthetic history was collectively authored at cursillos:

> This book is not simply the result of library research, nor is it the exclusive creation of a writer who enjoyed the privilege of knowing everything and having a monopoly of access to the available sources. It represents an effort that was sustained and coordinated by groups in various regions of the country, made up of peasants and intellectuals who participated with the undersigned in the design of the study, they discussed the manuscript with him at various stages and occasions, they contributed concrete facts to correct and enrich the text, and they oriented political or group action, when necessary, following the resulting analysis. For this reason, this book can in good measure be considered a collective product to which those of us interested in better knowing Colombian reality have contributed, [and] are driven by the urgency of acting upon this reality to advance the revolutionary process in our society. (Fals Borda 1975: vi)

The basic contours of *Cuestión agraria* emerged, more specifically, out of a 1973 cursillo held in a rural hamlet in Sucre, at which campesino participants analyzed ANUC's land struggle in light of regional agrarian history (1975: vii). Before the manuscript was published as a book, excerpts appeared in *Alternativa* and *Alternativa del Pueblo*, two magazines that were intended to serve as organs for disseminating the voice of social movements and which were sometimes read at cursillos (fig. 6.2).

The sedimentation of the magazine columns in *Cuestión agraria* reflects Fals's long-term research strategy of complementing activism with reflection in an alternating cycle. I have identified five columns in *Alternativa* that resemble parts of *Cuestión agraria* (and may be first attempts at organizing his historical narrative) and fourteen columns in *Alternativa del Pueblo* that replicate the book's chapters.[1] The following year, Fals wrote *Capitalismo, hacienda y poblamiento* (henceforth, *Capitalismo*; Fals Borda 1976), a volume that is structured similarly to *Cuestión agraria* but concentrates specifically on the Caribbean coast. Ultimately, the structure of the argument Fals articulated in

Figure 6.2   Montería cursillo, with man holding an issue of *Alternativa* (CDRBR/M, CF, 1400). Photo reprinted with permission of the Centro de Documentación Regional "Orlando Fals Borda," Banco de la República, Montería)

these publications would determine the historical metanarrative in *Historia doble*, now recast in an experimental format that foregrounds the process of co-analysis that preceded it.

The two relatively short volumes—*Cuestión agraria* is 160 pages in length and *Capitalismo* has only seventy pages—were written for peasant and working-class reading publics. Fals explains his choice of audience in the preface to *Cuestión agraria*: "The objective was—and continues to be—to provide global and methodical information about the national agrarian problem, directed principally at the training of cadres from the popular classes" (1975: vii). Books like these helped to initiate campesino intellectuals into a culture of reading. For example, an endnote informs readers how to navigate the bibliographic references contained in the volume, since it was not taken for granted that the audience was cognizant of academic conventions (1975: vii). Marginal entries highlight the themes of paragraphs or groups of paragraphs, directing readers' attention to key concepts (use value, superstructure, exchange, and so on), as do some school textbooks. Selected paragraphs are emphasized in italics to foreground the arguments detailed in the chapters, guiding readers in the process of analyzing historical events and then distancing readers from the specificities of historical experience to consider the broader historical processes at play. These publications might be thought of as intermediate steps in a process that began with cursillos and ended over a decade later with *Retorno*. A comparative look at the entire progression indicates that Fals intended that the contents of *Historia doble* reiterate and expand on these previous activities and publications.

The contents of both of the history textbooks (which I will call by their Spanish name, *cartillas*) were first presented at cursillos sponsored by the Fundación del Caribe in Sucre (Fals Borda 1975: vii; 1976: 5-6). I haven't been able to identify Fals's notes for these particular cursillos, but I discovered an undated outline of a workshop that more or less reproduces the general organization of the texts (CDRBR/M, 2190). The notes bear the title "peasant struggles." The categories around which Fals's lecture is organized move from a structural analysis of indigenous populations in the pre-Columbian era to resistance to Spanish rule by Native peoples and African slaves. The lecture notes narrate the process of capitalist expansion by highlighting hegemonic actors, such as the generals commanding troops during nineteenth-century civil wars or the owners of haciendas, and the forces of resistance from below, including mid-nineteenth-century artisans and guerrillas, twentieth-century socialist peasant leaders, and the organizations advocating agrarian reform in the years leading up to the formation of ANUC. The cartillas embed these topics in a narrative organized by modes of production; the lecture notes nod to the same template with their repeated references to class struggle.

The magazine columns and *Capitalismo* build upon the Fundación's tendency to privilege visual media for a semiliterate campesino audience. The history of the 14,000-hectare Mundo Nuevo hacienda—which was an object of ANUC land occupations in 1972 and merits its own dossier in Fals Borda's archives (CDRBR/M, 0271-0272)—was published in the second issue of *Alternativa* (Alt 2: 30-31). Here, Fals focuses on the introduction of cattle raising in the mid-nineteenth century, but he frames his account with a striking image of the 22 November 1973 assassination of ANUC leader Ismael Vertel (sometimes spelled Bertel), who died next to the barbed-wire fence enclosing the latifundio. Fals reminds us that barbed wire was a technology that opened the way for cattle to replace peons in the savannas of Córdoba and Sucre. The layering of previous texts and narrative techniques is evident here. Vertel's story is crafted into a testimonial piece by David Sánchez Juliao, a Lorica native and Fundación researcher who first circulated his chronicles as cassette recordings that he called a "radio program" for campesino communities (Sánchez Juliao 1975: 35-71). The *Alternativa* column is illustrated with portraits of the peasant leaders whose histories were resuscitated in Ulianov Chalarka's comics: El Boche, Vicente Adamo, Juana Julia Guzmán, and Alberto Licona. Past and present are juxtaposed through the presence of these campesino heroes, just as they are in the graphic histories.

From Cartillas to *Historia doble*

The structure and themes of *Cuestión agraria* and *Capitalismo* are comparable to Channel B of *Historia doble* insofar as they take a step back from the personal narratives Fals collected over his decade on the coast to cast a wider geographic net and to synthesize and conceptualize historical process. *Historia doble* amplifies the thematic structure of the cartillas with further archival and bibliographic research. It is a much more scholarly work than the cartillas, which are largely based on published sources and on Fundación publications. *Historia doble* relies much more heavily on Fals's explorations in archives and private collections, as well as focusing more pointedly on the oral narratives of local knowledge bearers. Fals dedicates more space here than he does in the cartillas to vignettes about particular places and historical actors. Unlike the cartillas, which are highly synthetic, Channel B of *Retorno* purposefully enters into dialogue with the personal experiences of narrators in Channel A. A detailed comparison of the cartillas with Channel B and a subsequent tracing out of the myriad dialogues that interweave the two channels of *Historia doble* would be somewhat cumbersome and long-winded. Instead, I will focus on a single chapter of *Retorno* to demonstrate how the earlier publications of the Fundación and La Rosca made their way into Fals's final text.

Chapter 5 of *Retorno* centers on the destruction provoked by late nineteenth- and early twentieth-century agrarian capitalism. Fals explains the nature of the enclave economies established by foreign investment in the Sinú in Channel B. The introduction of foreign investment in lumber, bananas, mining, and a host of other industries led to the proletarianization of the workforce and the introduction of the matrícula, as campesino settlers abandoned their properties to make way for the establishment of latifundia that originally were in the hands of foreign companies and a small number of local elites and subsequently sold to wealthy investors from the neighboring department of Antioquia (HDC IV: 112B–119B). Centers of economic influence like the riverine port of Lorica lost their sway as commerce moved to Montería (HDC IV 119B–127B). Fals draws here on chapters 6 and 7 of *Cuestión agraria*, as well as on chapter 4 of *Capitalismo*, but he declines to confine his analysis to Channel B. Instead, Channel B enters into conversation with Channel A, which contains vivid accounts of the exploits of individual investors who came to control regional politics, men he calls the "regional wizards" (HDC IV: 117A–118A).

Fals dedicates considerable space in Channel B of this chapter to the changing modes of control of the rural workforce, which included not only the matrícula but also other arrangements (HDC IV: 121B–125B). Basing himself on chapter 7 of *Cuestión agraria*, he illustrates how previous labor arrangements were redefined to sustain capitalist development, so that formerly cooperative types of wage labor gave way to more exploitative ones. Fals's systematic description is placed in dialogue with the story of El Boche in Channel A (HDC IV: 120A–122A), his major source being Ulianov Chalarka's comic. The story of Manuel Hernández as it is presented in the graphic history diverges, of course, from the accounts of other authors. In *Retorno* the reworked narrative is presented as historical fact and serves as the gateway into Fals's exposition of subsequent socialist organizing in the region.

It would be too simplistic, however, to conclude that Channel A sediments Costeño narratives while Channel B layers the contents of the cartillas. Certainly, that is partially the case, since Fals expands on and refocuses the thematic content with his synthetic analysis in Channel B. But materials from *Cuestión agraria* and *Capitalismo* are also relocated into Channel A, such as the founding of certain well-known haciendas. I would venture to guess that Fals's strategy of situating some of his vignettes in Channel A and his global interpretation in Channel B is meant to evoke the conversations at cursillos, which drew on local experience to construct a regional history. These exchanges were erased from the cartillas, which take a step back from the everyday lives and memories of the campesinos who participated in the workshops, so in them we only observe one half of the dialogue. Fals reincorporates the other side of the conversation into *Retorno* by plotting the process of critical recovery that took place in these workshops and in study groups in Bolívar, sometimes bringing inimitable local voices to the fore and sometimes submerging them into a more abstract discourse.

Fals Borda's Diary

After reading the four volumes of *Historia doble*, which weave together campesino narratives with Fals's historical synthesis, I was confused when I arrived at chapter 8A of *Retorno a la tierra*. Fals Borda's personal archives contain myriad interviews with campesinos and texts authored by ANUC cadres, but they are all reduced to background material in the only chapter he dedicates to ANUC. Here, the narrative is explicitly dominated by the sociologist. Instead of reproducing his extensive conversations with leaders like Moisés Banquett, Clovis Flórez, or Alfonso Salgado, the rise of ANUC is narrated through

Fals's field diary, making him, and not the ANUC leaders he accompanied, the narrator (Pernett 2015). His portrayal of external researchers as major protagonists carries over into chapter 8B. After analyzing the implementation of government agrarian policy in 1970s Córdoba and Sucre, Fals turns to an evaluation of the work of La Rosca. In effect, the two voices that are juxtaposed in this chapter are both Fals's, first as a participant and then as an external observer.

I puzzled for a long time over why, given his unprecedented access to campesino interlocutors, Fals would privilege his own voice in a chapter that crowns the four volumes with a distinctly utopian climax. If ANUC is heir to the heroes he anoints in its pages, why is he the most important character in its final act? I recalled my conversations with Alfredo Molano, who repeatedly asserted that the problem with *Historia doble* is that Fals *did not* compose it in the first person, that he was unable to "inhabit" his narrators; thus, we don't feel what his narrators experience but instead gain access to their insights on an intellectual level through the reproduction of his conversations with them. But now, unlike all the other chapters of *Historia doble*, in which he avoids using the first person, the very last chapter assumes the perspective of the author: not peasant reminiscences but Fals's autobiographical voice is seized upon as eyewitness to the apogee of ANUC.

This was not by accident. *Historia doble* is not only a campesino-inspired history of the Caribbean coast. It also invites readers to look over Fals's shoulder as he engages in action research; thus it is a variation on the field narrative. Until the final chapter of *Retorno* he is a supporting actor, although he is unmistakably present throughout the four volumes as the instigator of conversations in Channel A and as the academic lecturer, albeit ever attentive to his campesino interlocutors, in Channel B. As I have already described in this chapter, *Mompox y Loba*, the first volume of *Historia doble*, opens with an account of how Fals and a group of activists from San Martín de Loba, Bolívar, founded a study group to advocate for the establishment of a new Colombian administrative department, the Departamento del Río (HDC I: part 1, chap. 1A); in Channel B he explores the general characteristics of the regional culture (HDC I: 21B) and the notion of region itself (HDC I: 16B–26B). Fals closes the final volume, *Retorno a la tierra*, with a two-channeled assessment of the work of La Rosca (HDC IV: chaps. 8A and 8B). Consequently, the four volumes of *Historia doble*, whose experimental format embodies a dialogue between campesino knowledge and social science, are bookended by Fals's methodological project, in which he is the main protagonist. He thereby turns a regional history into a space for documenting his innovative methodology. For this reason, at the end of *Retorno a la tierra*, he goes it alone instead of reconstructing his conversations with his campesino allies.

The first paragraph of chapter 8A, "El destello de la ANUC" ["The Spark Ignited by ANUC"], explains why Fals appropriated the literary genre of the field diary to document ANUC's intense organizing drive:

> From my field notes and archive, with some necessary explanations, I take extracts of events that occurred between 1972 and 1974 and information on subsequent events. In this way we will have a picture, based on the very grassroots work of that intense process of organizing, conflict, and disintegration of the struggle for land that characterized the emergence of the National Association of Peasant Users (ANUC) in Colombian history and society, constituting the largest mass movement of this century in the country. It also gives an idea of the role that some engaged intellectuals played, especially in the departments of Córdoba, Sucre and Bolívar, where the peasant movement presented a resolute vanguard. (HDC IV: 170A)

A close comparison of chapter 8A with Fals's personal archive confirms that this portion of *Retorno* is a re-elaboration of his field notes, not a series of extracts from those diaries. The rewritten diary reproduces some quotations from the archival source (CDRBR/M, 0396, fol. 2237), but they have been radically rearranged. Fals's field notebook compiles a great deal of organizational information, mostly undated and organized topically. He also used his notes as a space to record discussions and debates taking place among the ANUC-Córdoba leadership. His diary is rounded out by facts and figures detailing who participated in the occupations of La Antioqueña and Mundo Nuevo and how they were organized, descriptions of the atmosphere among the occupiers, lists of supporting organizations, and some of the tactics used by large landowners to diffuse campesino dissent. The diary, as it appears in chapter 8A, transforms the notebook into a narrative. It tells a story that flows from one event to the next, and in each episode Fals observes the activities of the occupiers and participates in planning meetings, documenting along the way the founding of the Fundación del Caribe, the production of the graphic histories, and the proceedings of cursillos.

Fals's rendering of his field notes in *Retorno* is noticeably more didactic than the original diary. Take, for example, his description of a 20 October cursillo in Arroyón:

> *20 October.* First cursillo for campesino cadres in Arroyón, with the participation of teachers from the PCML, who expressed their agreement

with the program we are carrying out. It was organized by the new leadership of Arroyón, Alberto Guerra and Ismael Bertel. We began by singing "El Turbión."[2] We break with the official definition of "usuario" ["user"] (of State services), upon which the movement was founded, to suggest something else [that is] more ours: usuario is he who works with the rank and file and "gives use" to vital elements (his house, his money, his burro, his machete, his profession). We also redefined the rich as subversives, because they want to maintain an exploited class. We discussed concrete problems of the organization and the leadership, with the expectation of rationalizing and resolving them. We justified the land occupations as the right to work, to live our lives, and against hunger. We suggested that wives and women be mentored, so that they join in the struggle alongside their husbands (there were no women at this cursillo). At the end of the working day a dance was organized with a sound-system at the house of the town sheriff, which we all went to. Afterwards, repose in our hammocks. United in struggle, we will triumph! (HDC IV: 181A)

This is an indisputably literary adaptation of Fals's undated notes from a cursillo held at Arroyón. The workshop notes are organized into agenda points that lack further explanations of their contents (CDRBR/M, 1922) and closely follow the Fundación's cursillo manual (Centro Popular de Estudios 1972), in contrast to the vivid descriptions in the book passage. What leads me to correlate these cursillo notes with the *Historia doble* passage is an entry on the second page of the field notes that lists particular problems voiced by local participants, especially how to engage women in the struggle (CDRBR/M, 1922, fol. 10248, p. 2r).

Fals demonstrably supplemented the agenda stored in his personal archive with his memory—his "head notes"—and creative imagination to construct a teachable moment that opens a unique window into how cursillos connected external collaborators and ANUC leaders with the campesino rank and file. The passage from *Retorno* cogently illustrates how complex ideologies encoded in movement documents were made explicit and accessible to empower and inspire a neophyte audience that had only just begun to participate in the land struggle. Fals's reminiscence seizes on the name of the organization—the National Association of Peasant Users—which was bequeathed when ANUC was founded as a government-sponsored association, and imbues it with a new purpose. No longer would "users" be clients, which is the usual meaning of the term, but would, instead, collectively appropriate the use value of their tools, their bodies, and the land to drive off the landlords who had suffocated them for decades. Channel A of Fals's description of the rise of ANUC imparts an inspirational and educational story, meant to be emulated, a worthy capstone for the four volumes.

Chapter 8B initiates readers into the historical context needed to make sense of the field diary. In particular, Fals reminds his audience that the Colombian government used Sucre as a showcase for the government-sponsored peasant organization and for the launching of the agrarian reform on the Caribbean coast. He traces how campesinos subsequently became disenchanted with an official project that never seemed to achieve its lofty goals, leading to the founding of ANUC-Línea Sincelejo, which advocated radical revolutionary change instead of mere reform (HDC IV: 170B–186B). *Cuestión agraria* recounts the same developments (Fals Borda 1976: 126–130), although the *Retorno* version concentrates on their impact in Bolívar, Córdoba, and especially Sucre, allowing Fals to draw a parallel between the direct action of Channel A and the historical interpretations of Channel B. His pairing of a semi-fictional field diary with a history of the Línea Sincelejo accomplishes objectives similar to those he reaches in other chapters: he draws on personal experience—this time, his own experience—and reframes it as historical process. The second half of the chapter enters into a methodological dialogue with Channel A through a self-critical reflection on the work of La Rosca in Córdoba (HDC IV: 188B–193B). Just as the narrative of ANUC is presented as an inspiring model for future social movements, so is the story of action research.

Action research, as La Rosca conceived it, was a "science of and in the service of the people." The asymmetrical relationships traditionally established by researchers would be broken down through participation, political commitment, and empathy. At the end of *Historia doble* Fals ponders whether the researchers caught up by the events recounted in Channel A "tended to adjust their sociological writings, such as the graphic histories . . . to the perceptions that the people had of their own situation, and thus produce immediate [not sufficiently analytical] work" (HDC IV: 192B). In other words, he confesses that the team lost sight of the possible consequences of its actions and those of its subjects, thus limiting its success and impeding the evolution of its nascent methodology. Fals concludes by reminding his readers that "transcending existing ideology when defining the research problem and disputing it when presenting the results is, therefore, the fate of the engaged researcher" (HDC IV: 192B). The bridges he aspired to build between scientific practice and other forms of knowledge would necessarily have to transcend usual scientific knowledge if they were to be effective, but in order to achieve this, researchers would also have to move beyond the immediate needs of the grass roots. Thus, *Historia doble* closes with a call for others to take up the task where La Rosca and the Fundación del Caribe left off. He needs to close the four volumes not with the story of ANUC but with the story of action research, because by the mid-1980s the peasant movement had lost its momentum, but action research had caught the attention of researchers worldwide. This is another reason Fals is the main protagonist of the end of the book.

Conclusion

A close reading of *Historia doble* requires much more than the single chapter I dedicate to the topic in this book. I leave the task to other researchers of moving beyond a narrow focus on Fals's work in Córdoba and Sucre to inquire into the decade of research in Bolívar that encompasses the bulk of the first three volumes, engaging a close comparison between the book and Fals's personal archive (Arrieta 2015; McRae 2015; Robles Lomeli 2015, 2019). My purpose here has been more specific, dwelling in particular on how Fals narrates his research process in the early 1970s. *Retorno a la tierra* is a retrospective staging of one of the first large-scale applications of participatory action research. In it, Fals uses his empirically informed imagination to hold actors and events in a creative tension, juxtaposing their voices to a theoretical and historiographic assessment of Costeño history. *Historia doble* is an attempt at "performing" action research. The reader, forced to be an active participant, enters into an empathetic engagement with the methodology and with the history it narrates.

I have spent the great part of this book dwelling on particular features of Fals and the Fundación del Caribe's research practice during the first three years of his sojourn on the coast, concentrating especially on their graphic histories as an ethnographic window into the techniques they used and their general philosophy. From there, I cautiously branched out to look at other venues of participation, namely, the cursillos and the cartillas. An appreciation of the Fundación's craft has afforded me tools for reading *Historia doble* as a unique rendition of the research process. Nonetheless, the experience Fals records is not entirely replicable in the twenty-first century, given that his historical context is so different from today's. The full-time commitment of participatory-action researchers is not as feasible for lack of funding and the exigencies of the institutions in which they work; in addition, with the advent of the paramilitary at the turn of this century, the situation became considerably more dangerous for politically committed researchers and for grassroots activists. Moreover, in the ensuing forty years since the Fundación's work with ANUC, collaborative and participatory research methods have matured, as have social movements, whose schooled leaders are just as likely to engage in research themselves as to relegate it to outsiders. In my concluding chapter I meditate on what today's participatory researchers can glean from Fals Borda's and the Fundación del Caribe's experiences.

7

FALS BORDA'S LEGACY

Orlando Fals Borda would engage in many evaluative dialogues in the years following the shuttering of La Rosca. Especially notable was the 1977 World Symposium on Action-Research and Scientific Analysis, at which participatory researchers from five continents came together in Cartagena to evaluate the evolution of what they would come to call "participatory action research," or PAR (Simposio Mundial de Cartagena 1978). Fals and his Bangladeshi coauthor, Muhammad Anisur Rahman, reflect in retrospect on what was achieved in Cartagena: "We started to understand PAR not merely as a methodology of research with the subject/subject relationship evolving in symmetrical, horizontal or non-exploitative patterns in social, economic and political life. We saw it also as a part of social activism with an ideological and spiritual commitment to promote people's (collective) praxis" (Rahman and Fals Borda 1991: 25). The success of action research would be measured not only by its ability to reconfigure the research relationship, they argued, but by the contribution it makes to activist projects. Activism is, of course, a component of theory building, since PAR entwines theory and political practice in a productive dialogue.

My final chapter takes the results of my research to a series of Colombian grassroots organizations practicing PAR, with whom I met in 2018 in a series of workshops in which we evaluated the extent to which Fals's experiences in Córdoba in the 1970s are still relevant for today's activist researchers. Following the recommendation by

PAR advocates that academics share our research with the wider community (Osorio Sánchez 2017), I hoped to discover what these researcher activists, who also have at their disposal an array of approaches developed since the time of La Rosca by collaborative ethnographers and radical pedagogues, see as Fals's continuing contribution to their mission as activists and their craft as researchers. Certainly, one of my intentions behind organizing these workshops was to foreground the notion of critical recovery in our conversations. In fact, although I cannot claim to have consistently used PAR methodologies in the course of my project—I was not allied with an organization or social movement, and with the exception of the workshops, I worked alone—I explicitly organized our discussions around the idea of the critical recovery of La Rosca's organizing principles. This was a political choice, made in consultation with numerous colleagues engaged in participatory and collaborative projects in different parts of Colombia. The issues that emerged out of the workshops revealed to me that the notion of critical recovery has dropped out of the intellectual tool kits of many of the activists I spoke with and, with some notable exceptions, in many instances PAR has been defined by its practitioners as a collection of techniques rather than as a set of principles. Thus, I hope that the process of and the issues discussed in the workshops may serve as a wake-up call, contributing to the evolution of participatory and collaborative research methodologies by engaging the principle of critical recovery.

Before considering the insights I gleaned from my conversations with contemporary PAR activists, I will trace out the broader contexts in which they are working. After a brief look at how, after the 1970s, action research entered ever-widening spheres of application (while disappearing from the tool kit of ANUC in Córdoba) and at how it has been used in Colombia in particular, I introduce a series of other participatory approaches that interact in the contemporary scene with PAR. This overview sets the stage for the conversations that transpired in the workshops.

The Promise of Participatory Research in the New Millennium

In the four decades since Fals Borda's experiments with action research on the Colombian Atlantic Coast, participatory methodologies have become a mainstay of Latin American social movements and of minority organizing in the global North, with a small but significant academic following in Canada and the United States, particularly in education departments. I will concentrate here on PAR in Colombia in particular, providing only a bird's-eye view of its counterpart in the global North. The more radical currents of PAR in the United States—which Michelle Fine (2017) calls "Critical Participatory Action Research"—have especially flowered in communities of color, among immigrant youth, in schools and in prisons, and in Appalachia, also counting among their proponents community organizers, environmental activists, and health care advocates; they are deeply conscious of questions of race and class, particularly as they compute into educational advantage, gentrification, and the prison-industrial complex; and they immerse communities in powerful research exercises. They trace their methodological genealogies back to Jane Addams, W. E. B. Du Bois, and Myles Horton, among others, and are highly attuned to the methodology's activist potential (Fine 2017: chap. 5; Gaventa 1988; Park et al. 1993). Also included in this group are those participatory researchers based in the global North with considerable experience in Third World settings, some of whom, like Canadian Budd Hall (2005), were close associates of Fals Borda's and participated in the two Cartagena congresses he organized in 1977 and 1997.

Other action researchers based in Europe and to a lesser extent in North America, while politically progressive, have been less closely affiliated with social movements and more concerned with the operation of complex organizations, such as industrial cooperatives, local governments, and universities (Greenwood 1999, 2008; Greenwood and Levin 2007: part 1). This group of researchers was invited to the 1997 congress but, as Greenwood told me in a 2 September 2018 email, Fals was polite but somewhat distant with them, both because he felt they were "insensitive to power and political economy" and because he was largely concerned with the promotion of theory emerging from the global South. Nonetheless, the various applications of PAR in North America and Europe all exist on a common continuum and share core values.

Just as the topography of participatory research is complex in the global North, it is difficult to delimit PAR activities in Latin America. They run the gamut, including groups that expressly identify themselves as participatory practitioners, research collectives that include PAR as one of many approaches in their methodological tool kit, advocates of popular adult education, organizations and consultants who selectively employ participatory techniques within more conventional research frameworks, and collaborative ethnographers—all of whom will come up in the course of this chapter. Correspondingly, it is difficult to define who engages participatory methodologies in Latin America, because PAR is not a set of procedures but a principled stance favoring popular participation in research projects, a revaluing of what Fals called "people's knowledge" to admit the epistemologies of indigenous peoples and African descendants (an approach I will call "alternative epistemologies"), and a commitment to more equal control of the research process. On the whole, PAR has a broader following in Latin America than it has in the global North and is undeniably more closely associated with politically progressive and grassroots movements.

Colombian advocates of participatory research are involved in historical memory work with victims of violence (Osorio Sánchez 2017; Riaño-Alcalá 2006, 2009, 2013), harnessing research to campaigns for environmental justice and land rights (J. Gutiérrez 2016; Negrete Barrera 2008a, 2008b, 2018; Vélez Torres et al. 2012), developing community-generated intercultural curricula (Bolaños et al. 2004), and confronting inequality in urban areas (Naranjo Botero 2018). The Jesuit research institute CINEP, whose use of participatory research techniques in marginal urban communities dates back to the early 1970s (Archila 2013), promotes PAR among youth in urban and rural settings on the Caribbean coast (CINEP 2018) and has collaborated in unearthing local histories of coastal indigenous communities embroiled in environmental disputes with mining companies (Archila Neira 2015). The neoliberal system of privatization of public resources has become an arena for participatory research, as César Abadía and Héctor Ruiz recount in their collaboration with hospital workers in an inventory of the Instituto Materno Infantil, a publicly funded hospital in Bogotá, which, at the time of the research, was slated for closing (Abadía Barrero and Ruiz Sánchez 2018).

The contributions of Orlando Fals Borda and of Paulo Freire are recognized by all of these groups as laying the conceptual, methodological, and political basis for their combination of research with activism. Human rights, environmental, and ethnic activists have drawn on Fals in their appropriation of his notion of participation and the establishment of horizontal or equal relationships between external researchers and community members. Educational activists have seized in particular on Freire's pedagogical methods of raising consciousness by collectively analyzing those concepts that embody their social, political, and economic predicaments, as well as retooling endogenous ideas and practices that could help them to change their circumstances through collective action. The methodologies developed by Fals and Freire complement and enter into dialogue with each other, and in those instances in which activists are not familiar with their writings, the two figures function as icons positioned at the root of the genealogy of radical research methods (Santos 2018: 253–257).

Within the Colombian popular adult education community, which draws its inspiration from Freire, a participatory practice called "systematization" emerged in the late 1980s as an outgrowth of PAR (Cendales G., Mariño S., and Peresson T. 2016). Like PAR, systematization is an incompletely defined set of collaborative procedures for the collection of information and historical analysis aimed at documenting popular education projects. As with PAR, systematization is a collective tool for the critical interpretation of experience, its central objective being stimulating further action (Torres Carrillo 2010: 214). Most commonly, it takes into account the relationships that develop among researchers in the course of the project, in effect privileging process over contents, just as PAR does. In fact, proponents of systematization with whom I have come in contact in the Colombian indigenous movement see it as an approach that can be used in conjunction with PAR. Nonetheless, I have always found it difficult to get a handle on what groups do when they "systematize"— even after having myself participated in a systematization process (Bolaños et al. 2004; Rappaport 2005)—because the procedures vary by context, just as they do in PAR.

Some participatory researchers have also begun to include collaborative ethnography in their methodological tool kit.[1] Collaborative anthropologists, like their PAR counterparts, engage community researchers in a horizontal relationship, in addition to using participatory techniques. Unlike PAR practitioners, many contemporary Latin American collaborative ethnographers tend to limit their interventions to the research sphere, and their work is frequently more explicitly academic. This stands in contrast to Fals and his team, who favored the direct participation of researchers in political activism. Notwithstanding, some Latin American collaborative researchers explicitly see their work as one of political intervention, in which they share academic knowledge with their nonacademic counterparts—Argentine collaborative anthropologist Laura Kropff calls this "critical activism," as opposed to "activist research," emphasizing the activist rather than the research dimension of her practice (2014: 55). Nonindigenous collaborators with indigenous organizations tend in this direction, as well (Rappaport 2005: chap. 2).

Latin American collaborative ethnographers' distancing from activism is a response to the reality that many of the social movements with which they work are sufficiently mature to make their own political decisions and prefer to call on social scientists to fill specific gaps with their expertise, as opposed to serving as general advisors. Moreover, the expansion of opportunities in higher education to popular sectors in Latin America (Mato 2012) has led to a significant layer of indigenous, African descendant, and working-class researchers with academic credentials (Cojtí Cuxil 1997; Comunidad de Historia Mapuche 2012, 2015; Rivera Cusicanqui 2004). These emerging circles of scholars are more likely to engage in epistemological experiments in which local knowledge—especially indigenous knowledge—becomes a space for the generation of theory (Rappaport 2005; Rivera Cusicanqui 2010; Vasco Uribe 2002, 2011; cf. Alonso Bejarano et al. 2019), for confronting the state and corporations (Hale and Millaman Reinao 2018), and for enabling the sort of intercultural academic dialogue that could not have been imagined by the researchers of La Rosca in the 1970s (Casa de Pensamiento n.d.; Leyva Solano 2011; Leyva Solano and Speed 2015; RACCACH 2010). They are informed by explicitly culturalist theories that engage alternative epistemologies to a much greater degree than was the Fundación del Caribe (Guerrero Arias 2010; Santos 2014, 2018; Walsh 2009).

Some collaborative researchers have begun to define what they do by using the term *co-labor* instead of *colaborar* [collaborate], the former roughly translating as "to work in community" (Archila 2015: chap. 4; Leyva Solano and Speed 2015). This usage gives the sensation that external researchers are not "assisting" communities by means of a paternalistic relationship, but are sharing a common intellectual plane in which external and internal researchers work together to build relationships of equality. This is not unusual, as proponents of PAR have emphasized the process of conducting participatory research as being more significant than the results of that research (Reason and Bradbury 2008: 4). Such an attitude toward research makes possible cross-fertilizations across cultures and methodologies.

PAR, Conflict, and Post-Conflict

Participatory and collaborative approaches have become crucial tools for human rights activists in Colombia. According to Human Rights Watch, more than 7.7 million Colombians have been displaced by conflict since 1985 (Human Rights Watch 2018; see also Grupo de Memoria Histórica 2013). The Unit for Victims' Assistance and Restitution counts over 8.5 million victims over the five years of the conflict, including victims of massacres, threats, sexual offenses, enforced disappearances, antipersonnel mines, as well as forced displacement (Amnesty International 2018). The Grupo de Memoria Histórica calculates that the conflict has resulted in 177,307 civilian fatalities and 40,787 fatalities among armed actors, bringing the total dead to over 220,000 between 1985 and 2013 (2013: 32); this figure more or less resembles the number of fatalities in La Violencia of the late 1940s and the 1950s, the period that is commonly identified as the beginning of the Colombian conflict. They also tally 25,007 disappeared; 1,754 victims of sexual violence; 6,421 children recruited by armed groups; 27,023 kidnappings; and 10,189 victims of land mines in this period, and they point to the paramilitary as overwhelmingly responsible as perpetrators of massacres (2013: 32–39). The National Center of Historical Memory (CNMH) collected testimonies and published numerous reports on specific instances of such violations, the most relevant for the Caribbean coast being reports by Becerra Becerra and Rincón García (2017a, 2017b) and Machado and Meertens (2010).[2]

CNMH researchers have frequently employed participatory methodologies, following guidelines established in a handbook authored by anthropologist Pilar Riaño-Alcalá (2009), which offers a series of techniques that she used in her earlier memory work with urban youth in Medellín (Riaño-Alcalá 2006). Riaño's manual is especially directed at members of local communities who aspire to assemble their own reports of human rights violations, suggesting that the sorts of interventions made by external scholars like Fals Borda have in some instances ceded space to entirely local initiatives. Among the tools Riaño includes in her methodological survey is the mapping of human rights violations, instances of resistance to armed conflict, major events in community history, and local chronologies of land tenure and of displacement; she recommends that the maps be drawn collectively at meetings and during visits to sites of local significance (2009: 82–89). Riaño also highlights the technique of compiling time lines of significant events, a kind of a "visual biography" of the community (2009: 90–92); the Fundación also elaborated time lines, but they appear to have been prepared in their Montería office on the basis of the information they collected, as opposed to the participatory exercise encouraged by Riaño. Enlisting more conventional research techniques, Riaño explains in the manual how grassroots researchers might conduct interviews, collect life histories (2009: 99–104), and work with archivos de baúl (2009: 105–108).

None of these techniques is meant to stand on its own. They are intended to be combined into a collective framework in which community members share, listen to, and reflect on accounts of personal experience (2009: 110–112), thus emphasizing process over product; the objective is as much—if not more—that of healing as it is of collecting information. The manual provides a point-by-point agenda so that local leaders can structure their workshops in ways that promote democratic decision-making and dialogue (2009: 113–118). The success of Riaño's manual spurred the Centro Nacional de Memoria Histórica to publish an English-language version of the text (Riaño-Alcalá 2013). To be sure, the use of such techniques does not automatically make a project into PAR. The government Unit for Victims' Assistance and Restitution requires that its investigative staff prepare time lines and engage in social cartography with peasants with an eye to compiling legal evidence for the restitution of land rights (Carmen Ortega, personal communication, 23 June 2018), although the unit is not engaged in PAR and has only appropriated some of its techniques. Many researchers who have adopted Riaño's recommendations assume that by emulating the techniques she describes they are involved in participatory action research. In effect, they confuse technique with method. Tools like time lines or social cartography are techniques, while organizing a project democratically around political or social objectives linked to a grassroots organization is the method. As I am sure Riaño would agree, PAR is more than a set of techniques to be applied by rote but, instead, calls for a rethinking of what research is and how it is carried out. That is the intent of her manual.

Recent Colombian experiences in participatory research resemble the work of the Fundación del Caribe in some respects and diverge from it in others. They are the product of a different historical moment. As Alfredo Molano affirmed two decades ago, political conditions and the nature of research practice have changed radically since the 1970s:

> In Colombia, we have passed from the dictatorship of the bourgeoisie to the struggle for full respect for human rights, or in other words, we have stopped fighting against the State, and are now fighting for it. Before we were concerned with militancy; now, our eyes are on participation. It is as if Action Research had made us more modest. Today we are prepared to accept equality; we are undergoing a far-reaching redefinition of our own relevance. The idea that the people need to be led has fortunately been replaced by the excitement of being among the people and the wonder of its creative ability. Subjectivity has gained ground, and allowed the heart to win some points against the head. (Molano 1998a: 8)

Molano's observations reflect the changing nature of social protest across the globe, with the advent of neoliberal policies that bound popular movements to nongovernmental organizations, and, in the wake of the 1991 constitution, fostered electoral participation in new political parties as an alternative to direct action and dreams of overthrowing the current social order. Correspondingly, today's participatory projects are frequently smaller-scale and more localized than was the Fundación del Caribe's. The limitations of external funding cause their practice to be more episodic than continuous, in contrast to the three years during which the Fundación gave its full-time attention to ANUC. The Latin American academics who engage in participatory research labor in a public university system that denies them many of the basic research tools enjoyed by their North American and European counterparts (Hylton et al. 2018; Kropff 2014: 73–83; see also Greenwood 2008: 333–334), or, if they are affiliated with nongovernmental organizations, they are subject to funding cycles that strictly delimit their participation in communities.

In many respects, as Molano states, today's participatory researchers work within the system—the political system, public education and the university, nongovernmental organizations—in an attempt to reform it, as opposed to overturning it. They are forced to operate in a neoliberal environment in which collaboration is encouraged by the university system, so long as it coincides with institutional goals (Macfarlane 2017). Nongovernmental organizations, compelled to fill in the gaps in services abandoned by the state, must also conform to the dictates of their funders (Ismail and Kamat 2018); participatory research is, in turn, delimited by the sponsoring organization. In these spaces the hegemony of the capitalist system can only be timidly contested. Changing the system from within, as many educational and nongovernmental projects promise, presents substantial pitfalls. Charles Hale and Rosamel Millaman problematize this reformist turn by examining the position of the *indio permitido* [authorized Indian] in the neoliberal landscape. The indio permitido is a category of indigenous actors who operate as Native representatives within the bounds of a system that recognizes and promotes multiculturalism but limits indigenous agency (Hale and Millaman Reinao 2006). As a consequence of their insertion into institutions of power, today's PAR practitioners face different challenges and limitations than did the Fundación del Caribe, whose ultimate objective was to overturn the capitalist system.

Finally, at least in Colombia, participatory researchers frequently take greater risks than did the Fundación del Caribe. Especially during the presidency of Álvaro Uribe Vélez (2002–2010), but again under the current Iván Duque Márquez government, popular protest has met a continuous wall of violent reprisals from both official and informal armed agents. Víctor Negrete once told me that external collaborators frequently had to hide during cursillos because of police raids. If they were apprehended, they might spend a day or so in jail. Nowadays, he opined, they would pay for workshop participation with their lives.[3]

The changing topography of participatory research is also evident in its adoption by institutions that have no intention of replicating its emancipatory ethos. Multilateral lending organizations like the World Bank and similar nationally based institutions like the United States Agency for International Development, as well as administrators in the business world, have appropriated PAR as a means of lending legitimacy to projects aimed at maintaining the status quo (Fals Borda 2001: 31; Jordan 2003). I think, however, that the antipathy toward PAR that grows out of its application by powerful institutions is probably more widespread in the global North than in Colombia, where it has experienced a growing acceptance by grassroots organizations, in universities, and in the human rights community. Moreover, many Latin American PAR practitioners fully comprehend that to take up Fals Borda's legacy in this new landscape is to recognize their obligation to reinvent his methodology. Fals Borda's ideas cannot be applied literally, but must be reinscribed within a new reality.

The Political Legacy of Action Research

While PAR and its methodological outgrowths steadily gained currency over the four decades since the Fundación del Caribe's collaboration with ANUC, the peasant organization that was the focus of early explorations into action research did not enjoy the same trajectory. Perhaps Fals overstated his influence, or was too harsh on himself, when he and Rahman asserted that PAR's success should be gauged by the success of the social movements in which it is applied (Fals Borda and Rahman 1991). The organizations with which La Rosca collaborated experienced different trajectories of rise and decline, irrespective of the advocacy and participation of external researchers. PAR's contribution was only a small part of the story of organizations like ANUC.

Following ANUC's heyday in the first half of the 1970s, political infighting, a growing organizational bureaucracy, and a distancing of the leadership from the rank and file weakened the peasant movement. As I explained in chapter 1, ANUC's capacity for mobilization was also sapped by clashes with leftist political parties and their peasant supporters, as well as by government repression (Rivera Cusicanqui 1982: 154–182; Zamosc 1986b: chap. 9). Fals and his associates certainly attempted to ameliorate these problems, but the issues confronting ANUC were not confined to the Atlantic Coast. Consequently, the success or failure of the peasant movement cannot be attributed to a small group of action researchers working in the department of Córdoba. ANUC slowly began to revive in the 1980s (Celis 2013: chap. 3) but has not approached the zenith it enjoyed in the 1970s. Moreover, campesinos who participated in the land occupations of the 1970s that fueled the remarkable rise of ANUC found their communities irrevocably transformed in the 1990s by paramilitary violence, forced displacement, the expansion of industrial agriculture, environmental degradation, and urban migration. Thus, it would not be fair to gauge Fals's work on the Caribbean coast entirely by its political results, even if this was his original intention.

Nonetheless, the Fundación was relatively successful in the short term at political organizing. Its activists played a significant role in mobilizing the rank and file of the municipality of Montería during ANUC's heyday (Parra Escobar 1983; Rudqvist 1983, 1986). They were enormously successful in harnessing research to political recruitment, particularly thanks to their facilitation of cursillos. We don't know whether the educational materials they produced achieved the influence they hoped they would have, though. When ANUC-Córdoba began to fracture in 1974, the textbooks and graphic histories resulting from action research fell out of circulation; at the height of the factional disputes of 1974, copies of Chalarka's comics held in storage were destroyed by the departmental leadership of ANUC.[4] Notwithstanding, the Fundación left a significant political legacy, with members like Víctor Negrete relentlessly practicing PAR over the following forty years and mentoring a wide range of young activists in Córdoba, Sucre, and Bolívar (Negrete Barrera 2008a, 2008b).

If we move from action research's political impact to its legacy as an activist methodology, the scope for appreciating the work of Fals Borda broadens notably. It may be more productive to evaluate action research through an examination of its relative success in generating a new memoryscape in the regions where it operated in the 1970s. La Rosca's methods were highly effective in the indigenous southwest, where researchers nurtured CRIC, the Regional Indigenous Council of Cauca and other indigenous organizations (Archila and González 2010; Findji 1992; Rappaport 2005: 86–87). Historical investigations conducted by La Rosca members Víctor Daniel Bonilla (1977, 1982) and Gonzalo Castillo Cárdenas (1987) resulted in several highly influential products: a pamphlet-sized biography of the eighteenth-century Nasa hereditary lord don Juan Tama (Bonilla 1977), picture-maps of indigenous history (Bonilla 1982; Barragán León 2016), and the writings of early twentieth-century leader Manuel Quintín Lame (Lame 1971 [1939]). Research into indigenous political strategies of the past shaped CRIC's historical imaginary so profoundly that these figures have become emblematic to the indigenous historical memory, even in regions where they had minimal influence during their lifetimes. It would be a mistake to assume that this success owed to the exceptional talents of Bonilla and Castillo, in comparison to Fals Borda. The three were using broadly similar approaches. There are structural reasons why La Rosca was able to instill a new historical consciousness in indigenous communities but were not as successful with the Costeño peasantry. Native people in Colombia have always paid attention to history because they have depended on colonial documentation to defend their landholdings. As a result, the process of critical recovery was successful in indigenous communities, building on centuries-long institutions and practices of preserving historical memory.

Peasant organizing on the Caribbean coast was considerably more spo-
radic over the twentieth century, never achieving the historical depth or the
continuity of indigenous activism in the southwestern highlands. In addition,
the process of hacienda expansion in the nineteenth and twentieth centuries
was predicated on the continuous migration of campesinos from public lands
in one region to new settlements in another, forcing them to establish and
reestablish communities in new locations as they ceded their lands to larger
agricultural enterprises (LeGrand 1986). In the process, they were denied
the crucial ties to place that are so central to the construction of indigenous
memory (although sometimes, they developed attachments through a distinctive sense of landscape, which was effectively captured by Ulianov Chalarka
in *Tinajones*). Finally, the continuous experience of violent conflict by the
peasants of Córdoba has led some authors to surmise that memories of recent
massacres inhibit the retention of narratives of past conflicts (Machado and
Meertens 2010).

The persistence of memory in a population that has not traditionally co-
alesced around reminiscences of popular struggle presented a major challenge
for the Fundación del Caribe. It is only in the long run that we can discern
the Fundación's influence, as much in the work of today's PAR practitioners
as in the recent adoption by activists of the campesino heroes that Fals and
his associates celebrated. In the course of giving public presentations about my
research, I encountered intense interest in the Fundación's story on the part
of young researcher activists from popular sectors of Montería and Cereté, as
well as from ANUC members. Memories of figures like Juana Julia Guzmán and
Felicita Campos have been nourished in recent years by the ubiquitous reproductions of Ulianov Chalarka's drawings, which one encounters in a plethora of
local and national publications, usually unaccompanied by explanations. Gustavo Petro, the progressive candidate for president in 2018—who is from Cié-
naga de Oro, Córdoba, not far from Montería—revived their memory during
his political campaign in a tweet accompanied by a panoramic view of massive
attendance at one of his speeches in Montería. It reads, in the clipped language
of Twitter, "The Sinú River and its people. The Montería of Juana Julia Guzmán
and of 'El Boche' lives again, of Vicente Adamo. Terror could not overcome
culture. We are for a humane Colombia."[5] This is not the first time that Petro
reminded Costeños of their past. In a 2005 interview, he recalled the stories of
El Boche and of the Baluarte Rojo—which he compressed into a single episode
in which El Boche is described as a protégé of Vicente Adamo (Bonilla 2005: 67).
In the long run, the contributions of Fals and the Fundación have been resuscitated in the struggles of the present, each time taking a new form.

Even the Fundación's failures are a significant facet of its legacy. Their sometimes paternalistic attitude toward the peasant rank and file holds significant lessons for researchers seeking to collaborate with today's communities, who have wider access to information and ideas. The disappointing attempt to reintroduce baluartes into ANUC-occupied haciendas pushes the envelope on the possibilities of, and constraints to, the process of critical recovery. The Fundación's lack of comprehension of the political landscape in which they were operating, particularly with regard to their strained relationship with the Maoist left, points to the need for participatory and collaborative researchers to look beyond the communities with whom they are working and take into account their insertion into the wider political and ideological panorama. It should also move them to evaluate the conflicting and overlapping discourses and organizational practices that are unfolding around them (Martínez 2008). That is to say, embracing the Fundación's legacy requires simultaneous processes of critique and reappropriation. However ragged, limited, unfinished, and conflict-ridden the Fundación's project may have been, its work is "good to think," an inspiration to both scholars and participatory researchers today. I sensed an urgency to this history as I shared my research with Colombian activists.

A Participatory Evaluation

Once the central arguments of my research began to gel, I began to present my findings to academics and activists in Colombia. On one occasion, a member of an indigenous audience asked me to end this book with a chapter reflecting on what today's participatory researchers could learn from the experience of La Rosca and the Fundación del Caribe. It would have been less time-consuming to rely on my own thinking on this matter, but I decided instead to open a dialogue with Colombian organizations involved in participatory research. In June and July 2018, I facilitated eight workshops with community groups, social movements, and academic researchers working in rural and urban areas of the Caribbean coast, the southwest highlands, Bogotá, and Medellín.[6] Among the sponsoring organizations were three institutions with extensive experience in participatory research: CINEP, the Jesuit research institute that pioneered action research in the 1970s; ACIN, the Association of Indigenous Councils of Northern Cauca, an organization with which I have collaborated over the past decade; and the Corporación Con-Vivamos, a community organization in the periphery of the city of Medellín.

The CINEP team was led by researchers who had first been inspired in the 1970s by the Fundación del Caribe's methodology and, particularly, their graphic histories, to engage in similar projects with highland peasants (COPRORCO n.d.). These veterans were joined by younger researchers in the production of community histories from the Caribbean coast (CINEP 2018) and collaborated with indigenous communities confronting extractive industries (Archila 2015). ACIN's Education Program [Tejido de Educación] organized a workshop that brought together experienced Nasa educational activists with external collaborators whose long-standing affiliation with the organization has transformed them into organic intellectuals in an intercultural movement. ACIN is a zonal organization affiliated with CRIC, the Regional Indigenous Council of Cauca, one of the social movements in which La Rosca's researchers inserted themselves in the early 1970s. I also met with a heterogeneous group of neighborhood activists and politically committed academics at the Corporación Con-Vivamos, one of the groups in which Pilar Riaño participated during her study of youth and popular memory in Medellín (Riaño-Alcalá 2006). The Comuna I, where Con-Vivamos is located, was originally a *barrio de invasión* where poor city dwellers and rural migrants occupied the slopes overlooking the city and built precarious structures that, over time, have solidified into an urban neighborhood. Con-Vivamos has played a major role in promoting dialogue within the barrio, as well as with other social sectors, pursuing agendas in popular education and community development, in addition to engaging in PAR as a means of compiling local history.

I organized other workshops, some with audiences that were more cohesive than others. Several of the workshops brought together researchers and activists who had not worked together before: a collection of Medellín academics at a meeting held at the Universidad Nacional, a group of university students and ANUC leaders at the Banco de la República in Montería, health workers of the RedSaludPaz. I worked with a group of high school students in San Pablo (María la Baja), an Afrocolombian village near Cartagena. I was invited to present to the Escuela Nacional Orlando Fals Borda, a space in which young leftist activists meet twice a year for intensive training sessions that highlight research methodology and where they receive mentoring in order to develop their own action-research projects. Students came to the Bogotá meeting from local chapters, like IAPES, which hosted the workshop I facilitated in Popayán, cosponsored by the Autonomous Indigenous Intercultural University (UAIIN), CRIC's indigenous university. IAPES and the Escuela Nacional Orlando Fals Borda are affiliated with a national network of popular organizations called the Congreso de los Pueblos.

In other words, I tapped a diverse set of organizations, some of whose members I was familiar with and others I hadn't met before, a few of them seasoned PAR researchers and many others new to activist methodologies, of different ages and living in various parts of the country. In order to help readers keep them straight, I've included descriptions of the workshop groups in the Cast of Characters at the beginning of this book.

Workshops lasted from two to four hours, attracting between fifteen and fifty participants, including university students and academic researchers, community activists, members of indigenous and peasant associations, and representatives of nongovernmental organizations. After I presented the results of my research, emphasizing how Fals and the Fundación del Caribe carried into practice their notions of participation, critical recovery, and systematic devolution, I requested that participants forgo the usual question-and-answer session to instead consider a series of open-ended questions evaluating the Fundación del Caribe's project in the context of their own activities. I hoped to gauge participants' sense of the similarities and differences between their own PAR practice and action research in the 1970s, paying particular attention to changing research techniques, the relevance of the concept of critical recovery, and the appropriation of multiple activist research methodologies. Most of the workshops resulted in lively dialogue; my interventions were limited to my presentation, responses to some questions and, when requested, a final summation. I did not tape the proceedings but took copious notes, as did many of the participants. The workshop format permitted them to tailor the dialogue to their own organizational objectives, which they understood as overlapping with my goal of incorporating my findings into this book. Workshops are very common components of these organizations' activities, providing a crucial space for collective reflection. Therefore, participants were used to the framework and conscious of the fact that all of us would use the results to our own ends.

I ask myself why these eight organizations or institutions agreed to host these workshops, which deprived their members of an afternoon or an entire day of work, in order to satisfy the needs of a foreign scholar. Granted, I had worked with some of the organizations or was close to colleagues who placed me in contact with them. Most of the groups were aware of the fact that I had conducted collaborative research myself (Bolaños et al. 2004; Rappaport 2005), which may have spurred their interest. But I think that their willingness has much more to do with Fals Borda's legacy than with my own status as a scholar with collaborative inclinations. A reflection on how Fals's methodology worked on the ground would help them to fill in some of the gaps in their own activist genealogies; they intuited that it would enrich their own practice.

This doesn't mean that they hoped to replicate Fals Borda's work. Most of the participating groups do not enjoy the time nor the resources of the Fundación del Caribe, the only exception to this rule being the Tejido de Educación of ACIN, whose activists are engaged full-time in educational planning and, to a greater extent than other organizations, are empowered to adapt their methods to the needs of the moment, independent of the entities that fund them, because the major decision-making body to which they look for guidance is ACIN itself. Even the CINEP team, whose fundamental activity is research, complained that their work was limited by the whims of their funders and by the requirement of strict observance of the calendars imposed by their sponsors.[7]

Consequently, the participatory research that most of the workshop participants had conducted was of a more limited scope than that of the Fundación. Its thematic content ranged from community history to human rights, environmental degradation and extractive industries, and the evaluation of bilingual education projects. Not all of the attendees were experienced researchers. Some of them—particularly those at the Escuela Nacional Orlando Fals Borda (which I will refer to as the Bogotá training seminar), IAPES, and the graduate students who attended the workshop in Montería—had never conducted any prolonged research and were only beginning their careers as activists. They did not all enjoy close relationships with popular movements, a sine qua non for early action researchers (Vío Grossi 1981: 47). Their sparse experience contrasted with the workshops in CINEP, ACIN, and Con-Vivamos, which claimed decades-long experience in activist research and a close association with grassroots organizations.[8] Each of my audiences absorbed my narrative of the Fundación's work in its own way, adjusting it to its particular circumstances.

The seminars took place against a fraught political backdrop. Presidential elections held on 17 June 2018 brought to power Iván Duque Márquez, a conservative politician in the mold (some would say, in the thrall) of former president Álvaro Uribe Vélez. The latter's presidency, which extended from 2002 to 2010, was accompanied by massive human rights violations by the military and its paramilitary allies. Workshop participants expressed concerns that the peace process with the FARC guerrillas, negotiated by President Juan Manuel Santos and signed in 2016, would be truncated with Duque's coming to power. *Convivencia*—the peaceful coexistence of different parties to the conflict—was already straining at the seams due to unbridled attacks by armed right-wing actors against leaders of social movements. (As I make the final touches to my manuscript in March 2020, their fears are being realized, with growing attacks on popular leaders and the cutting of funding for peace initiatives.) In the face of these challenges, workshop participants repeatedly reiterated that Duque's opponent, Gustavo Petro, had earned eight million votes, an unprecedented following for a leftist candidate. They saw this as delivering an opening for progressive forces to press for a continuation of the peace process. PAR could contribute a time-tested methodology to meet such a challenge. As a sociologist from the School of Veterinary Medicine at the Universidad Nacional in Bogotá, who participated in the RedSaludPaz workshop, commented:

> PAR is an accumulation of diverse experiences that have the potential to generate a new concept of society. The peace accord implies constructing a new narrative, not just fulfilling the different points of the accord. The idea is to revive emancipatory and transformational categories, which will impact what science is. We have been subject to an epistemological colonization that we must transcend with the help of these new narratives.

The topic of the workshops was, therefore, timely and significant for participants, helping them to carve out an intellectual space in which to begin to construct these "new narratives."

Indeed, all of the workshop attendees (except for the high schoolers) were already aware of PAR and knew they could use it for community building and for crafting personal narratives of human rights violations, although they were not all fully cognizant of what the methodology involved. One of the participants at the workshop hosted by the Universidad Nacional in Medellín told listeners that when communities seek out university-trained experts, they frequently request that they use PAR methods, which suggests that among the grass roots, participatory action research is appreciated as a vital organizing tool, which academic consultants are expected to adopt. While they were all somewhat familiar with PAR, what was novel for my audiences was the level of ethnographic detail I presented, especially the nature of the Fundación's team dynamics and how political objectives were embedded in the research process.

All of the workshop groups found themselves struggling, in one way or another, with how the Fundación's history might inform their own practice, given the differences in the political and social environments of the early 1970s and 2018. As one of the Medellín participants so cogently expressed: "What do we do today, when the revolution is no longer around the corner? There is no unified program for social transformation that might resonate in the academic world, nor among intellectuals in social movements." How does the history of a research methodology steeped in universalist revolutionary ideologies inspire today's activists? Workshop participants' responses to this question allow me to conclude this book with an examination of how relevant the central concepts and practices that distinguished the Fundación del Caribe's methodology are today, thereby bringing Orlando Fals Borda's legacy into the present.

What Is PAR?

The first point of business at the workshops was to establish how the different groups envisaged the methodologies they draw on to conduct research. Some participants defined PAR as an amalgamation of research methodology, pedagogy, and politics, something that one of them called a "methodological-political horizon." Seeing it as more than a set of research techniques, the young leftist activists I met with at the Bogotá training workshop called it a "socio-critical strategy" and an "emancipatory political exercise." One participant—an education professor who served as a mentor for the Escuela Nacional Orlando Fals Borda—said it was "a philosophy of life, an emancipatory stand to confront the world," and a collectively constructed ethic. This echoes Fals Borda's equating of PAR, in one of his last writings, with a "philosophy of life" (Fals Borda 2007: 20; 2008a: 162).

Channeling Fals Borda's notion of the *sentipensante* or "thinking-feeling person," a member of the CINEP team observed that PAR is a process of coming to know something, although its meaning is different for each researcher. She reflected, in particular, on her experience with the indigenous Wayuu community of Provincial in the northeastern department of the Guajira, with which CINEP collaborated to stem the expansion of a massive coal mine, El Cerrejón: "The meaning of PAR isn't in a product, but a process. It's a healing process." She echoes Pilar Riaño's observation that local participatory memory workshops are intended to be healing experiences for the victims of conflict, more so than the spaces from which information is extracted. The healing, in the case of Provincial, is from the noise and pollution that inhibit its inhabitants from dreaming, which for the Wayuu is an essential part of their being; collaborative research was undertaken to organize a series of actions that would block further mining activity and allow the people of Provincial to dream again.

No one offered the suggestion that PAR was merely a set of research techniques, at least not explicitly. To the contrary, one of the young trainees of the Escuela Nacional Orlando Fals Borda said that in order for the methodology to function properly, groups that employ it must set their political objectives, because if they do not, PAR is merely a set of procedures that could be used by any institution conducting research. Their observations fall in line with participatory-action theorists, who place their greatest emphasis on PAR as an emancipatory process of discovery that strives toward practical outcomes, a verb rather than a noun, "a work of art emerging in the doing of it" (Reason and Bradbury 2008: 4).

Early proponents of participatory research were always somewhat unclear as to how their methodology was to be applied. They envisioned PAR as an epistemological stance that fostered horizontal relationships through a process of collective investigation and critical reflection, rather than as a set of procedures—a conclusion that was seconded in the workshops I facilitated. Fals lists four avenues that such research should follow: it should be collective, the group playing a central role in collecting and analyzing information; it should engage in the critical recovery of history; it should value and apply folk culture to mobilize the masses; and it should produce new knowledge through materials oriented to diverse publics (Fals Borda 1991: 8–9), all part of a core program that is still relevant in today's environment. There is no recipe for PAR, as Budd Hall reminds us:

> The literature on participatory research has always been vague on the question of methods. This is so because for participatory research, the most important factors are the origins of the issues, the roles that those concerned with the issue play in the process, the emersion of the process in the context of the moment, the potential for mobilizing and collective learning, the links to action, the understanding of how power relationships work and the potential for communications with others experiencing similar discrimination, oppression or violence. In addition participatory research is based on the epistemological assumption that knowledge is constructed socially and therefore that research approaches which allow for social, group or collective analysis of life experiences of power and knowledge are most appropriate. (1992: 20)

Not only is epistemology, rather than technique, the fundamental attribute of participatory research, but all epistemologies are necessarily local, emerging from the grass roots who participate in the research process.

In keeping with Hall's open-ended characterization of PAR, many of the workshop attendees had incorporated into their participatory practice a constellation of ideas and approaches that Boaventura de Sousa Santos (2014, 2018) calls "epistemologies of the South," which in the past few decades has gained purchase in Latin America thanks to the incorporation of indigenous and Afrodescendant forms of knowledge into the activist researcher's tool kit. Especially at the workshops sponsored by ACIN, CINEP, and IAPES—the workshops held with organizations collaborating with indigenous communities—these new epistemologies were foregrounded as models to be emulated or as knowledge bases with which participatory researchers felt the need to enter into dialogue. From 2009 to 2016, ACIN sponsored its own research institute, the Casa de Pensamiento [House of Thought], with the objective of providing a space in which to construct knowledge that indigenous leaders could translate into political action (Casa de Pensamiento n.d.). Casa reconceptualized the research process by situating it within a core group of values in Nasa culture, thereby coining new research strategies, at the same time that they advocated intercultural dialogue with nonindigenous ethnic groups and with collaborators from the dominant Colombian society. The Nasa researcher activists sought to ground knowledge production in techniques that not only engaged the five senses but also paid heed to shamanic practices, such as the interpretation of dreams and the reading of signs on the body. Furthermore, the spaces in which Casa members conducted research were determined by Nasa practices, leading them to privilege communal activities, such as collective work parties [mingas], rituals, and family conversations around the hearth, symbolically reproducing these venues at their meetings by, for example, placing three stones [tulpas] in the center of the room and lighting a fire there (Casa de Pensamiento n.d.: 14–18). A similar hearth fire burned at the center of the kiosk in which our ACIN workshop was held. Participants in most of the workshops were generally familiar with similar research strategies developed by indigenous organizations and, to a lesser extent, Afrocolombians. Given their knowledge of such alternative research practices, it was difficult for them to imagine PAR as anything other than open-ended, fluid, and contextual.

Accordingly, they were very much aware that their own definitions of PAR built upon, but were not identical to, Fals Borda's action research methodology. Some of the more experienced activists eschewed any discussion of particular techniques coined by Fals or, more recently, by the Centro de Memoria Histórica, in favor of a more inclusive and contextual approach to the generation of participatory research practices. PAR involves creativity, commented a participant at the ACIN workshop; it is not the rote application of techniques. One of the attendees cited the metaphor of the spiral, which is ubiquitous in Nasa political discourse (Rappaport 2005: chap. 5), to evoke the creative dimension of PAR: "The spiral involves a coming and going, it's never the same: we have to advance and retreat. We're not going to homogenize [research] formulas, but instead must use multiple referents to construct an interlacing of knowledge and wisdom . . . in all contexts of life."

Many of my interlocutors' investigative techniques grew out of the very activities in which they were immersed. For example, CINEP found it diffi-

Figure 7.1   Mural gallery in Comuna 1, Medellín, 2018 (photo by author)

cult to engage Wayuu youth in historical research and began to use clan genealogies as a participatory method for uncovering the indigenous past in an
idiom familiar to community members (Archila 2015), much like when Pilar
Riaño evoked the memories of violence-battered Medellín youth by creating
"soundscapes" out of popular songs that her respondents associated with pain-
ful events (Riaño-Alcalá 2006). The workshop I facilitated at the Corporación
Con-Vivamos was preceded by a visit to what they called a "gallery" of murals
painted by local artists with the collaboration of barrio youth. A painting facing the barrio's funicular station (fig. 7.1) depicts three mules making their way
up the hills, one of them carrying high-rise buildings in saddlebags on its back.
The image is framed on the top by the cable railway that connects the settlement to the Metro station below, representing the comuna's relationship to

the city. The mural builds on oral histories that young community researchers collected recounting how building materials were hauled up the mountain
on the backs of beasts, brick by brick.[9] Action researchers attentive to local
forms of memory were able to harness them to knowledge creation, just as the
Fundación sought to do in its depiction of the centrality of the Sinú River in
Tinajones.

Notwithstanding these innovative approaches and workshop participants'
desire to envisage PAR as an open-ended epistemological stance, more often
than not I discovered that in practice, less-experienced aspiring researchers
still engaged PAR as though it were a recipe book containing such procedures
as time lines and social cartography. At the Escuela Nacional Orlando Fals
Borda workshop, teams of budding PAR practitioners presented lists of the research *rutas* [paths] through which they aspired to intervene in marginal urban
environments. Some of these—particularly the time lines—seemed to me to
not always have much relevance to their projects. They were included almost
by rote, without any sustained reflection on how they fit into a participatory
research model, and there was scant discussion about whether they could be
articulated with the political objectives that the students had in mind (nor
was it always clear that these goals had been generated in dialogue with the
community). Minutes before, the same respondents had shared their lofty gen-
eralizations about PAR, but they remained at a loss as to how to connect these
values with their practice in the field. In other words, in some cases PAR is
more an ideal than a working concept.

The same might be said of some of the understandings of systematization I encountered. This methodology was chosen by IAPES as a tool for writing a history of its development as a popular educational institution. They
explained to the audience that they would proceed according to the following
steps (which I copied from their slide presentation): "(1) delimiting the experience, (2) contextualizing the experience, (3) creating an inventory of evidence
of the experience, (4) specifying the intentions of the systematization process, (5) arriving at a work plan." In other words, they had created a general
recipe for systematization out of which it was impossible for the audience
to decipher their specific political objectives and their connection to the research problem at hand. While it is true that this insistence on PAR as a set
of techniques was most evident at the workshops involving young activists
whose political and research experience was still nascent, it also cropped up in
some of the conversations with academics at the meeting held at the Universidad Nacional in Medellín, who zeroed in on social cartography as a stand-in
for PAR.

I did not always get the sense that all of the workshop participants understood research as something that unfolds in a dialogic relationship to political action, which, as I have explained, was one of the foundations of action
research as it was practiced by the Fundación del Caribe. When I mentioned
this to one of the women mentoring the young people gathered at the Escuela
Nacional Orlando Fals Borda, she responded that they were only just beginning to make the connection. I remember a Montería symposium several years
ago at which various student groups mentored by Víctor Negrete also seemed
to be involved in something that appealed to, but didn't quite achieve, a participatory methodology. Negrete's answer was similar to the Bogotá mentor's:
That's okay, we want to light a fire under them and don't expect them to reinvent PAR on their first try.

PAR as an Activist Methodology

How clearly workshop participants comprehended the dialogical relationship
between research and political action depended on their space of enunciation.
Among some of the more idealistic university students, who had only just become aware of the power of coupling research with activism, the relationship
between the two was one of proximity or coexistence rather than of synergy.
But in other instances, especially in ACIN, the fact that research nourished the
struggle and, in turn, political action influenced research was already baked
into their worldview. This is not surprising, given that the Caucan indigenous
movement emerged out of a program of direct action involving the occupation
of haciendas, which unfolded at the same time as it did in Córdoba (Archila
Neira and González 2010; Rappaport 2005) and was encouraged and supported
by La Rosca. CRIC, ACIN's parent organization, was in its early years affiliated
with ANUC and shared some of the same strategies and political objectives,
although they diverged in the early 1970s over whether alternative politics
was to be generated by the leadership or the rank and file. CRIC ultimately
separated from ANUC to become an autonomous organization (Tattay 2012:
69–71). Like ANUC in Córdoba, CRIC was nourished by a complex of cursillos,
providing the grass roots with training in the possibilities of political mobilization, the relationship between indigenous struggles and class struggle, and
the history of Native peoples in relation to the Colombian nation-state (2012:
62–63). These training workshops were frequently grounded in practical activities, such as organizing cooperatives (2012: 65). Such events promoted a culture of reading that was new to many indigenous activists, fostering the study
of Marxist texts, an organizational newspaper called *Unidad Indígena* (García

and Caballero Fula 2012), pamphlets produced by collaborating researchers (Bonilla 1977), and in some communities, mapas parlantes of Nasa history (Bonilla 1982), the latter two growing out of the association of La Rosca with CRIC in its early years.

In the past few years, the Nasa of northern Cauca have revived a strategy of civil disobedience that first brought their organization into prominence in the 1970s. Now rechristened as the "liberation of Mother Earth," local activists occupy commercially owned cane fields in the Cauca Valley, frequently provoking violent repression on the part of the military police (Dest 2019: 35–40). Participants in the ACIN workshop described their efforts as a way of regenerating their organizational memory through political practice. They said that by liberating Mother Earth they could teach today's activists that they are not "invaders" but *recuperadores*—political actors taking back what is theirs. Note that their concept of "research" is not that of collecting and systematizing information but of dredging up memories in the course of direct action. In this sense, the way in which they connect research to activism draws on something similar to the reconceptualization of research by the Fundación del Caribe; this is not by accident, given their common origins.

That does not imply, however, that my Nasa interlocutors rejected the contributions of conventional researchers—in contrast, they welcomed my collaboration over the years with the Casa de Pensamiento—but when I asked ACIN members which research projects they thought were most urgent, they responded by selecting issues that were inextricably connected to their political agendas and not to the academic agendas that ground the research of most scholars, even those who collaborate with the movement. One workshop participant advocated deciphering the multiple meanings that inhere in the various political structures that are currently replacing traditional *resguardo* (reservation) councils with more autochthonous organs derived from their study of Nasa cultural history. Another respondent hoped to use ethnography to develop strategies for incorporating youth into the indigenous movement so that they don't become actors in the armed conflict. One of the administrators of the education program said she was most concerned with constructing criteria for evaluating intercultural education projects. Yet another advocated reevaluating the long-term life plans [*planes de vida*] that indigenous communities developed in the 1990s in lieu of standard development plans (Gow 2008: chap. 3).

My CINEP interlocutors—who expressly defined themselves as researchers rather than as activists—seized the opportunity presented by the workshop to think through the possibilities of systematic devolution, the vehicle by means of which La Rosca harnessed research results to inspire popular mobilization, a term that wasn't brought up in discussion at other workshops. One of the CINEP participants confessed to the group that in their work with youth on the Caribbean coast they had neglected to pay sufficient attention to the process of devolution. In particular, they felt they needed to reflect more deeply on the pedagogical nature of the materials they produce and how to disseminate them to key audiences; they also recognized that it would be necessary to motivate people to read them.

The voicing of such concerns was driven by the participation of CINEP's communications team in the workshop. Our conversation touched on how the dissemination of research takes in more than the distribution of results to a passive readership. Instead, systematic devolution fosters a continuing dialogue spurring further reflection and political action, as took place in the work of the Fundación del Caribe. CINEP members reminded each other that devolution takes place at multiple points in the research process, not only in the diffusion of the final results but also in the work of communal analysis. PAR's participatory character is achieved by spurring the confrontation and combination of information collected by external researchers with local knowledge. This *diálogo de saberes* [dialogue of knowledges], which is what my CINEP interlocutors called this process, is generated out of the collective work of the imagination, paying meticulous attention to the formats in which this knowledge is encoded. For this reason, the communications staff was so fascinated by my analysis of Ulianov Chalarka's comics because I was able to trace the relationship between the collaborative procedures that governed the research and the writing of the graphic histories.

The diálogo de saberes is a practical, political dialogue. This was manifest in CINEP's evaluation of their collaboration with the Wayuu community of Provincial. Their research into Provincial's history and the environmental impact of coal mining was coupled with the staging of a *consulta autónoma* [autonomous consultation], whereby the indigenous population registered its approval or rejection of the mining company's plans to reroute a waterway that was a vital community resource (Archila 2015). Most ethnic communities confronting major public works or extractive industries undergo a *consulta previa* [previous consultation], which generally obliges communities to partially accede to the presence of external forces. Provincial opted to reject them entirely. Sharing historical and environmentalist knowledge created a vital space for mobilizing people to follow through with the consulta autónoma.

Critical Recovery in the Post-Conflict Era

One of the central precepts of action research as it was practiced by La Rosca was the concept of critical recovery, the uncovering of the history of institutions and values from the past that could be useful to promote the struggles of the present. Except for some of the older CINEP researchers, the Nasa activists, and the director of the community organization in Medellín, critical recovery was new to workshop attendees. A young member of the Escuela Nacional Orlando Fals Borda—the idealistic activist trainees in Bogotá—exclaimed, upon learning of critical recovery, that our workshop itself was a good example of critical recovery, insofar as the methodologies developed by Fals Borda became the object of reflection by young people.

How could critical recovery contribute to promoting the Colombian peace process? This was one of the central questions on the table at many of the workshops. The high schoolers of San Pablo, with whom I analyzed selected pages of *Felicita Campos* in lieu of presenting a detailed rendition of my research, found Chalarka's history of land loss in San Onofre to be compelling. Our communal reading of his panels led them to share their own experience of dispossession, of which Montes de María, the region in which San Pablo is located, has had more than its fair share. The drive from Cartagena to San Pablo imprinted on my memory the miles and miles of palm plantations that blanket the landscape and have gobbled up what were once subsistence plots owned by Afrocolombians, ceded during the past twenty years to commercial interests in the wake of paramilitary occupations (the story recounted in *Caminos condenados*). The high schoolers reflected on their own experience as they gazed at the comics pages, expressing their desire to study the environmental history of their community. They could imagine a process of critical recovery, but the lack of an organization in their village and the grinding poverty of their everyday lives would undoubtedly slow its progress. Other, more experienced respondents explicitly connected the concept of critical recovery to the challenges of the peace process. A leader from the Medellín comuna noted that an insistence on peace as an objective has led to a homogenization of political discourse, placing unusual emphasis on juridical language. He recommended that research into community history might revive local ways of thinking and acting that could expand the community's notion of what constitutes politics.

Participants from CRIC and ACIN, where La Rosca's project of critical recovery was successful, were, to my surprise, more hesitant to embrace the concept. While they did not deny that history could nourish activism in the present, they questioned who should engage in such research and how it should be conducted, with whom, and on what topics. Their questioning of the place of research draws on epistemological choices made by the indigenous movement. The research-based recovery of shamanic knowledge called *cosmovisión*, which has dominated the discourse and political practice of Native organizations during the past three decades (Rappaport 2005: chap. 6), has spurred internal debates over whether ancestral knowledge—the indigenous variant of Fals's "people's knowledge"—belongs only to shamans or can also be revealed in distinct registers, for example, those of young people and women. They wondered if it was possible to convert ancestral knowledge into action without running the risk of converting it into a kind of folklore that precludes meaningful routes for harnessing knowledge to action.

Who Is an External Researcher?

My Nasa interlocutors disparaged the dependency of community activists on external researchers. The ACIN members also questioned Fals Borda's paternalism, asking who generates the terms of research; they underscored the challenge of confronting power relations inside the research team itself, something that the indigenous movement has contended with over the years as they have negotiated the relationship between Native activists and collaborators (Rappaport 2005: chap. 2). They emphasized the importance of remembering that outside researchers would not stay with them forever, highlighting the fact that the most significant takeaway from PAR was not its final product but the assimilation of a research process that could potentially endure without the presence of external collaborators.

The pronouncements made by Nasa activists contrast with what I heard in other workshops, where university-educated community organizers interrogated the meaningfulness of pointing to a divide between local and academic researchers. Fals Borda hoped to bridge such a gap when he ventured to claim that committed outsiders could potentially acquire the status of an organic intellectual (Fals Borda 2010b: 189–190; Fals Borda and Brandão 1986: 26), an issue that is still under debate in many circles. In Medellín, both collaborators from the city center and educated comuna dwellers probed the problem of who, exactly, qualifies as an outsider. In an increasingly urbanized country, young people from working-class barrios fill the classrooms of public universities and obtain scholarships to private ones. Under such circumstances, workshop participants argued, the notion that a university-educated researcher is external to the community has become somewhat shopworn.

The question today is not whether those with a university education are outsiders but, instead, how researchers who are not affiliated with universities but have access to academic methods and ideas can contribute to the construction of new research methodologies. At first, I was surprised that community-university relations were so central to the two workshops in Medellín, in which academics emphatically displayed their community connections. Only after looking at the Con-Vivamos website did I discover that the issue has been debated at previous events, so it was very much on participants' minds (Con-Vivamos 2015). In fact, in all of the workshops I facilitated there were participants of humble origins who had completed, or were in the process of obtaining, university degrees. Fals Borda called attention to the gap between academics and the grass roots, my interlocutors told me, but today's PAR researchers must reconsider the meaning of the "great divide." At the Montería workshop Víctor Negrete reiterated Fals Borda's contention that it is necessary for *all* researchers to inhabit the research site and then distance themselves from it to create a space for reflection. But when researchers are at once academically trained and community members, what meanings inhere to the paired actions of drawing near to and withdrawing from the research context?

This could not have been imagined by Fals Borda in the 1970s, since the peasantry of Córdoba was largely unschooled and geographically isolated. He regarded his young collaborators—Víctor Negrete, Franklin Sibaja, and Ulianov Chalarka—as external researchers because of their urban residence and their education, but Negrete has repeatedly reminded me that he and his colleagues were only a generation away from being peasants themselves. Perhaps those of us reading Fals's field notes overlook the fact that the lines in the 1970s between people's knowledge and academic inquiry were already being blurred by the very members of the Fundación, various of whom were "amphibious researchers," who moved between and received sustenance from both the working class or the peasantry and educated sectors. As is the case today, they were not alone. They inhabited a local world in which there were many equally amphibious interlocutors or, at the least, many who aspired to be so: leftist militants, writers and poets, theater groups, university students. In overwhelming proportions, the young researchers in the comunas of Medellín and the offices of CINEP, the Bogotá-bred collaborators with ACIN, and even its indigenous activists all belong to what are called in Colombia the "popular classes" and are academically trained. They move across a network of non-governmental organizations and research institutes where they find many more who share their social profile. So they are "amphibious," just as were the members of the Fundación del Caribe. I was continually reminded of this in the workshop discussions.

Undeniably, the quandary facing external researchers—Who is external and who is *popular*?—depends on the locus of enunciation, on who is troubled by the role of outsiders in a participatory research project, and on who rejects the label of "outsider." The director of Con-Vivamos pointed out that individual positionalities are not the only spaces of enunciation that are relevant to participatory research. He compellingly argued that dialogue takes place not only between individuals but between institutions. Drawing on Fals Borda's experience, he pointed out that there was a difference between a campesino's relationship to ANUC and La Rosca's relationship with the peasant organization. In other words, intervention and dialogue occur simultaneously on multiple scales, where power differentials operate in distinct manners. Con-Vivamos and a research institute affiliated with the Universidad Nacional are equal players, while perhaps a university researcher and an older resident of the comuna find the establishment of a horizontal relationship more challenging, as a workshop participant without university training admonished us. She confessed that she felt used by academics, who accumulated information and then exerted control over it. The university, she asserted, should not speak for her, but should open a pathway for her to speak.

My respondents at CINEP expressed the concern that PAR researchers unwittingly create hierarchies in the very act of "returning" research results to communities, citing that

> systematic devolution . . . rings of messianism, paternalism. The attempt to create levels [of reception] through systematic devolution is something that collaborative research resists [by establishing] a more horizontal, more constant, relationship during the course of a project, with less differentiation between researcher and researched.

In other words, systematic devolution is the moment at which differences between internal and external researchers become more apparent. It marks those occasions at which certain actors end up controlling access to research results. The CINEP researchers therefore preferred to complement the Fundación del Caribe's model with collaborative ethnography as a modus for sharing the knowledge generated during the research process. This observation is not new: Carlos Rodrigues Brandão, one of Fals's early interlocutors, also points to the relevance of ethnography to the collaborative endeavor (Fals Borda and Brandão 1986). Of course, my friends at CINEP assume that collaborative anthropologists are more likely than PAR researchers to engage in collective authorship, which in reality occurs more smoothly when the external and internal researchers are evenly matched in terms of the academic skills they bring to the process but also depends on the extent to which community researchers are willing or able to demand control of it (that wasn't the case in the Córdoba of the 1970s). Xochitl Leyva Solano and Shannon Speed's analysis of their collaboration with indigenous academics from Chile, Ecuador, Nicaragua, Guatemala, and Mexico lays bare some of the contradictions that can ensue, even for those with advanced degrees. In the course of their research, participants on their team voiced tensions, not only over ethnic differences but also over gender, status, level of education, and political positions, making explicit some of the fault lines in their expectations of what the project would yield: how "useful" it would be, and for whom (cf. Briones et al. 2007). The differences that arise between academics and indigenous activists go to the heart of the collaborative academic project, questioning the extent to which we are free to produce critical analyses and whom we seek to serve when we engage in scholarly interpretation (Leyva Solano and Speed 2015: 468). In effect, we are still facing the same challenges that Fals and his associates experienced in Córdoba.

The Legacy of Orlando Fals Borda

A little over a year before his death Fals delivered the Martin Diskin Memorial lecture at the 2007 Congress of the Latin American Studies Association (Fals Borda 2007). As in many of his earlier papers and articles, he identifies the three "strategic tensions" that continue into the neoliberal era to characterize his approach: the relationship of theory to practice, of subject to object, and between different forms of knowledge. He sums up his methodological approach as one of "scientific humility and local realism" (2007: 20). It is difficult for me to ascribe humility to a scholar who openly rejected the major sociological currents of his time and resigned his post at a major university in favor of the audacious and risky alternative of collaboration with ANUC. I believe that Fals's use of the term "humility" is best construed as defining the terms of his relationship with popular sectors, rather than with his academic colleagues. His use of "local realism" is more thought-provoking to me. "Local realism" is broader than the shopworn concept of "local knowledge," which betrays an ethnographic scaffolding that precludes the political potential of other forms of knowledge. It is also more versatile than "people's knowledge," the concept Fals used in the 1970s as the counterpart to academic science. "Local realism" brings to mind a constellation of ideas that inhere in the philosophies of La

Rosca and the Fundación del Caribe, laying emphasis on lived experience [*vivencia*] and its analytical promise as an antidote to universal sociological models, thereby also redeeming empirical research. It emphasizes the possibilities of theorizing from multiple subject positions. It underscores the fact that all knowledge is local. "Local" implies paying attention to the depth and texture of experience—it requires empirical observation. But it redefines what is meant by "empirical" by reinterpreting what constitutes a "fact": it stipulates that truths emerge out of particular points of view that must be carefully identified by the researcher. These points of view are not, however, relative, as they would be in a caricature of postmodernism. Instead, they are profoundly real. Grassroots intellectuals are sentipensantes—thinking-feeling persons—who combine reason with sentiment and experience and who wield the truth, as Uruguayan writer Eduardo Galeano exclaims in his riff on Fals Borda in *Libro de los abrazos*: "Such wise doctors of Ethics and Morals are the fisherfolk of the Colombian coast, who invented the word sentipensante to define the language that tells the truth" (1989: 89). Finally, "local realism" recognizes that such points of view, especially those generated from below, not only are facts to be analyzed but form the basis for both action and further reflection.

Local realism at once reflects what action research in Córdoba hoped to achieve and expands on it. In the Spanish version of Fals's 2007 talk, he replaces his earlier concept of *ciencia popular* with *cosmovisión* (2007: 19). In the English translation of his lecture, "world view" is the unfortunate gloss used for *cosmovisión* (2008a: 161)—unfortunate because the ethnographic connotations of "world view" for English speakers do not reflect the political meanings that have come to adhere to cosmovisión in Latin America. The latter has become a buzzword for alternative epistemologies, especially but not exclusively associated with Native cultures. To some degree, I think cosmovisión erects a wall of radical otherness around the indigenous political project, which must necessarily act both within the Native sphere and confront the broader social system, which implies managing multiple discourses, practices, and epistemologies. But at the same time, cosmovisión supplies activists with an alternative notion of democracy built on historical introspection and interethnic dialogue (Santos 1998) and has allowed scholars to articulate with social movements through an appeal to epistemology (Hale and Millaman Reinao 2018). Cosmovisión clearly underlies the conversations that we had in the ACIN workshop. It is, I would argue, more potent at the current moment than "people's knowledge" because its scope is simultaneously broader and more precise.

The moderator of the workshop I facilitated for academics at the Universidad Nacional in Medellín summed up her appreciation of the contributions of

Fals and the Fundación del Caribe with the following three concepts: creativity, critical recovery, and activism. Fals Borda's appeal to "local realism" in his LASA address fuses these three ideas into a dynamic whole in which the lessons of the past are creatively resignified to contribute to social transformation. A researcher who is sentipensante combines different types of knowledge by means of the collective exercise of a series of investigative techniques, framed by a research paradigm that lends support to popular struggles and cedes at least partial control of the research process to them. The combination of academic and grassroots notions of research into a single process entails the bridging of substantial methodological, conceptual, and epistemological disparities, involving a dialogue between distinct knowledge bases in a conversation that encompasses not only their contents but also their form. As a result, the attitudes of external researchers and grassroots participants are transformed. By reconceptualizing ciencia popular as local realism, Fals implicitly recognizes the new waves of participatory and collaborative research that his work in Córdoba inspired.

For collaborative or participatory researchers to arrive at a common idiom involves not so much a process of reconciliation or compromise but a taking advantage of the confrontation between not entirely compatible worldviews that, in clashing, bear the potential to produce knowledge. Making sense of how much can be said and how it will be said requires the work of the imagination, just as much as it presupposes a recognition of the existence of diverse definitions of observable fact, dissimilar understandings of what constitutes rigor, and different philosophical or theoretical bases. Early PAR was typified by methodologies that engaged both external researchers and internal activists in a dynamic process of imagining.

What can today's PAR researchers learn from the experiences of the Fundación del Caribe? The Medellín moderator made it clear that Fals's concept of imputation—the collective work of the imagination—was the bridge that connected rigorous research to activism. It was not sufficient for Fals and his colleagues to be capable researchers or adhere to the politics of ANUC and steer their research toward political ends. The connection between the two could only be made by the exercise of imagination: entreating peasants to imagine their forebears—how they looked, how they suffered, what they built, how they fought—and cajoling external researchers and artists into placing themselves in the shoes of the actors in the scenarios that emerged from the mouths of the narrators, in order to resuscitate and refurbish the political tools of the past that the narrators revealed in their testimonies.

Appropriating Fals's notion of imputation, one of the participants in the CINEP workshop asked, "How can we impute to ourselves the researcher's craft?" [¿*Cómo imputarnos el oficio de investigar?*]. In the course of this book, I have demonstrated that imputation involves more than Fals Borda's experimental format in *Historia doble de la Costa*. It transcends the innovative formats in which Ulianov Chalarka and David Sánchez Juliao crafted their texts. Creativity was the primary foundation of the three-year dialogue between the Fundación and ANUC. Interviewers had to impute to peasant storytellers the capacity to transform the historical narrative, because at the time campesinos were not recognized as trustworthy witnesses. Narrators had to impute to Ulianov Chalarka the trust to reimagine their experience in pictures, because the comics they were crafting were new and unusual: not action heroes, but campesino heroes and heroines. Chalarka had to impute to the Fundación collective the authority to assemble the graphic histories, following some of his suggestions and rejecting others. The Fundación had to impute to the participants in ANUC cursillos the capacity to take hold of the past to inform their present. As one of the CINEP workshop participants underscored, the objectives of the Fundación were not only understanding or knowledge but also action, and the combination of knowledge and action is at the heart of imputation as a legal construct, which attaches to an individual the responsibility for an act.

Imputing the researcher's craft to unlikely actors was, precisely, what the Fundación del Caribe was all about. Remember that of the entire Fundación team, only Fals was trained as a researcher. Moreover, the stances Fals assumed in Córdoba—as an academic receptive to peasant historical narrative, as an external researcher willing to support ANUC's agenda, as a social scientist trained as a positivist in the global North who ultimately eschewed his schooling in favor of a Latin America–based theoretical corpus and who employed creative and collective analytical approaches—went against his own upbringing, as he reminisced in his 2008 Malinowski Award Lecture in acceptance of the honor bestowed by the Society for Applied Anthropology (Fals Borda 2008b: 359). His colleagues in the Fundación were forced to meet a different challenge, imputing to themselves the role of a radical researcher, balancing what little they knew about conventional research with their highly unconventional intervention in the politics of ANUC. The Fundación researchers were not strictly participant observers who took part in activities in order to learn about the local culture. Their participation was a great deal more practical than that. Their objective as researchers was not only to understand but to transform and build. The act they were imputing to themselves was not just to conduct research but to overturn the conditions they were observing. Fals's notion of imputation implies a particular brand of empathy that transcends standard ethnographic mimesis. This is what Fals meant by the word *sentipensante*: someone who not only analyzes and empathizes but takes action.

But the researchers of the Fundación del Caribe constituted only half of the equation. Empathy also ran in the other direction. Campesinos were encouraged to move into the cultural arena of the researcher, collaborating in the production of educational materials, facilitating cursillo sessions, guiding the selection of historical referents for critical recovery. In effect, it was not only Fals imputing the values of the campesinos to himself as an investigator but also the peasants imputing to themselves the tasks of the researcher. This cross-empathy was only made possible by redefining the researcher—whether internal or external—as someone who not only observes but takes political action, whose investigation is nourished by activism and whose activism is fueled by research. This is what distinguishes Fals Borda's project from the conventional exercise of the ethnographic or historical imagination.

The Fundación del Caribe project established a two-way street on which both external researchers and grassroots investigators encountered one another, but in the long run, Fals hoped that local researchers would be able to go it alone. In a sense, the workshops I facilitated demonstrated that this hope is being increasingly realized, although perhaps in ways that Fals had not envisioned when he and Augusto Libreros wrote their research manual. Today's PAR practitioners move between social movements and universities via routes that were not imaginable in the 1970s, when there were few peasants, shantytown dwellers, indigenous people, or people of color enrolled at Colombian institutions of higher education who had acquired the research skills necessary to nourish new imaginings. The cross-fertilization of the intervening four decades brings forth new questions.

The workshop participant who asked how she could impute to herself the researcher's craft was not concerned with how researchers like Fals Borda, or even the lower-middle-class Fundación del Caribe members, might have pondered their calling. As an Afrocolombian who can simultaneously claim membership in a community and as an academic, the speaker—one of my graduate students, who was invited to participate in the CINEP workshop—was thinking aloud in front of the other attendees about what her role might be in a participatory research project. Like Nasa researchers from CRIC, her frontier position affords her movement between the grass roots and the academy but, simultaneously, subjects her to the standards of both academics and nonacademics (Rappaport 2005: chap. 1). While she has grounded herself in diasporic theory and can draw on her own life experiences, if she is to take Fals Borda seriously, the only way that she can impute to herself the role of a scholar is to embrace his creative impulses and to harness her research in some way to broader activist projects.

This is the legacy of La Rosca. As Juan Mario Díaz Arévalo, a young historian working with Fals's archive, observed at a symposium commemorating the decade since his death, you cannot replicate Fals Borda's work; instead, it must inspire you to create something new (2018b). For this reason, I think that the PAR researchers with whom I came into contact in the workshops could not appropriate in any simplistic way what they learned from my presentation of Fals Borda's experience. What they needed to do was evaluate their own practices, using what new insights they could glean from Fals's legacy, and continue to impute to themselves the researcher's and activist's craft.

Introduction

1   ANUC was established as a government-sponsored initiative in the 1960s. As I will detail in the next chapter, peasants became increasingly aware of the failures of the agrarian reform, and in 1972, a significant portion of the ANUC membership split off to form a parallel organization that advocated direct action to reclaim large landholdings. Fals and his associates collaborated with this radical wing of the peasant movement.

2   When Fals Borda writes about Juana Julia, he refers to her by using her first and middle names (Fals Borda 1986). I have decided to adopt this more intimate usage as a way of underscoring her centrality to the Fundación's project. Following Spanish usage, individuals are sometimes identified by a combination of their patronymic (Fals) and matronymic (Borda), and at other times only by their patronymic; I employ the combined form in citations and in the bibliography. Thus, Orlando Fals Borda will sometimes be called "Fals Borda" and sometimes "Fals." The main protagonists of my narrative are listed in the Cast of Characters that opens this book.

3   *Historia doble* is a two-channeled book: the left-hand pages narrate the history of the coast, while the right-hand pages contextualize the narrative. My references to parts, chapters, or pages indicate whether they are located in channel A or channel B.

4   All ACHUNC/B documents cited are from the La Rosca series of the Fals Borda collection, identified by their box, folder, and folio numbers.

5   I return to this point in more detail in chapter 7, where I point out some of the fundamental differences between collaborative research in Latin America and in North America and Europe.

6   Freire was forced to leave Brazil by the military dictatorship and spent his exile at Harvard. While in the United States, he came into close contact with Myles Horton, the founder of the Highlander Center, a famous laboratory of activist research in Appalachia (Horton and Freire 1990).

7   Fals requested US $386,740 over three years from the National Committee on the Self-Development of People of the Worldwide Ministries of the Presbyterian Church, receiving approximately $75,000 a year from 1971 to 1973. This was an enormous amount of money at that time. See Presbyterian Historical Society, Philadelphia (henceforth, PHS/P), Worldwide Ministries, Self-Development of People, Correspondence, Reports on International Projects, 1970–88, box 2: "A

Self-Development Program for Colombian Destitute Groups" submitted by the Rosca de Investigación y Acción Social with the sponsorship of Church and Society in Latin America (ISAL), Colombia, 1970. They also received US $90,000 in 1975 (Gittings 1993: 69). Díaz Arévalo (2017), Moreno Moreno (2017b), and Pereira Fernández (2005) have examined Fals's ties to the Presbyterian Church.

8 Of course, things have changed since those days. As I will elaborate in chapter 7, many of today's "insiders" also have advanced training and are able to combine introspection with the systematic collection of information.

9 The index of Fals's papers at the Centro de Documentación Regional Orlando Fals Borda in Montería (henceforth, CDRBR/M) identifies documents by their item number—the box and folder numbers can be traced through the catalogue—and folio, although when a bound set of materials (such as a notebook) is numbered as a single folio, I also identify page numbers. CDRBR/M, CF is the abbreviation I employ for Fals's photographic collection in Montería, whose items are numbered, and CDRBR/M, CG for his digitized reel-to-reel tapes, also numbered.

10 As Fals observed in a dialogue with Colombian anthropologists, his use of imputation in his writings was profoundly personal, something that could not be replicated verbatim by other writers or researchers (ACHUNC/B, caja 50, carpeta 3).

Chapter 1. The Fundación del Caribe in Córdoba

1 Interviews with Negrete, 10 July 2016, Montería, and Sánchez Juliao, 4 August 2009, Bogotá. Composer and musician Máximo Jiménez worked closely with Sánchez Juliao on "protest vallenatos," using the popular Costeño ballad genre, which he performed to motivate peasants during land occupations (interview with Jiménez, 10 July 2019, Montería). The lyrics of the title song of Jiménez's recording "El indio del Sinú" (Jiménez 1975) were written by Sánchez Juliao. See also Zabaleta Bolaños (2017).

2 Members of the Fundación, their campesino contacts, and other intellectuals who worked with them are listed in the Cast of Characters at the beginning of this book. Beyond the innermost circle, other collaborators included José Galeano, a high schooler in Cereté who went on to become a leader of the student movement before he began to work with Víctor Negrete in the late seventies (interview with Galeano, 15 July 2016, Montería). Leopoldo Berdella, a founder of the Grupo "El Túnel" that in the mid-seventies brought together Córdoba's creative writers and artists, was also from Cereté; he later became a university professor in the southwestern city of Cali and an author of children's books. Matilde Eljach, who would become a faculty member at the Universidad del Cauca in Popayán, worked with the Fundación while she was a university student in Barranquilla. Prominent Costeño intellectuals frequently collaborated as facilitators of training workshops for ANUC leaders (CDRBR/M, 1922, 2177, 2180, 2183, 2185–2187, 2190, 2195, 2197). Among the most notable of the workshop facilitators were Cartagena-based folklorist Benjamín Puche, sociologist María Josefina Yance (who went on to direct the regional planning office and manage the Banco de la República), Roberto Yance (the regional *procurador agrario*, or agrarian prosecutor), and sociologist Raúl Pa-

niagua of the University of Cartagena. Some of these individuals, particularly those who were government functionaries, worked clandestinely with the Fundación, although they crop up in Fals Borda's photographic collection. Afrocolombian novelist Manuel Zapata Olivella, a native of Lorica, was another of Fals Borda's important interlocutors. Fals also drew on former students and colleagues in Bogotá and Cali to support and evaluate his work, including sociologists Gilberto Aristizábal, Darío Fajardo, Alfredo Molano, William Ramírez, and Alejandro Reyes Posada, as well as economist Ernesto Parra Escobar and Swedish development scholar Anders Rudqvist (interviews with Aristizábal, 17 July 2009, Cali; Fajardo, 12 August 2008, Bogotá; Molano, 19 July 2016, Bogotá; and Parra Escobar, 14 June 2016, Bogotá). Rudqvist drew on the evaluation for his doctoral dissertation (1986), while Parra Escobar published his study in book form (1983). Molano also penned a critical discussion piece on the work of La Rosca (ACHUNC/B, caja 49, carpeta 3, fols. 158–176).

3   The document goes on to emphasize that researchers should not arrive at the field site with long hair, should wear simple clothing, and that they should not carry the sort of tape recorder that could potentially lead local people to equate them with previous researchers. They should carry only "a pocket notebook, a pencil, and a small camera, their modesty leading people to assume that they are not 'dangerous elements'" (CDRBR/M, 0642, fol. 3578). The code of conduct was obviously composed for neophytes.

4   For those too young to remember, Instamatics were very simple cameras produced by Kodak, which were loaded with film cartridges instead of rolls of film.

5   Interview with Aristizábal.

6   The Fundación del Caribe reopened in 1979 and continued to function until 1981, when its core members established the Fundación del Sinú, which is still active promoting participatory action research in Córdoba (Negrete Barrera 1983, 2008a).

Chapter 2. Archives and Repertoires

1   Fals's donation to the Centro de Documentación Regional contains 180 manila folders and approximately twelve thousand numbered folios, although it assigns some notebooks and publications a single numeral, so the number of pages is in actuality greater. In addition to his field archive, he bequeathed three hundred books about the Atlantic Coast (substantially augmenting the Centro's library holdings), more than two thousand photographs, three sets of notes from historical archives, several paintings, and a number of complete collections of regional periodicals. Fals's ceding of his papers to a small repository located in a provincial city on the Caribbean coast is an indication of how he intended to frame his legacy. In part, he was responding to critics who had faulted *Historia doble* for its supposed lack of rigorous attention to empirical sources (Bergquist 1990; see also Martínez Garnica 2008–2009; Meisel Roca 2002), laying bare his use of a wide range of historical documentation. He also intended to place the wealth of material he had collected into circulation in the coast itself, so that future researchers could work on neglected regions like Córdoba, Sucre, and southern Bolívar and examine the

real-life experiences of peasants as opposed to limiting their analyses to local elites (Alex Pereira, personal communication). Fals was highly conscious of the fact that his corpus of field notes should be made available to future generations (Behrensmeyer 2011: 93).

2 I have not identified who assisted Fals in organizing the papers he donated to the Centro de Documentación in Montería, although I suspect that Víctor Jiménez, who has identified himself publicly as Fals's assistant, had a hand in the project. The other major fond I consulted, in the archives of the National University of Colombia in Bogotá, was assembled with the assistance of Gabriel Escalante, who continues as the custodian of the Fals papers (Escalante 2018).

3 Here, I am only concerned with comparing two sets of documentation. Readers interested in what Fals was doing during the intervening decades should consult the introduction.

4 Interview with Negrete, 23 June 2018, Montería.

5 Fals did not include the pamphlet in his papers; I consulted it in the Archivo de la Fundación del Sinú (AFS/M) in Montería but cite it as a bibliographic item because the archive is neither public nor catalogued.

Chapter 3. Participation

1 Iván was the nickname by which he was known in his neighborhood, but when combined with Tejada, it became a nom de plume; Fals sometimes called him "Iván Chalarka." Ulianov died in Montería in 1977, after a jeep ran him over in the wee hours and he died of complications from anesthesia weeks later; there is some dispute between the Chalarca family and Ulianov's colleagues and allies over the circumstances of the accident and his medical treatment. The personal reminiscences in this section come from conversations with Orlando Chalarca on 18 July 2016, 2–3 and 6 June 2017, and 11 July 2019 in Montería; sister Marta Chalarca on 5 July 2019 in Montería; and Utamaro Chalarca, Ulianov's nephew, on 12 and 16 June 2017 in Cartagena. (The Chalarca family commonly spells its surname with a c, but at the time of his collaboration with the Fundación, Ulianov Chalarka spelled his name with a k.) Utamaro created a Facebook page for Ulianov Chalarka, which reproduces family photos and a good selection of his drawings and paintings: https://www.facebook.com/UlianovChalarka/ (accessed 25 February 2020).

2 Leonardo Chalarca, Ulianov's father, was a journalist and a caricaturist. Although the drawing I describe is attributed to Ulianov, family members found it difficult to distinguish between Ulianov's caricatures and those drawn by his father, both of them bearing the same signature.

3 The 1985 edition in which these pamphlets appeared was published in commemoration of Chalarka by the Fundación del Sinú; a boutique edition by Bogotá-based Piedra, Tijera, Papel came out in 2019. The anthology of the four graphic histories is posted on the internet: http://babel.banrepcultural.org/cdm/ref/collection /p17o5coll2/id/71 (accessed 26 May 2020). *Lomagrande* (1972) was originally published in the name of the Municipal Association of Peasant Users of Montería (ANUCM); *El Boche* came out in 1973, under the authorship of the Association of Peasant Users

of Córdoba and the Centro Popular de Estudios, the legal entity under whose auspices the pamphlets were researched and composed. Authorship of *Tinajones* (1973) was ascribed to the Sindicato de Agricultores de Palermo, one of several local campesino organizations that had originally been affiliated with FANAL, the National Agrarian Federation [Federación Agraria Nacional]; FANAL was a rural labor organization originally set up by the Catholic Church to offset communist influence (Zamosc 1986b: 37–38), but in Tinajones it had a greater capacity for mobilization than ANUC. *Felicita Campos* (1974) was credited to the Felicita Campos Study Group, under the supervision of Florentino Montero, a peasant leader, and Néstor Herrera, a young Fundación researcher from Sincelejo. Chalarka sketched some fliers for ANUC events containing biting critiques of INCORA, the Colombian Institute for Agrarian Reform (CDRBR/M, 2145), on the occasion of the Día del Campesino [Day of the Campesino]. He depicts a police agent beating a peasant whose hands are in chains; a tiny turtle at the policeman's feet carries the label "IN-CORA" and out of its head emerges a thought balloon containing a question mark. Of course, Chalarka also drew the images for *¡Escucha cristiano!*—the pamphlet aimed at recruiting Protestant youth to the land struggle introduced in chapter 2.

4 This was an inversion of the process used to produce *¡Escucha cristiano!* The verbal script for the illustrated pamphlet written for Cereté Protestants came before the drawings.

5 Interview with Herrera, 13 July 2016, Sincelejo.

6 Interview with Eljach, 15 July 2009, Popayán.

7 Personal communication, Víctor Negrete, 3 October 2014. Fals Borda's experience with graphic materials began with his work in the 1950s with Andean peasants in Saucío, Cundinamarca (ACHUNC/B, Acción Comunal Saucío, Introducciones, Cocina Chula; Fals Borda 2010c: 73). I have found no further evidence of his familiarity with the alternative comics scene in Colombia or Latin America, although the national peasant movement produced a highly sophisticated comics pamphlet, which he undoubtedly read (ANUC n.d.).

8 Interview with Negrete, 4 June 2017, Montería.

9 Interview with Eljach.

10 Interview with Eljach. I located a very brief storyboard mapping out the last two pages of *Felicita Campos* (CDRBR/M, 1787), in which images are only noted by topic while the verbal contents of speech balloons and captions are written in detail, suggesting that the script was prepared after Chalarka had completed his images. Néstor Herrera, the researcher who organized the interviews in San Onofre, did not participate in the writing process (interview with Herrera, 13 July 2016, Sincelejo). Negrete told me that, likewise, he was not involved (interview with Negrete, 10 July 2016, Montería). Perhaps the layout of this graphic history—which originated in Sucre, where Fals's relationship with ANUC was not as intimate as it was in Córdoba—was outsourced. The comic is different from the other three graphic histories; it is so text heavy that at times the panels are oddly shaped to accommodate the combination of the verbal and visual materials.

11 I interviewed Negrete via Skype on 8 February 2015 and he immediately published the interview, with a few minor editorial changes, which I cite here as my source material (Rappaport and Negrete 2015).

12 Negrete describes the procedure for composing *Tinajones* and *Felicita Campos*; the interviews for *Lomagrande* had already been recorded before Chalarka joined the Fundación, so he listened to the tapes to conjure in his imagination the scenes he would depict (conversation with Negrete, 13 June 2017, Montería). *El Boche* is more fictional in nature than the other graphic histories; my speculations regarding its production can be found in chapter 5.

13 Interview with Negrete, 22 July 2009, Montería.

14 Interview with Negrete, 4 June 2017.

15 In her commentary on an earlier publication in which I analyze the Fundación's research process (Rappaport 2018), Claudia Briones (2018) underscores the significance of disagreement and negotiation in the collaborative research process, although I can only speculate on how it unfolded in the making of the graphic histories.

16 Interview with Herrera, 13 July 2016, Sincelejo.

17 Note that the local ANUC president quoted here was aligned with the Armenia Line of ANUC, although ANUC in Córdoba and Sucre was overwhelmingly affiliated with the more radical Sincelejo Line. *Tinajones* was prepared in collaboration with a peasant organization independent of ANUC, the Sindicato de Agricultores de Palermo. Fals identified the ANUC president in the early 1970s as a *politiquero*, or "machine politician" (CDRBR/M, 1921, fol. 19247, fol. 8r). Pablo García, director of the regional office of INCORA in Córdoba in the late 1970s, told Leon Zamosc that local peasant organizations grew out of the anti-Communist FANAL, the National Agrarian Federation (CINEP/B, doc. 9), which was the rural arm of the Union of Colombian Workers (UTC), a union federation supported by the Catholic Church and, at its inception, strongly anti-Communist; some of these local syndicates promoted their own demands, as occurred in San Bernardo del Viento (Zamosc 1986b: 37–38, 45–46).

18 I only note in passing that Cabrera was a mulatto. Peasants in the region called all the landowners *blancos* [whites], reflecting class position in addition to—sometimes in spite of—race. Manuel Zapata Olivella's *Tierra mojada*, which was one of the primary sources for *Tinajones*, underscores the racial tensions underlying the relationship between landlords and peasants in the region (Zapata Olivella 1964 [1947]: 161; see also Tillis 2005: 18–19). Fals's photographs of the campesinos of San Bernardo del Viento display a population that is largely Afrodescendant; in a July 2019 visit I discovered they consciously identify as Afrocolombians, and I was particularly struck when I met the grandson of the comic's narrator, who told me that his grandfather—whom he resembles—was black, notwithstanding the fact that he looks mestizo in the graphic history. In the comics, however, the peasants are depicted as mestizos, perhaps reflecting Fals's adherence to a discourse that erroneously celebrated the Caribbean coast as a site of a democratizing process of racial mixing (Figueroa 2009) or maybe in an effort to distinguish the peasants vi-

sually from Cabrera; when I elicited the opinion of the descendants of the activists depicted in the comic, however, they were unperturbed by Chalarka's depiction of them and instead observed that there had been no political discourse of blackness at the time the comic was produced. Nonetheless, Zapata Olivella, a Costeño and an Afrocolombian, would not have agreed with the Fundación on this count.

19 Interview with Eljach.

20 In July 2019 I held readings of the comics at several rural locations, at which the same dynamics occurred: *Felicita Campos* in San José de Uré, Córdoba, 6 July 2019, and *Tinajones* in San Bernardo del Viento, 5 November 2019.

21 Interview with Negrete, 25 June 2018, Montería.

Chapter 4. Critical Recovery

1 Interview with Eljach, 15 July 2009, Popayán.

2 Interview with Molano, 19 July 2016, Bogotá.

3 Molano doesn't do justice to Fals Borda's use of personal testimony. Fals also carefully crafted on the basis of multiple interviews the campesino voices he inserted into *Historia doble de la Costa* (McRae 2015; Robles Lomeli 2015, 2019). What is different is that he places these voices in dialogue with his own historical reconstructions, as I will explain further in chapter 5. Nonetheless, Molano's point about the importance of the first person is useful for comprehending the nature of the witnessing that occurs in the Fundación's graphic histories.

4 Interview with Orlando Chalarca, 11 July 2019, Montería.

5 Urbano de Castro was a young activist from Barranquilla who was killed during the massacre in Lomagrande in 1921. Another baluarte was named for Manuel Hernández, aka "El Boche," the protagonist of another of Chalarka's graphic histories that I examine in more detail in the following chapter.

6 Interview with Herrera, 13 July 2016, Sincelejo.

7 The large landowner with whom the peasants clashed, "El Turco" Malluk, was one of numerous Syrio-Lebanese immigrants who arrived on the Caribbean coast after the disintegration of the Ottoman Empire. The new arrivals started out as small merchants and eventually acquired landholdings (Fals Borda 1986: 116A; see also Jattin Torralvo 2019; Posada Carbó 1998: 323–328; Viloria de la Hoz 2003), later joining a cosmopolitan class of hacendados and investors from Europe and North America (Fals Borda 1986: chap. 5A). Not so much of a backwater, the coast has always been a very cosmopolitan place.

8 Conversation with Jesús Pérez, 23–26 July 2013, Montería. See also Fals Borda (1984: 21B).

9 The manuscript can be found in CDRBR/M, 1918; the published version is stored in CDRBR/M, 1923, fol. 10247. All citations will be from the published version of the text, which varies only very slightly from the manuscript.

10 The *derecho de pernada* [droit du seigneur], as this custom was called, is registered in both versions of *Tinajones*. In one of Chalarka's panels, Cabrera stands on the riverbanks of his Río Ciego hacienda, his arms crossed, observing workers unloading from El Caimán scores of burlap bags filled with rice, and demands: "Go to

Sicará and bring me a good fifteen-year-old for tonight" (Chalarka 1985: 33). A less vivid description can be found in the prose narrative (CDRBR/M, 1923, fol. 10249, pp. 16–17).

11 I was surprised to discover during my July 2019 visit to San Bernardo that the Sinú had been diverted a kilometer or so outside the town, so there is no longer a riverfront.

12 The main channel has been considerably reduced in size and the cañitos are in danger of disappearing due to the construction of buildings along the channels.

13 Interview with Eljach.

Chapter 5. Systematic Devolution

1 Interview with Negrete, 4 June 2017, Montería.

2 Interview with Negrete, 23 June 2018, Montería.

3 Interview with Santana Luna et al., 26 June 2018, Montería.

4 This document from the Fals archives in Montería has been miscatalogued. Its page number (fol. 1068v) does not correspond to an appropriate item number in the catalogue; I estimate it should probably be CDRBR/M, 0242 or 0243, located in caja 3, carpeta 4, which contains documentation of meetings of the Fundación del Caribe.

5 Participation of women in ANUC was limited in Córdoba and Sucre, where they served as negotiators for imprisoned male activists and as a front line to demand more respect from the police. They began organizing as women by the mid-1970s. ANUC's capacity for mobilization diminished in the 1980s, due to factionalism and government repression. It was thanks to the persistence of women in sustaining local-level activities that the movement survived. The murders of many male leaders during the paramilitary incursions of the 2000s left women's organizations at the forefront of peasant activism (Machado and Meertens 2010: chap. 5).

6 I consulted the pamphlet in the holdings of the Archivo de la Fundación del Sinú in Montería (AFS/M) but, since the archive is not catalogued, have listed it as an item in the bibliography.

7 Duplat made four documentary shorts in Guapi and Buenaventura using participatory-action methodologies (Fundación Patrimonio Fílmico Colombiano n.d.: 64; Higuita and López Diez 2011: 103–104, 182). He subsequently served as artistic director of *Alternativa*, belonging to what could be called the "Falsista" faction of the magazine's editorial staff (Agudelo 2007: 77–78, 80). It was through Duplat that the M-19 guerrilla group influenced *Alternativa*, and he, along with Fals's wife, María Cristina Salazar, was detained in 1979 after the security forces found a large cache of stolen arms buried in Salazar's garden (Agudelo 2007: 241–242).

8 Of course, graphic novels were not yet an established genre in the 1970s (Chute and DeKoven 2006: 770), which is why I call *El Boche* a "kind of" graphic novel.

9 Interview with Valencia, 15 July 2016, Montería.

10 Interview with Negrete, 4 June 2017, Montería.

11 Córdoba only became an independent administrative department of Colombia in 1952. Before that, it belonged to Bolívar, with its capital in Cartagena.

12 Interview with Parra Escobar, 14 June 2016, Bogotá.
13 Interview with Negrete, 4 June 2017, Montería.
14 The title is a riff on the short story "La increíble y triste historia de la cándida Eréndira y de su abuela desalmada" by Gabriel García Márquez (1979 [1972]).
15 I consulted this primer in the archives of the Fundación del Sinú (AFS/M) and cite it in the bibliography.

Chapter 6. Engagement and Reflection

1 It would be ponderous to parallel-track the magazine columns and *Historia de la cuestión agraria* (Fals Borda 1975). It suffices to draw interested readers' attention to my listings of *Alternativa* and *Alternativa del Pueblo* columns in the bibliography titled "La historia prohibida," "Historia de la cuestión agraria," and "La cuestión agraria." These columns become chapters of the cartilla, with only minimal changes. *Capitalismo, hacienda y poblamiento* (Fals Borda 1976) also makes use of those magazine columns that specifically refer to the Atlantic coast (Alt 1: 30–31; AP 26: 30; AP 30: 30–31).
2 A song that dates to the era of La Violencia in the 1950s. The lyrics were changed to reflect the revolutionary fervor of the 1970s: "The storm that makes my people tremble / oppressed and ravished by the law, / I grab the rifle in my hand / and I am filled by a new faith" (HDC IV: 178A).

Chapter 7. Fals Borda's Legacy

1 I confine my observations here to collaborative anthropology in Latin America. Its North American counterpart (Lassiter 2005; Lassiter et al. 2004) is more academically oriented and, while politically progressive, less activist than in Latin America, although collaborative anthropologists in the United States and Canada have a long tradition of working with tribal historians and other indigenous intellectuals (see, for example, Field 2008; Ridington and Hastings 1997), as well as with Native communities in Latin America (Hale and Stephen 2014). Following the lead of Hale (2006), some U.S. scholars have advocated for an "activist anthropology" that is more closely engaged with social movements than the traditional collaborative model (Checker 2005; Stuesse 2016) and that uses ethnography as an activist tool rather than a scholarly objective (Alonso Bejarano et al. 2019).
2 The future of the CNMH is uncertain under the Duque government, elected in 2018. Its current director refuses to recognize the armed conflict as political and has disparaged the center's insistence on collecting testimony from grassroots victims.
3 Since the 2016 signing of the peace accord with FARC, 486 defenders of human rights have been assassinated in Colombia, according to *El País* (27 July 2019).
4 Víctor Negrete shared this heart-rending reminiscence at a panel discussion at the Congress of the Action Research Network of the Americas, Cartagena, 13–15 June 2017.
5 6 April 2018. https://twitter.com/petrogustavo/status/982422319804141568?lang=en (accessed 6 September 2018).

6   The workshops are listed in the bibliography. With the exception of the San Pablo workshop, made up largely of high school students, the participants were adults engaged in some form or other of research combined with activism. No external funds were solicited for these workshops; the only expenditures were for the lunches served at some of the meetings, using the resources of the organizations themselves.

7   I didn't attempt this agenda with the high schoolers of San Pablo, who spent the workshop reading pages of Chalarka's graphic histories and thinking about the topics they would cover if they could write a comic book about the problems of their community.

8   The same could be said of UAIIN, but only a handful of its members were able to attend the workshop, due to conflicting obligations, and the workshop was facilitated by the younger and less experienced IAPES activists.

9   ACIN is engaged in a similar muralistic project (Segunda Minga Muralista del Pueblo Nasa 2016).

Archives

ACHUNC/B (Archivo Central e Histórico de la Universidad Nacional de Colombia, Bogotá). Colección Orlando Fals Borda. Catalogue: Accessed 8 November 2017. http://archistoricoun.wixsite.com/senderos-digitales/fondo-fals-borda-1.

AFS/M (Archivo de la Fundación del Sinú).

CDRBR/M (Centro de Documentación Regional "Orlando Fals Borda," Banco de la República, Montería, Córdoba). Colección Orlando Fals Borda. Catalogue: Accessed 8 November 2017. http://www.banrepcultural.org/sites/default/files/archivo -orlando-fals-borda.pdf.

CDRBR/M, CF (Colección Fotográfica Orlando Fals Borda).

CDRBR/M, CG (Colección de Grabaciones Orlando Fals Borda).

CINEP/B (Centro de Investigación y Educación Popular, Bogotá). Colección ANUC, Entrevistas.

PHS/P (Presbyterian Historical Society, Philadelphia). Worldwide Ministries, Self-Development of People.

Interviews

Aristizábal, Gilberto. Cali, 17 July 2009.

Castro, Carmen. Montería, 12 July 2016.

Chalarca, Marta. Montería, 5 July 2019.

Chalarca, Orlando. Montería, 18 July 2016, 2–3 and 6 June 2017, 11 July 2019.

Chalarca, Utamaro. Cartagena, 12 and 16 June 2017.

Eljach, Matilde. Popayán, 15 July 2009.

Fajardo, Darío. Bogotá, 12 August 2008.

Fals Borda, Orlando. Bogotá, 24 June 2008.

Findji, María Teresa. Cali, 16 July 2009.

Galeano, José. Montería, 15 July 2016.

Herrera, Néstor. Sincelejo, 13 July 2016.

Jiménez, Máximo. Montería, 10 July 2019.

Molano, Alfredo. Bogotá, 19 July 2016.

Negrete, Víctor. Montería, 22 July 2009, 8 February 2015 (Skype interview), 10 July 2016, 4 June 2017, 23 June 2018, 25 June 2018.

Ojeda, Diana, Pablo Guerra, Camilo Aguirre, Henry Díaz. Bogotá, 17 June and 7 July 2016.

Parra Escobar, Ernesto. Bogotá, 14 June 2016.

Pérez, Jesús. Montería, 23–26 July 2013.

Rojas, José María. Cali, 14 July 2013.

Sánchez Juliao, David. Bogotá, 4 August 2009.

Santana Luna, Adalgiza, Walberto Garcés, and Luis Pérez Rossi. Montería, 26 June 2018.

Valencia, Jorge, and Francisco Mendoza. Montería, 15 July 2016.

Workshops

Asociación de Cabildos Indígenas del Norte del Cauca Cxab Wala Kiwe (ACIN), Tejido de Educación, Caloto (Cauca), 4 July 2018.

Centro de Documentación Regional "Orlando Fals Borda," Banco de la República, Montería (Córdoba), July 2016, 25 June 2018, 11 July 2019.

Centro de Investigación y Educación Popular (CINEP), Bogotá, 19 June 2018.

Corporación Con-Vivamos, Comuna 1, Medellín, 14 June 2018.

Escuela Nacional Orlando Fals Borda, Bogotá, 1 July 2018.

Instituto de Investigación-Acción en Procesos Educativos y Sociales "Simón Rodríguez" (IAPES)/Universidad Autónoma Indígena Intercultural (UAIIN), Popayán, 7 July 2018.

Institutión Educativa Técnica Agroindustrial de San Pablo, San Pablo, María la Baja (Bolívar), 28 June 2018.

RedSaludPaz, Facultad de Veterinaria, Universidad Nacional de Colombia, Bogotá, 21 June 2018.

San Antero, Córdoba, 3 November 2019.

San Bernardo del Viento/Cañogrande, Córdoba, 6–7 July, 4 November 2019.

San José de Uré, Córdoba, 5 July 2019.

Universidad del Sinú, Trabajo Social, Montería, 10 July 2019.

Universidad Nacional de Colombia-Sede Medellín, Laboratorio de Fuentes Históricas/Corporación Cultural Estanislao Zuleta/Corporación Con-Vivamos, Medellín, 15 June 2018.

Alternativa (Alt)

Alternativa and *Alternativa del Pueblo* published most of their articles without bylines. While "Historia de la cuestión agraria" and other columns I cite were undoubtedly authored by Orlando Fals Borda, I list them anonymously, organized by issue and page number. *Alternativa* articles are cited in the text using the abbreviation "Alt" followed by the issue and page numbers; *Alternativa del Pueblo* is abbreviated as "AP," with the same mode of citation. The articles are arranged by date of publication.

"La historia prohibida II: Berástegui, hacienda de gamonales." *Alternativa* 1: 30–31 (15–28 February 1974).

"La historia prohibida 1: Los 'Nuevos Mundos' del Gallino Vargas y Cía Ltda." *Alternativa* 2: 30–31 (1–15 March 1974).

"La historia prohibida: La epopeya del palenque." *Alternativa* 10: 30–31 (24 June 1974).

"Habla Fals Borda: 'Sería absurdo un partido agrario.'" *Alternativa* 16: 9 (16–29 September 1974).

"Historia de la cuestión agraria en Colombia I." *Alternativa* 18: 30–31 (14–27 October 1974).

"Historia de la cuestión agraria en Colombia II." *Alternativa* 19: 30–31 (24 October–6 November 1974).

"'Alternativa' y 'Alterna-rosca': Debate sobre la prensa de izquierda." *Alternativa* 20: 5 (11–24 November 1974).

"Cartas del lector." *Alternativa* 20: 20–21 (11–24 November 1974).

"Cartas del lector." *Alternativa* 21: 22 (25 November–8 December 1974).

Alternativa del Pueblo (AP)

"La cuestión agraria en Colombia, parte 4: La tierra por merced." *Alternativa del Pueblo* 21: 30–31 (25 November–8 December 1974).

"Historia de la cuestión agraria, parte 5: Nace la hacienda." *Alternativa del Pueblo* 22–23: 46–47 (15 December 1974–15 January 1975).

"Historia de la cuestión agraria, parte 6: Se afirma el latifundio." *Alternativa del Pueblo* 24: 28–29 (20 January–2 February 1975).

"Historia de la cuestión agraria, parte 7: El papel sellado contra el hacha." *Alternativa del Pueblo* 25: 26–27 (3–15 February 1975).

"El Plan del Noroeste, engendro misionero contra la revolución colombiana." *Alternativa del Pueblo* 26: 12–13 (17 February–2 March 1975).

"Historia de la cuestión agraria, parte 8: La formación del campesinado." *Alternativa del Pueblo* 26: 28–29 (17 February–2 March 1975).

"Corralejas y poder terrateniente." *Alternativa del Pueblo* 26: 30 (17 February–2 March 1975).

"Historia de la cuestión agraria, parte 9: La rebelión de los cimarrones." *Alternativa del Pueblo* 27: 28–29 (3–17 March 1975).

"Declaración: La Rosca de Investigación y Acción Social se Retira de Alternativa del Pueblo." *Alternativa del Pueblo* 28: 10 (17–30 March 1975).

"Historia de la cuestión agraria, parte 10: Aparceros y colonos: Fuerza de choque." *Alternativa del Pueblo* 28: 28–29 (17–30 March 1975).

"Historia de la cuestión agraria, parte 11: La técnica al servicio de la explotación." *Alternativa del Pueblo* 29: 28–29 (31 March–13 April 1975).

"Historia de la cuestión agraria, parte 12: Máquinas y capital agrario." *Alternativa del Pueblo* 30: 28–29 (14–27 April 1975).

"Juana Julia Guzmán (1892–1975): Una luchadora." *Alternativa del Pueblo* 30: 30–31 (14–27 April 1975).

"Historia de la cuestión agraria, parte 13: La expansión del capitalismo." *Alternativa del Pueblo* 31: 28–29 (28 April–11 May 1975).

"Historia de la cuestión agraria, parte 14: La destrucción de los resguardos." *Alternativa del Pueblo* 32: 28–29 (12–26 May 1975).

"Historia de la cuestión agraria, parte 15: La descomposición del campesinado, el concierto forzoso." *Alternativa del Pueblo* 33: 28–29 (26 May–8 June 1975).

"Historia de la cuestión agraria, parte 16: De campesino a asalariado." *Alternativa del Pueblo* 24–25 (9–22 June 1975).

"El Instituto Lingüístico de Verano: ¿Filial de la CIA?" *Alternativa del Pueblo* 34: 18–19 (9–22 June 1975).

"Historia de la cuestión agraria, parte 17: El campesinado lucha por sobrevivir." *Alternativa del Pueblo* 35: 24–25 (23 June–6 July 1975).

"Los baluartes campesinos en Córdoba." *Alternativa del Pueblo* 36: 24–25 (21 July–3 August 1975).

"Carta al lector." *Alternativa del Pueblo* 38: 3–4 (4–17 August 1975).

Publications

Abadía Barrero, César Ernesto, and Héctor Camilo Ruiz Sánchez. 2018. "Enfrentando el neoliberalismo en Colombia: Arte y colaboración en un hospital en ruinas." *Etnográfica* 22(3): 575–603.

Acevedo, Juan. 1981. *Para hacer historietas*. Madrid: Editorial Popular.

Acevedo, Juan. 2015. *Mundo Cuy: Retrospectiva 1969–2015*. Lima: Instituto Cultural Peruano Norteamericano.

Achugar, Hugo. 1992. "Historias paralelas/ejemplares: La historia y la voz del otro." *Revista de Crítica Literaria Latinoamericana* 18(36): 51–73.

Agudelo, Carlos G. 2007. "Daring to Think Is Beginning to Fight: The History of Magazine Alternativa, Colombia, 1974–1980." PhD diss., Philip Perrill College of Journalism, University of Maryland, College Park.

Alonso Bejarano, Carolina, Lucia López Juárez, Mirian A. Mijangos García, and Daniel M. Goldstein. 2019. *Decolonizing Ethnography: Undocumented Immigrants and New Directions in Social Science*. Durham, NC: Duke University Press.

Altricher, Herbert, and Peter Gstettner. 1997. "Action Research: A Closed Chapter in the History of German Social Science?" In Robin McTaggart, ed., *Participatory Action Research: International Contexts and Consequences*, 45–77. Albany: SUNY Press.

Amnesty International. 2018. Colombia 2017/2018. Accessed 18 July 2018. https://www.amnesty.org/en/countries/americas/colombia/report-colombia/.

AMUCM (Asociación Municipal de Usuarios Campesinos de Montería). 1972. *Así luchamos por recuperar la tierra!* Montería: AMUCM.

ANUC (Asociación Nacional de Usuarios Campesinos). n.d. *La increible y triste historia de la reforma agraria y su INCORA desalmado*. N.p.: ANUC.

Archila Neira, Mauricio. 1973. "Proyecto de una metodología de acción social." Typescript. La María.

Archila Neira, Mauricio. 1986. "Retorno a la investigación social." *Boletín Cultural y Bibliografico* 7: 107–110. Bogotá.

Archila Neira, Mauricio. 1991. *Cultura e identidad obrera: Colombia 1910–1945*. Bogotá: CINEP.

Archila Neira, Mauricio. 2008. "El maoísmo en Colombia: La enfermedad juvenil del marxismo-leninismo." *Revista Controversia* 190: 148–195.

Archila Neira, Mauricio. 2013. "La investigación activa en Cinep." In Fernán González, ed., *Una apuesta por lo imposible, Cinep 40 años*, 239–265. Bogotá: CINEP/Programa por la Paz.

Archila Neira, Mauricio. 2015. *"Hasta cuando soñemos": Extractivismo e interculturalidad en el sur de La Guajira*. Bogotá: CINEP/Programa por la Paz.

Archila Neira, Mauricio, and Nidia Catherine González. 2010. *Movimiento indígena caucano: Historia y política*. Tunja: Sello Editorial Universidad Santo Tomás.

Arcila Aristizábal, Zoraida. 2017. *Ciencia y compromiso social: La instauración de la Sociología en la Universidad Nacional de Colombia, sede Bogotá, 1959-1970*. PhD diss., Facultad Latinoamericana de Ciencias Sociales, Sede Académica México, Mexico City.

Arrieta Fernández, Nohora. 2015. "Literatura y política en la 'reconstrucción' de Jegua en *Resistencia en el San Jorge*: Una lectura de los archivos personales de Orlando Fals Borda." *Tabula Rasa* 23: 105-129.

Barnet, Miguel, and Esteban Montejo. 2016 [1966]. *Biografía de un cimarrón*. Havana: Editorial Letras Cubanas.

Barragán León, Andrea Natalia. 2016. *Mapas parlantes: Memoria y territorio en el pueblo nasa-paéz, Cauca-Colombia*. Master's thesis, Universidad Nacional Autónoma de México, Mexico City.

Barthes, Roland. 1981 [1980]. *Camera Lucida: Reflections on Photography*. Translated by Richard Howard. New York: Hill and Wang.

Bartolomé, Miguel Alberto, Nelly Arevelo de Jiménez, Guillermo Bonfil Batalla, Esteban Emilio Mosonyi, Víctor Daniel Bonilla, Darcy Ribeiro, Gonzalo Castillo Cárdenas et al. 1971. "Declaración de Barbados." 30 January. http://www.servindi.org/pdf/Dec_Barbados_1.pdf.

Barz, Gregory F. 1996. "Confronting the Field(Note) In and Out of the Field: Music, Voices, Texts, and Experiences in Dialogue." In Gregory F. Barz and Timothy J. Cooley, *Shadows in the Field: New Perspectives for Fieldwork in Ethnomusicology*, 45-62. Oxford: Oxford University Press.

Becerra Becerra, Carmen Andrea, and John Jairo Rincón García. 2017a. *Campesinos de tierra y agua: Memorias sobre sujeto colectivo, trayectoria organizativa, daño y expectativas de reparación colectiva en la región Caribe 1960-2015: Campesinado en el departamento de Córdoba*. Bogotá: Centro Nacional de Memoria Histórica. Accessed 29 August 2017. http://www.centrodememoriahistorica.gov.co/informes/informes-2017/campesinos-tierra-agua.

Becerra Becerra, Carmen Andrea, and John Jairo Rincón García. 2017b. *Campesinos de tierra y agua: Memorias sobre sujeto colectivo, trayectoria organizativa, daño y expectativas de reparación colectiva en la región Caribe 1960-2015: Campesinado en el departamento de Sucre*. Bogotá: Centro Nacional de Memoria Histórica. Accessed 29 August 2017. http://www.centrodememoriahistorica.gov.co/informes/informes-2017/campesinos-tierra-agua.

Bechdel, Alison. 2006. *Fun Home: A Family Tragicomic*. New York: Mariner.

Bedoya Ortiz, Carlos Andrés. 2011. "Marta Rodríguez: Memoria y resistencia." *Nómadas* 35: 201-212.

Behar, Ruth. 1986. *Santa María del Monte: The Presence of the Past in a Spanish Village*. Princeton, NJ: Princeton University Press.

Behrensmeyer, Anna K. 2011. "Linking Researchers across Generations." In Michael R. Canfield, ed., *Field Notes on Science and Nature*, 89–108. Cambridge, MA: Harvard University Press.

Berger, John. 1987. "To Take Paper, to Draw: A World Through Lines." *Harper's Magazine* 267: 57–60.

Berger, John. 2001. "Drawn to That Moment." In Geoff Dyer, ed., *Selected Essays: John Berger*, 41–44. New York: Pantheon.

Berger, John. 2015. *Bento's Sketchbook*. London: Verso.

Bergquist, Charles. 1990. "In the Name of History: A Disciplinary Critique of Orlando Fals Borda's *Historia doble de la Costa*." *Latin American Research Review* 25(3): 156–176.

Berrocal Mendoza, Barney. 2017. "'El Boche,' las dos caras de una tragedia a orillas del Sinú." Accessed 12 January 2018. http://rionoticias.co/el-boche-las-dos-caras-de-una-tragedia-a-orillas-del-sinu/.

Bleichmar, Daniela. 2012. *Visible Empire: Botanical Expeditions and Visual Culture in the Hispanic Enlightenment*. Chicago: University of Chicago Press.

Boal, Augusto. 1985 [1974]. *Theatre of the Oppressed*. Translated by Charles A. and Maria-Odilia Leal McBride. New York: Theatre Communications Group.

Bolaños, Graciela, Abelardo Ramos, Joanne Rappaport, and Carlos Miñana. 2004. *¿Qué pasaría si la escuela . . . ? Treinta años de construcción educativa*. Popayán: Programa de Educación Bilingüe e Intercultural, Consejo Regional Indígena del Cauca.

Bologna, Marco, Fiorella Foscarini, and Gabriella Sonnewald. 2017. "Historical Sedimentation of Archival Materials: Reinterpreting a Foundational Concept in the Italian Archival Tradition." *Archivaria* 83: 35–57.

Bonilla, María Elvira. 2005. *Grandes conversaciones, grandes protagonistas*. Bogotá: Grupo Editorial Norma.

Bonilla, Víctor Daniel. 1972 [1968]. *Servants of God or Masters of Men? The Story of a Capuchin Mission in Amazonia*. Translated by Rosemary Sheed. Harmondsworth, UK: Penguin.

Bonilla, Víctor Daniel. 1977. *Historia política de los paeces*. Mimeo. Bogotá: Carta al CRIC 4.

Bonilla, Víctor Daniel. 1982. "Algunas experiencias del proyecto 'Mapas Parlantes.'" In Juan Eduardo García Huidobro, ed., *Alfabetización y educación de adultos en la región andina*, 145–161. Pátzcuaro, Mexico: UNESCO.

Bonilla, Víctor Daniel, Gonzalo Castillo, Orlando Fals Borda, and Augusto Libreros. 1972. *Causa popular, ciencia popular: Una metodología del conocimiento científico a través de la acción*. Bogotá: La Rosca de Investigación y Acción Social.

Bonilla, Víctor Daniel, Carlos Duplat, Gonzalo Castillo, Orlando Fals Borda, and Augusto Libreros. 1971. *Por ahí es la cosa: Ensayos de sociología e historia colombianas*. Bogotá: La Rosca de Investigación y Acción Social.

Brandão, Carlos Rodrigues. 2005. "Participatory Research and Participation in Research: A Look between Times and Spaces from Latin America." *International Journal of Action Research* 1(1): 43–68.

Bredehoft, Thomas A. 2011. "Style, Voice, and Authorship in Harvey Pekar's (Auto)(Bio)Graphical Comics." *College Literature* 38(3): 97–110.

Bringel, Breno, and Emiliano Maldonado. 2016. "Pensamento crítico latino-americano e pesquisa militante em Orlando Fals Borda: Práxis, subversão e libertação." *Revista Direito e Práxis* 7(13): 389–413.

Briones, Claudia. 2013. "Conocimientos sociales, conocimientos académicos: Asimetrías, colaboraciones, autonomías." Working Paper Series No. 39, desiguAL-dades.net, Research Network on Interdependent Inequalities in Latin America. Accessed 16 April 2018. http://www.desigualdades.net/Resources/Working_Paper /39_WP_Briones_Online.pdf.

Briones, Claudia. 2018. "Research through Collaborative Relationships: A Middle Ground for Reciprocal Transformations and Translations?" *Collaborative Anthropologies* 9(1–2): 32–39.

Briones, Claudia, Lorena Cañuqueo, Laura Kropff, and Miguel Leuman. 2007. "Assessing the Effects of Multicultural Neoliberalism: A Perspective from the South of the South (Patagonia, Argentina)." *Latin American and Caribbean Ethnic Studies* 2(1): 69–91.

Brown, Joshua. 1988. "Of Mice and Memory." *Oral History Review* 16(1): 91–109.

Campbell, Bruce D. 2009. *¡Viva la historieta!: Mexican Comics, NAFTA, and the Politics of Globalization*. Jackson: University Press of Mississippi.

Cardoso, Fernando H., and Francisco C. Weffort. 1973. "Ciencia y conciencia social." In Antonio Murga Frassinetti and Guillermo Bolls, eds., *América Latina: Dependencia y Subdesarrollo*, 77–104. San José, Costa Rica: Editorial Universitaria Centroamericana.

Casa de Pensamiento de la Çxhab Wala Kiwe-ACIN. n.d. *Pensando la investigación/Herramientas para la investigación*. Santander de Quilichao, Cauca: Casa de Pensamiento/ Corporación Ensayos para la Promoción de la Cultura Política.

Casagrande, Joseph B. 1960. *In the Company of Man: Twenty Portraits by Anthropologists*. New York: Harper.

Castillo Cárdenas, Gonzalo. 1987. *Liberation Theology from Below: The Life and Thought of Manuel Quintín Lame*. Maryknoll, NY: Orbis Books.

Cataño, Gonzalo. 1986. *La sociología en Colombia: Balance crítico*. Bogotá: Asociación Colombiana de Sociología/Departamento Nacional de Planeación/Plaza & Janes.

Celis, Leila. 2013. "Les mouvements sociaux dans le contexte de conflits armés: Causes et effets de la défense des droits humains (1980–2012)." PhD diss., University of Ottawa.

Cendales G., Lola, Germán Mariño S., and Mario Peresson T. 2016. "Dimensión Educativa, 40 años: Haciendo camino al andar." *Aportes* 60: 6–29.

Centro Nacional de Memoria Histórica (CNMH). 2018. *Desaparición forzada: Balance de la contribución del CNMH al esclarecimiento histórico*. Bogotá: Centro Nacional de Memoria Histórica. Accessed 26 March 2020. http://centrodememoriahistorica.gov .co/wp-content/uploads/2020/01/BALANCE_DESAPARICION_FORZADA.pdf.

Centro Popular de Estudios. 1972. *Manual para cursillos campesinos para cuadros del movimiento campesino*. Montería: Centro Popular de Estudios.

Centro Popular de Estudios. 1974. *Nuestra cartilla*. Montería: Centro Popular de Estudios.

Chakrabarty, Dipesh. 2000. *Provincializing Europe: Postcolonial Thought and Historical Difference.* Princeton, NJ: Princeton University Press.

Chalarka, Ulianov. 1985. *Historia gráfica de la lucha por la tierra en la Costa Atlántica.* Montería: Fundación del Sinú.

Checker, Melissa. 2005. *Polluted Promises: Environmental Racism and the Search for Justice in a Southern Town.* New York: New York University Press.

Chute, Hillary L. 2006. "Gothic Revival: Old Father, Old Artificer: Tracing the Roots of Alison Bechdel's Exhilarating New 'Tragicomic,' *Fun Home.*" *Village Voice,* 4 July. https://www.villagevoice.com/2006/07/04/gothic-revival-2/.

Chute, Hillary L. 2012. "Comics as Archives: Meta*Meta*Maus." *E-misférica* 9. Accessed 6 April 2016. https://hemisphericinstitute.org/en/emisferica-91/9-1-essays/comics-as -archives-metametamaus.html.

Chute, Hillary L. 2014. *Outside the Box: Interviews with Contemporary Cartoonists.* Chicago: University of Chicago Press.

Chute, Hillary L. 2017. "A Man Alone in a Comic Book." NYR *Daily,* 1 May. http://www .nybooks.com/daily/2017/05/01/a-man-alone-in-a-comic-book-guy-delisle/.

Chute, Hillary L., and Marianne DeKoven. 2006. "Introduction: Graphic Narrative." *Modern Fiction Studies* 52(4): 767–782.

CINEP (Centro de Investigación y Educación Popular). 2018. *De aquí no nos sacan: Recorridos de investigación local de jóvenes en el Caribe.* Bogotá: CINEP.

Clifford, James. 1983. "Power and Dialogue in Ethnography: Marcel Griaule's Initiation." In George W. Stocking Jr., ed., *Observers Observed: Essays on Ethnographic Fieldwork,* 121–156. Madison: University of Wisconsin Press.

Cojtí Cuxil, Demetrio. 1997. *Ri maya' moloj pa iximuleu/El movimiento maya (en Guatemala).* Guatemala: Editorial Cholsamaj.

Comunidad de Historia Mapuche. 2012. *Ta iñ fijke xipa rakizuameluwün: Historia, colonialismo y resistencia desde el país Mapuche.* Temuco: Ediciones Comunidad de Historia Mapuche.

Comunidad de Historia Mapuche. 2015. *Awükan ka kütrankan zugu Wajmapu meu: Violencias coloniales en Wajmapu.* Temuco: Ediciones Comunidad de Historia Mapuche.

Con-Vivamos. 2015. "Diálogo de saberes universidad-comunidad." Corporacion Con-Vivamos, Accessed 26 March 2020. http://www.convivamos.org/web25w/?p=773.

COPRORCO. n.d. *Historias que nadie cuenta.* N.p.

Crampton, Jeremy W. 2009. "Cartography: Performative, Participatory, Political." *Progress in Human Geography* 33(6): 840–848.

Dávila Flórez, Manuel. 1912. *Código de policía del Departamento de Bolívar, con las modificaciones introducidas por las Ordenanzas posteriores á la 54 de 1892.* Cartagena: Tip. de Vapor "Mogollón."

de Certeau, Michel. 1984 [1980]. *The Practice of Everyday Life.* Translated by Steven Rendall. Berkeley: University of California Press.

de Schutter, Antón [and Lola Cendales]. 1985. "El proceso de investigación participativa." *Aportes* 20: 54–72.

Dest, Anthony. 2019. "After the War: Violence and Resistance in Colombia." Doctoral diss., University of Texas at Austin.

Díaz, Antolín. 1935. *Sinú: Pasión y vida del trópico*. Bogotá: Editorial Santafé.

Díaz Arévalo, Juan Mario. 2017. "Orlando Fals-Borda or The Ethics of Subversion: Towards a Critique of Ideology of Political Violence in Colombia, 1948–1974." Doctoral diss., University of Roehampton, London.

Díaz Arévalo, Juan Mario. 2018a. "The Making of an Intellectual: Orlando Fals-Borda, 1948–1958." *Revista de Estudios Colombianos* 52: 6–15.

Díaz Arévalo, Juan Mario. 2018b. "Tras bambalinas: Los orígenes de la idea fundacional de La Rosca y el debate académico sobre la investigación acción (1969–1974)." Balance y Perspectivas de la Investigación Acción Participante (IAP), Universidad Nacional de Colombia, 9–11 August.

Díaz Arrieta, Alvaro. 2010. "La pesadilla del Boche." *ADA: Los escritos de Alvaro Díaz Arrieta* (blog), 29 April. https://alvarodiazarrieta.blogspot.com.co/2010/04/la-pesadilla -del-boche.html.

Dilley, R. M. 2002. "The Problem of Context in Social and Cultural Anthropology." *Language and Communication* 22(1): 437–456.

Douglas, Jennifer. 2013. "What We Talk about When We Talk about Original Order in Writers' Archives." *Archivaria* 76: 7–25.

Douglas, Jennifer. 2015. "The Archiving 'I': A Closer Look into the Archives of Writers." *Archivaria* 79: 53–89.

Douglas, Jennifer, and Heather MacNeil. 2009. "Arranging the Self: Literary and Archival Perspectives on Writers' Archives." *Archivaria* 67: 25–39.

D'Salete, Marcelo. 2019 [2017]. *Angola Janga: Kingdom of Runaway Slaves*. Translated by Andrea Rosenberg. Seattle: Fantagraphic Books.

Durango Espitia, Cristóbal Andrés. n.d. *Historia de Santo Domingo Vidal Villadiego: Religiosidad popular*. Bogotá: Mincultura.

Durango Padilla, Alba Lucía. 2012. "El papel de la hacienda en la configuración del espacio urbano y regional en Córdoba." Master's thesis, Facultad de Artes, Universidad Nacional de Colombia.

Dyrness, Andrea. 2008. "Research for Change versus Research as Change: Lessons from a 'Mujerista' Participatory Research Team." *Anthropology and Education Quarterly* 39(1): 23–44.

Eil, Philip. 2016. "John Lewis Marches On: 'Our Struggle Is a Struggle to Redeem the Soul of America.'" *Salon*, 8 August. http://www.salon.com/2016/08/08/john-lewis -marches-on-our-struggle-is-a-struggle-to-redeem-the-soul-of-america/.

El Refaie, Elisabeth. 2012. *Autobiographical Comics: Life Writing in Pictures*. Jackson: University Press of Mississippi.

Ernst, Nina. 2015. "Authenticity in Graphic Memoirs: Two Nordic Examples." *Image and Narrative* 16(2): 65–83.

Escalante, Gabriel. 2018. "El fondo Orlando Fals Borda: Un legado histórico, fundamental para la historia social y política en Colombia." Balance y Perspectivas de la Investigación Acción Participante (IAP), Universidad Nacional de Colombia, 9–11 August.

Exbrayat Boncompain, Jaime. 1939. *Reminiscencias monterianas*. [Montería?]: Editorial "Esfuerzo."

Exbrayat Boncompain, Jaime. 1994 [1971]. *Historia de Montería*. Montería: Alcaldía Mayor de Montería.

Fals Borda, Orlando. 1955. *Peasant Society in the Colombian Andes: A Sociological Study of Saucío*. Gainesville: University of Florida Press.

Fals Borda, Orlando. 1957. *El hombre y la tierra en Boyacá: Bases sociohistóricas para una reforma agraria*. Bogotá: Ediciones Documentos Colombianos.

Fals Borda, Orlando. 1959. "El vínculo con la tierra y su evolución en el departamento de Nariño." *Revista de la Academia Colombiana de Ciencias Exactas, Físicas y Naturales* 10: 9–14.

Fals Borda, Orlando. 1969. *Subversion and Social Change in Colombia*. Translated by Jacqueline D. Skiles. New York: Columbia University Press.

Fals Borda, Orlando. 1971. *Cooperatives and Rural Development in Latin America: An Analytic Report*. Geneva: United Nations Research Institute for Social Development.

Fals Borda, Orlando. 1975. *Historia de la cuestión agraria en Colombia*. Bogotá: Publicaciones de La Rosca.

Fals Borda, Orlando. 1976. *Capitalismo, hacienda y poblamiento: Su desarrollo en la Costa Atlántica*. Bogotá: Punta de Lanza.

Fals Borda, Orlando. 1978. *El problema de como investigar la realidad para transformarla: Por la praxis*. Bogotá: Ediciones Tercer Mundo. Summarized and translated into English in 1979c.

Fals Borda, Orlando. 1979a [1957]. *El hombre y la tierra en Boyacá*. Bogotá: Punta de Lanza.

Fals Borda, Orlando. 1979b. *Historia doble de la Costa: Tomo 1, Mompox y Loba*. Bogotá: Carlos Valencia Editores.

Fals Borda, Orlando. 1979c. "Investigating Reality in Order to Transform It: The Colombian Experience." *Dialectical Anthropology* 4(1): 33–55.

Fals Borda, Orlando. 1981. *Historia doble de la Costa: Tomo II, El Presidente Nieto*. Bogotá: Carlos Valencia Editores.

Fals Borda, Orlando. 1984. *Resistencia en el San Jorge: Historia doble de la Costa—3*. Bogotá: Carlos Valencia Editores.

Fals Borda, Orlando. 1985. *Knowledge and People's Power: Lessons with Peasants in Nicaragua, Mexico and Colombia*. New Delhi: Indian Social Institute.

Fals Borda, Orlando. 1986. *Retorno a la tierra: Historia doble de la Costa—4*. Bogotá: Carlos Valencia Editores.

Fals Borda, Orlando. 1987a. "The Application of Participatory Action-Research in Latin America." *International Sociology* 2(4): 329–347.

Fals Borda, Orlando. 1987b [1970]. *Ciencia propia y colonialismo intelectual: Los nuevos rumbos*. Bogotá: Carlos Valencia Editores.

Fals Borda, Orlando. 1991. "Some Basic Ingredients." In Orlando Fals Borda and Mohammad Anisur Rahman, eds., *Action and Knowledge: Breaking the Monopoly with Participatory Action-Research*, 3–12. New York: Apex.

Fals Borda, Orlando. 1998. *Participación popular: Retos del futuro*. Bogotá: ICFES/IEPRI/ Colciencias. [*People's Participation: Challenges Ahead*. Bogotá: Colciencias/IEPRI/TM Editores, 1998.]

Fals Borda, Orlando. 1999. "Fuentes y encrucijadas de la identidad sinuana." *Aguaita* 2: 78–81.

Fals Borda, Orlando. 2001. "Participatory (Action) Research in Social Theory: Origins and Challenges." In Peter Reason and Hilary Bradbury, eds., *Handbook of Action Research: Participative Inquiry and Practice*, 27–37. London: Sage.

Fals Borda, Orlando. 2007. "La investigación-acción en convergencias disciplinarias." *LASA Forum* 38(4): 17–22. Translated into English in 2008a.

Fals Borda, Orlando. 2008a. "Action Research in the Convergence of Disciplines." *International Journal of Action Research* 9(2): 155–167.

Fals Borda, Orlando. 2008b. "The Application of the Social Sciences' Contemporary Issues to Work on Participatory Action Research." *Human Organization* 67(4): 359–361.

Fals Borda, Orlando. 2009. *Una sociología sentipensante para América Latina*, ed. and intro. Víctor Manuel Moncayo. Buenos Aires: CLACSO.

Fals Borda, Orlando. 2010a [1993]. "El reordenamiento territorial: Itinerario de una idea." In *Antología Orlando Fals Borda*, 273–282. Preface by José María Rojas Guerra. Bogotá: Editorial Universidad Nacional de Colombia.

Fals Borda, Orlando. 2010b [1981]. "La ciencia y el pueblo: Nuevas reflexiones sobre la investigación-acción." In *Antología Orlando Fals Borda*, 179–200. Preface by José María Rojas Guerra. Bogotá: Editorial Universidad Nacional de Colombia.

Fals Borda, Orlando. 2010c [1959]. "La teoría y la realidad del cambio sociocultural en Colombia." In *Antología Orlando Fals Borda*, 65–93. Preface by José María Rojas Guerra. Bogotá: Editorial Universidad Nacional de Colombia.

Fals Borda, Orlando, and Carlos Rodrigues Brandão. 1986. *Investigación participativa*. Montevideo: Instituto del Hombre/Ediciones de la Banda Oriental.

Fals Borda, Orlando, and Mohammad Anisur Rahman, eds. 1991. Preface to *Action and Knowledge: Breaking the Monopoly with Participatory Action-Research*, vii–viii. New York: Apex.

Field, Les. 2008. *Abalone Tales: Collaborative Explorations of Sovereignty and Identity in Native California*. Durham, NC: Duke University Press.

Figueroa, José Antonio. 2009. *Realismo mágico, vallenato y violencia política en el Caribe colombiano*. Bogotá: Instituto Colombiano de Antropología e Historia.

Findji, María Teresa. 1992. "From Resistance to Social Movement: The Indigenous Authorities Movement in Colombia." In Arturo Escobar and Sonia Alvarez, eds., *The Making of Social Movements in Latin America: Identity, Strategy, and Democracy*, 112–133. Boulder, CO: Westview.

Fine, Michelle. 2017. *Just Research in Contentious Times: Widening the Methodological Imagination*. New York: Teachers College Press.

Flora, Cornelia Butler. 1984. "Roasting Donald Duck: Alternative Comics and Photo-novels in Latin America." *Journal of Popular Culture* 18(1): 163–188.

Foote, Nelson N., and Leonard Courell. 1955. *Identity and Interpersonal Competence*. Chicago: University of Chicago Press.

Freire, Paulo. 1970. "The Adult Literacy Process as Cultural Action for Freedom." *Harvard Educational Review* 40(2): 205–225.

Freire, Paulo. 2005 [1970]. *Pedagogy of the Oppressed*. Translated by Myra Bergman Ramos. New York: Continuum.

Fundación Patrimonio Fílmico Colombiano. n.d. *Documentales colombianos en cine, 1950–1992*. Accessed 6 February 2018. http://cine.8manos.in/wp-content/uploads /DocumentalesCol-101212.pdf.

Galeano, Eduardo. 1989. *Libro de los abrazos*. México: Siglo XXI.

Garcés González, José Luis. n.d. "Réquiem por El Percal." In Grupo "El Túnel." *La palabra compacta: Textos de El Túnel, siglo XXI*, 56–60. Montería: El Túnel.

Garcés González, José Luis. 1992. *Los locos de Montería*. Montería: Domus Libri.

García, Santiago. 1979. "La creación colectiva como proceso de trabajo en 'La Candelaria.'" *Taller de Teatro* 1(1): 5–16. Bogotá.

García, Vianney Judith, and Jorge Caballero Fula. 2012. "Unidad Indígena: Un periódico en la estrategia de comunicación del proceso indígena caucano." In Daniel Ricardo Peñaranda Supelano, ed., *Nuestra vida ha sido nuestra lucha: Resistencia y memoria en el Cauca indígena*, 275–307, Bogotá: Centro de Memoria Histórica. http://www.centrodememoriahistorica.gov.co/descargas/informes2012/cauca.pdf.

García Márquez, Gabriel. 1979 [1972]. *Innocent Eréndira and Other Stories*. Translated by Gregory Rabasa. New York: HarperCollins.

García Márquez, Gabriel. 1986 [1970]. *The Story of a Shipwrecked Sailor*. New York: Alfred A. Knopf.

Gaventa, John. 1988. "Participatory Research in North America." *Convergence* 21(2): 19–28.

Getz, Trevor R., and Liz Clarke. 2016. *Abina and the Important Men: A Graphic History*. Oxford: Oxford University Press.

Gittings, James A. 1993. *From Dream to Reality: A Contextual History of Twenty Years of the Presbyterian Self-Development Program*. Philadelphia: Presbyterian Committee on the Self-Development of People.

Glass, Liliane, and Víctor Daniel Bonilla. 1967. "La Reforma Agraria frente al minifundio nariñense." *Tierra* 5: entire issue.

Gómez Buendía, Blanca Ines. 2007. *Viajes, migraciones y desplazamientos: Ensayos de crítica cultural*. Bogotá: Editorial Pontificia Universidad Javeriana.

González Casanova, Pablo. 1969. *Sociología de la explotación*. Mexico City: Siglo XXI.

Gow, David D. 2008. *Countering Development: Indigenous Modernity and the Moral Imagination*. Durham, NC: Duke University Press.

Greenwood, Davydd J. 1999. *Action Research: From Practice to Writing in an International Action Research Development Program*. Amsterdam: John Benjamins.

Greenwood, Davydd J. 2008. "Theoretical Research, Applied Research, and Action Research: The Deinstitutionalization of Activist Research." In Charles R. Hale, ed., *Engaging Contradictions: Theory, Politics, and Methods of Activist Scholarship*, 319–340. Berkeley: University of California Press.

Greenwood, Davydd J., and Morten Levin. 2007. *Introduction to Action Research*. 2nd ed. Thousand Oaks, CA: Sage.

Groensteen, Thierry. 2007. *The System of Comics*. Translated by Bart Beaty and Nick Nguyen. Jackson: University Press of Mississippi.

Groensteen, Thierry. 2013. *Comics and Narration*. Translated by Ann Miller. Jackson: University Press of Mississippi.

Grupo de Memoria Histórica. 2013. *¡Basta ya! Memorias de guerra y dignidad*. Bogotá: Centro Nacional de Memoria Histórica.

Grupo El Túnel. n.d. *La palabra compacta: Textos de El Túnel, siglo XXI*. Montería: El Túnel.

Guber, Rosana. 2013. *La articulación etnográfica: Descubrimiento y trabajo de campo en la investigación de Esther Hermitte*. Buenos Aires: Editorial Biblos.

Guerra, Pablo. 2010. "Panorama de la historieta en Iberoamérica." In Jaime Correa, ed., *El comic, invitado a la biblioteca pública*, 36–53. Bogotá: Centro Regional para el Fomento del Libro en América Latina y el Caribe.

Guerrero Arias, Patricio. 2010. *Corazonar: Una antropología comprometida con la vida: Miradas otras desde Abya-Yala para la decolonización del poder, del saber y del ser*. Quito: Abya Yala/Universidad Politécnica Salesiana.

Guilbert, Emmanuel, Didier Lefèvre, and Frédéric Lemercier. 2009. *The Photographer: Into War-torn Afghanistan with Doctors Without Borders*. Translated by Alexis Siegel. New York: First Second.

Gutiérrez, Gustavo. 2012 [1971]. *A Theology of Liberation: History, Politics, and Salvation*. Translated by Sister Caridad Inda and John Eagleson. Maryknoll, NY: Orbis Books.

Gutiérrez, José. 2016. "Participatory Action Research (PAR) and the Colombian Peasant Reserve Zones: The Legacy of Orlando Fals Borda." *Development Education Review* 22: 59–76.

Guzmán Campos, Germán, Orlando Fals Borda, and Eduardo Umaña Luna. 1980 [1962]. *La Violencia en Colombia*. 2 vols. Bogotá: Carlos Valencia Editores.

Hale, Charles R. 2006. "Activist Research vs. Cultural Critique: Indigenous Land Rights and the Contradictions of Politically Engaged Anthropology." *Cultural Anthropology* 21(1): 96–120.

Hale, Charles R., and Rosamel Millaman Reinao. 2006. "Cultural Agency and Political Struggle in the Era of the *Indio Permitido*." In Doris Sommer, ed., *Cultural Agency in the Americas*, 281–304. Durham, NC: Duke University Press.

Hale, Charles R., and Rosamel Millaman Reinao. 2018. "Privatization of the 'Historic Debt'? Mapuche Territorial Claims and the Forest Industry in Southern Chile." *Latin American and Caribbean Ethnic Studies* 13(3): 305–325.

Hale, Charles R., and Lynn Stephen. 2014. *Otros Saberes: Collaborative Research on Indigenous and Afro-Descendent Cultural Politics*. Santa Fe, NM: SAR Press.

Hall, Budd. 1982. "Breaking the Monopoly of Knowledge: Research Methods, Participation and Development." In Budd L. Hall, Arthur Gillette, and Rajesh Tandon, eds., *Creating Knowledge: A Monopoly?* 13–26. New Delhi: Society for Participatory Research in Asia.

Hall, Budd. 1992. "From Margins to Center? The Development and Purpose of Participatory Research." *American Sociologist* 23(4): 15–28.

Hall, Budd. 2005. "In from the Cold? Reflections on Participatory Research from 1970–2005." *Convergence* 38(1): 5–24.

Haraway, Donna. 1991. "Situated Knowledges: The Science Question in Feminism and the Privilege of Partial Perspective." In *Simians, Cyborgs, and Women: The Reinvention of Nature*, 183–202. New York: Routledge.

Heinrich, Bernd. 2011. "Untangling the Bank." In Michael R. Canfield, ed., *Field Notes on Science and Nature*, 33–48. Cambridge, MA: Harvard University Press.

Higuita, Ana María, and Nathalí López Diez. 2011. "Memoria e imagen: Cine documental en Colombia, 1960–1993." Tesis de grado, Universidad de Antioquia.

Hinds, Harold E., Jr. 1977. "'No hay fuerza más poderosa que la mente humana': Kalimán." *Hispamérica* 6(18): 31–46.

Hirsch, Marianne. 1992–1993. "Family Pictures: Maus, Mourning, and Post-Memory." *Discourse* 15(2): 3–29.

Hirsch, Marianne, and Leo Spitzer. 2006. "Testimonial Objects: Memory, Gender, and Transmission." *Poetics Today* 27(2): 353–383.

Holland, Edward C. 2015. "Mapping Bosnia: Cartographic Representation in Joe Sacco's Graphic Narratives." In Daniel Worden, ed., *The Comics of Joe Sacco: Journalism in a Visual World*, 85–100. Jackson: University of Mississippi Press.

Horrocks, Dylan. 2010. *Hicksville*. Montreal: Drawn and Quarterly Publications.

Horton, Myles, and Paulo Freire. 1990. *We Make the Road by Walking: Conversations on Education and Social Change*. Edited by Brenda Bell, John Gaventa, and John Peters. Philadelphia: Temple University Press.

Human Rights Watch. 2018. "Colombia: Events of 2017." Accessed 18 August 2018. https://www.hrw.org/world-report/2018/country-chapters/colombia.

Hylton, Forrest, Aaron Tauss, and Juan Felipe Duque Agudelo. 2018. "Remaking the Common Good: The Crisis of Public Higher Education in Colombia." NACLA, 16 November. https://nacla.org/news/2018/11/17/remaking-common-good-crisis-public -higher-education-colombia.

Ismail, Feyzi, and Sangeeta Kamat. 2018. "NGOs, Social Movements and the Neoliberal State: Incorporation, Reinvention, Critique." *Critical Sociology* 44(4–5): 569–577.

Jaramillo Jiménez, Jaime Eduardo. 1996. "*Campesinos de los Andes*: Estudio pionero en la sociología colombiana." *Revista Colombiana de Sociología* 3(1): 53–82.

Jaramillo Jiménez, Jaime Eduardo. 2017. *Estudiar y hacer sociología en Colombia en los años sesenta*. Bogotá: Editorial Universidad Central.

Jaramillo Marín, Jefferson. 2012. "El libro *La Violencia en Colombia* (1962–1964): Radiografía emblemática de una época tristemente célebre." *Revista Colombiana de Sociología* 35(2): 35–64.

Jattin Torralvo, Alexis. 2019. *Colonia siria y libanesa en Lorica y sus cercanías*. N.p.

Jiménez, Máximo. 1975. "El indio del Sinú." Medellín: Discos Sonolux, 993–688.

Jordan, Steven. 2003. "Who Stole My Methodology? Co-opting PAR." *Globalisation, Societies and Education* 1(2): 185–200.

Karl, Robert A. 2017. *Forgotten Peace: Reform, Violence, and the Making of Contemporary Colombia*. Berkeley: University of California Press.

Ketelaar, Eric. 2001. "Tacit Narratives: The Meanings of Archives." *Archival Science* 1: 131–141.

Kropff, Laura. 2014. "Acerca del posicionamiento: Investigación activista, crítica cultural o activismo crítico." In Débora Betrisey and Silvina Merenson, eds., *Antropologías contemporáneas: Saberes, ejercicios y reflexiones*, 71–91. Buenos Aires: Miño y Dávila.

Lame, Manuel Quintín. 1971 [1939]. *En defensa de mi raza*. Ed. and intro. by Gonzalo Castillo. Bogotá: Comité de Defensa del Indio. English translation in Castillo Cárdenas 1987.

Larcom, Joan. 1983. "Following Deacon: The Problem of Ethnographic Reanalysis, 1926–1981." In George W. Stocking Jr., ed., *Observers Observed: Essays on Ethnographic Fieldwork*, 175–195. Madison: University of Wisconsin Press.

Lassiter, Luke Eric. 2005. *The Chicago Guide to Collaborative Ethnography*. Chicago: University of Chicago Press.

Lassiter, Luke Eric, Hurley Goodall, Elizabeth Campbell, and Michelle Natasya Johnson, eds. 2004. *The Other Side of Middletown: Exploring Muncie's African American Community*. Walnut Creek, CA: AltaMira.

Laurent, Muriel, Rubén Egea, and Alberto Vega. 2013. *El antagonista: Una historia de contrabando y color—novela gráfica*. Bogotá: Ediciones Uniandes.

Leal, Claudia, and Shawn Van Ausdal. 2013. "Landscapes of Freedom and Inequality: Environmental Histories of the Pacific and Caribbean Coasts of Colombia." Working paper 58, desiguALdades.net, Research Network on Interdependent Inequalities in Latin America. http://www.desigualdades.net/Working_Papers/Search-Working-Papers/working-paper-58-_landscapes-of-freedom-and-inequality_/index.html.

LeGrand, Catherine C. 1986. *Frontier Expansion and Peasant Protest in Colombia, 1850–1936*. Albuquerque: University of New Mexico Press.

LeGrand, Catherine C. 2013. "Legal Narratives of Citizenship, the Social Question, and Public Order in Colombia, 1915–1930 and After." *Citizenship Studies* 17(5): 530–550.

Lewis, John, Andrew Aydin, and Nate Powell. 2013–2016. *March*. 3 vols. Marietta, GA: Top Shelf Productions.

Leyva Solano, Xochitl. 2011. "Walking and Doing: About Decolonial Practices." *Collaborative Anthropologies* 4: 119–138.

Leyva Solano, Xochitl, and Shannon Speed. 2015. "Hacia la investigación descolonizada: Nuestra experiencia de co-labor." In Xochitl Leyva Solano, Camila Pascal, Axel Köhler, Hermenegildo Olguín Reza, and María del Refugio Velasco Contreras, eds., *Prácticas otras de conocimiento(s): Entre crisis, entre guerras*, vol. 1, 451–480. San Cristóbal de las Casas, Mexico: Cooperativa Editorial Retos.

Low, Carlos, and Marta Herrera. 1988. "Orlando Fals Borda: El Retorno a la Tierra." *Huellas*, Barranquilla 22: 43–47.

Lutkehaus, Nancy. 1990. "Refractions of Reality: On the Use of Other Ethnographers' Fieldnotes." In Roger Sanjek, ed., *Fieldnotes: The Makings of Anthropology*, 303–323. Ithaca, NY: Cornell University Press.

Macfarlane, Bruce. 2017. "The Paradox of Collaboration: A Moral Continuum." *Higher Education Research and Development* 36(3): 472–485.

Machado, Absalón, and Donny Meertens. 2010. *La tierra en disputa: Memorias de despojo y resistencia campesina en la costa Caribe (1960–2010)*. Bogotá: CNRR-Grupo de Memoria Histórica/Ediciones Semana. Accessed 9 March 2012. http://www .centrodememoriahistorica.gov.co/informes/informes-2010/la-tierra-en-disputa.

MacNeil, Heather. 2008. "Archivalterity: Rethinking Original Order." *Archivaria* 66: 1–24.

Malinowski, Bronislaw. 1965 [1935]. *Coral Gardens and Their Magic*. Vol. 1. Bloomington: Indiana University Press.

Malinowski, Bronislaw. 1984 [1922]. *Argonauts of the Western Pacific*. Prospect Heights, IL: Waveland.

Martínez, Alsal (Alfonso Salgado Martínez). 1973. *14 preguntas sobre economía política: Textos para cuadros campesinos*. Montería: Centro Popular de Estudios.

Martínez, Samuel. 2008. "Making Violence Visible: An Activist Anthropological Approach to Women's Rights Investigation." In Charles R. Hale, ed., *Engaging Contradictions: Theory, Politics, and Methods of Activist Scholarship*, 183–209. Berkeley: University of California Press.

Martínez Garnica, Armando. 2008–2009. *"Historia doble de la Costa*: El Legado que nos queda." *Aguaita* 19: 117–122.

Mata Caravaca, María. 2017. "The Concept of Archival 'Sedimentation': Its Meaning and Use in the Italian Context." *Archival Science* 17: 113–124.

Mato, Daniel, ed. 2012. "Educación superior y pueblos indígenas y afrodescendientes en América Latina: Constituciones, leyes, políticas públicas y prácticas institucionales." In *Educación superior y pueblos indígenas y afrodescendientes en América Latina: Normas, políticas y prácticas*, 13–98. Caracas: Instituto Internacional de la UNESCO para la Educación Superior en América Latina y el Caribe (ESALC-UNESCO).

McCloud, Scott. 1993. *Understanding Comics: The Invisible Art*. New York: William Morrow.

McRae, Douglas. 2015. "El hombre hicotea y la ecología de los paisajes acuáticos en *Resistencia en el San Jorge*." *Tabula Rasa* 23: 79–103.

McTaggart, Robin. 1994. "Participatory Action Research: Issues in Theory and Practice." *Educational Action Research* 2(3): 313–337.

McTaggart, Robin, ed. 1997. "Guiding Principles for Participatory Action Research." *Participatory Action Research: International Contexts and Consequences*, 25–43. Albany: SUNY Press.

Meehan, Jennifer. 2010. "Rethinking Original Order and Personal Records." *Archivaria* 70: 27–44.

Meisel Roca, Adolfo. 2002. "Mesa Redonda: *El Presidente Nieto*, de Orlando Fals Borda." In Haroldo Calvo Stevenson and Adolfo Meisel Roca, eds., *Cartagena de Indias en el siglo XIX*, 263–305. Bogotá: Universidad Jorge Tadeo Lozano and Banco de la Republica, Seccional del Caribe.

Merino, Ana. 2003. *El cómic hispánico*. Madrid: Cátedra.

Mills, C. Wright. 1959. *The Sociological Imagination*. Oxford: Oxford University Press.

Molano, Alfredo. 1998a. "Cartagena Revisited: Twenty Years On." In Orlando Fals Borda, ed., *People's Participation: Challenges Ahead*, 3–10. Bogotá: Colciencias/IEPRI/ TM Editores.

Molano, Alfredo. 1998b. "Mi historia de vida con las historias de vida." In Thierry Lulle, Pilar Vargas, Lucero Zamudio, eds., *Los usos de la historia de vida en las ciencias sociales*, 102–111. Bogotá: Centro de Investigaciones sobre Dinámica Social de la U. Externado de Colombia.

Mora Vélez, Antonio. 2010. "Cómo se formó el barrio La Granja." *Capuniá* 24(17): 8–9. Montería.

Moreno Moreno, Mónica Cecilia. 2017a. "Construyendo una noción de campesinos con un método." *Revista Latinoamericana de Metodología de las Ciencias Sociales* 7(2). https://www.relmecs.fahce.unlp.edu.ar/article/view/RELMECSe028 /8919.

Moreno Moreno, Mónica Cecilia. 2017b. "Orlando Fals Borda: Ideas, prácticas y redes, 1950-1974." PhD diss., Universidad Nacional de Colombia.

Morrison, Toni. 1995. "The Site of Memory." In William Zinsser, ed., *Inventing the Truth: The Art and Craft of Memoir*, 83–102. Boston: Houghton Mifflin.

Naranjo Botero, María Elvira. 2018. "Aportes de los viviendistas colombianos a la paz en el posacuerdo: Un ejercicio de Investigación Acción Participativa con fundadores barriales." *Revista Colombiana de Sociología* 41(1): 157-174.

Negrete Barrera, Víctor Manuel. 1981. *Origen de las luchas agrarias en Córdoba*. Montería: Fundación del Caribe.

Negrete Barrera, Víctor Manuel. 1983. *La investigación-acción participativa en Córdoba*. Montería: Fundación del Sinú.

Negrete Barrera, Víctor Manuel. 2007. *Lucha por la tierra y reforma agraria en Córdoba*. Montería: Universidad del Sinú Elías Bechara Zainúm.

Negrete Barrera, Víctor Manuel. 2008a. "A la memoria del maestro Orlando Fals Borda: Bases y desarrollo de la investigación-acción participativa en Córdoba (Colombia)." *International Journal of Psychological Research* 1(2): 85-97. Bogotá.

Negrete Barrera, Víctor Manuel. 2008b. "Orlando Fals Borda en Córdoba: Bases y desarrollo de la investigación acción participativa." *Revista Peri-feria* 7. Neiva.

Negrete Barrera, Víctor Manuel. 2018. *Los humedales en Córdoba 1987-2007: ¿Cuántos hemos perdido y deteriorado? ¿Es posible su recuperación?* Montería: Fundación del Sinú/Centro de Estudios Sociales y Políticos, Universidad del Sinú Elías Bechara Zainám.

Ocampo, Gloria Isabel. 2003. "Urbanización por invasión: Conflicto urbano, clientelismo y resistencia en Córdoba (Colombia)." *Revista Colombiana de Antropología* 39: 237-272.

Ocampo, Gloria Isabel. 2007. *La instauración de la ganadería en el valle del Sinú: La hacienda Marta Magdalena, 1881-1956*. Medellín: Editorial Universidad de Antioquia.

Ocampo, Gloria Isabel. 2014. *Poderes regionales, clientelismo y estado: Etnografías del poder y la política en Córdoba, Colombia*. Bogotá: Odecofi-CINEP.

Oesterheld, H. G., and F. Solano López. 2013 [1957-1959]. *El eternauta*. Barcelona: Norma.

Ojeda, Diana, Pablo Guerra, Camilo Aguirre, and Henry Díaz. 2016. *Caminos condena-dos*. Bogotá: Pontificia Universidad Javeriana.

Ojeda, Diana, Jennifer Petzl, Catalina Quiroga, Ana Catalina Rodríguez, and Juan Guillermo Rojas. 2015. "Paisajes del despojo cotidiano: Acaparamiento de tierra y agua en Montes de María, Colombia." *Revista de Estudios Sociales* 34: 107–119.

Ortega Valencia, Piedad, and Alfonso Torres Carrillo. 2011. "Lola Cendales González, entre trayectos y proyectos en la educación popular." *Revista Colombiana de Educación* 61: 333–357.

Osorio Sánchez, César. 2017. "Participatory Action Research for Recovery of the Senses and Sources of Historic Memory." In Lonnie L. Rowell, Catherine D. Bruce, Joseph M. Shosh, and Margaret M. Riel, eds., *Palgrave International Handbook of Action Research*, 807–821. London: Palgrave.

Ottenberg, Simon. 1990. "Thirty Years of Fieldnotes: Changing Relationships to the Text." In Roger Sanjek, ed., *Fieldnotes: The Makings of Anthropology*, 139–160. Ithaca, NY: Cornell University Press.

Park, Peter, Mary Brydon-Miller, Budd Hall, and Ted Jackson, eds. 1993. *Voices of Change: Participatory Research in the United States and Canada*. Westport, CT: Bergin & Garvey.

Parlato, Ronald, Margaret Burns Parlato, and Bonnie J. Cain. 1980. *Fotonovelas and Comic Books—The Use of Popular Graphic Media in Development*. Report. Washington, DC: Office of Education and Human Resources, Development Support Bureau, U.S. Agency for International Development.

Parra Escobar, Ernesto. 1983. *La investigación-acción en la Costa Atlántica: Evaluación de La Rosca, 1972–1974*. Cali: Fundación para la Comunicación Popular (FUNCOP).

Parra Salazar, Mayra Natalia. 2015. *¡A teatro camaradas!: Dramaturgia militante y política de masas en Colombia (1965–1975)*. Medellín: Fondo Editorial FCSH (Facultad de Ciencias Sociales y Humanas de la Universidad de Antioquia).

Parsons, James. 1970. "Los campos de cultivos pre-hispánicos del bajo San Jorge." *Revista de la Academia Colombiana de Ciencias* 12(48): 449–458.

Pedri, Nancy. 2011. "When Photographs Aren't Quite Enough: Reflections on Photography and Cartooning in *Le Photographe*." *ImageTexT: Interdisciplinary Comics Studies* 6(1). http://www.english.ufl.edu/imagetext/archives/v6_1/pedri.

Pekar, Harvey, and R. Crumb. 1996. *Bob and Harv's Comics*. New York: Four Walls Eight Windows.

Pell, Susan. 2015. "Radicalizing the Politics of the Archive: An Ethnographic Reading of an Activist Archive." *Archivaria* 80: 33–57.

Pereira Fernández, Alexander. 2005. "El itinerario ideológico de Fals Borda, 1925–1957." Trabajo de grado, Universidad Nacional de Colombia.

Pereira Fernández, Alexander. 2008. "Fals Borda: La formación de un intelectual disór-gano." *Anuario Colombiano de Historia Social y de la Cultura* 35: 375–411. Bogotá.

Pereira Fernández, Alexander. 2008–2009. "Orlando Fals Borda: El nacimiento de una vocación." *Aguaita* 19: 101–116.

Pérez, Jesús María. 2010. *Luchas campesinas y reforma agraria: Memorias de un dirigente de la ANUC en la costa caribe*. Bogotá: Grupo de Memoria Histórica. http://www.centrodememoriahistorica.gov.co.

Pernett, Valentina. 2015. "De cómo Moisés Banquett y Orlando Fals Borda hablan de la ANUC." *Tabula Rasa* 23: 23–36.

Plazas, Clemencia, and Ana María Falchetti. 1981. *Asentamientos prehispánicos en el bajo río San Jorge*. Bogotá: Fundación de Investigaciones Arqueológicas Nacionales.

Plazas, Clemencia, Ana María Falchetti, Thomas van der Hammen, and Pedro Botero. 1988. "Cambios ambientales y desarrollo cultural en el bajo río San Jorge." *Boletín del Museo del Oro* 20: 55–88.

Poggi, Alfredo Ignacio. 2015. "De lo etnográfico a lo teológico-político: Investigación-acción ecuménica de *La Rosca* en comunidades protestantes de Córdoba, Colombia." *Tabula Rasa* 23: 59–77.

Polack, Gillian. 2014. "Novelists and Their History." *Rethinking History* 18(4): 522–542.

Polo Acuña, José Trinidad. 2018. "Los franceses en el valle del río Sinú (Colombia). El caso de la familia Lacharme en Montería: Sus actividades económicas 1850-1950." *Memorias, Revista Digital de Historia y Arqueología desde el Caribe Colombiano* 14(36): 31–56.

Posada Carbó, Eduardo. 1998. *El Caribe colombiano: Una historia regional (1870-1950)*. Bogotá: Banco de la República/El Áncora.

Puche Puche, Edgardo. 1998. *Crónicas y estampas de Montería*. Montería: Gerco Editores.

RACCACH (Red de Artistas, Comunicadores Comunitarios y Antropólogos de Chiapas). 2010. *Sjalel kibeltik/Sts'isjel ja kechtiki'/Tejiendo nuestras raíces*. Accessed 24 July 2015. http://jkopkutik.org/sjalelkibeltik/.

Rahman, Muhammad Anisur, and Orlando Fals Borda, eds. 1991. "A Self-Review of PAR." In *Action and Knowledge: Breaking the Monopoly with Participatory Action-Research*, 24–34. New York: Apex.

Randall, Margaret. 1992. "¿Qué es, y cómo se hace un testimonio?" *Revista de Crítica Literaria Latinoamericana* 18(36): 23–47.

Rappaport, Joanne. 2005. *Intercultural Utopias: Public Intellectuals, Cultural Experimentation, and Ethnic Pluralism in Colombia*. Durham, NC: Duke University Press.

Rappaport, Joanne. 2008. "Beyond Participant Observation: Collaborative Ethnography as Theoretical Innovation." *Collaborative Anthropologies* 1: 1–31.

Rappaport, Joanne. 2015. "La investigación como trabajo de la imaginación." *Revista Señas (Revista de la Casa del Pensamiento de la Çxab Wala Kiwe—ACIN)* 4: 117–123. Santander de Quilichao, Colombia.

Rappaport, Joanne. 2018. "Rethinking the Meaning of Research in Collaborative Relationships." *Collaborative Anthropologies* 9(1–2): 1–31.

Rappaport, Joanne, and Víctor Negrete. 2015. "La IAP con las comunidades: El caso de los folletos ilustrados." *Documentos para la reflexión 10*, 37–44. Montería: Centro de Estudios Sociales y Políticos, Universidad del Sinú Elías Bechara Zainúm.

Rässler, Susanne, Donald B. Rubin, and Nathaniel Schenker. 2003. "Imputation." In Michael Lewis-Beck, Alan E. Bryman, and Tim Futing Liao, *The Sage Encyclopedia of Social Science Research Methods*, 477–482. Thousand Oaks, CA: Sage.

Reason, Peter, and Hilary Bradbury, eds. 2008. Introduction to *The Sage Handbook of Action Research: Participative Inquiry and Practic*, 1–10. 2nd ed. London: Sage.

Restrepo, Gabriel. 2002. *Peregrinación en pos de omega: Sociología y sociedad en Colombia*. Bogotá: Universidad Nacional de Colombia.

Reyes Posada, Alejandro. 1978. *Latifundio y poder político: La hacienda ganadera en Sucre.* Bogotá: Editorial CINEP.

Riaño-Alcalá, Pilar. 2006. *Dwellers of Memory: Youth and Violence in Medellín, Colombia.* New Brunswick: Transaction Publishers.

Riaño-Alcalá, Pilar. 2009. *Recordar y narrar el conflicto: Herramientas para reconstruir memoria histórica.* Bogotá: Grupo de Memoria Histórica. Accessed 23 June 2012. www.centrodememoriahistorica.gov.co/index.php/informes-gmh/informes-2009/caja-de-herramientas.

Riaño-Alcalá, Pilar. 2013. *Remembering and Narrating Conflict: Resources for Doing Historical Memory Work.* Bogotá: Centro Nacional de Memoria Histórica. http://blogs.ubc.ca/historicalmemory/files/2015/02/0_RememberingNarratingConflict_V2.pdf.

Ridington, Robin, and Dennis Hastings. 1997. *Blessing for a Long Time: The Sacred Pole of the Omaha Tribe.* Lincoln: University of Nebraska Press.

Rivera Cusicanqui, Silvia. 1982. *Política e ideología en el movimiento campesino colombiano: El caso de la ANUC (Asociación Nacional de Usuarios Campesinos).* Bogotá: CINEP.

Rivera Cusicanqui, Silvia. 2004. "El potencial epistemológico y teórico de la historia oral: De la lógica instrumental a la descolonización de la historia." *Peri-feria* 4: 16–24. Neiva.

Rivera Cusicanqui, Silvia. 2010. *Ch'ixinakax utsiwa: Una reflexión sobre prácticas y discursos descolonizadores.* Buenos Aires: Tinta Limón.

Robles Lomeli, Jafte Delean. 2015. "El tatarabuelo a la sombra del caudillo: Efectos y defectos testimoniales de la voz Mier en *El Presidente Nieto* de Orlando Fals Borda." *Tabula Rasa* 23: 37–57.

Robles Lomeli, Jafte Delean. 2019. *La doble historia del testimonio en la costa colombiana: Aproximaciones a una episteme alternativa.* PhD diss., Georgetown University.

Rojas Guerra, José María. 2010. "Semblanza y aportes metodológicos de un investigador social: Orlando Fals Borda." Paper presented at the Simposio Internacional de Investigadores en Ciencias Sociales, Medellín, Universidad de Antioquia, 30 November–3 December. http://aprendeenlinea.udea.edu.co/revistas/index.php/ceo/article/viewFile/7591/7028.

Rojas Guerra, José María. 2014. *Orlando Fals Borda: Fundador de la sociología científica en Colombia.* Medellín: Centro de Estudios de Opinión, Universidad de Antioquia.

Rosca de Investigación y Acción Social. 1974. *"La verdad es revolucionaria": Manifiesto de la Fundación Rosca de Investigación y Acción Social.* Bogotá: Fundación Rosca de Investigación y Acción Social.

Rosemblatt, Karin Alejandra. 2014. "Modernization, Dependency, and the Global in Mexican Critiques of Anthropology." *Journal of Global History* 9(1): 94–121.

Rudqvist, Anders. 1983. "La organización campesina y la izquierda: ANUC en Colombia, 1970–1980." Informes de Investigación no. 1, Centro de Estudios Latinoamericanos, Uppsala University, Sweden.

Rudqvist, Anders. 1986. *Peasant Struggle and Action Research in Colombia.* Vol. 3. Uppsala, Sweden: Research Reports from the Department of Sociology, Uppsala University.

Sacco, Joe. 2000. *Safe Area Goražde: The War in Eastern Bosnia 1992–95.* Seattle: Fantagraphics Books.

Sacco, Joe. 2002. "Joe Sacco: Presentation from the 2002 UF Comics Conference." *ImageTexT: Interdisciplinary Comics Studies* 1(1). http://www.english.ufl.edu/imagetext/archives/v1_1/sacco/index.shtml.

Sacco, Joe. 2012. *Journalism*. New York: Metropolitan Books.

Sacco, Joe, and Hillary Chute. 2011. "Interview." *Believer*. June 1. http://www.believermag.com/issues/201106/?read=interview_sacco.

Sacco, Joe, and W. J. T. Mitchell. 2014. "Public Conversation." *Critical Inquiry* 40(3): 53–70.

Sánchez Juliao, David. 1975. *Historias de Raca Mandaca*. Montería: Fundación del Caribe.

Sánchez Juliao, David. 1999 [1974]. *¿Por qué me llevas al hospital en canoa, papá?* Bogotá: Plaza & Janés.

Sanjek, Roger, ed. 1990a. "A Vocabulary for Fieldnotes." In *Fieldnotes: The Makings of Anthropology*, 92–121. Ithaca, NY: Cornell University Press.

Sanjek, Roger, ed. 1990b. "The Secret Life of Fieldnotes." In *Fieldnotes: The Makings of Anthropology*, 187–270. Ithaca, NY: Cornell University Press.

Sanjinés, Jorge, and Grupo Ukamao. 1979. *Teoría y práctica de un cine junto al pueblo*. Mexico City: Siglo XXI.

Santos, Boaventura de Sousa. 1998. "The Fall of the *Angelus Novus*: Beyond the Modern Game of Roots and Options." *Current Sociology* 46(2): 81–118.

Santos, Boaventura de Sousa. 2014. *Epistemologies of the South: Justice against Epistemicide*. London: Routledge.

Santos, Boaventura de Sousa. 2018. *The End of the Cognitive Empire: The Coming of Age of Epistemologies of the South*. Durham, NC: Duke University Press.

Schecter, Ronald, and Liz Clarke. 2014. *Mendoza the Jew: Boxing, Manliness, and Nationalism, a Graphic History*. Oxford: Oxford University Press.

Segunda Minga Muralista del Pueblo Nasa. 2016. *Revista Ya'ja: Tejiendo en comunidad*. Toribío: Autoridades Tradiciones de los Cabildos de San Francisco, Toribío y Tacueyó/CECIDIC/Centro Nacional de Memoria Histórica/Colectivo Cultural Wipala. September. http://www.centrodememoriahistorica.gov.co/micrositios/minga-muralista/revista-ya-ja.pdf.

Serrano Suárez, Beatriz Elena. 2004. "The Sinú River Delta on the Northwestern Caribbean Coast of Colombia: Bay Infilling Associated with Delta Development." *Journal of South American Earth Sciences* 16: 623–631.

Shaull, M. Richard. 1967. "The Revolutionary Challenge to Church and Theology." *Theology Today* 23(4): 470–480.

Simposio Mundial de Cartagena. 1978. *Crítica y política en ciencias sociales: El debate sobre teoría y práctica*. 2 vols. Bogotá: Punta de Lanza.

Smith, Robert J. 1990. "Hearing Voices, Joining the Chorus: Appropriating Someone Else's Fieldnotes." In Roger Sanjek, ed., *Fieldnotes: The Makings of Anthropology*, 356–370. Ithaca, NY: Cornell University Press.

Smith, T. Lynn, Justo Díaz Rodríguez, and Luis Roberto García. 1944. *Tabio: Estudio de la organización social rural*. Bogotá: Editorial Minerva.

Sociedad de Jóvenes Cristianos, Primera Iglesia Evangélica. 1973. *¡Escucha cristiano!* Cereté, Córdoba: Sociedad de Jóvenes Cristianos.

Sontag, Susan. 1973. *On Photography*. New York: Farrar, Straus & Giroux.

Sousanis, Nick. 2015. *Unflattening*. Cambridge, MA: Harvard University Press.

Spiegelman, Art. 1973. *Maus: A Survivor's Tale*. New York: Pantheon.

Spiegelman, Art. 1986. *Maus: A Survivor's Tale II: And Here My Troubles Began*. New York: Pantheon.

Spiegelman, Art. 2011. *MetaMaus: A Look inside a Modern Classic, Maus*. New York: Random House.

Stavenhagen, Rodolfo. 1971. "Decolonializing Applied Social Sciences." *Human Organization* 30(4): 333–357.

Stoler, Ann Laura. 2002. "Colonial Archives and the Arts of Governance." *Archival Science* 2: 87–109.

Stoller, Paul. 1994. "Embodying Colonial Memories." *American Anthropologist* 96(3): 634–648.

Striffler, Luis. 1920 [1880]. *El río San Jorge, aumentado con una relación histórica y geográfica de sus principales poblaciones por Eugenio Quintero A.* Cartagena: Tipografía de El Anunciador.

Striffler, Luis. [1990?] [1875]. *El Alto Sinú: Historia del primer establecimiento para extracción de oro en 1844*. Barranquilla: Ediciones Gobernación del Atlántico.

Stuesse, Angela. 2016. *Scratching Out a Living: Latinos, Race, and Work in the Deep South*. Berkeley: University of California Press.

Swantz, Marja-Liisa. 1982. "Research as Education for Development: A Tanzanian Case." In Budd L. Hall, Arthur Gillette, and Rajesh Tandon, eds., *Creating Knowledge: A Monopoly?*, 113–126. New Delhi: Society for Participatory Research in Asia.

Tandon, Rajesh. 1988. "Social Transformation and Participatory Research." *Convergence* 21(2–3): 5–18.

Tattay, Pablo. 2012. "Construcción del poder propio en el movimiento indígena del Cauca." In Daniel Ricardo Peñaranda Supelano, ed., *Nuestra vida ha sido nuestra lucha: Resistencia y memoria en el Cauca indígena*, 52–83. Bogotá: Centro de Memoria Histórica. http://www.centrodememoriahistorica.gov.co/descargas/informes2012/cauca.pdf.

Taylor, Diana. 2003. *The Archive and the Repertoire: Performing Cultural Memory in the Americas*. Durham, NC: Duke University Press.

Tejada Cano, Luis. 1977. *Gotas de tinta*. Bogotá: Biblioteca Básica Colombiana, Instituto Colombiano de Cultura.

Tillis, Antonio D. 2005. *Manuel Zapata Olivella and the "Darkening" of Latin American Literature*. Columbia: University of Missouri Press.

Thon, Jan-Noël. 2013. "Who's Telling the Tale? Authors and Narrators in Graphic Narrative." In Daniel Stein and Jan-Noël Thon, eds., *From Comic Strips to Graphic Novels: Contributions to the Theory and History of Graphic Narrative*, 67–99. Berlin: De Gruyter.

Torres Carrillo, Alfonso. 2010. "Generating Knowledge in Popular Education: From Participatory Research to the Systematization of Experiences." *International Journal of Action Research* 6(2–3): 196–222.

Torres Restrepo, Camilo. 1985. *Obras escogidas*. Bogotá: Fundación Pro-Cultura/Comité de Solidaridad con los Presos Políticos/Revista Solidaridad/Movimiento de Cristianos por el Socialismo.

Trouillot, Michel-Rolph. 1995. *Silencing the Past: Power and the Production of History*. Boston: Beacon.

Trudeau, Garry. 2017. "The Comic Strip's Heyday in 'Cartoon Country.'" *New York Times Book Review*, 11 December: 1, 20.

Universidad Nacional de Colombia, Unidad Nacional de Archivo. 2004. *Archivos de investigadores de la Universidad Nacional de Colombia: Inventario Documental Orlando Fals Borda, 1644-2002*. Bogotá: Universidad Nacional de Colombia.

Uribe, María Tila. 1994. *Los años escondidos: Sueños y rebeldías en la década del veinte*. Bogotá: CESTRA-CEREC.

Valencia Hernández, Lucy Margarita, and Paola Andrea Márquez Meza. 2012. "Guillermo Valencia Salgado y su influencia en la literatura del Sinú." Trabajo de grado, Universidad Tecnológica de Pereira. Accessed 2 May 2018. http:// recursosbiblioteca.utp.edu.co/tesisd/textoyanexos/9289861V152.pdf#page =3&zoom=auto,-95,46.

Valencia Molina, Jorge. 1987. "La primera radionovela: Entrevista a Jorge Valencia Molina (periodista)." *La Revista (Academia de Historia de Córdoba)*, April: 16-17.

Valencia Salgado, Guillermo (Compae Goyo). 1980. *El Sinú y otros cantos*. Montería: UniCórdoba/El Túnel.

Van Ausdal, Shawn. 2008. "Un mosaico cambiante: Notas sobre una geografía histórica de la ganadería en Colombia, 1850-1950." In Alberto Guillermo Flórez-Malagón, ed., *El poder de la carne: Historias de ganaderías en la primera mitad del siglo XX en Colombia*, 47-117. Bogotá: Pontificia Universidad Javeriana.

Van Ausdal, Shawn. 2009. "Potreros, ganancias y poder: Una historia ambiental de la ganadería en Colombia, 1850-1950." *Historia Crítica*, no. especial 1: 126-149.

Vasco Uribe, Luis Guillermo. 2002. *Entre selva y páramo: Viviendo y pensando la lucha indígena*. Bogotá: Instituto Colombiano de Antropología e Historia.

Vasco Uribe, Luis Guillermo. 2011 "Rethinking Fieldwork and Ethnographic Writing." *Collaborative Anthropologies* 4: 18-66.

Vázquez, Laura. 2010. *El oficio de las viñetas: La industria de la historieta argentina*. Buenos Aires: Paidós.

Vega Cantor, Renán. 2002. *Gente muy rebelde: 2. Indígenas, campesinos y protestas agrarias*. Bogotá: Ediciones Pensamiento Crítico.

Velasco Puche, Carlos. 1963. *La bruja de Tucurá*. Cartagena: Imprenta Departamental.

Vélez Torres, Irene, Sandra Rátiva Gaona, and Daniel Varela Corredor. 2012. "Cartografía social como metodología colaborativa de investigación en el territorio afrodescendiente de la cuenca alta del río Cauca." *Cuadernos de Geografía-Revista Colombiana de Geografía* 21(2): 59-73.

Viloria de la Hoz, Joaquín. 2003. *Lorica, una colonia árabe a orillas del río Sinú*. Cartagena: Centro de Estudios Económicos Regionales, Banco de la República, Cuadernos de Historia Económica y Empresarial 10.

Vío Grossi, Francisco. 1981. "Socio-Political Implications of Participatory Research." *Convergence* 14(3): 43-51.

Walsh, Catherine. 2009. "Interculturalidad crítica y pedagogía de-colonial: apuestas (des) de el in-surgir, re-existir y re-vivir." UMSA *Revista (entre palabras)* 3.

Warman, Arturo, Margarita Nolasco, Guillermo Bonfíl, Mercedes Olivera, and Enrique Valencia. 1970. *De eso que llaman antropología mexicana*. Mexico City: Nuestro Tiempo.

Watson, Julia. 2008. "Autographic Disclosures and Genealogies of Desire in Alison Bechdel's *Fun Home*." *Biography* 31(1): 27–58.

Whyte, Kyle. 2017. "Indigenous Climate Change Studies: Indigenizing Futures, Decolonizing the Anthropocene." *English Language Notes* 55(1–2): 153–162.

Wright, Steve. 2012. "'I Came Like the Thunder and I Vanish Like the Wind': Exploring Genre Repertoire and Document Work in the Assemblea Operai e Studenti of 1969." *Archival Science* 12: 411–436.

Yie Garzón, Soraya Maite. 2015. *Del patrón-Estado al Estado-patrón: La agencia campesina en las narrativas de la reforma agraria*. Bogotá: Editorial Pontificia Universidad Javeriana.

Yúdice, George. 1992. "Testimonio y concientización." *Revista de Crítica Literaria Latinoamericana* 18(36): 311–332.

Zabaleta Bolaños, Ivo. 2017. "El vallenato de 'protesta': La obra musical de Máximo Jiménez." Master's thesis, Universidad Nacional de Colombia.

Zamosc, Leon. 1986a. "Campesinos y sociólogos: reflexiones sobre dos experiencias de investigación activa en Colombia." In Orlando Fals Borda et al., *IAP en Colombia: Taller Nacional, Bogotá, noviembre 14 al 16 de 1985*, 19–42. Bogotá: Punta de Lanza/Foro Nacional por Colombia.

Zamosc, Leon. 1986b. *The Agrarian Question and the Peasant Movement in Colombia: Struggles of the National Peasant Association 1967-1981*. Cambridge: Cambridge University Press.

Zapata Olivella, Manuel. 1964 [1947]. *Tierra mojada*. Madrid: Editorial Bullón.

Zapata Olivella, Manuel. 1974 [1964]. *En Chimá nace un santo*. Barcelona: Seix Barral.

Note: Page numbers in italics refer to illustrations and captions.

Fals Borda and, 10; in *Felicita Campos*, 75–76, 76; Fundación and, 49, 61, 71–72; shortcomings of, 23, 43. *See also* action research

collaborative anthropology, 201, 225–226, 241n1 (2nd)

collaborative ethnography, 199, 201

collective history and memory, 159, 186

collectives, 1, 16, 99, 105, 215; agrarian, 36, 129. See also *baluartes*; socialism

Colombia: civil wars in, 73, 154, 172, 180; colonial, 48, 172, 181; constitution of, 176, 204; inequality in, 29, 32; maps of, 4, 178; national government and politics of, 6, 7, 9, 11, 32, 33, 134, 156, 191, 200–206, 212–213, 219, 241n2 (2nd); PAR in, 12, 198, 200–201, 202–206; Presbyterian synod of, 58, 59. *See also* Caribbean coastal plain

Colombian Institute for Agrarian Reform. *See* INCORA

comics. *See* comics panels; Fundación del Caribe (Caribbean Foundation), graphic histories by; graphic histories

comics panels, 85, 89, 117, 132, 184–85; cadence in, 165; captions in, 77, 81, 91, *103*, 104; conventions and elements of, 72, 77; designing, 66–67, 84–90, 139; dynamic pictorial space of, 164–165; of *El Boche*, 145, 147, *148*, *149*, *150*, 152, *153*; of *Felicita Campos*, 74, 75; of *Lomagrande*, 102, *103*, 104, 132; perspective in, 90; speech balloons in, 81; of *Tinajones*, 86–90, 87, 89; verbal scripts of, 61, 71, 78–79, 81. *See also* Fundación del Caribe (Caribbean Foundation), graphic histories by; graphic histories

common sense, 133, 157

Communism, Communists. *See* leftists; Maoism, Maoists; Marxism; PCML; socialism, socialists

Communist Manifesto (Marx and Engels), 138

community: campesinos and, 39, 65, 203; memory and, 126, 132, 158; researchers and, xviii, 58, 64

composite characters, 141–142

Comuna 1 (Medellín barrio), xvi, 210; mural gallery in, *217*, 217–218

Conflict in Colombia, 202–206

Congreso de los Pueblos, xvi, 210

conocimiento popular. *See* people's knowledge

conscientização (critical consciousness; Freire), 13

Consejo Regional Indígena del Cauca. *See* CRIC

Conservative Party, 6, 7, 32, 33, 134

convivencia (peaceful coexistence), 212

cooperatives, 31–32, 38

Córdoba department, *4*, 48, 143, 176, 180, 234n2, 235n1, 240n11 (2nd); action research in, 173, 226; Agrarian Reform agency and, 122, 123; ANUC in, 131, 238n17; baluartes in, 25, 39; description of, 5; El Boche legend in, 145; Fals Borda in, xix, 22, 35, 45, 54, 55, 170, 185; La Rosca in, 45, 154; PCML in, 57–58; in *Retorno a la tierra*, 194; Sinú River and, 110; social landscape of, 35, 50, 133–134, 155

Corozal (Sucre), xiv, 31, 181

Corporación Con-Vivamos, xvi, 210, 212, 225; sponsors PAR evaluative workshops, xvi, 209, 224

Corporación Cultural Estanislao Zuleta, xvi

corralejas (bullfighting festivals), 22, 180, 184

cosmovisión (indigenous knowledge), 223, 226

Costeño (Coastal region), 83, 181; ethos of, 56–57, 95–96, 109; folklore and storytellers of, 36, 172; music of, 175, 234n1; peasants in, 20, 21, 114; social landscape of, 99, 134, 136, 173

costume, Chalarka's attention to, 85, 86, 104

Courell, Leonard, 53

creativity and imagination, 20, 98, 228, 229

CRIC (Consejo Regional Indígena del Cauca; Regional Indigenous Council of Cauca), xi, xv, xvi, xx, 92, 137, 207, 219; La Rosca and, 15, 210, 220

critical activism (Kropff), 201

critical consciousness (*conscientização*), 13

elders, 22, 84, 140, 166

El Eternauta (Argentine graphic narrative), 76–77

El hombre y la tierra en Boyacá (Fals Borda, 1957), preface to, 33

Eljach, Matilde, 96, 128, 243; Fals Borda and, 75; Fundación and, xiii, 79, 234n2; on Juana Julia Guzmán, 90–91, 161

"El Mello" (The Twin). *See* Silgado, Ignacio

El Presidente Nieto (Fals Borda, 1981), 21, 172, 174

El Retiro de los Indios (Córdoba), 59

El Soldado inlet (Córdoba) atrocities, 89

El Tiempo (Bogotá daily), 112

El Túnel, literary group, 175, 234n2

empathy, 194, 229–230; empathetic imagination and, 98

English language, 79, 85, 111, 132, 144, 203, 227

enunciation, space of, 225

environmental justice, 200

environment of Sinú River Valley, 109, 117

epistemology, epistemologies: alternative, 199, 202; PAR and, xviii, 215; social movements and, 227

EPL (Ejército Popular de Liberación; Popular Liberation Army), 134

equality, relationships of, 202

Escalante, Gabriel, 236n2 (1st)

¡Escucha cristano! (Fundación graphic history, 1973), 37, 237n3, 237n4; as action research experiment, 59–64; Evangelicals and, 57–59

Escuela de Cuadros (Cadre School), 136, 139, 140, *140*, 167

Escuela Nacional Orlando Fals Borda, xvi; PAR evaluative workshops in Bogotá and, 210, 212, 218; trainees of, 214, 219, 222

Espitia, Felipe, 89

ethnographic mimesis, 98, 229–230

ethnographic research and writing, xii, xx–xxi, 10–11, 59, 97

ethnography, ethnographers, xi, xviii, 15, 47, 71, 241n1 (2nd); collaborative, xx, 26, 198, 199, 225–226; Fals Borda and, 52, 116

ethos, 116, 181; Costeño, 95–96, 109

Evangelical Church, Evangelicals, 68, 134; in Fals Borda's archives, 57–59, 61

Exbrayat Boncompain, Jaime, 100, 146

external researchers, 190, 200, 228; identifying, 223–226

factionalism, 26, 43–45, 131, 207, 240n5, 240n7

Fajardo, Darío, xii, 154, 235n2, 243

Fals Borda, Orlando, 99–100; academic training and career of, xxi, 6–7, 52, 112; *Alternativa* and, 45, 169, 240n7; Banquett and, xiii–xiv; campesinos and, *3*, 94, 105; collaboration by, 5, 9, 19, 172; in Córdoba, 14, 45; criticisms of, xx, 44; falsistas and, 45; field notes and field diary of, 114, 190–195; García Márquez and, 21; government work of, 33, 176; honors awarded, 226, 228, 229; identified, xi–xii; imputation and, 20–22; interviews and, 102, 113, 176, 239n3, 243; Juana Julia Guzmán and, 1, 30, 99, 102, 178–183, 233n2; La Rosca and, xi, 15; legacy of, 11, 26, 43, 211, 226–231; paternalism of, 223; photographs taken by, 67, *68*, 71, 107, 122, *123*; Presbyterianism and, 15, 16, 58, 233n7; presentations by, 12, 137, 199; students of, 95, 235n2; at symposia and conferences, 12, 199; wife of, 48

Fals Borda, Orlando, archives of, xii, xiv, xv, xix–xx, xxii, 17, 26, 38, 48, 154–155; archivos de baúl in, 158–159; description and history of, 235–236n1; dossiers in, 57–58, 59, 60–61; El Boche legend in, 146; as epistemological experiment, 50; evidence of consciousness-raising in, 59; *Felicita Campos* in, 72, *73, 74*, 75–76, *76*, 81, 237n10; field notes and field diary in, 20, 23–24, 46–47, 52, 53–54, 84, 111, 188, 192, 236n1 (1st); *Historia doble* compared to, 174–175, 195; interviews in, 117, 174; as map/gateway to his activism, 46, 49; material on cursillos in, 132, 135–139, *139*; material on graphic histories in, 40, 67, *68*, 71, 144–145; material on Juana Julia Guzmán in, *101*, 159; material on

INDEX

INDEX

www.ingramcontent.com/pod-product-compliance
Lightning Source LLC
Chambersburg PA
CBHW061716270326
41928CB00011B/2001